Statehood and Security

American Academy Studies in Global Security

Carl Kaysen, John Steinbruner, and Martin B. Malin, editors

Robert Legvold, ed., *Thinking Strategically: The Major Powers, Kazakhstan, and the Central Asian Nexus*

Robert Legvold and Celeste A. Wallander, eds., *Swords and Sustenance: The Economics of Security in Belarus and Ukraine*

Steven E. Miller and Dmitri V. Trenin, eds., *The Russian Military: Power and Policy*

Bruno Coppieters and Robert Legvold, eds., *Statehood and Security: Georgia after the Rose Revolution*

The American Academy Studies in Global Security book series is edited at the American Academy of Arts and Sciences and published by The MIT Press. Please direct any inquiries about the series to:

American Academy of Arts and Sciences

136 Irving Street
Cambridge, MA 02138-1996
Telephone: (617) 576-5000
Fax: (617) 576-5050
e-mail: ciss@amacad.org
Visit our Website at www.amacad.org

Statehood and Security: Georgia after the Rose Revolution

Bruno Coppieters and Robert Legvold, editors

American Academy of Arts and Sciences
Cambridge, Massachusetts

The MIT Press
Cambridge, Massachusetts
London, England

This book was set in ITC Galliard by Anne Read.
Printed and bound in the United States of America.

Library of Congress Cataloging-in-Publication Data

Statehood and security : Georgia after the Rose Revolution / Bruno Coppieters
  and Robert Legvold, editors.
     p.   cm. — (American Academy studies in global security)
  Includes bibliographical references and index.
  ISBN 0-262-03343-7 — ISBN 0-262-53276-X (pbk.)
  1. National security—Georgia (Republic). 2. Georgia (Republic)—Foreign
  relations—1991– . 3. Georgia (Republic)—Politics and government—1991– .
  I. Coppieters, Bruno. II. Legvold, Robert. III. American Academy of Arts and
  Sciences. IV. Series.
  DK678.18.S73 2005
  327.4758'009'051—dc22   2005050477

Contents

Foreword

This book is the last of five volumes on security challenges to the international community posed by developments within the vast territory of what was once the Soviet Union. It would take a very long series indeed to explore in detail all of the security relationships among the successor states of the former Soviet Union. The issues selected for further study in this series we believe are among the most important. The approach to these issues is a practical one: rather than settle for generalizations driven by broad analytical categories, each book deals with a specific manifestation of a selected problem and studies it from the "ground up."

The current volume addresses the relationship of mutual to national security in the Caucasus region, using Georgia as the telling case. Not only has that country undergone a painful political and economic transformation since the collapse of the Soviet Union, but it also suffers from violent internal conflicts that resonate with interregional tensions. Add to this the involvement of many external players, as well as the influence of oil politics, and the picture grows very complex. All this creates very large tasks for the new Georgian leadership that came to power following the Rose Revolution in fall 2003. This volume attempts to explain how Georgia's present and past leaders, faced with an enervated state and an alienated public, have dealt with the challenge of secession, attempted to create a defense establishment, thought about the role of the military in foreign policy, and managed military relations with Georgia's neighbors and outside powers.

The previous volume in the series, *The Russian Military: Power and Policy* (2004) deals directly with the military profile of the key country in the region, Russia. Not much can be said about the broader international significance of security trends within the former Soviet Union without having some sense of what kind of military power Russia is today. The Russian armed forces remain a scaled-down and much battered version of their Soviet predecessor. This book examines how the Russian military has absorbed the shock of the collapse of empire and simultaneously resisted efforts at serious reform. The authors draw the many dimensions of Russia's military physiognomy—the evolution of defense policy, the socio-economic condition of the military, Russia's use of force in regional conflicts, and its approach to nuclear weapons—into a single composite picture. The book provides a broad assessment of how Russia fits into both regional and international contexts as a military actor.

Another volume in the series, *Swords and Sustenance: The Economics of Security in Belarus and Ukraine* (2004), tackles the problem of how economic factors impinge on the national security policies of the states of this region. Unique as some features of Belarus and Ukraine are, the way that economic considerations shape and complicate their national security agendas applies in crucial respects to virtually all of the post-Soviet states because of their geopolitical environment and legacy as Soviet republics. Their environment means Russia looms large as potential partner or potential threat, while Europe and the United States are potential partners or problems as well. Their legacy of political and economic integration within the Soviet Union created a high level of dependence on Russia and distance from the Western global economy, affecting the costs and benefits of alternative security policies. The intermingling of economic and security factors is further deepened by the fact that these countries remain in the earlier stages of their post-Soviet political and economic transitions, rendering their choice often a matter of national sovereignty and survival.

The first volume in the series, *Thinking Strategically: The Major Powers, Kazakhstan, and the Central Asian Nexus* (2003), assesses how systematically, ambitiously, and skillfully the major powers have thought about and pursued their vital stakes in Central Asia. It does so by comparing the policies of China, Japan, Russia, Europe, and the United States toward a key country in this crucial region, Kazakhstan. Without pretending that the knowledge generated in a specific case study can be applied perfectly to the policies of the major powers in other parts of the former Soviet Union, the book's basic insights, made richer by the concrete instance from which they are derived, deepen our understanding of what roles the major powers are playing in the massive hinterland of Europe and Asia.

A forerunner to the books in the series, *Belarus at the Crossroads* (1999), shares the same conception and examines what kinds of security issues are overlooked when the complex challenges raised by the larger post-Soviet space are reduced to the single dimension of Russia's relationship with the West. The book illuminates the way in which Belarus in its external relations considerably complicates European security issues as NATO expands and analytical energies are focused on resolving Russia's relationship with it.

We thank the Carnegie Corporation of New York for its support of the project, which has been carried out under the auspices of the American Academy of Arts and Sciences and its Committee on International Security Studies. Robert Legvold is the intellectual and organizational force behind the entire project. We are grateful for the important work he has done to advance our understanding of the international implications of developments within the post-Soviet space.

Carl Kaysen and John Steinbruner
Co-Chairs, Committee on International Security Studies
April 2005

Acknowledgments

Neither this book nor its three predecessors in this series would have been possible without the support of the Carnegie Corporation, the project's key sponsor. Deana Arsenian, the program chair in International Peace and Security at the Foundation, has been a particularly encouraging, efficient, and gracious counsel to the project. Its home has been the Committee on International Security Studies under the auspices of the American Academy of Arts and Sciences. This carries special advantages, and none greater than the assistance provided by the Committee's staff. Martin Malin, program director, provided us the same care and good-spirited supervision that he has given the other books in the project. Two of Marty's colleagues, Leigh Nolan and Leigh's successor, Helen Curry, were indispensable, coordinating our efforts, minding the detail of the work, and running interference for us throughout. We are also grateful to Leslie Berlowitz, the Academy's Executive Officer, for the interest she has taken in the project and the promotion she has given it. From beginning to end of the project of which this book is part, Carl Kaysen and John Steinbruner, the co-chairs of the Committee, have lent their wisdom, gentle encouragement, and good names to the effort.

Our gratitude is particularly great to our fellow authors whose work forms the core of this book. Not only have they shared their knowledge and talents with us; they tolerated with grace what seemed to them at times unending demands on our part. Our host for an author's meeting in Bruges February 2004 was UNU-CRIS, the United Nations University program on Comparative Regional Integration Studies, and we are grateful to its director, Luk Van Langenhove, and to Pascale Vantorre for affording us this congenial setting. Brenda Shaffer served as the outside commentator on draft chapters prepared for this meeting, as did Oksana Antonenko, who afterwards became a part of the project, and all of us benefited handsomely from their insights and prodding. Viacheslav

Chirikba, George Hewitt, and Magaly Rodriguez Garcia read and commented on several of the chapters, and we thank them for their special assistance. Two anonymous outside reviewers read the manuscript with exceptional thoroughness and intelligence, and all of us in the project benefited greatly from their constructive, highly informed advice. We also want to thank Alla Rachkov for carefully checking the accuracy of the book's footnotes. Finally, we want to express particular gratitude to John Grennan, who copy-edited the volume with remarkable skill and efficiency.

Bruno Coppieters
Robert Legvold
April 2005

Glossary of Acronyms

AER	Assembly of European Regions
AIOC	Azerbaijan International Operating Company
AO	Autonomous Region (Soviet Union)
ASSR	Autonomous Soviet Socialist Republic
AWACS	Airborne Warning and Control System
BLACKSEAFOR	Black Sea Naval Cooperation Task Force
BMOs	border monitoring operations
BTC	Baku–Tbilisi–Ceyhan Pipeline
BSEC	The Black Sea Economic Cooperation Organization
CFE	Treaty on Conventional Armed Forces in Europe
CIS	Commonwealth of Independent States
CIS PKF	The Commonwealth of Independent States Peacekeeping Force
CIVPOL	United Nations Civilian Police
CMPC	Confederation of the Mountain Peoples of the Caucasus
CPC	Confederation of the Peoples of the Caucasus
CSCE	Conference on Security and Cooperation in Europe
CUG	Citizens' Union of Georgia
EC	European Commission
ENP	European Neighborhood Policy
EvrazES	Eurasian Economic Community
GKChP	State Committee for the Emergency Situation
GTEP	Georgia Train and Equip Program
GUUAM	Georgian, Ukraine, Uzbekistan (until May 2005), Azerbaijan, Moldova (Organization)
IDP	internally displaced person

IFC	International Finance Corporation
IFES	International Foundation for Election Systems
INOGATE	Interstate Oil and Gas Transport to Europe (Program)
IPAP	Individual Partnership Action Plan
IRI	International Republican Institute
ISAB	International Security Advisory Board
ISFED	International Society for Fair Elections and Democracy
JCC	Joint Control Commission
JPKF	Joint Peacekeeping Force
KGB	Committee for State Security (Soviet Union)
LINKS	London Information Network on Conflicts and State-building
MCA	Millennium Challenge Account
NDI	National Democratic Institute
NGO	nongovernmental organization
NSC	National Security Council (Georgia)
OSCE	Organization for Security and Cooperation in Europe
PACE	Parliamentary Assembly of the Council of Europe
PfP	Partnership for Peace
SRSG	Special Representative-of the Secretary-General of the UN
SSOP	Sustainment and Stability Operations Program
SSR	Soviet Socialist Republic
TRACC	Transnational Crime and Corruption Center
TRACECA	Transport Corridor Europe Caucasus Asia
UNDP	United Nations Development Program
UNHCR	United Nations High Commissioner for Refugees
UNOMIG	United Nations Observer Mission in Georgia
USAID	United States Agency of International Development

Map 1. Administrative Map of Georgia

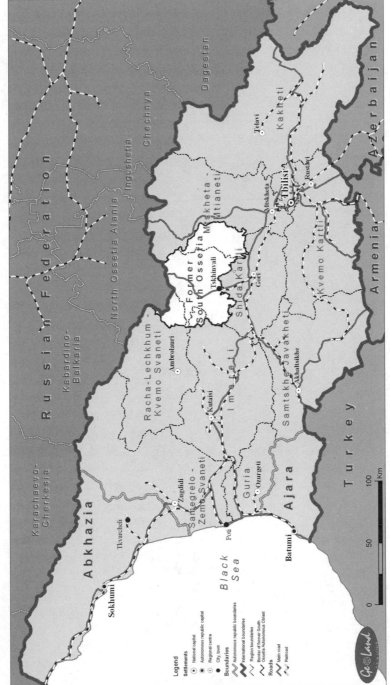

Legend

Settlements
- ● National capital
- ◉ Autonomous republic capital
- ◎ Regional centre
- ● City/town

Boundaries
- Autonomous republic boundaries
- International boundaries
- Region boundaries
- Border of former South Ossetia Autonomous Oblast

Roads
- Main road
- Railroad

Map courtesy of the International Crisis Group (www.crisisgroup.org).

Map 2. Map of the UNOMIG-Mission in Georgia

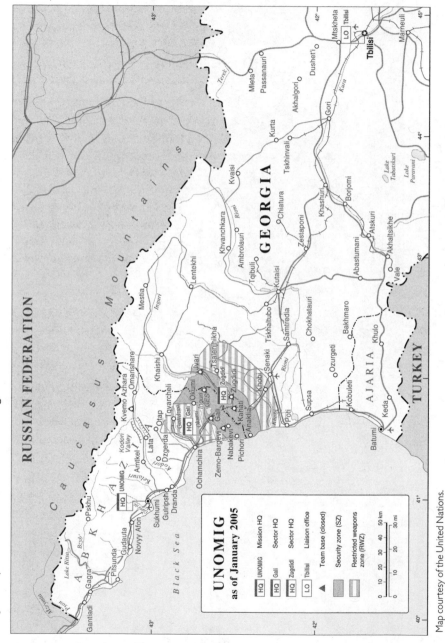

Map courtesy of the United Nations.
UNOMIG, no. 3837 Rev. 43E, January 2005, The United Nations Cartographic Section, http://www.un.org/Depts/Cartographic/english/htmain.htm.

Outlining the Challenge

ROBERT LEGVOLD

E veryone knows that Russia lives in a troubled neighborhood. Weak and unstable states on its borders threaten to export their problems to it or to become conduits for the threats brewing in Afghanistan, Iran, Iraq, and the Middle East. Yet other post-Soviet states face an even more daunting environment, and Russia occupies a large part of it. Scarcely any of these states, with the exception of the three Baltic states now nestled under Europe's protective wing, enjoy anything approaching a secure existence. On the contrary, many confront not only dangers on their borders, but fundamental sources of insecurity generated from within. All are suffering the uncertainties, setbacks, and miseries of inventing themselves from the ruins of the Soviet Union; many are beset by explosive internal conflicts and, in four cases, rebellious provinces that refuse to be a part of a common state.

If only a few post-Soviet countries were facing these perils, the outside world could look the other way. However, virtually no state in any of the subregions of the former Soviet Union—Central Asia, the Caucasus, and the "new lands in between" (Belarus, Moldova, and Ukraine)—is free from the threats posed by uncertain domestic transformations, potential civil strife, and regional violence.[1] Again, if one or all of these subregions (or for that matter the post-Soviet space as such) were located at the outer edges of the international system, other states, including major powers, could afford to ignore failures in meeting these challenges. But the post-Soviet space is the hinterland of the two most important strate-

---

[1] The notion of Belarus, Ukraine, and Moldova as the "new lands in between" is developed in Robert Legvold and Celeste A. Wallander, eds., *Swords and Sustenance: The Economics of National Security in Belarus and Ukraine* (Cambridge, MA: The MIT Press, 2004).

gic regions in the contemporary international system—East Asia and Europe—and of the cauldron where its gravest security threats boil—the Muslim south. In addition, each of the subregions within the post-Soviet space merges uneasily into some of the world's most unstable areas.

Thus, the issue for the larger international community and its leading powers is not and never has been Russia alone, but rather Russia in geographical context. Yet even this does not do justice to the way this part of the world should be thought of and approached. Each of the subregions is capable of generating disorder menacing the stability or adding to the instability of neighboring regions. Each harbors trends toward domestic political illiberalism, spoiling the casual hopes many in the West had that the post-Soviet states would form the core of the next democratic wave. And each already serves as a corridor through which all manner of contaminant—drugs, arms, contraband, trafficked humans, and potentially supplies for weapons of mass destruction—make their way into the outside world.

No subregion better illustrates or incorporates more of these threats than the Caucasus, and no country is more afflicted with these hazards than Georgia. In addition, no country in any of the subregions is more central than Georgia in determining whether these threats will affect others. That is the first reason for this book.

For virtually all of Georgia's existence as an independent state, the country's peace and well-being have been under siege, undermined by violent separatist conflicts. The simmering problems of Abkhazia and South Ossetia evoke national security in its most primal form—namely, as a threat to the territorial integrity of the state itself. Complicating this peril, Georgia's original leaders faltered in guiding the country through the transition from its Soviet past to a more modern political and economic order, leaving the country weakened and poorly positioned to address the security challenges confronting it. Superimposed on the trouble that Georgia faces within its borders is the instability that prevails beyond them. To the south, the tension surrounding the unsettled issue of Nagorno-Karabakh leaves Armenia and Azerbaijan in a quasi-state of war. To the north, the ongoing insurgency in Chechnya makes Russia, already seen by Tbilisi as aggressive and ill-intentioned, still more on edge and overweening.

All of these factors create an immensely complex and intractable security challenge for Georgia's new government. It has been more than a year since the political opposition, following transparently manipulated elections, mobilized the streets and chased Eduard Shevardnadze's regime from power. The Rose Revolution of November 2003 and the presidential and parliamentary elections that followed installed leaders determined to break with past practices and face this challenge head on. At home, the new president, Mikheil Saakashvili, and his principal partners, the former Prime Minister Zurab Zhvania and parliamentary leader Nino Burjanadze, moved swiftly to reinvigorate the state, strengthen executive power, pare back corruption in government, disrupt criminalized networks, restore central authority in the often quarrelsome province of Ajara, create a trustworthy domestic police force, and collect taxes to sustain a revenue-starved government.

But the new government has accomplished these goals in what one of this book's authors calls a "prolonged revolutionary syndrome" and with tactics that by the first anniversary of the Rose Revolution had civil society advocates, many of whom were the new regime's original supporters, questioning just how pluralistic and open a society the new government would tolerate.[2] Moreover, in attempting to compel progress on the agonizing core issue of Abkhazian and South Ossetian separatism, the new leadership's impetuous initiatives during spring and summer 2004 reheated the embers of conflict, roiled relations with Russia, and brought admonitions from otherwise well-disposed Western governments. One year after the Rose Revolution, the central questions remained: As promising as the intentions and first steps of the new government were, could it surmount the profound challenges facing the country? Could it overcome the lethal sources of the country's insecurity?

If the deficiency of outsiders is their failure to assess judiciously their stake in Georgia's developments (as is true of the Russians) or to give adequate weight to their stake in them (as is true of the Europeans and the Americans), the weakness on the Georgian side is conceptual: the failure to think through the many dimensions of Georgia's security problem and their complex interconnections. Beyond a visceral sense of frustration and danger over the ethnically-charged regional conflicts, the inability of earlier governments to come to grips with the country's problems, and

---

[2] The quote is from Ghia Nodia and is cited in Jaba Devdariani, "Georgia's Rose Revolution Grapples with Dilemma: Do Ends Justify Means?" *Eurasia Insight,* October 26, 2004.

the Russian threat (each real enough), relatively little sophisticated conceptual thinking about Georgian national security had been done, at least not in official circles. In late 2000, the Shevardnadze government issued a formal document called, "Georgia and the World: A Vision and Strategy for the Future." It was an effort to articulate Georgia's approach to foreign and security challenges, but rather than grappling with the hard conceptual issues, it settled for a loose statement of basic principles and a wish-list of what it hoped to see happen, particularly in relations with Europe and the United States. The new Saakashvili government, as David Darchiashvili notes in his chapter, has given military reform a new impulse, and by spring 2005 it appeared ready to release a new national security concept for parliamentary and public discussion. Whether this document would at last capture the complexity of the threats facing the country and offer a systematic, realistic, and concrete response to them remained to be seen.

Thinking through the challenge to Georgian national security provides this book's second justification. The authors of this volume have tried to bring greater clarity to the task of identifying the key dangers facing Georgia and their complicated interaction. True, Georgia's security problem is often acknowledged to be multi-tiered, with the secessionist threat, the corrosion of state institutions, and Russian mischief-making treated as parts of a whole. And many have noted, although not spelled out, the linkage between insecurity within Georgia and instability within the region. But simply listing the different dimensions of the security problem without considering the synergy among them or without exploring the precise connection between trouble inside and outside the country makes it hard to devise a national security concept that does justice to the challenge. Second, and even more important when it comes to assessing the significance of Georgia and its security problems for the wider world, the failure to situate Georgia within a broader regional context leads policymakers in Washington, Brussels, and almost surely in Moscow as well to underestimate and distort their stake in the outcome of the challenges facing Georgia. That they care about Georgia because they have stakes in the region is not the same as recognizing the way that regional dynamics intersect. Nor is their genuine but general desire to see the new Saakashvili government advance toward democracy and draw closer to Europe any guarantee that they will muster policies suited to the intricate domestic and foreign environment in which Georgia operates.

We have, therefore, given ourselves three tasks in this book: First, to untangle the many different layers of the security challenge arising both within and outside Georgia and to explore the complicated ways they intersect and influence one another. Second, to explain why the challenge confronting this country matters to more than Georgia and its immediate neighbors—indeed, why it should be a problem taken seriously by major Western powers and their allied institutions, a problem requiring more than the material aid at the heart of current efforts. And third, to consider what the Georgians, their immediate neighbors, and the West ultimately can and should do in response. How, in short, might Georgians, Russians, Europeans, and Americans improve the situation in ways that enhance each party's national security while strengthening mutual security? And how might this be done within the realm of the politically feasible?

THE ESSENCE OF THE PROBLEM

For Russia and all other post-Soviet states, except arguably the Baltic states, security begins at home, because the turbulence and uncertainties surrounding their efforts to fashion new or at least viable political and economic systems after the collapse of the Soviet Union remain their single greatest preoccupation. In the case of Georgia, however, even before getting to the traumas of this task, its leaders confront the risk that the homeland they hope to reconstruct may not survive intact. Hence, security for them begins in the most tangible fashion—with preserving the territorial integrity of the country, and short of that, with restoring sovereign authority over broad swaths of territory where it has been lost.

Achieving this objective, however, is only the beginning of Georgia's security agenda. The anxieties of knowledgeable Georgians are not only prompted by the threat of separatism, but by the fear that neither the Georgian state nor Georgian society has the will or capacity to stand up to the threat. They worry that institutions, including those expressly designed to provide security, have so weakened, have been so corrupted, and have so become the preserve of families, clans, and special interests that they no longer have the strength to defend either the individual or the country from harm. Georgians even contemplate uneasily the possibility that they are the source of the problem: that what underpins Georgian identity ends up fracturing the larger community. These apprehensions explain why the Rose Revolution has become such a watershed—

because it represents Georgian hopes of at last breaking free of these shackles and reversing the downward descent.

Formidable as the internal sources of Georgian insecurity are, if the country enjoyed a benevolent or at least an unthreatening environment beyond its borders, the nature of the challenge would be more confined (albeit still not easy). On the contrary, Georgia's neighborhood offers trouble, not relief. Violence, either active or latent, surrounds the country. If intrastate conflict poisons Georgia's domestic life, regional conflict defines international relations in Georgia's immediate neighborhood. The absence of dialogue—often even of practical or economic intercourse, let alone the rudiments of community—in the South Caucasus leaves Georgia without support from its neighbors or, more important, the opportunity to concentrate on its own problems. It also creates the risk of conflicts in one area bleeding into another or generating tensions among neighbors forced to choose among contending parties. In particular, the uncertainty and violence in the Northern Caucasus, especially in Chechnya, make Russia a more aggressive and impatient neighbor. This, in turn, compounds a basic problem: even if Chechnya were at peace and the rest of the Northern Caucasus securely a part of the Russian Federation, Russia would still cast a large shadow over Georgia, given Moscow's slow and painful adaptation to its loss of control over a region that has been a strategic salient for two centuries.

These are the immediate, practical sources of Georgian insecurity. On a deeper level, history and geography conspire to create more permanent, structural impediments to Georgia's security. Georgia is part of the Black Sea region, which through the millennia, dating back to the Greeks and Scythians, has been dominated by the rise and fall of empires—Roman, Byzantine, Persian, and Ottoman—or by the interplay of dueling empires, such as the Persian and Ottoman from the sixteenth through eighteenth centuries and the Russian and Ottoman in the nineteenth century. Over time, smaller societies were simply absorbed into these imperial domains or, as in the case of the Caucasus, turned into buffer zones (between Roman and Parthian, Byzantine and Arab, and Persian and Russian empires).[3] For only a single century—the "Golden Age" of the Bagratid monarchy beginning with the liberation of Tbilisi from the

---

[3] For an elegant recent retelling of this history, see Charles King, *The Black Sea: A History* (New York: Oxford University Press, 2004).

Seljuks in 1122 and ending with the Mongol invasion in 1220—was Georgia master of its own fate. For nearly all of the last two hundred years, it remained a dominion of the Russian and then Soviet empire. During interludes of relative freedom, Georgia's choices ranged narrowly from seeking protection at the expense of autonomy (as with Erekle II's approach to the Russians at the end of the eighteenth century) to watching the country fracture (as under Alexander I's sons in the fifteenth century) or be partitioned (as under the Turks in the sixteenth century).

Now that Georgia is again independent, it faces the small power's predicament of existing alongside a large and less than beneficent neighbor, particularly when, as Jaba Devdariani stresses in his chapter, historical memory sets the two countries at odds. Georgia enters this new era without natural allies or a history of reliable alliances. As Thomas de Waal notes in his chapter, rarely has Georgia, when buffeted among competing great powers, been able to fall back on a united front with its Caucasian neighbors. The fissures and tensions that keep the Caucasus in disarray are not new; they have long-standing historical antecedents. As a result, Georgia is, to use de Waal's expression, "without a secure regional security environment."

Pronounced as these historical patterns are, nothing says that they must prevail or cannot be escaped. Choices matter: the choices Georgia's leaders make in facing domestic challenges, in dealing with the breakaway territories, in helping to fashion greater cooperation in the region, and in responding to the policies of external actors—in short, in playing the hand they are dealt. Alas, the choices made by Georgian leaders and their counterparts in the decade and half of independence have fallen considerably short of optimal. As a consequence, until recently the inertia of historical patterns and the force of contemporary trends were reinforcing rather than distinct. The unanswered question is whether the Saakashvili regime can divorce them.

Georgia's security challenge is large, dramatic, and complex. Its essence, however, can be thought of as two-part: At its core, Georgian security is about statehood; beyond this core, it reflects the unhappy reality that an insecure Georgia exists within a region of insecure states. The insecurity of statehood and the insecurity of neighborhood combine to produce the kind of security dilemma endured by only the most endangered countries.

To say that security for Georgia is about statehood contains, but does not convey, the underlying nature and full scope of the issue. What strikes the outsider with particular force (as it presumably will strike many read-ers of this book) is how much the question of Georgia's very existence dominates Georgian thinking about security. It is not that Georgian policymakers and political analysts are oblivious to the dangers of violence within the region they inhabit; or are incapable of imagining how conflict between states might escalate to war; or are inattentive to the importance of a conventional defense policy addressed to conventional military needs; or are unmindful of the perils inherent in a badly managed relationship with Russia. It is simply that all these considerations pale alongside anxieties over Georgia's future and particularly its incapacity to find some means by which to draw the lost territories of Abkhazia and South Ossetia back into the national fold.

Most countries, including the United States, Russia, and the European states, approach the question of national security by first laying out the character and range of threats they face. Georgia, however, in sharp contrast, begins not with the topic of threats, but with that of security—that is, by defining security itself. In the "National Security Concept for Georgia" proposed by the Strategic Research Center (Tbilisi) in November 1998, the authors place the uncertainties surrounding Georgian statehood squarely at the center of their formulation.[4] They start from the premise that Georgia is in peril because state institutions are enfeebled, because society has lost its sense of common purpose, and because the nation has failed to create a locus around which to rally different ethnic communities. While not all official and unofficial voices are as explicit as the Strategic Research Center, most implicitly share a similar perspective.

According to the security concept developed by this group, security depends less on Georgia's ability to fashion a security strategy than to create a development strategy. Security will be the product of conscious and effective efforts to give the country a focus inspiring loyalty and a constitutive direction appropriate to Georgia's cultural identity, yet suited

---

[4] *National Security Concept of Georgia* (Tbilisi: Strategic Research Center, November 1998), http://www.src.ge/policy_papers/national_security.html. Although the authors of the report are not identified, the founders of the center are David Iakobidze, former minister of finance; Irakli Menagarishvili, former minister of foreign affairs; Niko Melikadze, the executive director of the center; and Natela Sakhokia, the center's director. I cite this report not because of its political impact—my impression is that it had little if any influence on policy—but as representative in the spectrum of Georgian thinking.

to the changing imperatives of a globalizing international environment. This, however, requires a sovereign Georgia—that is, a Georgia able to make choices for itself, free of interference from outside forces. Hence, in this argument, the chain goes from a "national development strategy" to statehood to sovereignty to security. It is true that there is a circularity to this argument, because security *qua* sovereignty must underpin a strategy for domestic transformation, but the relationship between statehood and security is clear: statehood precedes security.

Ghia Nodia's chapter in this book argues along similar lines. Security, he maintains, is the freedom of a people to pursue the "idea of what they want to be." He calls it the "national project," and anything that threatens to undermine or divert it constitutes a security challenge. In order for the national project to work, Nodia insists that it must respect "some kind of unique national identity," whether based on language, culture, or "spirituality," but it must also aspire to something more. In Georgia's case, the "more," he says, is the desire to emulate the liberal democratic model of European states. Yet as Nodia acknowledges, how can one be sure of what the national project is and who subscribes to it? If there are competing national projects, which has legitimacy? These questions push the problem to a deeper level and reverse the relationship between security and statehood.

The roadblocks to the national project in Georgia are considerable. According to Nodia, they include: "ethnic exclusivity" among the Georgians themselves; a Soviet institutional legacy aiding fragmentation; powerful "alternative national projects;" and an array of potential sources of tension, from Armenian and Azerbaijani irredentism to unintegrated ethnic groups. These obstacles are the internal dimension of the national security challenge; they are the threat to the national project, the threat to statehood. But they, by his light, do not alone constitute the problem. The deeper dimension resides in the faltering of political institutions, which accentuates the roadblocks to the Georgian national project, not the other way around. It is not that these obstacles explain the failure of institutions, but rather that the troubled condition of institutions account for the magnitude of these obstacles.

Hence, in Nodia's view, to penetrate to the heart of Georgia's security problem, one must explain the reasons for the weak state. His explanation takes him back to an essential duality in Georgian popular values: fancying, on the one hand, the liberal democratic model, but prejudicing it, on the other hand, with an antipathy to the state and a readiness to hijack it for private purpose. Dig a bit deeper, and the problem appears to stem from the nature of the Georgian public's stake in the Western model: it accepts the democratic model, because it wants to be Western, and it wants to be Western to affirm its independence from Russia. In this chain, however, a commitment to the liberal Western model is for security's sake, not because of a strong attachment to the model's intrinsic worth.[5] Add to this the Georgian public's instinctive mistrust of the state—any state, democratic or otherwise—because of what the state came to represent in Soviet times, and the prospect of overcoming state weakness by promising democracy dims, particularly when for many Georgians, democratic values compete with other values embedded in Georgian society and at times fostered by the Georgian Orthodox Church.

Other knowledgeable Georgians argue from the same basic point of departure. David Darchiashvili, another author in this book, elsewhere suggests that the future of Georgia's Rose Revolution depends "on its ability to mobilize around a national idea," something that cannot be done by simply assuming civil society will carry the day.[6] Rather, the "project" requires "emotion, even romanticism." Hence, he argues, in order to succeed, Georgia's "democratic forces," must "draw on [Georgian] nationalism to strengthen their project," provided—and here is the rub—that it can be cleansed of "its dangerously ethnic flavor." In effect, Georgian nationalism must be rescued from its unholy alliance with corrupt officialdom and the criminal element, and deployed by democrats to legitimate a state capable of capturing the support of the alienated citizen.

So Darchiashvili is among the commentators who believe that Georgia's security problem starts from the frailty of statehood and that its most dangerous manifestation is the inefficacy of state institutions. In his explanation, however, the hollowing of institutions is due to rampant

---

[5] This is my interpolation. Nodia insists that among most Georgians the commitment to liberal values and the democratic model is genuine, not instrumental, indeed, more so than in most other post-Soviet states.

[6] David Darchiashvili, "Georgian Security Problems and Policies," in Dov Lynch, ed., *The South Caucasus, A Challenge for the EU,* Chaillot Papers no. 65 (Paris: Institute for Security Studies, European Union, December 2003), p. 126, http://www.iss-eu.org/public/content/chaile.html.

corruption, which has led to three effects: first, "the privatization of security"—that is, state agencies responsible for national and public safety have become the preserve of corrupted state officials who subordinate them to private interests; second, the re-empowering of armed groups that only a few years earlier were thought to have been contained; and third, the entwining of "politics, crime, and clans."[7] Georgian officials at all levels "are deeply involved in dubious commercial deals that involve the open or hidden privatization of state assets," all of which fosters in the public a sense that criminality is a normal and acceptable ethos.

The links among corruption, including its worst manifestation, the criminalized state, the enervation of institutions, and the erosion of national security all figure widely in most analyses of Georgia. Darchiashvili, however, makes them the core of his story. He is not alone. Pavel Baev goes further, contending that "Georgia's troubles," whatever the mischievous actions of outsiders have been, derive principally from "the anomalies and distortions of its own society, political institutions, and elites," and that these stem less from "ethnic grievances, or past injustices, or communist legacies [than from] the all-penetrating shadow economy and corruption."[8] Indeed, he traces the rise of paramilitaries such as the National Guard and the Mkhedrioni at the outset of independence, the civil war in the early 1990s, and even the eruption of war over Abkhazia to "clan-based corruption," whose roots had grown thick and sturdy during the Soviet period. What the Soviet era had wrought, the economic devastation following its collapse, the end of normal economic activity, and the rise of the shadow economy unleashed in still more virulent form.

In this volume, Darchiashvili looks specifically at the destructive interplay among the enfeebled state, corruption, and the military. Unlike a number of other former Soviet republics, such as Ukraine, Belarus, and Kazakhstan, Georgia could not simply nationalize standing Soviet forces deployed on its territory and use them as the basis for a new Georgian military. Instead, during the rule of Georgia's first post-independence

---

[7] Darchiashvili, "Georgian Security Problems and Policies," p. 113.

[8] Pavel K. Baev, "Civil Wars in Georgia: Corruption Breeds Violence," in Jan Koehler and Christoph Zürcher, eds., *Potentials of Disorder* (Manchester, UK: Manchester University Press, 2003), p. 128. (Baev recognizes that corruption and the shadow economy also formed part of the communist legacy.)

president, Zviad Gamsakhurdia, the void was filled by a variety of paramilitary groups, only some of which were loyal to him and all of which owed their first allegiance to the often criminal figures who commanded them. The first challenge for Gamsakhurdia's successor, Eduard Shevardnadze, therefore, was to bring these semi-renegade military elements to heel and achieve some degree of state control over their actions. Shevardnadze, Darchiashvili contends, went about the task by adopting a strategy of "divide and rule," picking off key paramilitary figures one by one. By its nature, however, this strategy stood in the way of rationalizing a new Georgian military, because it worked against a clear-cut centralization of military authority.

Darchiashvili explores in detail the painful, desultory stages by which Gamsakhurdia and then Shevardnadze sought to discipline the criminalized, ragtag, freewheeling military groupings used to fight Georgia's initial battles and to turn them into a proper military responsive to national leadership, under civilian authority, and subject to democratic overview. Until the end of the Shevardnadze era, notwithstanding numerous commissions, dozens of "reforms," and considerable input from the United States and other NATO countries, Georgia had not gotten very far in its military reform efforts. Darchiashvili lays the blame on Georgia's leadership, particularly on Shevardnadze's "divide and rule" strategy for dealing with the military and security forces he mistrusted and his willingness to ignore corruption among elements whose support he sought. To complete the vicious circle, Shevardnadze's inability or unwillingness to do what was necessary to create a reformed, well-institutionalized military was compounded by the failure to settle on a larger strategic concept to guide the effort. But this failure also traced back to the regime's incoherent, narrowly opportunistic approach to the military needs of the country.

Whatever the contrasts in emphasis, nearly all Georgian analysts understand the core of the country's security problem to be the compromised condition of statehood. What makes the issue so difficult, however, is that everything is a piece of a larger puzzle. Analyses that seek to locate the precise source of Georgia's security problem generally end up being circular, such as that of the Strategic Research Center mentioned earlier. It is a chicken-and-egg problem *par excellence*: what comes first, institutions capable of securing public loyalty and overcoming noxious forms of nationalism, or the transformation of nationalism permitting the emergence of institutions capable of commanding general support? Restoring the state in order to attack corruption or attacking corruption in order to restore the state? Devising the "national project" or a "national development strategy" to consolidate statehood as a foundation for sovereignty *qua* independence, or battling for sovereignty to permit the pursuit of the national project?

Then there are the internal contradictions: Georgians, particularly Western-oriented foreign policy intellectuals and policymakers, commonly insist that however one gets there, the goal should be to create a liberal democratic system, but one that protects Georgians' unique cultural, social, and historical identity. Yet liberal democratic systems require that conflicting identities be reconciled, if necessary by affording less protection to the predominant nationality. In addition, the equally frequent exhortation to predicate statehood on the reconciliation of warring national identities has no answer if a group refuses to be conciliated.

It is here that the outside world enters the Georgian situation. Its entry is often for ill, and when for good, usually more a promise than a fact. If the essence of Georgia's security problem is statehood, its agonizing form is truncated sovereignty—that is, the absence of national authority over whole provinces, and, as Darchiashvili stresses, even the territory adjacent to these breakaway territories.[9] The reality that South Ossetia and Abkhazia are de facto mini-states within Georgia's borders, that Georgian writ has no standing in areas seen as integral to the Georgian state, and that the national government remains powerless to change the situation appears to focus the question of national security as nothing else can.

Because Russia is universally perceived as originally a party to Abkhazian separatism, subsequently as an obstacle to a Georgian–Abkhazian settlement, and ultimately as manipulating the Russian–Abkhazian relationship to pressure Tbilisi, the internal dimension of Georgian security automatically becomes international and highly inflammatory. Russia, viewed from the Georgian perspective, constitutes the single most dangerous factor in Georgia's international environment. The reasons are many: Russia is seen as having stalled on the removal of its remaining military bases in Georgia in order to intimidate Georgia's leaders or at least to prevent these facilities from falling into U.S. or NATO hands; it is viewed as bullying and willing to violate Georgian sovereignty if it thinks

---

[9] Darchiashvili, "Georgian Security Problems and Policies," p. 109.

its war in Chechnya warrants it; it is assumed to be behind past attempts to assassinate former President Shevardnadze; and it is suspected of doing everything from interrupting gas services to conniving with the regime's opponents in order to dictate Georgia's choices. But what consolidates these impressions and gives them special resonance is Russia's assumed readiness to abet Abkhazian and Ossetian separatism or, at a minimum, to exploit these conflicts with the aim of weakening or pressuring Georgia's national leadership.

REGIONAL CONFLICT AND GEORGIAN NATIONAL SECURITY

It is not that Georgian observers ignore the nuances that make the Russian threat less clear-cut. They are aware that at times Russian trouble-making may have been more the work of freebooters than by the design of those in power in Moscow. They accept that the tension and ill-will may not have been generated only on the Russian side.[10] And they realize that while an issue like global terrorism may be used prejudicially against the Georgians by the Russians, Russia's stake in this issue is genuine, not merely instrumental, and consequently has the support of others, such as the United States, whose goodwill is important to Georgia.

This more subtle appreciation of the factors burdening the Georgian–Russian relationship is evident in Jaba Devdariani's chapter in this volume.[11] He sees the Russian dimension of Georgia's national security challenge as complex and rooted in the deepest levels of Georgia's national psychology. The clash of what he calls "national myths" gives a far greater resonance to contemporary frictions than they might otherwise have, particularly at a time when both countries are struggling to fashion new national identities. The fact that Georgians find inspiration—and the Russians offence—in the notion that Georgia has long been defiled and oppressed by Russian imperialism, however, does not distinguish Georgia from several other former Soviet republics. The difference between, for example, Georgia and Ukraine would appear to be in how

---

[10] See the interview with Tedo Japaridze, "Georgia's Interim Foreign Minister: Russian Security Depends on Georgian Stabilization," by Giga Chikhladze, *Eurasianet*, January 6, 2004, http://www.eurasianet.org/departments/insight/articles/eav010604.shtml.

[11] See also Jaba Devdariani, "Georgia on a Fault Line," *Perspective*, vol. 13, no. 3 (January–February 2003), pp. 1, 6–8.

uniformly this sentiment is shared throughout the population.[12] Segments of the Ukrainian population, particularly in the western half of the country, think as the Georgians do on this issue, but people in other parts of the country, particular the eastern half, do not. As a result, attitudes toward Russia, rather than being a unifying backdrop to policy, become a divisive factor in domestic Ukrainian politics.

Dueling national myths, however, shape the context within which Georgia and Russia deal with the tensions that divide them; they do not create the tensions. These arise out concrete circumstances—out of disputes over the liquidation of military bases or the imposition of visa regimes; out of activities seen as ill-intentioned or subversive; and out of frustration over conflicts, such as Abkhazia and Chechnya, where the other side is perceived as unhelpful or, worse, malevolent. Devdariani does not blame Moscow alone for all that has gone wrong in Georgian–Russian relations. Even when the Russians have, in his view, behaved aggressively, a part of the blame belongs to Georgia. He argues that when Georgia is focused, firm, and willing to assert itself in measured ways, the Russians act with restraint. A prime example of this was the Ajaran crisis in April 2004, when the Saakashvili government drove from power a local political boss who, with Russian complicity, had long defied the central government. Thus, Devdariani too is brought back to the problem of Georgian statehood. He too sees Georgian security—in his case, the Russian dimension—diminished by weakness on the Georgian side: by unsteady foreign policies, by leaders who use Russian actions to obscure their own failings, and by the corruption and infirmity of government itself, which encourages the Russians to treat these as exploitable vulnerabilities.

In the end, however, Devdariani and most Georgians do worry that Russia remains less than fully reconciled to its imperial demise and is determined to preserve as much control in Georgia and the Caucasus as possible. No part of Georgia's security agenda raises this concern more acutely than the problem of the separatist territories, particularly Abkhazia. Georgians know that the roots of Abkhazian and South Ossetian defiance reach deep into ethnic, cultural, historical, and political differ-

---

[12] Here I speak of the dominant ethnic group. Several minority groups in Georgia do not share the Georgian view of Russia, if one accepts Devdariani's representation of it.

ences. They know equally well that these differences were exacerbated by policies adopted by Georgian leaders, particularly in the 1990–91 period under Gamsakhurdia. True, as both Nodia and Christoph Zürcher discuss in their chapters, the spiral leading to the open break between the central government and these regions was the work of both sides. Whether the moves of Abkhazian leaders in 1988 to detach their region from the Georgian Soviet Socialist Republic or the menacing measures adopted by the Georgian side in 1989 started the escalation to violence cannot be easily settled. Whatever the starting point, however, the rapid and convulsive interaction between Tbilisi on the one hand and Sukhumi and Tskhinvali on the other spun out of control in a matter of months (these developments are traced in detail by Zürcher in his chapter). The Georgian leadership's neuralgic fear of Abkhazian and Ossetian "disloyalty" was more than matched by the Abkhazian and Ossetian fears of Georgian repression and, in the case of Abkhazian and Ossetian elites, fear of losing the privileged positions they held within their locales. But for the threshold of bloodshed to be breached—at least in the Abkhazian case—Zürcher maintains that yet another pathology was required: Georgia's tragedy stemmed from military and paramilitary elements that, unrestrained by a debilitated state, triggered the violence in order to protect lucrative criminal activity. He calls these groups "entrepreneurs of violence."

Once this threshold was crossed, Russia became a crucial factor. Georgians almost universally believe that the Russians abetted the Abkhazian side in the 1992–93 war, help that many Georgians still think was decisive in turning the tide against them. Their only uncertainty is whether the Russian role was orchestrated from Moscow or at the initiative of Russian military commanders and units in Abkhazia. In her chapter, Oksana Antonenko relates a far more complex story, one—and this is symptomatic of the deep emotions that flow at the base of this problem—that few Georgians, including most of those who contributed to this book, would buy. Indeed, the Russian military was involved, but in her view, its involvement was split. Parts of the military did supply or sell arms to the Abkhazian rebels, and Georgian troops were attacked by aircraft belonging to the Russian Air Force. At the same time, the command of the Transcaucasus Military District (inherited by Russia from the Soviet era) had transferred large stocks of arms to the Georgian military, including a sizable quantity of tanks on the eve of the August 1992 Georgian attacks on Abkhazia. And in the initial phases of combat, Georgian forces were backed by Russian naval units in the Black Sea. Symptomatically, Antonenko argues, the political lineup back in Moscow was equally divided between segments of the elite (including the president, foreign minister, and minister of defense) who supported a "stronger unified Georgia" and others (such as parts of the military and security forces, regional leaders, and activists in the North Caucasus) who wanted a "pro-Moscow Abkhazia."

In the longer run, by Antonenko's account, Russia complicates the Abkhazia issue less because of malicious intent than because of the way it goes about its mediating role. In carrying out a Russian-dominated Commonwealth of Independent States (CIS) peacekeeping mission in Abkhazia, Moscow's primary concern has been to prevent renewed violence, which from the Georgian perspective has had the perverse effect of securing Abkhazia's border and solidifying its autonomy. It is true that Russia's second war in Chechnya has given a darker cast to Russia's role in Georgia since 1999. The Russians, beginning with President Vladimir Putin, see the Georgians as too sympathetic to the Chechen cause and, at a minimum, as uncooperative in helping to cut off outside support for the insurgents. They have retaliated by sharply criticizing Georgian leaders, threatening to act preemptively to quash an alleged Chechen threat from the Georgian side of the border, and, on occasion, apparently allowing Russian military aircraft to strike targets inside Georgia. Russia also began to enhance ties with Abkhazia after 1999—opening their common border, lifting a blockade that had been (loosely) in place since 1992, and extending citizenship to the Abkhazian population while imposing visa restrictions on the Georgian population, although it is difficult to know whether these actions were meant to pressure Tbilisi or were the lowest-common-denominator outcome of domestic political conflicts within Russia. In any event, they left the Georgians still more convinced that Russia could not or would not play the role of honest broker in the secessionist conflicts rending the country. Nor did Moscow do much to soften this image by tenaciously resisting a larger peacekeeping or peacemaking role for others, including international organizations.

Yet to push Antonenko's argument further, the challenge Russia poses for Georgia is far more subtle and intricate than Georgians generally appreciate. It starts not so much from a tendency on Russia's part to pursue openly aggressive aims as from a policy intended to have one's cake and eat it too. That is, in the Abkhazian case, Russia is not out to favor one side over the other but rather to preserve its influence with both. It is formally (and probably genuinely) committed to preserving the territorial integrity of Georgia, but it also does all that it can to foster ties with Abkhazia. It almost certainly wants a stable Georgia within a stable South Caucasus, but it also is jealous of its own power in the region and resents the idea of others such as the United States, Turkey, NATO, or even the UN and the Organization for Security and Cooperation in Europe (OSCE) intruding in what it views as its security sphere. Moreover, as Antonenko shows, specific Russian actions that on the surface appear malign or spiteful, such as imposing visa requirements on Georgian citizens, granting Russian citizenship and waving visa requirements for Abkhazian and South Ossetian residents, opening rail links to Abkhazia, and doing little to promote constructive international initiatives directed at a Georgian–Abkhazian settlement turn out to have a much more complicated basis. For these reasons, therefore, dealing with Russia requires a more astute and nuanced policy than Georgian leaders have devised to this point.

Both Antonenko and Devdariani, however, detect signs that Russians and Georgians at the outset of Saakashvili's tenure were ready to explore the possibility of putting some of the past behind them. Devdariani points to solid pragmatic (principally economic) reasons for the two parties to dampen tensions and seek a more stable relationship. Antonenko agrees and identifies what at the time seemed like a series of potential areas of economic cooperation. She also senses that based on Russian actions during flare-ups over Abkhazia and South Ossetia in late spring 2004, Moscow had grown less resistant to greater cooperation between Russia and NATO in the Caucasus and between the CIS peacekeeping force and the UN monitoring group in Georgia. Still, notwithstanding these initial hopeful signs, the bedrock of mistrust and frustration between the two leaderships remained, and, if anything, further hardened in the months that followed. By early 2005, Saakashvili, in a scarcely veiled reference, spoke of Georgia facing "the strongest and most aggressive—perhaps not the strongest but certainly the most aggressive—forces in the world."[13] And, as one source close to Putin's entourage noted at

---

[13] Saakashvili said this in his annual state-of-the-nation report to the Georgian Parliament, February 10, 2005, http://www.kvali.com/kvali/index.asp?obiektivi=show&n=126.

about the same time, Saakashvili stirs in Putin roughly the same animus that "Fidel Castro does for U.S. politicians."[14]

THE EXTERNAL CONTEXT: VORTEXES AND CONCENTRIC CIRCLES

Nonetheless, in the end, barring an improbable geographical miracle moving Georgia to another place on the globe, Georgians know that they must find a way to live with their large northern neighbor. They also hope, as Georgia's former Foreign Minister Tedo Japaridze expressed it, that Russians also know—or will come to know—that their security "depends on Georgian stabilization."[15] The difficult circumstances between these two countries, however, create a dilemma. Can Georgian–Russian relations be normalized bilaterally, or considering the hurdles, will progress depend on finding a broader framework? Devdariani argues the latter and suggests the possibility of a constructive triangle drawing in the United States, a more active role for the European Union (EU), or the invigoration of alignments such as GUUAM—the loose association of Georgia, Ukraine, Azerbaijan, Moldova, and before Spring 2005 Uzbekistan. None of these alternatives, however, as he realizes, appears to be a very bright prospect. Herein lies the dilemma: It may be that the Georgian–Russian relationship resembles other relationships, such as the Israeli–Palestinian, North Korean–South Korean, and, until lately, the Indo–Pakistani, where the two parties alone are incapable of finding a way out. Yet "multi-tiered" solutions, to use Devdariani's phrase, face their own structural obstacles, making them scarcely more accessible.

Imagining a three-way conversation among the Americans, Russians, and Georgians to ease the Georgian–Russian bilateral relationship out of a dead end is fine in the abstract, but it soon confronts the reality that the U.S.–Russian strategic interaction in the Caucasus over the last decade has been far more competitive than cooperative.[16] Thus, Georgia, rather than benefiting from the dynamic of U.S.–Russian relations in this part of

---

[14] Interview in Moscow, March 24, 2005.

[15] Chikhladze, "Georgia's Interim Foreign Minister: Russian Security Depends on Georgian Stabilization."

[16] The continuing Russian apprehension over the United States' military role in the post-Soviet space is evident in Svetlana Babaeva, Ekaterina Grigoreva, and Nikolai Khorunzhii, "Oni uzhe nikogda ne uydut ottuda," *Izvestiya*, January 25, 2004.

the world, has tended to be its victim. It is true that at important points—such as after Russian military incursions into Georgia, Putin's September 2002 arrogation of the right of preemption, and Russian foot-dragging on withdrawing from its military bases in Georgia—Washington has urged Moscow's restraint. Both the nature and the effect of U.S. intervention, however, more closely corresponded with a competitive than a cooperative model. It hardly led Russian authorities to rethink the underlying relationship with Georgia. If anything, it induced those Russians who see U.S. encroachment in the Caucasus as a direct threat to argue their case even more adamantly.

In truth, Georgia is dragged in the wake of U.S.–Russian relations and cannot realistically expect to appropriate them for its own purposes. This unfortunate fact is only the first of several dimensions complicating Georgia's strategic position. Two metaphors capture the heart of the problem. They also begin to suggest why the stakes are considerable for more than Georgia alone. The two metaphors are a vortex and a series of concentric circles.

To begin with the first of these, conflict cleaves the Caucasus, north-south and east-west, creating a large obstacle to more constructive forms of cooperation within the region. As Bruno Coppieters argues elsewhere, until the Nagorno-Karabakh, Abkhazian, and South Ossetian conflicts are resolved, regional integration cannot go forward.[17] Moreover, unlike other regions of the former Soviet Union, conflict does more than create political divisions and generate tensions; it dominates every aspect of the region's international relations. Others have accurately described just how amorphous, fractured, and malign relations are in the South Caucasus. In Dov Lynch's retelling, the South Caucasus is about as politically impoverished as a region can be.[18] Disputed borders, economic blockades, disrupted rail and road links, and punitive visa regimes not only obstruct the moderating effects of commerce and contact, they serve as both the source and the amplification of widespread tension. To say the region

---

[17] Bruno Coppieters, *EU Policy on the Southern Caucasus,* Policy Paper for the Committee on Foreign Affairs, Human Rights, Common Security, and Defense Policy of the European Parliament (January 20, 2004), p.7, http://www.europarl.eu.int/meetdocs/committees/afet/20040120/wider%20europe%20caucasus.pdf.

[18] Dov Lynch, "A Regional Insecurity Dynamic," in Lynch, *The South Caucasus,* pp. 9–21.

lacks the institutions present in other areas, from Southeast Asia to Western Europe, is a risible understatement of how absent any form of community—institutionalized or not—is among Armenia, Azerbaijan, and Georgia. In addition, each of the three states in the region, like other post-Soviet states, is struggling to recast itself as a political, economic, and national entity—indeed, to do all three things simultaneously. These three countries, more than others, however, suffer from the feebleness and corruption of political institutions critical to this effort. Uniformly weak states in an amorphous, conflict-ridden setting obviously would pose a security challenge to Georgia even were its own internal picture healthy. Because the picture is not, trouble outside the country's borders risks mixing with trouble on the inside, making both more serious threats.

De Waal, however, stresses not only the politically fractured nature of the Caucasus, but Georgians' delinquency in doing much about it. Indeed, as de Waal writes, Georgia, Azerbaijan, and Armenia are so remote from one another, so unengaged economically that they scarcely constitute a region. As he says, on most counts "the three Caucasian countries are painfully estranged from one another." Economically, they remain divided, not least because of "strong criminalized vested interests" that obstruct any kind of a "Caucasian common market." Yet over time the Georgians have done little to alter this circumstance. Under Gamsakhurdia, Georgia pursued what de Waal calls a "messianic image of Georgia as a special European country," largely divorced from the tortured life of the region and bent on distancing itself as much as possible from Russia. Shevardnadze, Gamsakhurdia's successor, devoted himself to forging closer ties with the United States, and, in de Waal's words, "showed almost no interest in enhancing political or economic integration with Georgia's neighbors." Thus, rather than mediating between its neighbors Armenia and Azerbaijan over Nagorno-Karabakh, Georgia scarcely lifted a finger, leaving that role to the OSCE and the Russian government.

At the center of a region so charged with tension, Georgia, rather than emerging as a hub of stability, the metaphor that should be its natural lot, risks—in part of its own making—turning into a vortex of instability. If progress stalls and disorder follows, a Georgia in crisis could well pull neighbors in, if only to defend co-ethnics, protect material stakes, or prevent spillover effects from infecting their own domestic strife. On the other hand, it is not only the failings within Georgia that create the danger of the country's fission; unrest along Georgia's borders could easily seep across, and in the case of its northern border with Russia, already does. Thus, the danger remains that Georgia, rather than being a steadying influence within the region or an engine of regional integration, could yet turn into the opposite. In addition, if developments elsewhere in the Caucasus, including to the north, explode, Georgia has a much better chance of getting itself into trouble at home.

None of these danger points had dissipated a year and a half into Saakashvili's tenure. The conflict over Nagorno-Karabakh wavered uncertainly between, on the one hand, glints of hope that the Armenians and Azerbaijanis were making progress in their bilateral talks, perhaps enough to merit a new initiative from the OSCE Minsk Group, and, on the other, signs that Baku really was considering military action to force the issue. In Chechnya, the war dragged on, with all the attendant uncertainty of where its collateral effects might erupt next and what the Russians might do in response. And in Georgia, after the ill-considered effort of the new leadership to achieve a breakthrough on the South Ossetia stalemate in summer 2004, frustration continued to simmer when Saakashvili presented a new, and by most lights generous, peace plan to the Parliamentary Assembly of the Council of Europe in January 2005, only to see it utterly thwarted by a recalcitrant South Ossetian leadership backed by Moscow.

The images of the Caucasus as swept with instability and of Georgia as potentially a vortex rather than a hub of stability capture a crucial part of the picture, but not all of it. They convey the essential character of fragmentation and instability in the region's international relations. Yet there is a great deal more to the political geography of the area, for the Caucasus is not an enclave, but an arena where other powers are also active, which brings us to the second metaphor: Georgia at the heart of a series of concentric circles. Historically, of course, the Caucasus has been the fought-over outer wedge of empire. The empires (Persian, Ottoman, and Russian) are gone, but their rump successor states—Iran, Turkey, and Russia—once more jostle against one another in this space, sometimes directly, more often indirectly. Russia remains more resistant to Iranian and Turkish intrusion into the area than Iran and Turkey are toward Russia's dominant role, but Tehran and Ankara generally view Russia's actions in the Caucasus warily, particularly when it comes to energy politics and often welcome the chance to curtail Moscow's influence.

Turkey and Iran's real impact in the Caucasus is more direct and, while both positive and negative, arguably more the latter than the former. They do create opportunities for some of the Caucasian states: Turkey provides aid to Azerbaijan and economic options for Georgia, while Iran helps to reduce Armenia's political and physical isolation. That said, however, Iran and Turkey's more powerful effect on the international relations of the Caucasus stems more from the challenge they pose to other states. Iran constitutes, after Russia and Armenia, a third major security concern for Azerbaijan. The sources of potential tension, as Arif Yunusov has noted, are multiple: the stirrings of the large Azerbaijani population in Iran, disputed access to the Caspian gas fields, and Iran's policies toward the Shia of Azerbaijan, the country's dominant religious group.[19] Iran, it is true, has not attempted to exploit trouble in the region, including Nagorno-Karabakh, and for a fleeting moment in the early 1990s even sought to help mediate the Azerbaijani–Armenian conflict.[20] Yet Iranian restraint in this one sphere is quickly lost among Azerbaijanis amid the other sources of disquiet.

For Armenia, Turkey represents the preoccupation. Rather than a shadowy influence on the periphery of the Karabakh conflict, Turkey occupies a central place, allied to Azerbaijan, a critical link in the blockade of Armenia, and insistent on a resolution of the Karabakh issue before any real progress toward a normalization of Turkish–Armenian relations will be entertained. Notwithstanding halting steps to move beyond the past (including the 1915 massacres of Armenians) during the first years of Armenian independence, Armenian resentment over Turkey's position on Karabakh reinforces the long-held popular conviction that the Turks dream of restoring dominion over the Caucasus and would happily see the annihilation of Armenia as a means to that end.[21]

To add to the tangle, these bilateral enmities feed seamlessly, albeit at some remove, into a larger architecture of competition and conflict in the Caucasus. Not only do Azerbaijan's close ties with Turkey aggravate its

---

[19] Arif Yunusov, "Azerbaijan's Security Problems and Policies," in Lynch, *The South Caucasus*, p. 146.

[20] For a brief account of the one ill-fated Iranian attempt to bring the two sides of the Nagorno-Karabakh conflict together in May 1992, see Thomas de Waal, *Black Garden: Armenia and Azerbaijan through Peace and War* (New York: New York University Press, 2003), p. 180.

[21] De Waal makes the point and then illustrates it in *Black Garden*, pp. 274–75.

relationship with Iran, given the frictions between Iran and Turkey. And not only do Armenia's dealings with Iran have much the same effect on Turkey. They also extend alignments generated in the equally unstable regions to the south and west: The link between Azerbaijan and Turkey reaches to Israel; the link between Iran and Armenia extends to Greece. This dynamic draws the international politics of the Caucasus into the next concentric circle of international relations and carries the potential of bringing the politics of the Near East and the Balkans into the Caucasus. Consequently, weakness and instability in the Caucasus mixes with weakness and instability in adjacent regions.

The outer and last concentric circle is political rather than geographical. It is the level at which the major powers enter the Caucasus. Both the United States and the Europeans, including the European Union, also see their interests implicated in the region. The oil and gas in and around the Caspian Sea constitute the most obvious stake, and devising the means for getting it to European markets creates both foreign policy and commercial challenges. Because the politics of Caspian oil and gas is more about transport than production, no countries care more about influencing outcomes than the United States and Russia, which adds to the competition between the two countries. The U.S. determination, tracing back to the middle years of Bill Clinton's presidency, to ensure that the oil and gas flow east to Turkey—not south, lest it strengthen the Iranian regime; and not only north, lest it leave Moscow with too much leverage over the energy-producing states in the region—has stimulated a response in kind from the Russians. As a result, the new pipeline from Baku through Georgia to the Turkish port of Ceyhan, long championed by the U.S. government, has been more a bone of contention between Washington and Moscow than a basis for cooperation.

The international politics of oil and gas in the Caspian Sea region cannot be explored here—beyond the account provided in Damien Helly and Giorgi Gogia's chapter—other than to point out that the field of play is broad, involving Central Asia as well as the Caucasus; populated with important third-party players, such as the Europeans, Iranians, Turks, Chinese, and the oil majors; and governed by cooperative as well as competitive rules. Even the often politically contentious issue of pipelines has a positive side to it, and at times, as in the case of the Caspian Pipeline System (CPS), the United States and Russia have worked together. This, however, has not been true for the Baku–Tbilisi–Ceyhan (BTC) Pipeline, the major pipeline crossing Georgia. The BTC Pipeline has from the beginning stirred Russian discontent, particularly in the Ministry of Foreign Affairs, casting another shadow over the Georgian–Russian relationship.

The U.S. agenda in the Caucasus, of course, involves more than oil, and, indeed, has evolved markedly in recent years. As Brenda Shaffer and others have noted, since September 11, Georgia and Azerbaijan (especially Azerbaijan) have taken on a special importance in Washington's war on terrorism.[22] In a way that oil considerations did not, the new American preoccupation with global terrorism emboldened the Bush administration to override Congressional restrictions on aid to Azerbaijan and has prompted the Pentagon in particular to pay attention to ways these countries can be useful pieces in the mosaic of its strategic planning. Here too, however, while the United States and Russia share a common concern about global terrorism and cooperate in many respects in the fight against it, in the Caucasus their notions of the threat and how to respond are less in tandem. Thus, even on a question where the United States and Russia generally see eye to eye, their competing views of the conflicts in the Caucasus and where terrorism fits in make it hard for Georgia to mobilize a relationship with one of these countries in order to avoid yielding to the other. As a result, for Georgia, the war on terrorism affords neither a firm basis for building ties with the United States nor a very helpful context in which to deal with Russia.

Georgia, Azerbaijan, and Armenia all tend to see Russia and the United States as the decisive actors in the region. Given the region's impasses, bloody-mindedness, and disarray, the natural instinct is to assume that help and conceivably solutions must come from the outside. Because Moscow and Washington, however, are not viewed as equally benevolent, Tbilisi, Baku, and Yerevan feel forced to choose between them and then to labor to ingratiate themselves with the one they have chosen. But, because a thoroughgoing alliance with the United States is unavailable and such an alliance with Russia is unwanted (even by Armenia), each country in the South Caucasus must protect its options with both of the major powers. Again, realities are harsh, requiring a delicate balancing act.

---

[22] Brenda Shaffer, "U.S. Policy," in Lynch, *The South Caucasus*, pp. 58–59.

Thus, a remarkably formidable array of interlaced problems stands behind the stark notion of the twin security challenge facing Georgia: the "insecurity of statehood" within an "insecure neighborhood." Seeing how interconnected and tangled the many sides of the statehood problem are, it is disconcerting, although perhaps understandable, that Georgia has done so little to collect its thoughts and articulate a strategic doctrine to address the challenges facing it. In his chapter, Darchiashvili rehearses the various false starts in this direction—the diverse attempts to outline something that might serve as a defense agenda. None, beginning with the so-called military doctrine adopted by the Georgian Parliament in 1997 and ending with one last abortive effort by the government in 2003, ever made it off the shelf. All of these efforts, including the military's own 2002 White Paper and the official 2000 "Vision and Strategy for the Future," were either not vetted sufficiently within the political establishment to gain general acceptance or, worse, not sufficiently refined and attuned to the hard realities facing Georgia to be useful.

The 2000 "Vision and Strategy for the Future" well illustrated the problem. It spoke in sweeping terms of strengthening Georgian citizens' "feelings of loyalty to the Constitution and a sense of common citizenship" and of the "need to consolidate the unity of the state by building a stronger sense of nationhood among its people and regions."[23] It also acknowledged the need for a "long-term national program," but this only served to recognize a problem, not to conceptualize it; to highlight a challenge, not to break it down into its constituent parts. General principles—such as respecting territorial integrity, protecting human rights, abjuring blockades, and preserving the environment—are fine, but they are at best a lodestar, not the starting point for disaggregating threats and devising a strategy by which to respond.

As Darchiashvili reports in his chapter, President Saakashvili and his colleagues have set in motion an effort to create a national security concept more directly relevant to the concrete challenges facing Georgia, and by spring 2005 it was about to appear. How close the new leaders would come to accomplishing this goal, and how easily they would overcome the lethargy and bureaucratic indifference of the past stood as a major test of their ability to transcend the limitations of their predecessors.

---

[23] "Georgia and the World: A Vision and a Strategy for the Future," October 10, 2000.

Without a fundamental guide of this sort, as Darchiashvili stresses, it is difficult to devise a working military strategy, determine the necessary size of forces, and assign missions. The 2000 "Vision and Strategy for the Future" did contain a section devoted to defense strategy that effects a somewhat closer connection between need and response. Georgia, it says, must be able to defend the pipelines crossing its territory, defeat "attacks by modest size forces," prevent "smaller-scale infiltration of border areas," and "deal with potential unrest or disruption along the borders that might result from violence in neighboring regions." Although it also casually demands a military capable of "defeating any type of armed forces that might seek to divide Georgia or to change, by force of arms, its political system or form of government," elsewhere the document speaks more realistically of an ability to "counter threats until assisted by the international community."[24] Still, as Darchiashvili notes, the task of spelling out a practical, well-defined defense posture entails much more.

THE OUTSIDE WORLD

If Georgian efforts to think hard about the elaborate and intricate nature of the security challenge facing their country have fallen short, how well have the major outside powers done in identifying their stakes in Georgia and the best way of securing them? As Damien Helly and Giorgi Gogia argue in their chapter, until recently, not very well. Not only have the Europeans and the Americans for much of the period after the collapse of the Soviet Union failed to treat the challenge of Georgia and the region in its full interlocking complexity, they, unlike the Georgians, had long underestimated the stakes involved.

In fairness to the Americans and Europeans, it was easy to underestimate the stakes. Were it not for the oil, it well might be thought that those on the outside would be wise simply to wall themselves off from the chaos, tension, and backwardness of the region—in effect, creating a (political) "sarcophagus" around it much like that for the Chernobyl reactor. The Iranians and Turks, even though they border the Caucasus, have good reason to want to concentrate on their primary foreign policy fronts, which lie elsewhere. The Europeans have their hands full closer to home and, indeed, within their home. The United States scarcely needs

---

[24] "Georgia and the World."

yet another corner of the globe to police or remake. Even the Russians
might be better off if they could distance themselves from the uncertainties in the Caucasus, and focus on countries and regions—such as
Ukraine, Belarus, and Central Asia—that are economically, strategically,
and politically more critical to them.

None of these states, of course, will do anything of the kind. They cannot and will not in the first instance because of the inertia of past behavior—because of the assumptions, prejudices, aspirations, fears, and actions
that have gotten them to this point. So for the foreseeable future, most of
the players, including Russia, are likely to do more or less what they have
been doing in the Caucasus, unless the course of events within the region
changes fundamentally or, in the case of Russia, the summer and fall 2004
surge of terrorism tied to the war in Chechnya provokes the Putin administration into a suddenly more assertive policy. Putin's renewed talk of
attacking wherever necessary beyond Russian borders against terrorists—
Chechen and otherwise—and careless rumblings within the Russian political elite about securing Russia's position in Abkhazia and South Ossetia by
extending recognition to these territories are straws in the wind. Still, for
the moment, the safer bet is that none of the outside countries, including
Russia, is likely to assert itself dramatically in the Caucasus. At the same
time, however, neither in all likelihood will any of them walk away from
the region. Thus, on the one hand, they are unlikely to invest heavily in
recasting relationships, forcing change, or, alas, facilitating peace. On the
other hand, they are equally unlikely to run great risks to exploit instability, displace rivals, or build strategic outposts.

The second reason that these outside countries cannot—or best not—
forget Georgia and the Caucasus is the one normally offered by policymakers and analysts when exhorting their governments to pay attention.
Wherever the region ranks in the grand scheme of things, it has the
capacity to produce things good and bad on a scale justifying Brussels,
Berlin, London, Paris, Washington, and others' interest. The usual list
begins with oil and gas—gas being more important to the Europeans, oil
to the Americans, while both are important to the Iranians, Turks, and
Russians.[25] Then comes the trouble—the flow of drugs, arms, and the

---

[25] The point is often made that the United States actually has a very low stake
even in oil from this region, because it represents such a small a percentage of
U.S. imports. This ignores the very real interest the United States has in getting as much oil as possible to the world market.

like, particularly in and around the breakaway territories; the risk that
unresolved conflicts in Abkhazia and South Ossetia will reignite; and the
prospect of terrorists gaining a foothold. The Iranians, Turks, and Russians all have reason to contemplate how instability anywhere in the
region could spill across their shared borders, and, with the entry of Bulgaria and Romania into the EU in 2007, the Europeans will also become
immediate neighbors to the Caucasus. As Helly and Gogia underscore,
Europe will never be entirely secure if the Caucasus is left out of Europe's
security purview.

The Americans, since September 11, have a different concern: they
see the region, particularly a state like Azerbaijan, as a battlement in their
new war with global terrorism. Allied states with Muslim-majority populations are few and far between, and Washington values them not just for
the facilities they may lend, but also for the examples they provide. Russia, it scarcely needs saying, views the region as an organic extension of its
domestic agenda, beginning with the war in Chechnya and including the
basing needs of its military, as well as a field of opportunity for Russian
state monopolies and quasi-public corporations in communications, electricity, and the like.

According to Helly and Gogia, despite a range of initiatives and a fair
volume of assistance, for most of the last decade neither the Europeans
nor the Americans framed the challenge posed by Georgia quite as it
merited. The United States and Europe, it is true, were more generous to
Georgia on a per capita aid basis than to almost any other post-Soviet
state, but they were slow to use this aid in a brutally direct way to induce
institutional change and a serious struggle with corruption. They showed
sympathy for Georgia's position on the breakaway territories, but they
were unwilling to take the lead in forming an international monitoring
group that would relieve Georgia of its dependence on the Russians.
They had at various points, including the 2004 rise in tensions, sought to
keep the lid on in South Ossetia, but they had been reluctant to back a
more assertive role for the OSCE in the conflict. The EU had toyed with
developing a "strategy for the South Caucasus," but then left it largely in
abeyance. The United States had sided with Georgia at moments of height-
ened tension between Tbilisi and Moscow, but had done very little to
mediate a long-term normalization of relations between the two countries.

Since the Rose Revolution, the engagement of the United States, the
EU, and NATO has palpably grown. The "donor fatigue" of Shevard-

nadze's last years has disappeared, replaced by a new surge in economic assistance, including $1 billion pledged by the international community at the June 2004 Brussels donors conference. In addition both NATO and the EU have clearly energized their approach to the country. Each has quickly moved to map out steps by which Georgia can bring itself more in line with the needs and practices of their organizations. President Bush's visit to Georgia in May 2005, the first by a U.S. president, graphically underscored Washington's eagerness to give the new regime its seal of approval and, in the process, to signal its stepped up concern over Moscow's churlish behavior toward Tbilisi.

The task ahead, however, is formidable, and, if Europe and the United States truly mean to make a difference, they will have to go beyond the measures they have already undertaken. State-building and the arduous process of fashioning institutions capable of addressing corruption and restoring public confidence should be the priority of Western aid, but progress must also be achieved in thawing Georgia's frozen conflicts over Abkhazia and South Ossetia. Helly and Gogia credit the West with understanding that the outside world can contribute here only if the effort is genuinely multilateral, allowing the resources and influence of all parties, including Russia, to be brought to bear. Alas, they say, Russia has done little to foster a multilateral approach, and the West has not done enough to make what multilateralism there is effective. Matters were not helped in January 2005, when the Georgian leadership laid out an unusually generous peace plan for South Ossetia to the applause of Americans and Europeans, only to receive a stony dismissal from the South Ossetian leader Eduard Kokoiti, then on a visit to Moscow—and his Russian hosts made no effort to contradict him.

This still leaves an important vulnerability in Georgia's relations with the West, one noted by many of the authors in this book: the gap in expectations between Georgia's hopes for integration into the West and, unsurprisingly, the West's hesitancy to provide firm assurances that it will happen. Georgia's new Western-oriented leadership not only desires Georgia's membership in NATO and the EU, but believes membership in one or both is within reach. Washington and Brussels do not want to discourage Georgia or remove an incentive to domestic reform, but they are still not ready to embrace the prospect. The resulting ambiguity built into even positive steps such as Georgia's action plan with NATO and the EU's new European Neighborhood Policy reflect genuine ambiguity on the West's part, but this uncertainty carries the risk of, at some point, casting Georgia into the negative limbo that long characterized Ukraine's relationships with NATO and the EU and that has only begun to dissipate in the wake of the Orange Revolution.

Important as these considerations are, they underestimate the stakes the outside world, including the United States and Europe, has in Georgia's fate and the fate of its neighborhood. To appreciate these stakes at this other level, developments across the post-Soviet area must be factored in. True, what once was the Soviet Union no longer hangs together; it is a disintegrating space, with countries immersed in their subregions, and the subregions slipping away from the Russian core and fusing with often troubled neighboring areas. Yet, notwithstanding this fragmentation, trends within the post-Soviet space are similar, do interact, and have their greatest significance for the larger international setting as a composite. Viewed from this perspective, Georgia and its neighbors matter far more than most outsiders recognize in three respects.

First, with the collapse of the Soviet Union, many on the outside, particularly in Europe and the United States, casually assumed that the bulk of the new states would soon be part of the "third wave of democratization," that is, would want to create open, democratic political orders buttressed by market-oriented economies. Over the intervening years, the scales fell from the eyes of these outsiders as the post-Soviet countries struggled and stumbled. But none of the major powers, including those closest to the post-Soviet space, had faced up to the danger that the bulk of these states at the outset of the new century were not in transition to some form of genuine democracy, however imperfect, but settling for an illiberal, counterfeit version. Not many policymakers in Washington, Brussels, or Tokyo (and unsurprisingly, in Beijing or Moscow) gave much thought to what the failure of most post-Soviet states to make it to democracy would mean for their own countries.

Until the Rose Revolution, the Orange Revolution, and the turmoil in Kyrgyzstan in March 2005, the pattern was scarcely encouraging. The politically unreconstructed countries—Belarus, Turkmenistan, and Uzbekistan—remained so, but rather than forming a doomed circle of increasingly isolated remnants of the past, they were joined by a steadily increasing number of states ready to imitate them, at least in part. Virtually the whole of Central Asia—including Kyrgyzstan, whose leader's democratic aspirations were genuine at the start—had slowly slid from the path of open political competition, meaningful political parties, transparent decision-making, and relative freedom of expression. Ukraine drifted further from, not toward, democracy in the initial rounds of the 2004 presidential election, until the regime overreached and provoked a public reaction much like the one in Georgia in 2003, only with still more dramatic consequences. In Russia's case, few were able to explain how the Russians could turn an oxymoron like "managed democracy" into anything resembling a liberal democratic order. And in the Caucasus—in Armenia and Azerbaijan, not just in Georgia—the 2003 parliamentary and presidential elections veered powerfully in the wrong direction.

It may be that the revolutions in Georgia, Ukraine, and Kyrgyzstan represent a historic countertrend capable of stemming and perhaps reversing the general tide away from democratic reform. But for that to be so, those who led them must prove that they have reopened the door to democratic progress while simultaneously demonstrating that they have the ability to mitigate, if not solve, their countries' problems. While it remains to be seen whether the Saakashvili government can prevail against the enormous obstacles facing it—or even whether in the process it can preserve its commitment to a more pluralistic and open political order and a more transparent and competitive economic order—the mere fact that leaders have come to power who believe these goals should be their guide breaks the discouraging general trend among post-Soviet states.

It would be naïve to take what happened in Georgia, Ukraine, let alone Kyrgyzstan as certain to inspire publics elsewhere while cowing their high-handed leaders, particularly since the events in these countries have yet to prove self-sustaining.[26] Yet if orderly, progressive change within the post-Soviet space is important to stability there and beyond, every wisp of hope—every fragment of a positive model—deserves strong outside support. Moreover, as the post-Soviet space loses cohesion, the

---

[26] Indeed, if anything, leaderships in a number of states, including Belarus, Kazakhstan, Uzbekistan, Tajikistan, Azerbaijan, and Russia were treating the Georgian case as a negative object lesson and taking steps to ensure that opposition groups were not able to mobilize street demonstrations around varied, but mounting grievances. Matters were not helped by chaos and political self-seeking among Kyrgyz politicians in the immediate weeks after the March 2005 upheaval in Bishkek.

effect of one state on another shrinks to its own immediate vicinity. Change is likely to be subregional, and each subregion will likely require its own constructive example of a state that has halted the slide toward illiberalism and resumed progress toward democracy. In an ideal world, the most influential candidate in Central Asia would be Kazakhstan (not Kyrgyzstan); in the west, Ukraine; and in the Caucasus, Georgia. That is not the way strategists in any of the world's major capitals yet think.

Second, there is a critical factor checking the centrifugal forces within the post-Soviet space: Russia. Russia continues to be the single most powerful external influence on the political and economic life of every post-Soviet state, with the exception of the Baltic states. While weak in comparison to its former Soviet self, not to mention in comparison to other major powers, Russia has more economic, political, and military capacity to help or hinder its new neighbors than any other power. It also continues to see its stakes in these countries as greater than any other power does. Thus, to the extent that China, India, Pakistan, and the United States have interests in Central Asia, as they surely do; or Iran, Turkey, the EU, and the United States do in the Caucasus; or the United States and the EU do in Ukraine, Moldova, and Belarus, effective policy must cope with the Russian factor. No interested party can simply ignore the Russian dimension or assume that it will take care of itself.

The obverse is still more important: From the beginning, despite the original neglect, it has been apparent that the direction and character of Russian policy in the newly independent states would play a large role in defining the overall condition of Russian foreign policy. Invariably, therefore, it was certain to matter in Russia's relations with other major powers. In the global contest that was the cold war, the axes of Soviet interaction with the United States, Europe, China, and Japan were direct—at the Elbe, in the Middle East, and across the nuclear divide. They have been replaced, in the murkier and more remote circumstances of the post–cold war world, by indirect encounters, as Russia maneuvers to preserve its influence among its new independent neighbors and the West goes about its own separate agenda in these states. Thus, if the United States, Europe, China, or Japan wants to put relations with Russia on a different footing or to enhance cooperation and manage discord, it will have to take account of the chemistry with Russia in these new intermediate regions. The same holds true for Russia in its relations with the other major powers.

In the 1990s, the chemistry between the West, particularly the United States, and Russia had grown progressively less promising. Gradually, the dynamic within the post-Soviet space had begun to take on the quality of strategic rivalry—over pipelines, NATO Partnership for Peace exercises, key bilateral relationships, and the overall direction of NATO policy. After September 11 and the equanimity with which Putin initially accepted the deployment of U.S. and other forces in Central Asia and U.S. Special Forces in Georgia, the trend toward rivalry appeared to dissipate. It now seems that this trend is anything but over. Although less openly and stridently, Putin and his people have made it plain over the last two years that they have no intention of ceding a dominant voice to the United States or any other combination of powers in the Caucasus, Central Asia, and the former western republics. Sometimes with military resources or assertive diplomacy, but more often with economic clout, Moscow has underscored its determination to compete with any outside player, especially the United States, which is seen to be attacking Russia's presence and influence.

Thus, if the United States and Europe hope to see the historically vexed issue of Russia's relationship with the West resolved and Russia integrated into its universe, and if Russia wants something similar, the two sides will have to find ways of making the post-Soviet space an area of constructive, rather than destructive, interaction. No part of the post-Soviet space poses this challenge more sharply than the Caucasus and no country presents it in more neuralgic form than Georgia. Ukraine, Uzbekistan, and Kazakhstan may all be bigger prizes, but in none of them, with the obvious exception of Ukraine, does perceived U.S. involvement arouse Moscow's instant and emotional jealousy as intensely as in Georgia. And in Washington, no region raises more suspicion of Russia's ill intentions than the Caucasus and no country seems more the object of Russia's impatience and heavy-handedness than Georgia. Figuring out how the United States and Russia can work together rather than at cross purposes in Georgia, therefore, is not only crucial in addressing the security challenge facing Georgia, but vital to the kind of mutual relationship Moscow and Washington can build between themselves. Although Russia's relationship with the EU is richer and more ramified, it too faces something of the same challenge.

Third, the future of much of the post-Soviet space remains a question mark. At this point, there is no way of knowing whether most, or even any, of these new states will fashion stable political and economic orders; whether they will be able to manage the animosities that bubble up from within and threaten from without; whether they can overcome the maladies, including the corruption of values and institutions, that have taken root during the formative period of their independence; and whether they can escape the deformed politics that have kept other regions of the world in turmoil and ruin. Some states, of course, have a better chance of surviving these threats than others, and it is crucial to the entire post-Soviet region that Russia appears to be one of them, although its progress is likely to be uneven. If, however, there is a part of the post-Soviet space that represents the question mark in darkest outline, it is the Caucasus. It is the hard case.

Thus, if the major powers—not just the United States and the Europeans, but China, Japan, and for these purposes Russia as well—recognize the importance of seeing the uncertainty that hangs over the post-Soviet space resolved in a way that adds to the vitality and stability of the world outside, they need to give coherence and depth to their currently disparate, scattered, and incomplete engagements in this part of the world.[27] If they come to see, as they should, the wisdom of laboring seriously to begin untangling the sources of tension and conflict widely prevalent throughout the post-Soviet space, the Caucasus is as good a place to start as any. More than any other region, it combines everything that can go wrong: war-torn societies and war-divided states; ethnic divisions; corrupted political societies; embattled reforms; economic failure; the scourge of drugs, illegal arms, and terrorists; as well as natural resources that others covet and that the haves are too ready to use against the have-nots.

If achieving progress on the hard case is the best way to create and temper a capacity for dealing with a generic problem, then the outside world has a reason to focus on Georgia and the Caucasus, one that again transcends the intrinsic significance of the region. I would not make the

---

[27] It is, of course, characteristic of European, Chinese, and Japanese policy that none of these countries has seen its stakes as extending to all parts of the post-Soviet Space. For China and Japan, this has left the Caucasus largely beyond their purview. In a companion volume to this book, I have made an argument why this is shortsighted. See Robert Legvold, ed., *Thinking Strategically: The Major Powers, Kazakhstan, and the Central Asian Nexus* (Cambridge, MA: The MIT Press, 2003), especially the introduction.

indefensible argument that ameliorating Georgia's security problems and, in particular, its separatist challenges is more important for the peace and stability of the Caucasus than finding a way out of the Nagorno-Karabakh impasse. Both problems, in fact, constitute the nucleus of the mutual insecurity problem in the region. The international politics of the area will not change fundamentally until both are resolved; although, as one untangles a dense knot by picking at one strand and then another, the same method might be applied in the Caucasus. No method, however, is likely to produce much, unless it is underpinned by an appreciation of how complex and ramified the security environment is for Georgia and its neighbors.

For that, we invite the reader to turn to the contributions of our co-authors. Ghia Nodia begins the book by probing the most profound "inner" dimension of the problem: the interplay between the burden of the past and the challenges as well as failures on the path to state-building and reform, and how all of this has shaped the way national security has been addressed under successive regimes. His core concept is the "national project," by which he means the normative ideal that defines the sources of state sovereignty and the desired political order. He locates the main "sources of Georgian insecurity" in the failure to integrate competing national projects, a criminalized economy, and ineffective constitutional and institutional reform.

In the second chapter, Christoph Zürcher turns to the failure of the Georgian state to prevent violent mobilizations during its transition to independence, most particularly in the loss of South Ossetia in 1991 and of Abkhazia in 1993. David Darchiashvili then analyzes the various stages in the development of a Georgian defense posture. He deals directly with the military dimension of national security, including the construction of the armed forces, the devising of strategic doctrine, the management of civil–military relations, and the taming of renegade military actors. In chapter four, Jaba Devdariani looks at the Russian dimension of Georgian security, and in the following chapter, Oksana Antonenko zeroes in on the Russian role in the Georgian–Abkhazian conflict.

In the sixth chapter, Damien Helly and Giorgi Gogia consider U.S. and European policies toward Georgia as part of their approach to security in the Caucasus, including support for state-building and economic development. Tom de Waal, in the seventh chapter, turns to what might be thought of as the indirect regional factors complicating Georgian national security: the energy and the security stakes of various players in the oil and gas pipelines in Georgia; second, the impact of regional conflicts in which Georgia may not be directly involved but suffers the effects nonetheless (Nagorno-Karabakh, Armenia–Turkey, and Azerbaijan–Iran), and finally, regional organizations that bear on security, such as the unsteady collaboration among Georgia, Ukraine, Azerbaijan, and Moldova (GUAM).[28] Finally, in the conclusion to this volume, my co-editor, Bruno Coppieters, reframes the security challenge facing Georgia by placing it in a spatial context that features the varied dynamics in center–periphery relations and then offers thoughts on what the future holds.

---

[28] GUUAM has once again become GUAM, since Uzbekistan no longer finds Georgia and Ukraine after their revolutions to be attractive partners.

CHAPTER I

Georgia: Dimensions of Insecurity

GHIA NODIA

G eorgia has been an insecure and unstable country since regaining
independence in 1991. Over the intervening years, it has suffered two bloody and protracted secessionist wars, both of
which the central government lost. These produced two zones of unresolved conflict centered on two unrecognized states (Abkhazia and South
Ossetia) that together constitute nearly 15 percent of the country's territory. In these areas, political uncertainty, insecurity, and crime fester, with
a substantial portion of the population living as "internally displaced people."[1] Until May 2004, Ajara constituted a third area of uncertain jurisdiction within the country. Although Ajara never proclaimed independence, it did not comply with the Georgian constitutional order either.

In addition, Georgia has not had an orderly and constitutional transfer of power since the Communists lost the 1990 elections. Instead, it has
had two rebellions, revolutions, or *coups d' état* (depending on who is
describing them)—one of them bloody, the other peaceful and fairly
orderly. The first led to several years of near anarchy; the second triggered
a tense crisis between Tbilisi and Ajara. Moreover, even in those areas of
the country where the government's political control has not been
openly challenged, its capacity to ensure basic order and security has
often been questionable. For example, the Pankisi Gorge region has
acquired the reputation of being a safe haven for terrorists and criminals.
Georgia's relations with Russia, its most powerful neighbor and former
imperial master, remain extremely unstable and have been on the brink of
military confrontation several times. Georgian public revenues are minis-
cule (even allowing for the country's essentially dysfunctional economy),

---

[1] According to the 2002 Georgian census, the number of internally displaced persons in Georgia was 264,000, although some observers believe this figure to be
exaggerated.

and public sector salaries are as a rule well below subsistence levels. No wonder Georgia is often defined as a "weak state" or, even more radically, as a "failing state."

This chapter outlines Georgia's core insecurities and vulnerabilities, including "objective" threats and challenges. Objective threats include those realities that Georgia had to face when building its statehood on the debris of the Soviet Union, realities whose existence did not depend on choices made by the Georgian state, its political elite, or the public: factors such as Georgia's geography, its size and resources, its ethnic diversity, the specific settlement pattern of its ethnic groups, and the legacy of Soviet ethnic-based quasi-federalism. For example, ethnic secessionist conflicts emerged from a combination of pre-existing factors such as the presence of ethnic minorities not only concentrated in border regions, but also benefiting from ethnically based institutions on which they could rely in pursuit of their own nationalist political programs, coupled with considerable support from neighboring Russia. But this chapter also takes account of the "subjective" factor—that is, how the Georgian state and public responded to these threats and challenges. This includes both the policies chosen and capacities developed to implement those policies—in other words, the sphere in which Georgia earns the sobriquet of a "weak" or "failing" state. In this case, the focus switches from the analyses of pre-existing factors to the way Georgian actors tackled them.

The sources of the security challenges facing Georgia can be divided into internal and external categories. The most obvious external source of Georgia's insecurity resides in its relations with its former imperial patron, Russia. Over the years since Georgian independence, these relations have been mainly bad and at times particularly tense. Otherwise, Georgia has not faced serious threats from any other state. Because Georgian–Russian relations are treated elsewhere in this volume,[2] here the Russian dimension will be considered only as its bears on the internal sources of Georgia's insecurity.

THE GEORGIAN NATIONAL PROJECT

When we speak about security or insecurity, we always mean security of a certain actor: this may be an individual, a group, or a political body—that

---

[2] See Jaba Devdariani and Oksana Antenenko's chapters in this volume.

is, a polity. In political analysis, security issues are primarily discussed with regard to the state. It is usually assumed that all states are more or less uniform in what they regard as in their own interests and that differences on this issue mostly depend on objective factors, such as a state's size, geography, and resources.

While these factors are obviously important dimensions in determining a state's security, they are not sufficient conditions. States belong to specific collections of people—called "nations," "peoples," or "populations"—or sometimes simply to "elites." Different peoples or different elites may define the kind of public order they want and what constitutes the "national interest" quite differently. I refer to this process of determining a national interest as the "national project." The national project is a normative idea expressing the nature of the public order that state institutions are expected to define and protect, as well as defining whose institutions they are. Understanding this project lies at the heart of what is usually meant by "the national interest."

The national project reflects the ambitions of different people (or of the elites representing them), as well as the political values, ideologies, and orientations prevalent within a society or key parts of it. People may seek to create states that try to play an active role in shaping the world beyond their national borders, or they may just choose to be "consumers" of public goods produced within the international order. They may seek to create a "nation-state" for a specific people (or "nation"). Or they may think that unifying different "nations" is the task of their state. They may want their state to be based on liberal and democratic values, on patriarchal values, on communitarian values, or on something else.

Depending on the choices they make, states and the societies upon which they are based will have very different kinds of security problems. The same factors that threaten a certain nation's aspirations might not be perceived as threats if the national project had been formulated differently. For instance, a group that pursues a project of ethnic self-preservation (i.e., of preserving its identity) does not necessarily defend the same priorities as another otherwise similar group that is committed to setting up a full nation-state crowned with a UN seat, and therefore may face a different set of threats and challenges. A nation with superpower aspirations might consider a certain development to be a threat, while a nation with more modest ambitions would not even discuss this same development in the language of "threats" (e.g., Russia considers NATO expansion to be a national security threat, while Ukraine does not). A nation trying to build a democratic order will likely see threats differently from one that is aspiring to build either a traditional or modernizing autocracy. Contrary to what Lord Palmerston thought, not only does Britain (as any other country) not have permanent friends and enemies, neither does it (or any country) have permanent interests.[3]

Of course, it is legitimate to ask where these national projects come from. Nations consist of many individuals who disagree on issues of great importance and who are, especially in democracies, eager to express these disagreements. Obviously, these national projects do not grow on trees or emerge spontaneously from the "national soil." They are created—or constructed, as a postmodern sociologist would prefer to say. People who take the lead in formulating ideas behind a national project are usually elites, especially intellectuals and politicians.[4] However, the development of a national project never depends solely on the arbitrary decisions of individuals. Different versions must compete in the marketplace of ideas before one set of normative concepts gains critical acceptance.

It is also true that there is never a full consensus within a nation about what the national project should be, but strong majorities can usually be rallied around its central ideas. Politicians, especially when in government, like to frame many issues as security threats, because it is easier to mobilize people on matters said to endanger core national interests (and to enhance the incumbent government's standing or influence in the process).

There are many factors that shape the formulation of a national project, but one is particularly important: that of a *role model*. Most nations are so-called "late developers"—that is, they began constructing themselves as modern nations after other nations had already defined what it means to be developed or advanced, and after the major parameters of the world order were already in place. The national projects of late developers tend to imitate the successes of more advanced nations, while at the same time trying to find a niche that respects their own political personality.

---

[3] See very intelligent observations on this subject in Robert Cooper, *The Breaking of Nations* (London: Atlantic Books, 2003), pp. 38–39 and pp. 127–138.

[4] Cooper writes that, "It is the function of political leadership to define what people want, even before they may know it themselves: [Winston] Churchill's policy was based not on a calculus of interest, but on a deep insight into the British people and their history" (Cooper, *The Breaking of Nations*, p. 133). In many countries, intellectuals have provided this kind of leadership.

These role models are usually found among: (1) those states that are successful on a global scale (in the modern world, this is "the West"); (2) those that were once imperial masters and brought aspects of modernization, even if they were imposed (these may or may not be countries of the West); (3) countries that are culturally "like us" and/or geographically close to us, but at the same time that have been more successful in key respects (for instance, Spain and Portugal for Latin American countries). These role models may complement or contradict each other. The advanced countries of Europe and North America may provide general models of development, but if they are culturally distant, a late developer's effort to imitate their model will lack legitimacy, because people care about identities, not merely development models. This dilemma has developed dramatic dimensions—for instance, in many Islamic countries. Therefore, a culturally relevant role model, a "country like us," is easier to emulate.

Georgians do not have a single specific role model—no culturally similar country that serves as a model for imitation (as Azerbaijan arguably has in Turkey). One can say that Europe in general serves as a role model for Georgia, although one has to note here that the model is the European nation-state, rather than the European Union. More proximate models may be the more successful postcommunist countries of Eastern Europe such as the Baltic states, Poland, and even Serbia (the regime change in Georgia in November 2003 was consciously modeled on Slobodan Milošević's ouster in Serbia). This general orientation implies that Georgia's great project is to become a "normal" European nation and be recognized as such.

This simple and hardly original normative model for a national project implies several conditions that are far from simple to guarantee. First, that a nation exists—that is, there is a political body united around a more or less uniform vision of the national project. Second, that it exists as an internationally recognized independent state and a respected member of a community of nations. Third, that it has a political order similar to a normal European country—in other words, a liberal democracy. Fourth, it must have an economic order that ensures a reasonable level of well-being for its citizens and, at the same time, allows the country to be a part of the international economic system. However, it must also preserve what is unique to its national identity (language, national culture, even "spirituality").

One may legitimately ask, "How do we know that these ideas really define the aspirations of the Georgian people? How widely shared are such priorities? Are they simply an elite fantasy?" It would, of course, be wrong to argue that all Georgians are sure about their "Westernness" or "Europeanness." A certain nostalgia for the Soviet Union persists among parts of the population, and there have been events and movements reflecting an anti-Western backlash. In addition, ethnic minorities[5] do not necessarily share in all aspects of the predominant Georgian vision. However, even if countervailing ideas, such as a closer integration with Russia or developing some kind of "Georgian way" based on the Eastern Orthodox religion have been advanced and defended, they have failed to gain a significant place in Georgian political life or public discourse.

This background provides a basis for judging the sources of insecurity in Georgia. Security threats are those trends and forces that menace the national project. Whatever endangers goals essential to the project represents a principal security threat. Moreover, in Georgia's case, a special vulnerability stems from the tension between the country's normative model and its pre-existing realities.

BECOMING ONE NATION: ETHNICITY, AUTONOMY, AND CONFLICTS

Becoming one nation has proven to be the greatest challenge Georgians have faced since gaining independence. This kind of challenge is typical among countries that embark on nation-building after multinational empires have crumbled. Nations are not built on a *tabula rasa*; they start from a specific population mixture and an institutional design left over from the *ancien régime*. Nations-to-be, however, differ in the multiplicity and complexity of challenges they face, and in their capacities to deal with them. In the Georgian case, the challenges have been greater than in other postcommunist states, and, alas, the response of the Georgian public and political elite has been much less effective, particularly in the early stages of the country's independence.

When the Soviet Union collapsed, Georgian society faced an intricate web of fissures based on ethnicity, religion, and sub-ethnic regional loyal-

---

[5] According to the 1989 Soviet census, ethnic minorities made up approximately 30 percent of the Georgian population. According to the 2002 census (which did not include Abkhazia and parts of South Ossetia), minorities represent 16.3 percent of the Georgian population.

ties, fissures which were often reinforced by territoriality and administrative structures. The ethnic issue has proven to be the most important one. There are a number of ethnic minority populations in Georgia that differ in their size, settlement patterns, and attitudes toward the project of the Georgian state. Most importantly, at the time of Georgian independence, there were two ethnic-based autonomous territories (Abkhazia and South Ossetia) and one religious-based autonomous territory (Ajara) that had enjoyed certain administrative privileges in the Soviet era.

Whether or not Georgia's complex ethnic mix represents a challenge largely depends on the central idea of the national project and specifically how one defines a Georgian. Georgians, as is often true in Eastern Europe, have defined belonging to a nation in an ethnically exclusivist way.[6] For the vast majority of Georgians, a "Georgian" was a person who shared both a (mythological) common origin (that is, who was a Georgian "by blood") and a Georgian culture (especially Georgian language). For many (but not all) Georgians, this also included the Eastern Orthodox religion. Therefore, Georgian political nationalism was also ethnic: it implied that Georgians as a nation deserved an independent and indivisible state of their own, but only ethnic Georgians were considered full members of the nation.

This naturally left open the question about the status of ethnic minorities within Georgia. Most Georgians consider their nation to be

---

[6] There is a rather vast literature on the differences between civic or political (inclusive) versions and ethnic (exclusive) versions of nationalism, but most authors agree that most nationalisms to the east of France tend to be exclusive. Notably, however, Lord Acton drew this line between Great Britain and France, arguing that (to use contemporary terms) the French concept of nation was ethnic while the British concept was a more civic one. This illustrates that while the distinction between the two ideal types is more or less obvious, its application to specific cases may be rather problematic. See John Emerich Edward Dalberg Acton, *Essays on Freedom and Power* (Boston, MA: The Beacon Press, 1948); Eugene Kamenka, "Political Nationalism—The Evolution of the Idea," in Eugene Kamenka and John Plomenatz, eds., *Nationalism: The Nature and Evolution of the Idea* (London: Edward Arnold, 1973), pp. 2–20; and Rogers Brubaker, *Citizenship and Nationhood in France and Germany* (Cambridge, MA: Harvard University Press, 1992). Jack Snyder makes a good point linking predominance of ethnic over civic nationalism to late development. See Jack Snyder, *From Voting to Violence: Democratization and Nationalist Conflict* (New York: W. W. Norton & Company, 2000), p. 77.

especially tolerant, and with good reason. While some radicals have urged minority representatives to buy one-way tickets to their "historical home-lands," most Georgians have not questioned minorities' right to live in the country. Unlike in Latvia or Estonia, granting citizenship to ethnic minorities was never seriously contested, and in due time all those people who resided in Georgia at the time of the Soviet Union's disintegration had no problem becoming citizens.[7] Most people in Georgia do not object to granting what in the West are called "minority rights." For example, teaching minority languages in Georgian educational institutions is not questioned. But in this era of democracy, in contrast to the medieval period, it is not enough just to *tolerate* "the other"; a state must find a way to *integrate* "the other"—to make him a willing participant in the national project. As long as minorities are not integrated in this sense, their very existence may be seen as a challenge to the state.

This set of circumstances explains the rather confused and inconsistent attitudes on ethnic issues prevailing in Georgian politics even today. While an ethnically pure nation may theoretically be ideal for ethnic nationalists, even the most radical Georgian nationalists understood from the beginning that this was not a realistic policy option. The predominant assumption has been that ethnic minorities have the right to stay in Georgia and to maintain their cultural otherness, but only under the condition that they are loyal and support the national project. By this logic, any manifestation of disloyalty on the part of minorities constituted sufficient moral grounds for coercive action, including expulsion. Because most minorities were thought to be at least potentially disloyal, they were under constant pressure to affirm their trustworthiness.

This mindset is quite typical for ethnic nationalisms in the postcommunist world, and the Balkans and the Caucasus represent the areas where, in the early stages of the transition, it had been most predominant. In the Georgian case, this mindset is associated with the rule of Zviad Gamsakhurdia, the first leader of independent Georgia (1990–1992).[8] In his political vocabulary, ethnic minorities were often referred to as "guests."

---

[7] This was not true for ethnic Georgians who happened to live in other parts of the Soviet Union at the time of independence and attempted to return to Georgia.

[8] Gamsakhurdia became chairman of the Georgian Supreme Soviet in November 1990, and therefore the national leader. He was not elected president until May 1991. This, however, did not significantly alter his real power.

They could stay if they behaved, but if they started to question the fundamentals of the Georgian national project or express nationalist aspirations of their own, they could legitimately be pressed to move to their respective "historical homelands," where they could pursue their own nationalist agendas. If particular ethnic minority elites espouse their own exclusivist nationalist ideologies and can mobilize support for them, these attitudes constitute a recipe for violent conflict with the central government. Georgia has had two such conflicts (in Abkhazia and South Ossetia), and in both cases Georgian forces were defeated.

Military defeat and a general breakdown in Georgia during the mid-1990s discredited the aggressive ethnic nationalism espoused by politicians such as Gamsakhurdia. The ideologists of Eduard Shevardnadze's regime condemned Gamsakhurdia as a "parochial fascist." Ethnic minorities were no longer assigned the status of "guests"—a label that carried the tacit threat of expulsion. This brought an end to open ethnic tensions, but did not mean that a more inclusive civic concept of Georgian nationalism had triumphed over ethnic nationalism. Rather, this sensitive problem was tabled for discussion at a later date. During the beginning of Shevardnadze's reign, no one attacked ethnic minorities in Georgia or questioned their loyalty, but neither was any effort made to integrate them into public life and create conditions that would facilitate their genuine political participation. Abkhazia and South Ossetia were turned into "frozen conflicts"—there was no war, but neither was there a settlement promising a lasting peace.

Moreover, public discussions in Georgia on some pieces of legislation—for instance, on the ethnic nationality registration requirement in Georgian citizens' identity documents—displayed quite vividly that an ethnic understanding of nationhood still predominated. There was a public outcry when "reformers" in the government initiated legislation eliminating Soviet-style ethnic nationality fields in official identity documents in 2000, and the pro-Western elite that promoted a non-ethnic definition of nationhood found itself on the defensive.[9] This small elite, however,

---

[9] See Oliver Reissner, "'Test ground for Cosmopolitanism' or 'Ethnic Zoo'? The Debate about the Item 'Ethnicity' in the IDs for Georgia's Citizens" (paper presented at the conference "Potentials of (Dis-)Order: Former Yugoslavia and Caucasus in Comparison," Berlin, June 11–13, 1999). See also David Losaberidze, "Citizenship Regimes in the South Caucasus," in Carine Bachmann, Christian Staerklé, and William Doise, eds., *Reinventing Citizenship in the*

proved powerful enough to delay the adoption of legislation containing an expressly ethnic concept of a nation. However, as Shevardnadze's popularity plummeted at the end of his rule, his government tried to encourage ethno-nationalist sentiments for its own advantage. For instance, in the 2003 national election campaign, official representatives of the government party frequently alluded to the hidden Armenian roots of the main opposition leaders, implying that an ethnic Armenian heritage by itself disqualifies a person from a political leadership role in Georgia.[10]

The problem of national unity based on ethno-cultural factors continues to be one of the chief challenges facing Georgia. An ethnically exclusivist concept of nation remains at the heart of this problem. Moreover, exclusivist attitudes are no less, if not more, characteristic of minorities than of the Georgian majority, so a civic understanding of nationhood among the dominant Georgian population would not in itself guarantee the successful political integration of society. That said, considering that this mindset is typical for most postcommunist nations, it is also important to describe those factors of an ethno-nationalist nature—such as myth of origin, language, religion, or formal status of different groups within the political space—that do distinguish Georgia and help to explain why the problem of unity has been so difficult.

The first relevant factor is the link between ethnic diversity and institutional legacy, and specifically, the presence of autonomous formations in Georgia. The Soviet Union was built as a three-tier ethnic federation (or quasi-federation) that many compared to the Russian *matrioshka* doll. The highest level, that of the union, was notionally supranational, although it was perceived as "Russian" by both the outside world and the non-Russian population. The second level was represented by union republics—that is, quasi-nation-states within this supranational structure. On the third level, there existed ethnically based autonomous entities—

South Caucasus: Exploring Dynamics and Contradictions between Formal Definitions and Popular Conceptions (Zürich: Scientific Cooperation between Eastern Europe and Switzerland (SCOPES), Swiss National Science Foundation, 2003), p. 50, http://www.cimera.org/en/research/citizenship.htm.

[10] For instance, Irina Sarishvili, spokesperson for Shevardnadze's United Georgia bloc, spoke of the Armenian descent of Zurab Zhvania and Mikheil Saakashvili, and even alleged that Richard Miles, the U.S. ambassador to Georgia, was representing the interests of the Armenian lobby in the United States. See "Georgian Government-backed Bloc Spokeswoman Takes Swipe at U.S. Envoy," *BBC Monitoring Former Soviet Union*, August 12, 2003.

that is, quasi-nation-states of second rank embedded in the union republics. Autonomous republics ranked ahead of autonomous *oblasts*, which ranked ahead of national *okrugs*,[11] thus implying that some ethnically based autonomous entities had greater formal powers and a more elaborate web of state agencies than others.

The terms "quasi-federalism" and "quasi-nation-state" better describe this arrangement, however, because the division between the façade (or the formal institutional structure) and the real mechanisms of power constituted an essential and often underestimated part of the Soviet political system.[12] The façade was represented by the constitution—a quasi-federal, quasi-democratic document that put supreme power in elected parliaments (supreme soviets) and even allowed Soviet republics to secede—something that genuine federations rarely accept. The real mechanism of power, meanwhile, was the Communist Party and its coercive apparatus, which included the KGB, the army, and the police. It was strictly centralized and based on repression rather than democratic practice. The constitution could afford to look relatively democratic because the Communist Party was expected to dominate the actual mechanisms of power indefinitely.

Even in the Soviet case, the façade could not be fully isolated from the "real thing." With the benefit of hindsight, it is evident that the Soviet constitutional structure had an especially important influence on the way nationalist movements and agendas were formed in the wake of the Soviet Union's breakup. Soviet federalism might have been a hoax in terms of the real workings of power, but it contributed to the creation of national bureaucratic and intellectual elites, as well as national educational, academic, and cultural systems—all of which were crucial to post-Soviet nation-building. As a result, the Soviet quasi-federalist façade had a greater bearing on nationalism than its creators had intended.[13]

---

11 "Oblast" is the Russian word for region and "okrug" means district.

12 Noting this discrepancy is also important for understanding the workings of postcommunist political systems, as well as public attitudes toward them. One of the legacies of communism may be a widely shared assumption that it is normal to have a gap between the political façade that is intended for outside consumption and real mechanisms of political and economic power. No wonder many Western political scientists talk about "façade democracies" or "Potemkin democracies" in post-Soviet countries. See, for instance, Charles King, "Potemkin Democracy: Four Myths about Post-Soviet Georgia," *The National Interest*, no. 64 (summer 2001), pp. 93–104.

13 See Rogers Brubaker, "Nationhood and the National Question in the Soviet

Therefore, once the repressive Soviet system started to crack and newly emerging political movements could call on the Soviet Constitution to bolster their case, it turned out that the quasi-nation-states looked, felt, and eventually tried to behave like real ones. Unfortunately for Georgia, however, this was also true of the quasi-nation-states of the second order. As the Soviet Union collapsed, the autonomous units below the level of union republics represented excellent institutional platforms for launching secessionist movements. Georgia had three such units at the time of independence. In two of them, Abkhazia and South Ossetia, fully fledged secessionist movements developed.

Preexisting institutional forms like these ethnically based autonomous units were important, because they made it easier to put forward ethnonationalist programs on behalf of existing territorial entities rather than according to more amorphous ethnic groupings. Moreover, within the Soviet system, autonomy had nothing to do with freedom (contrary to what the term suggests), but with privilege. It created a sense of special status among both local bureaucratic and intellectual elites, as well as among the general public. At the same time, it bred a sense of being *under*privileged when compared to groups who were represented by union republics. Once the overarching structure of the Soviet Union gave way, conflicts were hard to avoid, because autonomous republics sought to enhance their status. From the perspective of the union republics, this assertion of status by autonomous units meant secession.

ALTERNATIVE NATIONAL PROJECTS:
THE CASE OF ABKHAZIA AND SOUTH OSSETIA

Soviet ethnic federalism created the preconditions, but not sufficient grounds, for open conflicts. These were provided by alternative ethnonationalist programs, such as those put forward by the Abkhazians and

---

Union and Post-Soviet Eurasia: An Institutionalist Account," *Theory and Society*, vol. 23, no. 1 (1994), pp. 47–78; Rogers Brubaker, *Nationalism Reframed: Nationalism and the National Question in the New Europe* (Cambridge: Cambridge University Press, 1996); and Yuri Slezkine, "The USSR as a Communal Apartment, Or How a Socialist State Promoted Ethnic Particularism," *Slavic Review*, vol. 53, no. 2 (summer 1994), pp. 414–452. These authors show quite well how Soviet institutions effectively encouraged nationalism, but fail to explain why Communist framers created a system that obviously contradicted their interests and ideology.

Ossetians (but not the Ajarans). The Abkhazians and Ossetians constitute ethnic groups that are linguistically unrelated to Georgians, while Ajarans speak Georgian and consider themselves to be (ethnically) Georgian. It is also important to note in this context that the Abkhazians and Ossetians are ethnically kin to North Caucasian peoples that already enjoyed autonomy. For example, a majority of Ossetians live in the North Ossetian Autonomous Republic in Russia.[14] Meanwhile, the Abkhazians are linguistically close to other North Caucasian peoples, such as the Adyghean, Circassian, and Kabardin. The national projects of Ossetians and Abkhazians can be summarized as follows: "We are not Georgians. We are the only autochthonous population on the territory that we occupy. Other groups, including Georgians, who live on this territory are guests (migrants) or, worse, 'occupiers.' The territory where we live is not Georgian and should be separate from Georgia. Uniting with our brethren in the North Caucasus is highly desirable."[15]

All of these assumptions, save for the first, ran exactly contrary to what Georgians thought. Georgians viewed the territories at issue an inseparable part of the historical Georgian homeland and considered themselves to be the autochthonous population of these lands.[16] Both Abkhazia and South Ossetia had already been the scenes of violent conflict during the first Georgian attempt to create an independent state from 1918 to 1921. This is not to say that the clash of Georgian, Abkhazian, and Ossetian national projects inevitably had to lead to violent conflicts. In the case of Abkhazia, the violent stage of the conflict could have been avoided.[17] But wars happened in both cases—both of which

---

[14] South Ossetia, on the other hand, had the lower rank of autonomous *oblast,* or autonomous region. This distinction, to Georgians at least, underscored that North Ossetia was the primary or "real" homeland of the Ossetians.

[15] In the Ossetian case, this meant simply unification with North Ossetia, while the Abkhazians thought of creating a confederation of North Caucasian peoples.

[16] It was the Ossetians whom Georgians considered "guests" on this territory—which is why the term "South Ossetia" itself was unacceptable to Georgians. With regard to the Abkhazians, the situation was more complex. Most Georgians would concede that the Abkhazians were also an autochthonous population of Abkhazia, although during the Georgian independence movement, another theory gained currency: that the Abkhazians were actually relatively recent migrants from the North Caucasus.

[17] Ghia Nodia, "The Conflict in Abkhazia: National Projects and Political Circumstances," in Bruno Coppieters, Ghia Nodia, and Yuri Anchabadze, eds.,

ended in military defeats for the Georgian side, creating two zones of "frozen conflict."

Currently, these conflicts represent the greatest strategic challenge to Georgia's security. Since these regions achieved quasi-independence in the early 1990s, people living in secessionist territories have evolved into societies that are separate from Georgia. With each passing year, the prospect of reintegration becomes more and more problematic. At the same time, Georgians still have strong feelings about these territories and just writing them off as lost for good is not considered an option. Displaced populations constitute an economic burden and a potentially destabilizing factor in the internal politics of Georgia. Until a solution for these conflicts is found, the resumption of hostilities could occur at any time, however successful the international community may be in momentarily discouraging politicians on all sides from resorting to the language of war in their speeches.

Apart from the internal problems they raise, these frozen conflicts also do major damage to Georgia's international image. Their persistence serves as the first (albeit not the only, or even the main) argument against Georgia's ambition of joining NATO and the European Union (EU). In addition, unresolved conflicts complicate Georgia's relations with Russia. They also have the practical effect of blocking transport routes between Georgia and Russia, the country that is destined to be Georgia's major economic partner. Parts of Georgia adjacent to Abkhazia have no way to get their products to the international market. Last but not least, these disputed areas are a breeding ground for crime and smuggling, which in turn make it harder for Georgia to clean up and strengthen its own state institutions. Georgian partisan groups operating on the border between Abkhazia and Megrelia were essentially private armies that served as a cover for smuggling and extortion. They created problems not only on the Abkhazian, but also on the Georgian side of the border. No wonder moving against these groups was one of the first steps President Mikheil Saakashvili took in western Georgia. Similarly, South Ossetia has turned into a haven for smuggling. In both cases, at least until Saakashvili's government launched its anti-crime campaign, corrupt Georgian law enforcement services were believed to be largely implicated in these illicit activities.

Georgians and Abkhazians: The Search for a Peace Settlement (Köln: Sonderveröffentlichung des Bundersinstituts für Ostwissenschaftliche und Internationale Studien, 1998), pp. 14–48, http://poli.vub.ac.be.

The Saakashvili government indicated that it considered such conditions in Abkhazia and South Ossetia to be intolerable and would take active measures to resolve the conflicts. As soon as the crisis in Ajara was surmounted in May 2004 (see the next section of this chapter), the government focused on the South Ossetian issue (since it looked easier to address than the Abkhazian conflict). The Georgian strategy in South Ossetia included several components: (1) showing good faith toward Ossetians residing in the region by starting to pay their retirement pensions, broadcasting in the Ossetian language, undertaking charity actions, and criticizing some past actions of the Georgian government like the abolition of South Ossetian autonomy in December 1990;[18] (2) undermining the economic basis of the separatist regime through a crackdown on smuggling; (3) military intimidation by moving some federal troops into South Ossetia, while formally claiming to keep within the quota of Georgian peacekeepers allowed in the region; and (4) intense diplomatic and public relations work with the Russians and other international players.[19] However, these measures led to increasing tensions within the region, including shootouts that resulted in casualties and a new tide of mutual accusations between Tbilisi and Moscow. Although the Georgian government proved prudent enough not to allow the situation in South Ossetia to deteriorate into a new all-out war, this episode became the first major failure of the new Georgian government.

AUTONOMOUS BUT NOT FREE:
THE CASE OF AJARA

The case of Ajara is rather peculiar. Among outside observers, it is often compared to Abkhazia and South Ossetia—a comparison that angers many Georgians. On the surface, the comparison may look plausible: Ajara was once an autonomous republic within Georgia, and, until May 2004, the Georgian central government exercised little control over it.

---

[18] "Georgian Leader Says It Was 'Mistake' to Abolish Breakaway Region's Autonomy," *ITAR-TASS*, June 12, 2004.

[19] The Georgian strategy for solving the South Ossetia issue was articulated in an interview with Giga Bokeria, an influential Georgian MP. See "Tbilisi Wants to Regain South Ossetia through Pro-Georgian Campaigning," *Civil Georgia*, http://www.civil.ge/eng/detail.php?id=7489. See also "Georgia to Adopt 'New Strategy' on South Ossetia—Minister," *Kavkasia-Press*, June 30, 2004.

However, Ajarans, unlike Abkhazians and Ossetians, consider themselves to be ethnic Georgians. Nor was there ever a separate Ajaran national project, which makes Ajara very different from South Ossetia and Abkhazia. Thus, even when Ajaran authorities defied Tbilisi, they never did so as ideological separatists. On the contrary, Ajara's former leader, Aslan Abashidze, loved to portray himself as a champion of Georgian unity.

Ajaran autonomy was first established in the 1921 Georgian Constitution and then confirmed in the October 1921 Treaty of Kars between Turkey and a Bolshevik-controlled Georgia, Armenia, and Azerbaijan. The arrangement was meant to protect the right of Georgian Muslims to practice their religion. During the period of Georgian independence (1918–21), Ajara was often referred to as "Muslim Georgia." Of course, allowing this kind of religious-based autonomy in a communist state that was committed to atheism was a contradiction in terms.

After Georgia achieved independence in 1991, the religious factor never seriously affected relations between Tbilisi and Ajara. Even when tension reached its climax after the November 2003 revolution, Abashidze never tried to invoke the religious factor. If anything positive can be said about Abashidze's rule, it was that Ajara had a higher level of religious tolerance than many other Georgian regions. It is also important to note that, according to the 2002 Georgian census, Muslims constitute a minority within Ajara.[20]

Thus, in Ajara the conflict was institutional and political, not ethnic. As in Abkhazia and South Ossetia, the root of the problem did start from the institutional setup inherent in the Soviet system of autonomous units. In the Ajaran case, Abashidze used the ambiguity of the autonomous units system to fashion a small personal fiefdom. His disobedience included, among other things, preventing Tbilisi from controlling customs points and the port of Batumi (two especially lucrative sources of income for Abashidze's regime), not paying tax revenues to the central government, and gradually building up a private army. The state under Shevardnadze was weak and intimidated by the disastrous results from the use of force in the South Ossetian and Abkhazian cases, circumstances that Abashidze skillfully exploited to mount his "separatist bluff"—that is, if Tbilisi tried to meddle in Ajaran affairs, he would opt for real separatism.

---

[20] The 2002 Georgian census reported that 30.6 percent of Ajara's population was Muslim and 54.0 percent was Eastern Orthodox.

With Ajara's defiance of the central government, the coexistence of two distinct political regimes within the same country further impeded Georgian state-building and added another source of conflict. While Georgia could not claim to have stable democratic institutions, it did have a fairly high level of political pluralism and civic freedom. Ajara, on the other hand, represented a one-man autocracy without any space for political pluralism. While the local and parliamentary elections in Georgia were always competitive (although not necessarily fair), in Ajara electoral contests were a pure fiction: the number of eligible voters was inflated and the turnout was always close to 99 percent, with 95 to 98 percent voting in favor of Abashidze's party.

This situation created a problem, and not just from a civil rights perspective. In the Georgian system of proportional parliamentary representation, when a local leader can distort the number of eligible voters, voter turnout, and results, he becomes a disproportionately powerful figure on the national level. In the 1999 parliamentary elections, Abashidze led the major opposition coalition (including some Tbilisi-based parties) and was even believed to have a reasonable chance of winning. Shevardnadze's Citizens' Union, therefore, was driven to run a (successful) scare campaign warning that Abashidze, if elected, would extend Ajaran-style autocracy to the whole of Georgia. In the November 2003 elections, the Ajaran factor (in addition to general fraud) was one of the major reasons for the crisis, without which the Rose Revolution might never have occurred. Abashidze's Revival Party was declared to have received 20 percent of the vote,[21] seemingly forcing Shevardnadze's Citizens' Union to form a coalition with it in order to control parliament. This prospect stirred fears that Abashidze's growing influence in Tbilisi would lead the "Ajarization" of the entire country, which was a major factor in galvanizing the protest movement leading to Shevardnadze's resignation.

As in all of Georgia's crisis regions, the Russian factor played an important role. Russia retained its military base in Ajara and considered Abashidze to be its key ally within Georgia. In the eyes of Russian geostrategists fearful (or even paranoid) about trends in the South Caucasus, Ajara served as an important instrument discouraging Georgia from forging a closer relationship with Turkey. Moreover, Abashidze

---

[21] This was achieved predominantly through votes in Ajara, although, according to the 2002 census, Ajara's share of Georgia's total population is only 8.6 percent.

certainly considered the Russian base to be a guarantee of his political security.

President Saakashvili made it clear from the beginning of his term that he would not put up with Abashidze's defiance. He took a dual-pronged approach to Ajara. On the one hand, he helped strengthen local resistance to Abashidze's rule (the local opposition was genuine, but previously too intimidated to act). At the same time, he used the power of the central government to apply outside economic and political pressure on Ajara. This strategy was intended to force the Ajaran leader to accept greater control from the center. Saakashvili's government did fear that Abashidze would be more prepared than Shevardnadze had been to use force to defend his position, but it proceeded decisively nonetheless. On May 2, 2004, Abashidze ordered the bridges between Ajara and the rest of Georgia to be blown up. He presumably hoped this action would provoke a military showdown with Tbilisi, in which case he counted on Russia's intervention to protect Ajara. If this was Abashidze's calculation, however, it proved wrong. In the end, it was the Ajaran people, and not Georgian troops, who took to the streets of Batumi and forced him to flee. Ironically, it was the Russian envoy, Igor Ivanov, who ultimately convinced Abashidze to leave Ajara.

After this crisis ended, the Georgian government promised that Ajara's autonomous status would be preserved, despite calls from some opposition parties to abolish it.[22] In effect, however, amendments to the Georgian Constitution and the new Law on the Status of the Autonomous Republic of Ajara enacted on July 1, 2004, significantly abridged the powers of the autonomous republic and reinstated central control in all the strategic areas of governance.[23] Elections for the Supreme Council of Ajara in June 2004 led to a strong victory for the pro-presidential party (which received 72.1 percent of the vote). The new supreme council elected a Saakashvili loyalist, Levan Varshalomidze, to the post of Ajaran prime minister and amended Ajara's constitution to put it into compliance with Georgia's legislation.

---

[22] Notably, they proposed to abolish this status through plebiscite of the residents of Ajara rather than unilateral action from Tbilisi. See "Party of New Rights Started Gathering of Signatures among Achara Residents for Plebiscite on Status of Achara," *Black Sea Press,* June 14, 2004.

[23] "Georgian Parliament Defines Autonomous Status of Ajara," *Prime-News,* July 1, 2004.

While the new definition of Ajaran autonomy may be criticized as too centralist, what matters most is that so far there have been no signs of it being resented by Ajara's population. They may not like their government being appointed from Tbilisi—but this is increasingly true in other Georgian regions as well. It seems that the problem of Ajara's challenge to Georgia's statehood is now solved. This does not mean that there are no questions about how the new autonomous regime will work. In a more democratic Ajara, some Georgians fear that the religious factor may lead to tensions in the future. There are Georgians who resent the very existence of Georgian Muslims and think that belonging to the Orthodox Church is part and parcel of "Georgianness." Ajaran Muslims are aware of this sentiment, and it could generate new frictions.

POTENTIAL IRREDENTISM? ARMENIANS IN
JAVAKHETI AND AZERBAIJANIS IN KVEMO KARTLI

The Abkhazians and the Ossetians had never been the largest ethnic minorities in Georgia. When the Soviet Union broke up, Armenians, Russians, and Azerbaijanis (8.1 percent, 6.3 percent, and 5.7 percent of the population, respectively) were the largest ethnic minorities in Georgia. The 2002 Georgian census revealed a shift in this breakdown. Following the large-scale emigration of Russians, as well as the de facto secession of Abkhazia (where many Russians and Armenians lived), Azerbaijanis became the largest ethnic minority (6.5 percent of the Georgian population), followed by Armenians (5.7 percent). Large groups of Azerbaijanis and Armenians are concentrated in border areas with Azerbaijan (Kvemo Kartli) and Armenia (Samtskhe-Javakheti), respectively. Only a minority of Azerbaijanis and Armenians in Georgia speak Georgian. For the most part, members of these two communities have a weak sense of Georgian identity and a strong emotional attachment to their ethnic homelands.

This means that these two areas could theoretically become areas of irredentist conflict similar to Nagorno-Karabakh. This concern exists in some Georgian quarters, although it has diminished over time since there have been no signs of such conflicts thus far. Why did these "dogs fail to bark?" There are several reasons. First, unlike the ethnic groups in autonomous entities, the Armenians and Azerbaijanis had no administrative platform from which to launch alternative ethno-nationalist projects.

Second, the earlier experiences in Abkhazia and South Ossetia made Georgians more cautious when dealing with minority issues in general. And, third, because of their heavy involvement in the Nagorno-Karabakh conflict, Armenia and Azerbaijan needed to have good relations with Georgia and could not afford to support separatist movements there.

Still, while general conditions in the minority regions of Javakheti and Kvemo Kartli are similar, there are greater concerns about the Armenian-populated Javakheti region than the Azerbaijani community in Kvemo Kartli. Javakheti is a small region that includes the Akhalkalaki and Ninotsminda districts, where over 95 percent of the population is ethnic Armenian.[24] No other part of Georgia is as dominated by a minority population. The Georgian language is hardly used there and—in defiance of the Georgian legislation—the Russian ruble rather than Georgian lari served as the main currency in both regions until June 2004. Against the backdrop of Georgian nationalism and the turmoil following President Gamsakhurdia's ouster in 1992, a local Armenian militia was created under the umbrella of Javahk, an Armenian nationalist organization. In the early 1990s, the Georgian authorities had considerable difficulty controlling the region, but by the mid-1990s, they had managed to re-establish their control through deals with local clans or patronage networks that dominated the most lucrative parts of local business. Javahk split into several organizations (including Virk, an unrecognized party) and lost most of its influence. Their agenda is territorial autonomy for Javakheti Armenians—something that, following Georgia's experience with its three autonomous units, is unacceptable to Georgians. Although voiced from time to time, the idea of autonomy for Javakheti has not become a basis for political mobilization.

In Azerbaijani-populated regions of Georgia, there has been no activism of this nature, and no slogan of territorial autonomy has appeared. The difference between regions may be explained by the character of the local communities and the remoteness of Javakheti as compared to Kvemo Kartli. However, external geopolitical factors have also played a role. The political behavior of local Armenians and Azerbaijanis

---

[24] Javakheti is part of Samtskhe-Javakheti, an administrative region in southern Georgia that includes six administrative districts; its population is 54.6 percent Armenian and 43.4 percent Georgian. The name Javakheti usually applies to two districts, Akhalkalaki and Ninotsminda, which are fully dominated by ethnic Armenians. However, Javakheti is not a formal administrative unit.

is largely influenced by the actions of the governments in their ethnic homelands. The governments of Georgia and Azerbaijan have common interests. They both have uneasy relations with Russia and seek closer relations with Turkey and the United States. Armenia, on the other hand, has a very close partnership with Russia and considers Turkey to be its "historical enemy." These divergent policies create a certain level of mistrust between Georgia and Armenia, which has the potential to influence Georgia's Armenian community.

The presence of the Russian military base in Akhalkalaki is the most important factor in this context. For Javakheti Armenians, the military base is a source of livelihood (many locals were employed there until spring 2004, and the base contributes to the local economy in other ways as well), but most importantly they also see it as a security shield against Turkey, as well as against a possible resurgence of Georgian nationalism. In contrast, most Georgians and their government consider the Russian base to be a threat to Georgia's security and want the Russian military to withdraw from it. Thus, the base constitutes a latent source of tension between Georgia's Armenian community and the Georgian state.

IMPORTED CONFLICT: THE CASE OF PANKISI

Pankisi Gorge is a tiny area in the northern mountains of Georgia where a small community of approximately 7,000 Kists reside. Kists are Muslims and are related to the Chechens. However, they are also relatively well-integrated into Georgian society, speak fluent Georgian, and have Georgian-sounding names.

Until the two wars in Chechnya, many Georgians did not even know where Pankisi was. The place became especially famous in 1999, when thousands of Chechen refugees fleeing the war arrived in Pankisi.[25] In addition to refugees, Chechen fighters easily infiltrated the region's porous mountainous borders, and this led to a serious problem between Georgia and Russia. Moscow accused Georgia of harboring terrorists.[26] These events also created grave internal problems for Georgia. Pankisi soon degenerated into an area outside effective state control and into a haven for illegal trade in arms and drugs, and, what was especially scan-

---

[25] There had been no similar inflow of refugees following the first Chechen war that started in 1994.

[26] See the contribution of Jaba Devdariani in this volume.

dalous, kidnapping for ransom. Pankisi became another symbol of state failure and disintegration.[27] As a matter of fact, Georgian law enforcement officials gave up on policing the area. In private, Georgian politicians said that trying to establish order in Pankisi would draw Georgia into the Chechen war, so the best possible course of action was to isolate it from the rest of Georgia.

However, if only because of the kidnappings, isolation of Pankisi proved to be impossible. Residents in the neighboring region of Akhmeta created a militia and threatened to establish order on their own, and this militia became a problem in its own right. In October 2001, a group of Chechen fighters that had entered Pankisi by mysterious means (some said with the help of Georgian law enforcement) found itself near Abkhazia and tried unsuccessfully to fight its way into the renegade province. While the Georgian central government's lack of capacity partially explains the authorities' inability to control the situation in Pankisi, it also appears true that corrupt law enforcement agents allowed an environment that permitted them to profit from the criminal business thriving in the area.

After September 11, 2001, the global war on terrorism changed both Georgian and international attitudes toward areas like Pankisi. Uncontrolled enclaves within failing states—especially if they happened to be populated by Muslims—were seen as possible sources of terrorism. After the top U.S. diplomat in Georgia, Philip Remler, said al-Qaeda was active in Pankisi in mid-February 2002, Georgia came under pressure from both Russia and the United States to do something about it, and this pressure produced results.[28] Georgian law enforcement agencies undertook several operations in Pankisi and gradually succeeded in improving the situation, but only after corrupt officials in the ministries of internal affairs and security were dismissed. The Pankisi problem led the United States to launch its Georgia Train and Equip Program in 2002, which sent 200 U.S. Special Forces soldiers to Georgia in order to help train the Georgian military.

---

[27] This provoked headlines in the Western media like Patrick Cockburn, "Collapse of Georgia Is Ignored by the World," *The Independent*, January 14, 2002.

[28] Ariel Cohen, "Moscow, Washington, and Tbilisi Wrestle with Instability in the Pankisi," *Eurasia Insight*, February 19, 2002, http://www.eurasianet.org/departments/insight/articles/eav021902.shtml.

THE PROBLEM OF POLITICAL INTEGRATION

In Pankisi, as well as other conflict zones in Georgia, the basic concern is that Georgia faces threats of fragmentation. In each of these problem areas, ethnic or religious factors are involved, but ethnic diversity on its own does not explain the outcome. Rather, the institutional structures of the Soviet period and the uncertainties created by the transition from the multilayered quasi-federation of the Soviet Union to independent nation-states have proven to be the strongest predictor of conflict in the early stages of state-building. The threat of fragmentation also strongly correlates with Russian military involvement, either directly (as in Abkhazia, South Ossetia, Ajara, and Javakheti), or as a collateral effect of Russia's military activity (in Pankisi). Where the institutional underpinning for fragmentation and negative outside influence is absent (as in Kvemo Kartli), the challenge is much less acute.

This, of course, does not lead to the simplistic conclusion that all of Georgia's internal problems are masterminded by Russia or some other external actor. Several fissures that are less obvious also contribute to Georgia's insecurity and its perception of vulnerability. Ethnic issues are the most important among them. Even if we do not count effectively separated Abkhazia and South Ossetia, ethnic minority groups constitute 16.3 percent of the Georgian population, with Azerbaijanis and Armenians being the two largest of these groups.[29] While there are no genuine grounds for fear of potential irredentism among these two groups, the main problem is their marginalization within Georgian society. Most of them do not speak Georgian, which is the country's only official language.[30] In addition, most of them only take part in the affairs of their local area and not national public life. While some minority representatives serve in the Georgian Parliament, their presence tends to be purely ceremonial, and there are almost no minority representatives in national political parties.

Lack of knowledge of the official language is only one reason for Armenians' and Azerbaijanis' passivity and marginalization. The real problem appears to be uncertainty over their status within Georgian

---

[29] These figures are from the 2002 census, which does not include Abkhazia or South Ossetia.

[30] The Abkhazian language has official status in the territory of Abkhazia, but this has purely symbolic relevance until the conflict is settled.

society. On what basis are they to be integrated? For instance, should integration be based on "ethnicity-blind" approaches, on formal or informal ethnic quotas, or on something else? After the experience of the Abkhazian and Ossetian conflicts, state officials and much of Georgian society simply want to duck the problem, hoping that it will take care of itself. It is not likely to do so.

In practice, these circumstances have ultimately led to the (greater) "Georgianization" of the state and, at the same time, a continuation of Soviet ethnic policies. Ethnic minorities have genuine mechanisms by which to preserve their cultural identities, such as education in their native languages, but these mechanisms only reinforce their isolation in ethnic ghettoes. Finding a proper formula for integration is hampered both by the reluctance of the majority to conceive of minority populations as part of the nation and the tendency of minorities to see any integration as the first step on the road to assimilation. The other solution would be to institutionalize existing ethnic enclaves through a system of ethnic federalism. This is politically untenable for the moment, however, because Georgians see the creation of ethno-federal units as a stepping stone to separatism. It also probably means giving up on the prospect of integration. Yet, until some formula is found, the existence of disenfranchised ethnic minorities in Georgia will continue to loom as a potential threat.

Some of the Saakashvili government's new policies suggest that the government recognizes the problems of ethnic minorities in Georgia and is willing to do something about them. Soon after he came to power, broadcasting was resumed in minority languages. In February 2005, in his annual address to the Georgian Parliament, he mentioned integration of ethnic minorities as one of the most important issues for the country and announced a program to train three hundred young minority representatives in Georgian universities with the aim of preparing them for future government positions.[31] It is not enough, however, to say that minority integration issues are going to be treated as a priority or that the government has a coherent plan of action in this regard. Yet the new government cannot neglect the problem. Previous research on the situation in ethnic minority areas allows this author to conclude that the main

---

[31] "Georgian President Delivers Annual Address to Parliament," *BBC Monitoring Newslife*, February 10, 2005.

method of preserving ethnic stability by the Shevardnadze government was through co-opting minority elites into corrupt patronage networks. Preserving these methods will run counter to the general reformist agenda of the new government, but undermining them without having some proactive policy of integration and addressing grievances of ethnic minorities may be destabilizing.

A second form of fissure within Georgia is regional identities and linguistic minorities among ethnic Georgians. Regional identities have a long history in Georgia. From its "Golden Age" in the eleventh and twelfth centuries to its gradual incorporation into the Russian Empire in the nineteenth century, Georgians lived in various princedoms that had some loose sense of unity, but were often in conflict with one another. When the liberal intelligentsia in nineteenth-century Georgia started to work on fostering a sense of common national belonging, they considered these *kutkhuroba* (territorial loyalties) to be a major impediment to nation-building. Paradoxically, it was the Georgian Soviet Socialist Republic that considerably strengthened Georgians' sense of belonging to a nation. Even today, however, these regional identities raise anxieties. While these identities rarely figure in the public discourse, many Georgians fear that under certain circumstances, regional loyalties could still pose a threat to national unity.[32] Traces of them show up, for example, in discussions of whether Georgia should acquire a federal model of government. In 1993 and 1994, President Shevardnadze created a new subnational unit of governance, the *mkhare*, which coincided with historical provinces such as Kakheti, Imereti, Guria, and Samegrelo. This plan, however, proved too controversial, and no agreement on a territorial arrangement for the country was achieved during the constitutional debates in 1995. This most important area of state-building remains a blank in the Georgian constitution, and the *mkhare*—which in fact has become a powerful level of governance—only exists by presidential decree.[33] Georgians still fear that turning historical provinces into admin-

---

[32] For instance, Georgian scholars have written about the influence of regional loyalties (which they define as "tribalism") on the composition of bureaucratic patronage networks. See Koba Kikabidze and David Losaberidze, *Institutionalism and Clientelism in Georgia*, Discussion Paper (Tbilisi: UNDP Discussion Paper Series, 2000), pp. 19–21.

[33] The official Georgian government explanation for the failure to put the territorial arrangement of the country into the constitution was that secessionist con-

istrative units will reinvigorate regional loyalties, which would further undermine Georgia's unity.

Out of all of these regional identities, two—Megrelian and Svan—stand out because these two groups speak languages that are related to Georgian but incomprehensible to other Georgians. Of the two, Megrelian is considered to be the more important group because it is much larger.[34] Some Western observers even wonder why Megrelians have not sought independence.[35] In 1918, 1921, and in the current period of post-Soviet independence, however, Megrelia has been a region where Georgian nationalism was and is especially strong. Zviad Gamsakhurdia, a Georgian nationalist and the country's first president, was of Megrelian heritage. This eventually caused a problem, because after Gamsakhurdia was deposed, Megrelia became a stronghold of resistance to Shevardnadze's government. Attempts to establish control over the region turned into punitive campaigns against the local Megrelian population. Moreover, most of the Georgians in Abkhazia were Megrelians, who were then expelled as a result of the Abkhazian conflict. Thus, Megrelians believe they have suffered disproportionately from the Georgian civil wars of the 1990s and, to make matters worse, believe that their suffering goes unrecognized by the remainder of the country. Megrelians have not developed anything like a separatist agenda, but the trauma of recent conflict does distance them from other Georgians.

The Rose Revolution may have healed the wound between Megrelians and other Georgians. Saakashvili gave preference to Megrelia in his campaign against Shevardnadze's regime, and it was this region that provided him with the strongest support during the November protests. After the revolution, Saakashvili took steps to rehabilitate Gamsakhurdia's image, something welcomed by most Megrelians. People close to Saakashvili say that "mainstreaming" Megrelia had long been part of his strategy for bringing Georgia together.

---

flicts in Abkhazia and South Ossetia had to be resolved first. In reality, however, it was finding an internal Georgian consensus on the issue that created a problem.

[34] There are no official statistics on carriers of different regional identities, but according to the 2002 Georgian census, the population of the regions traditionally considered Megrelian exceeded 450,000, while for the Svan regions the population was in the vicinity of 40,000.

[35] Neal Ascherson, *Black Sea* (New York: Hill and Wang, 1995).

Having strong regional identities that in some ways compete with a national identity is normal for a modern nation and does not necessarily imply a challenge to national unity. In Georgia, surviving the turmoil of the early 1990s proved that these regional loyalties by themselves (including in Megrelia) are not necessarily a challenge to Georgia's unity. If ever a restless people might have wanted to separate themselves from the central government, the government's breakdown immediately after independence would have been the time to do it. This was the period when the weakness of Georgia's political institutions presented the greatest threat to national unity.

While Shevardnadze's policy after the ethno-political wars of the early 1990s was to contain the damage and prevent further disintegration, Georgia's new president Saakashvili has put Georgian reunification at the top of his agenda. So far he appears to have been successful in overcoming the psychological trauma of Megrelia's estrangement and in surmounting the administrative and personal sources of the Ajaran problem. Solving problems of separatist entities and genuinely integrating major ethnic minorities, however, appear to be tougher challenges.

THE NEW STATE ORDER: ANARCHIC FREEDOM, NEO-PATRIMONIALISM, AND THE SOCIAL CONTRACT

A state's weakness often has two major dimensions: a deficit in its institutional capacity and its lack of legitimacy for the exercise of power. Trying to figure out which of these two aspects lies at the core of a state's weakness may simply lead to a chicken-and-egg question.[36] It is difficult to build efficacious state institutions when there is no agreement on what kind of state they are to serve and whose state it should be. Yet, who can take the lead in nation-building other than political elites acting through state institutions? In addition, the effective performance of a state can be a powerful source of its legitimacy. Conversely, the breakdown of a state is often a reason that secessionist conflicts turn into bloody wars (not vice versa).

---

[36] Dov Lynch speaks about these two aspects of state weakness with regard to South Caucasus countries in Dov Lynch, "A Regional Insecurity Dynamic," *The South Caucasus: A Challenge for the EU*, Chaillot Papers no. 65 (Paris: Institute for Security Studies, European Union, December 2003), pp. 12–15.

The strength of the Georgian state can be measured in two ways: (1) the stability and sustainability of its institutions, and (2) by these institutions' effectiveness—that is, their capacity to fulfill the functions normally expected of government.[37] By both of these measures, the Georgian state is weak, as demonstrated by its failure to enforce effective control over the whole territory of the country. It has also been evident in the central government's failure to enforce a monopoly over the legitimate use of force within the country—thereby falling short of the minimal Weberian criterion of effective statehood. This inadequacy was greatest from the time of the coup in the winter of 1991–1992 until the Georgian government cracked down on the Mkhedrioni, the most powerful of the private armies, in the fall of 1995. Even after 1995, however, the state tolerated the existence of paramilitary groups, such as those operating in Megrelia and Abkhazia, as well as a militia that was created in the context of the Pankisi crisis.

The weaknesses of the Georgian state, however, go beyond the inability to establish control over the legitimate use of violence and include its failure to master the constitutional transfer of power. Both Gamsakhurdia and Shevardnadze were forced to leave office rather than giving way to legitimate successors chosen through elections. Similar weakness is evident in the Georgian government's insufficient control over the armed forces. In 1991, it was the leaders of the armed forces that initiated the ouster of Gamsakhurdia, the first president of Georgia. In addition, Tengiz Kitovani, who was head of the Georgian National Guard, is often charged with primary responsibility for instigating the military conflict with Abkhazia in August 1992. Since April 1994, when a former Soviet general became the Georgian minister of defense, the army has lowered its political profile—but between 1998 and 2001, several mutinies in the army erupted, seriously challenging public order. Although neither the police nor security forces ever displayed open disloyalty to the state, they

---

[37] There are different ways to define state weakness. The Weberian criterion of exercising monopoly over the legitimate use of force may be considered as the minimal criterion. Joel S. Migdal, in his frequently quoted book, provides a more extensive list of state capacities as "capacities to *penetrate* society, *regulate* social relationships, *extract* resources, and *appropriate* or use resources in determined ways." See Joel S. Migdal, *Strong Societies and Weak States: State-Society Relations and State Capabilities in the Third World* (Princeton, NJ: Princeton University Press, 1988), p. 4.

are widely believed to be entangled in various criminal activities, such as smuggling, narcotics trafficking, and kidnapping. In addition, during the late Shevardnadze period they were largely perceived as machines for extorting businesses and citizens.

There is also the Georgian state's failure to raise public revenue and adequately fund state institutions. Georgia is usually considered to have the largest shadow economy among the post-Soviet states (estimated to be 40 to 70 percent of the country's overall economy).[38] As a result, public revenues are very limited. In 2003, they constituted only 11.2 percent of Georgia's GDP, compared to nearly 50 percent among European Union countries.[39] This has led to very meager state salaries and retirement pensions in Georgia, most of which are well below a living wage.[40] As a result, the state has had difficulty attracting honest and competent personnel (in the last years of Shevardnadze's rule, a minister's salary was not even close to that of a simple secretary in an international organization), leading many to use their office for private gain. Finally, corruption—the most obvious and widely discussed indicator of state weakness—is recognized as the principal reason for many of Georgia's other failings. According to the well-known Transparency International Corruption Perceptions Index, Georgia was tied for 124th place among the 133 rated nations in 2003.[41]

---

[38] According to official data from the Georgian State Department of Statistics, the share of Georgian shadow ("non-recorded") economy from 2000 to 2003 was between 32 and 34 percent of the country's total economy (*Georgian Economic Trends,* Quarterly Review, no. 2–3, 2003, p. 10). On the other hand, in the opinion of Nikolay Hadjiyski, a European Bank for Reconstruction and Development expert, this figure is "certainly more than 50 percent." See Daan van der Schriek, "Illicit Traders Work the Georgia–Turkey Shuttle," *Eurasia Insight,* August 6, 2003, www.eurasia.net.

[39] Galt and Taggart Securities, *Georgia: Weekly Stock Market Commentary,* January 26, 2004. This is based on official (relatively low) estimates of the size of the shadow economy. If it is presumed to be higher, then the share of public revenues as a percentage of GDP should be even lower.

[40] According to the data of the Georgian State Department of Statistics, the average nominal monthly salary of hired employees in Georgia in 2002 was 104.9 lari (equivalent to about $50), while a working person's subsistent minimum was estimated to be 127.9 lari. See *Georgian Economic Trends,* Quarterly Review, no. 2–3 (2003), pp. 50–51.

[41] Only Myanmar, Paraguay, Haiti, Nigeria, and Bangladesh were ranked below Georgia. See http://www.transparency.org/cpi/2003/cpi2003.en.html.

The relationship between a high rate of corruption and state weakness, however, is not always so obvious. There are many countries around the world where corruption is high, but the level of the state control is also high. While uncorrupted governments are, of course, generally preferable to corrupt ones, in some countries corruption serves as a lubricant enabling state mechanisms to function properly. It is the particular character of corruption that matters. Under Shevardnadze, the state depended on income from corruption, but no single center controlled it. As a Georgian expert put it, "Economic capital in Georgia is not structured into a single neo-patrimonial pyramid."[42] The state tacitly licensed public servants to use their offices for private gain: The leadership sold offices to be used for extortion, and then shared the funds it collected. These corrupt pyramids existed as multiple networks that did not necessarily coordinate with each other. President Shevardnadze mediated between different corrupt interests in order to maintain the general stability of the system, but did not try to enforce common rules. This setup, according to some informal sources, made the system of corruption in Georgia especially unpredictable (and hence destructive). Moreover, when efforts were made to attack corruption, they not only failed, but made the situation even messier and more unpredictable.

Why is the Georgian state so weak? Georgian intellectuals tend to speak about a "non-state mindset" or the alienation of individuals from state institutions.[43] Many Georgian intellectuals say that the modern state is something imposed by the Russian Empire, and therefore marked as "foreign." The Georgian experience with communism simply deepened that sense of alienation. This transforms the state into something defined by restrictions, repression, and deception, rather than by protection. Due to these experiences, many Georgians view the state as something to be avoided. The other side of a strategy of avoiding the state is a reliance on personalistic networks, which in turn are the root of clientelism, neo-patrimonialism, and corruption.

---

[42] Marina Muskhelishvili and Anna Akhvlediani, *Democratization in Georgia: Economic Transformation and Social Security*, Discussion Paper no. 8 (Stockholm: International Institute for Democracy and Electoral Assistance (IDEA), May 2003), p. 15.

[43] See, for instance, Mamuka Bichashvili, "Krizisi da misi tsnobierebis modipikaciebi," in Gia Chumburidze (ed.), *Chkua vaisagan* (Tbilisi: Caucasian Institute for Peace, Democracy and Development, 1994), pp. 83–108.

While this may be a valid argument, it can in no way be restricted
to Georgia alone. Modernity feels foreign to much of the non-Western
world, since it, as with anything imposed by outsiders, also destroys traditional values and living patterns. In this case, the alienating effect of
modernity also correlates with state weakness. Thus, the weakness of the
state constitutes a generic problem in much of the developing world.[44]
Beyond this, however, the communist system's addiction to corruption,
repression, and deception has stimulated an anti-political mindset in a
country like Georgia.[45]

But Georgia's political institutions are arguably more volatile than
those of other post-Soviet countries. Why is this? One explanation may
be that Georgia simply has had to face more diverse challenges than other
post-Soviet states. Even if there are grounds for making this claim, however, measuring and comparing potential challenges is a murky business.
For instance, arguably, there was no less potential for ethnic conflicts in
the three Baltic states, but they did not erupt, because political leaders
acted more skillfully. It is more plausible to argue that Georgia's suscepti-
bility to disorder is linked to the tension between the (self-imposed) normative model of liberal democracy and Georgians' use of pre-existing survival strategies based on their actual social experiences. The choice in
favor of a Western liberal democratic model in Georgia, it seems, is
largely identity-driven: Georgians feel they have to be democratic because
they have to be Western. However, the country's social and historical
experience with "Westernness" is minimal. Never in its history has Georgia been in close contact with the West. In medieval times, it was socialized mainly through ties with Byzantium (not an area that the modern
West claims as part of its heritage), followed by ties with the Ottoman
Empire and Persia. Western modernity came to Georgia only in the early
nineteenth century, and then by way of the Russian Empire. The Russian
version of modernity, however, was second-rate. No wonder Georgians
now want direct access to the "real thing," as represented by Europe and
the United States. The Georgian national project derives out of this
desire for access to Western modernization.

---

[44] See Mark R. Beissinger and Crawford Young, eds., *Beyond State Crisis? Post-
colonial Africa and Post-Soviet Eurasia in Comparative Perspective* (Washington, DC: Woodrow Wilson Center Press, 2002).

[45] See George Konrád, *Antipolitics* (San Diego: Harcourt Brace Jovanovich,
1984).

The collapse of the Russian Empire in 1917 and of the Soviet Union in 1991 afforded Georgia opportunities for direct access to Western modernization. The social capital that Georgians could actually invest in the Westernizing project, however, was and remains limited by Georgians' anarchic understanding of freedom as a lack of restraint, their intuitive mistrust toward state institutions, and their reliance on personalistic networks. This mindset has had the advantage of helping Georgians to defeat attempts to establish autocratic rule, both in the personalistic and populist version of Gamsakhurdia and the oligarchic version of Shevardnadze. However, it has not helped Georgians to construct sustainable and effective state institutions.

The most important feature of the Rose Revolution is not that Georgians once again rejected a nondemocratic leadership. Its greatest achievement may be the fact that it was fairly orderly, nonviolent, and involved a minimal derogation of the Georgian Constitution. It was the government, not the opposition, that had tampered with democratic institutions, and the people who enforced constitutional order by forcing the president to resign. With Shevardnadze's resignation, events again unfolded within the constitutional framework. It was the orderly and nonviolent character of the revolution that made Georgians, as well as many outside observers, believe that Georgians' European ambitions may be more justified than previously thought. In particular, it is widely believed that the Rose Revolution prompted the European Union to include countries of the South Caucasus into its neighborhood policy in 2004, contrary to its previous decision in 2003 to leave this question open. Georgian society used the period between the two extra-constitutional changes of power in 1992 and 2003 to develop some of the social capital necessary for building critical civil society institutions.

Whether Georgians' social capital is also sufficient for creating functional institutions that will make new revolutions (velvet or otherwise) unnecessary is an open question. The answer largely depends on the ability of Georgian political elites to formulate a new social contract that will be acceptable to the majority of the Georgian people. "The fight against corruption," the trademark issue of the post-revolutionary government, only makes sense against this backdrop. What Western advisors and Georgian democratic activists or politicians call corruption is for many Georgians a normal way to do business when the state is a presumed to be an adversary. Shevardnadze, like many other post-Soviet leaders, was simply trying to redefine in somewhat new terms what some American Sovietologists had called "the Brezhnev social contract."[46] This essentially entailed the state turning a blind eye to massive corruption among its civil servants and citizens in exchange for their political loyalty. Shevardnadze's rule was stable as long as this tacit contract survived. Rejecting the Brezhnev/Shevardnadze social contract formed the ideological basis for the Rose Revolution.

The Saakashvili government has demonstrated that strengthening the state and cracking down on corruption are its first priorities. Paramilitary groupings like the partisans in Megrelia and armed groups under Aslan Abashidze were crushed. One could say that save for separatist regions, Georgia now meets the Weberian criterion of statehood—the monopoly over the legitimate use of force. Since Saakashvili came to power, a number of high-level officials have been imprisoned on corruption charges, and improvement in tax collection has increased the level of public revenues by more than a half within a few months.[47] In order to reduce corruption in government offices, the government created a foundation that pays competitive salaries to some 11,000 public servants. It received funding from international and Georgian sponsors, including the United Nations Development Program (UNDP) and the American philanthropist George Soros, although it is supposed to be entirely funded by the Georgian state within three years.[48] The new authorities started to aggressively cut down personnel in government agencies so that in a few years time all employees who remain can be paid adequately from the state budget. Dramatic reductions in police forces (which were considered almost untouchable under Shevardnadze) were especially impressive. A radical program of privatization that calls for "selling everything but our conscience" is part of the same strategy.[49]

---

[46] See George Breslauer, *Five Images of the Soviet Future: A Critical Review and Synthesis* (Berkeley, CA: University of California Institute of International Studies, 1978); and Linda Cook, *The Soviet Social Contract and Why it Failed* (Cambridge, MA: Harvard University Press, 1993).

[47] Based on the data of the first nine months of 2004, the rate of tax collection increased by approximately 78 percent as compared to the similar period the previous year. See Galt and Taggart Securities, *Georgia: Weekly Stock Market Commentary*, October 11, 2004.

[48] Author's interview with Kote Kublashvili, the director of the foundation, July 2004.

[49] This program was announced by Georgia's new minister of economy, Kakha Bendukidze. See "A Different Sort of Oligarch," *The Economist*, July 27, 2004.

However, it is too early to say how successful these measures will be in creating a new relationship between Georgian citizens and the state. They could even be destabilizing in the short run, because these measures threaten a social order under which Georgians have lived for decades. Trying to replace this order with a new set of social practices that satisfy Western criteria of transparency and accountability is something other states have tried to do and failed, destabilizing their countries in the process. In these periods of transition, governments face the extremely difficult dilemma of tolerating a certain level of corrupt practices without being sucked into them. On the other hand, there is the danger of being carried away by a revolutionary Jacobin zeal for national purification and recasting all institutions from scratch.[50] This creates a temptation to resort to authoritarian modernization in the name of establishing liberal democracy. In this case, democratic political institutions are not based on a balance between different societal interests, but rather are imposed on society by "progressive" and enlightened elites. Widespread criticism of Saakashvili's government for skewing the power balance in favor of activist executive power at the expense of other institutions and actors, and for cutting corners of established democratic procedures, reflects this structural problem.[51] The problem cannot be solved unless a workable middle way is found between accepted social practices and the ideal type of the modern liberal state.

---

[50] Based on an analysis of 1998 survey results, German sociologist Theodor Hanf described part of the Georgian society dedicated to democratic values as "pious Jacobins" (pious because they displayed an unusually high level of religiosity). See Theodor Hanf and Ghia Nodia, *Lurching to Democracy: From Agnostic Tolerance to Pious Jacobinism: Societal Change and People's Reactions* (Baden-Baden: Nomos Verlagsgesellschaft, 2000).

[51] See on this, for instance, *Honouring of Obligations and Commitments of Georgia*, Resolution 1415 (2005) of the Parliamentary Assembly of the Council of Europe, http://assembly.coe.int/Mainf.asp?link=http://assembly.coe.int/documents/adoptedtext/ta05/eres1415.htm, accessed May 10, 2005; Tinatin Khidasheli, "The Rose Revolution Has Wilted Georgia," *International Herald Tribune*, December 8, 2004; Ghia Nodia, "Avtoritaruli modernizatsia lait tu demokratiuli institutebi?" *24 Saati*, January 28, 2005; Irakly Areshidze, "Bush and Georgia's Faded 'Rose,'" *Christian Science Monitor*, May 9, 2005.

'CULTURAL SECURITY': WESTERN VALUES AND NATIONAL TRADITIONS

The success of a new social contract upon which modern liberal democratic institutions can be based in Georgia depends on, among other
things, whether this social contract is ideologically reconciled with the
concept of the Georgian identity. This implies some linkage to traditional
values, because national identities cannot be defined without acknowl-
edging these values. The fact that democracy is unevenly spread between
civilizations (the widely discussed issue of the lack of democracy in Muslim-majority countries is the most dramatic example of this phenomenon)
suggests that it is not enough to explain why liberal democratic institutions are better from a rational point-of-view (or less bad than other systems, to borrow from Winston Churchill's phrase). People must also
believe that liberal democratic institutions can become "their institutions" and be compatible with their culture.

In this regard, there is a certain tension between two aspects of Georgia's national project. On the one hand, Georgia's insistence on being a
liberal democracy is largely identity-driven, in the sense that the country
wants to be a liberal democracy in order to prove that it is Western and
that it can be a modern nation-state without depending on Russia. On
the other hand, in the course of implementing the project of liberal
democracy in Georgia, it will be very difficult to avoid a clash with
accepted social practices that are deeply entrenched from years of experience with a foreign and repressive regime. This will require new norms
and institutions to be crafted by educated elites. In the process, however,
these elites will create an ideological opening for their political opponents, who can present existing social practices as the embodiment of
national values and traditions threatened by a new "foreign" modernizing project.

This is why modernizing projects often cause a nativist backlash. In
order to prevail, modernizers must demonstrate their ability to protect
and strengthen national identity, rather than weakening it. In other words,
the modernizing project should be ideologically embedded within the
national political tradition. Modernizing elites must be able to present
modernization as a continuation and enhancement of a domestic political
tradition or, at a minimum, as something that poses no threat to it.

This problem can also be described from sociological and political
perspectives. The gap between the normative model and available social
capital also translates into a social and cultural gap between "enlight-

ened" young modernizing elites on the one hand and the "backward" populace and old elites on the other. In the Georgian case, these new elites are represented mainly by political groups (such as Mikheil Saakashvili and Zurab Zhvania's circle that started as "young reformers" within the Shevardnadze-led Citizens' Union of Georgia), nongovernmental organizations, the media, academics, cultural figures, and parts of the new business community. These are the people who inspired and organized the force behind the Rose Revolution, although a minority of them rejected the revolution on the basis of strict interpretation of liberal constitutionalism. They acted in opposition to elite networks in the state bureaucracy and to business people of the old type (those who had vested interests in preserving practices that the reformers characterized as corrupt).

Ideological fights between these modernizing and conservative elites largely revolved around the social and cultural gap described in the previous paragraphs. Do efforts to change the ways in which things have been done in Georgia constitute a fight against corruption and the eradication of vestiges of an old political and economic order imposed by a foreign communist regime? Or is it a fight against Georgian national identity and values, a fight in which the West has a hidden agenda of undermining Orthodox culture? Are the reformers new national leaders who want to make their country stronger, or are they stooges of foreign influence who are, either intentionally or unwittingly, diluting Georgian national identity by introducing Western (or global) values and institutions into the country?

In Georgia, these two main opposing discourses have not led to the creation of opposing political parties based on reformist and conservative agendas. Nor have ethno-nationalist parties of the extreme right emerged to represent a nativist backlash against modernization. This may in part be explained by the fact that political parties in Georgia are not based on values and ideologies, but rather serve the political interests of specific personalities and groups.[52] A further explanation may be that the general legitimacy of the orientation toward democratic change in Georgia is rather strong. This may be measured both by sociological data that not

---

[52] Ghia Nodia, *Political Parties in Georgia*, Discussion Paper no. 8 (Stockholm: International Institute for Democracy and Electoral Assistance (IDEA), May 2003), pp. 8–14.

only demonstrate widespread support for basic democratic principles, but also—and even more importantly—the absence of significant antidemocratic discourses in Georgia. This distinguishes Georgia from a number of postcommunist countries at roughly the same level of development.[53] Players on the extreme right have never been able to establish viable political movements nor have they successfully challenged Georgia's orientation toward European values.[54] Were Georgia's pro-Western orientation to be questioned, this would most likely come from pro-Russian or neo-communist groups rather than from ethno-nationalist groups, but so far the former have failed to create any kind of credible political force.

This does not mean that the two discourses regarding modernization do not exist in Georgia. Instead, what is happening is that major political groups are trying to combine them. The idea that propagating liberal democracy and a market economy poses a threat to Georgia's traditional values and national identity has been present in the public discourse, although expressed in different ways. Discussions surrounding various versions of the "national security concept," a document that was supposed to define Georgia's major priorities for security policy, serves as an illustration.[55] One of the most divisive issues in these discussions was whether such a concept should discuss threats to national identity and

---

[53] For comparative sociological data, see John S. Dryzek and Leslie T. Holmes, *Post-Communist Democratization: Political Discourses across Thirteen Countries* (Cambridge, MA: Harvard University Press, 2002), pp. 147–157. On the general attitudes of the Georgian public towards democratic values and institutions, see Hanf and Nodia, *Lurching to Democracy,* and Marina Muskhelishvili and Luiza Arutiunova, "Political Views of Georgia's Population," unpublished paper.

[54] In my criticism of Guram Sharadze, the informal leader of the "extreme right" discourse and action in Georgia, I stated that his activities undermined the chances of Georgia's integration with the West. Remarkably, this was the only part of my criticism that he strongly denied. See Ghia Nodia, "Rogor Gavigot, Aris Tu Ara Guram Sharadze Rusetis Spetssamsaxurebis Agenti Da Aqvs Tu Ara Amas Mnishvneloba," *24 Hours,* July 10, 2002. Mr. Sharadze replied on television.

[55] After all these discussions, no such text was produced, apart from a document entitled *Georgia and The World: A Vision and Strategy for the Future* that was, according to credible sources known to this author, really written by Western consultants and was never widely publicized by the Georgian government, although it was posted on the NATO website, http://www.nato.int/pfp/ge/d001010.htm.

traditions as well as ways of dealing with them. Those more attuned to the modern Western discourse on security believed such references would complicate the document unnecessarily, but others argued that no concept of national security can or should avoid discussing threats to national identity.

There is a similar (and broader) discussion in Georgia about the concept of "national ideology." The proponents of such an idea insist that the lack of an ideology is one of Georgia's major problems. By "ideology," they mean some concept that would define values and strategies for the nation and the state. Such a concept, they argue, should be an official document sanctified by the state and thus made obligatory for all institutions and citizens. Opponents contend that there already is such a document—the Georgian Constitution—and that there is no need for another. While the supporters of a national ideology have never clearly defined what the structure or content of such a document should be, most discussions make it plain that the notion of national ideology refers to national identity and to strategies for preserving and empowering it.[56]

While it may seem easy to dismiss those who call for an official document spelling out a national ideology as people who cannot escape Soviet habits of thought, something more profound is involved. The quest for a national ideology also expresses, albeit rather clumsily, the feeling that Georgia lacks a clear sense of direction. Values of liberal democracy are viewed as being too abstract to provide this direction. These values have not been firmly planted in Georgian soil by the political elites, and the impression lingers that these elites use liberal democratic values more as a convenient political façade rather than as a program for action.

The nativist backlash's most dramatic expression has been the aggressive ideology of intolerance and violence against religious minorities. This backlash can be called "religious nationalism," and it arguably represents Georgia's version of the extreme right. Religious extremists in Georgia maintain that the Eastern Orthodox religion historically constitutes the core of Georgian identity. Therefore, they believe, the proselytizing activities of other churches—particularly Jehovah's Witnesses, other Protestant churches, and Catholics—are aimed at diluting Georgian identity. According to these religious nationalists, Georgian society and the state

---

[56] I reviewed this discussion in Georgian in "Ideologia: Erovnuli Da Sxva," *Apra*, no. 5 (1998), pp. 157–169.

should consider other religions besides Eastern Orthodoxy to be a major security threat. These attitudes were most evident during the wave of religious violence in Georgia from 1999 to 2003. In addition to violating human rights principles, this religious-inspired violence vividly demonstrated the weakness of the state. Officials did not institute the formal restrictions on minority churches demanded by the religious nationalists, but neither did they punish religious fanatics who engaged in open violence either. Moreover, in many instances, the police were largely sympathetic to the perpetrators.

Not that Georgia risked anything like a large-scale religious conflict, since the wave of intolerance was mainly directed against very small churches and not against larger minority confessions, such as Muslims or the Armenian Apostolic Church. Yet repeated acts of unpunished violence contributed to the erosion of the state's legitimacy. In addition, the very fact that religious aggression was primarily targeted against churches associated with the West was an indirect indication that there are members of the Georgian population who viewed the West as a threat to Georgian identity. The mainstream Georgian Orthodox Church formally distanced itself from the violent acts (most of them led by a defrocked Orthodox priest). But in official documents, the church also described "liberal ideology" as the major threat to the Orthodox tradition in Georgia. This is particularly important, because the Orthodox Church is the most respected institution in Georgia. A considerable portion of the Georgian public approved of the violent acts, while another portion disapproved of violence *per se* but showed hostility toward religious minorities and considered restrictions against them justified.[57] After the

---

[57] According to a 2004 survey, 32.7 percent or those polled supported violent disruption of meetings of religious "sects" such as Baptists or Jehovah's Witnesses, and 46.9 percent supported destroying their literature. In addition, 43.6 percent of respondents wanted the law to prohibit activities of sects like Baptists or Jehovah's Witnesses, and 34.4 percent wanted to restrict them. With regard to "traditional" religions like Catholicism or Islam, the idea to prohibit or restrict them was supported by 20.6 and 38 percent of those polled, respectively. See George Nizharadze, Iago Kachkachishvili, Rusudan Mshvidobadze, George Khutsishvili, and Emzar Jgerenaia, "Kartuli martlmadidebeli eklesia da religiuri umciresobebi sazogadoebrivi azris chrilshi: Sociologiuri kvlevis shedegebi," *Saertashoriso Konperentsia Religia Da Sazogadoeba—Rtsmena Chvens Tskhxovrebashi. Moxsenebata Mokle Shinaarsebi* (Tbilisi: International Conference Religion and Society: Faith in Our Life,

Saakashvili government came to power in November 2003, however, the tide of religious violence went down, and several of its perpetrators have been jailed.

The early post-Shevardnadze period has shown that while elements of a nativist backlash still exist, its magnitude no longer poses a serious challenge to Georgia's pro-Western national project. Accusations of "inadequate Georgianness" failed to discredit Georgia's new reformist leaders. After the revolution of November 2003, pro-Western modernizers came to power, and the subsequent presidential and parliamentary elections demonstrated their overwhelming popularity.[58] Many of the people now in office are the same individuals who earlier pushed for liberal reforms, including the less popular principle of religious freedom. Despite their current popularity, Saakashvili and his allies know that the gap between their liberal democratic modernizing agenda and prevailing social practices in Georgia still makes them vulnerable to a nativist backlash. For this reason, they need to develop their own alternative version of nationalism.

The nationalism of democratic modernizers in Georgia is that of a strong and effective state. As in the other post-Communist countries of Eastern Europe, joining the West through membership in organizations such as NATO and the European Union stands at the top of their agenda, but they do not want to give up national pride or the idea of the nation-state as a model of statehood. Membership in Western institutions is seen as the best mechanism for safeguarding the Georgian state and identity. Since the Georgian Orthodox Church remains the most powerful symbol of Georgian identity, however, pro-Western modernizers are careful to ensure that no one can question their loyalty to the church. While still cooperating with Shevardnadze, they sponsored a controversial "concordat" (constitutional agreement) between the state and the Georgian Orthodox Church in October 2002. The agreement highlighted the status of the church as the predominant religious institution in Georgia,

---

2004), pp. 11–14. See also David Zurabishvili, *Freedom of Confession and Religious Minorities in Georgia*, Discussion Paper no. 7 (Stockholm: International Institute for Democracy and Electoral Assistance (IDEA), May 2003), pp. 24–27; and Nodar Ladaria, *Religioznyi ekstremizm v gruzii*, http://www.pankisi.info/analitic/?page=ge&id=43.

[58] Mikheil Saakashvili won the January 2004 Georgian presidential elections with 96.27 percent of the vote; the National Movement-Democrats won the parliamentary elections with 66.24 percent of the vote.

although it fell short of formally establishing it as the state church. This led to criticism from many pro-democracy activists in Georgia, including some who later became part of Saakashvili's government.

While the concordat arrangement violates the liberal democratic model, it was a relatively safe way for the reformers to demonstrate their commitment to safeguarding national identity without directly under-mining religious freedoms. During his presidential inauguration cere-monies on January 24, 2004, Saakashvili took a holy oath at the Gelati Cathedral in the western Georgian city of Kutaisi.[59] There was a double symbolism in this gesture. On the one hand, he received the blessing of the church (rather like a medieval monarch). On the other hand, Gelati is where the greatest Georgian king of the eleventh century, David the Builder, is buried. By receiving the blessing at Gelati, Saakashvili, who wants a strong Georgian state, was symbolically alluding to a period of history when Georgia had such a state.

In general, Saakashvili attaches a large importance (some say too large) to symbols. One of his first steps after the Rose Revolution was to push the Georgian Parliament, even before his inauguration, to change the country's flag. The previous flag had been created by the Georgian Social Democratic government in 1918. It had colors similar to those of the German flag, although with dark red occupying the greatest part of the flag in honor of social democratic ideological preferences.[60] The new flag, introduced by Saakashvili's National Movement when it was still in the opposition, has one large cross and four small red crosses set against a white background. His opponents claimed that it was a Catholic flag, but it has also been used by the Georgian Orthodox Church in recent years. Some historians argue that this flag can be traced back to the golden age of Georgia in the eleventh and twelfth centuries—which is yet another way to evoke the idea of a strong Georgia.

Apart from being a strong state by medieval standards, the Georgian kingdom of that period also cooperated with Christian Crusaders. While Georgia's European vocation is sometimes challenged by Westerners on historical grounds—Georgia has never been part of the European histori-

---

[59] "Catholicos-Patriarch to Bless Saakashvili as President of Georgia," *InterPress*, January 24, 2004.

[60] The independent Georgian Republic was created in 1918 under the patronage of Germany.

cal experience, they insist[61]—the connection to the Crusaders provides a rare occasion when Georgia can claim to be affiliated with Europe.[62] Although the Crusades' relevance to the modern European idea is another matter, Saakashvili does appear to be reaching out not only to Georgia's glorious past, but also to the time when Georgia was strong enough to contribute to European projects. In his inaugural speech, Saakashvili said, "Not only are we old Europeans, but we are ancient Europeans."[63] The statement contained an allusion to Donald Rumsfeld's distinction between "old Europe" and "new Europe"—a sensitive issue, because Saakashvili must balance between the Americans and Europeans. But more importantly, he meant to stress that Georgia's European vocation is rooted in ancient times. At his inaugural ceremony, there were two flags: the new Georgian flag with its ancient symbolism and the European flag—the flag used by the Council of Europe and the European Union—with its symbolism of modernity.

CONCLUSIONS

The security challenges facing Georgia are multilayered. The two most dramatic and closely interlinked—the unresolved territorial conflicts in Abkhazia and South Ossetia and the failure to find a modus vivendi in relations with Russia—constitute the outside layer. In trying to solve these issues, Georgia's options are rather limited. The debacle in South Ossetia in summer 2004 demonstrated these fundamental limitations: an attempt to change the situation on the ground and accelerate a solution

---

[61] See, for instance, William Pfaff, "'Europe' Has Historical Limits: The Baltics vs. the Caucasus," *The International Herald Tribune*, February 28, 2004. Pfaff writes that, "The new president [Saakashvili] says he is committed to leading Georgia back into the Euro-Atlantic fold. Back? Georgia was under divided Persian and Turkish rule from the 16th to 18th centuries, then was a Russian colony for two centuries, and from 1921 to 1991 was a constituent republic of the Soviet Union." But the point is that Saakashvili justifies the policy of going *back* to Europe by citing much more ancient experiences.

[62] In 2005, the image of the Crusaders resurfaced when Saakashvili—together with his Ukrainian friend and counterpart Viktor Yushchenko—started a joint Georgian program of summer camps for Georgian and Ukrainian youths called "Young Crusaders."

[63] "Georgian President Optimistic about Future in Inauguration Speech," *BBC Monitoring Former Soviet Union*, January 25, 2004.

may only have made things worse, yet the alternative appeared to be passively accepting the status quo. Georgia simply lacks the resources to solve these issues. International experience shows that when it comes to territorial conflicts, especially when they reach the status of "frozen conflicts" where both parties are entrenched in their positions, either powerful outsiders impose a solution by force or blatant pressure or the parties remain in limbo for many decades. Georgians have good reason to fear that they may have to live with the tensions surrounding the country's "frozen conflicts," including troubled relations with Russia, for quite a long time.

Other instances of fragmentation—such as the problem of Ajara, sensitive regional identities, and non-integrated and potentially irredentist ethnic minorities—represent the next layer of security challenges. Georgia can deal with these problems based on its own resources, and its record since independence suggests that, on balance, the dynamics are positive. The peaceful removal of Abashidze's repressive regime and effective incorporation of Ajara into the Georgian political space may have been the greatest strategic success in Georgia's nation-building since independence. Megrelia appears to have overcome the trauma lingering from the civil conflict of the early 1990s. Important problems remain: Armenian and Azerbaijani minorities are only superficially part of the Georgian political nation, and attempts to integrate them may prove controversial in the future. However, Georgians appear to have overcome the worst phase of aggressive ethnic nationalism, while the Azerbaijani and Armenian minorities—despite many grudges—have not shown readiness to mobilize around separatist programs even in the worst of times.

Issues related to the creation of effective, stable, and legitimate state institutions lie at the core of Georgia's security problems. They are central because they define the ability of the Georgian state to face the issues that lie on the surface. Here, the record is mixed, and the jury is still out. While the Georgian people have expressed their commitment to the normative idea of democracy, they have yet to pass the most basic test of sustainable democracy: namely, an orderly constitutional transfer of power. "Corruption" has become the buzzword in Georgia—as it has in many other countries in the world—but what it really denotes is a disconnect between the normative Weberian idea of the modern state and the entrenched practices or survival strategies typical for societies that were late in embracing this idea. The new government of Mikheil Saakashvili has demonstrated a genuine resolve to fight specific manifestations of corruption. But the repressive-revolutionary methods predominant in this fight and the total mistrust of the existing civil service may prove counterproductive if this campaign is not backed up by a more mundane effort aimed at building a new and sustainable civil service.

The tenacity of Georgia's "national project" to be a modern liberal state may be the most promising element of Georgia's experience since independence. Gamsakhurdia and Shevardnadze's failed policies have not led to an anti-Western backlash, although these policies were notionally pro-Western. Openly illiberal ideological currents—neocommunism, nativist ethnic nationalism, anti-modern religious fundamentalism—did emerge, but after Gamsakhurdia's ouster they remained marginal. Georgians may not have yet mastered routine democratic procedures. However, as the Rose Revolution showed, the basic values of democracy and human rights are internalized by a critical mass of the people. Strict liberals may not like privileging the dominant Orthodox Church or the rhetoric of strong-state nationalism characteristic of the pro-Western modernizers now in power. But the latter know that success of their reforms depends on finding the proper formula for marrying traditional Georgian values and identity with modern liberal ideals. Still, a strong illiberal-nativist force may emerge and work to unravel Georgia's current national project. Thus far, however, Georgia's experience shows that the way to a secure and stable country can only be paved by a new social contract rooted in a combination of modern Western values and safeguards for the national identity.

CHAPTER 2

Georgia's Time of Troubles, 1989–1993

CHRISTOPH ZÜRCHER

T he crisis of Soviet communism and the eventual breakup of the Soviet Union in 1991 was obviously a major factor triggering the civil wars in the Caucasus.[1] In 1987, Mikhail Gorbachev launched an ambitious reform project. His policies of *perestroika* and *glasnost* had for the first time in the history of the Soviet Union created a public sphere where political grievances could be voiced. National movements were among the first to occupy that public space. By 1989, many

---

* This chapter has greatly benefited from comments and suggestions by Jonathan Cohen, George Hewitt, Robert Legvold, Bruno Coppieters, Ghia Nodia, Viacheslav Chirikba, and Jonathan Wheatley.

[1] This chapter draws on my previous work, mainly *Institutionen und organisierte Gewalt. Konflikt und Stabilitätsdynamiken im (post-)sowjetischen Kaukasus* (Berlin: Habilitationsschrift, Free U Berlin, 2003), and Christoph Zürcher, Jan Koehler, and Pavel Baev, "Internal Violence in the Caucasus," *The Economics of Political and Common Violence* (Washington, DC: The World Bank Development Economic Research Group, 2002). See also Svante Cornell, "Autonomy in the South Caucasus: A Catalyst for Conflict" (paper presented at the ASN Fifth Annual World Convention, New York, NY, April 12–15, 2000); Nikola Cvetkovski, "The Georgian–South Ossetian Conflict," (PhD diss., Aalborg University, n.d.), chapter 4, http://www.caucasus.dk/publication5.htm; Stephen F. Jones, "Georgia: A Failed Democratic Transition," in Ian Bremmer, and Raymond Taras, eds., *Nation and Politics in the Soviet Successor States* (Cambridge: Cambridge University Press, 1993), pp. 288–310; Darrell Slider, "Democratization in Georgia," in Karen Dawisha and Bruce Parrott, eds., *Conflict, Cleavage, and Change in Central Asia and the Caucasus* (Cambridge: Cambridge University Press, 1997), pp. 156–200. Jonathan Wheatley's forthcoming book *Georgia from National Awakening to Rose Revolution: A Story of Delayed Transition in the Former Soviet Union* (Ashgate) proved to be a very valuable source of inspiration and knowledge.

Map 3. Autonomous Republics and Autonomous Regions (*oblasts*) in Georgia (1991)

Central Intelligence Agency Map, courtesy of the University of Texas Libraries, The University of Texas at Austin, http://www.lib.utexas.edu/maps/commonwealth/georgia.gif

of these movements had adopted radical positions advocating secession from the Soviet Union. Popular organizations in the Baltic states began the process, but the national movements of Armenia, Azerbaijan, and Georgia followed shortly thereafter—with no less passion, and with more dramatic consequences.

In 1991, the Soviet Union imploded and left behind fifteen successor states that had very low state capacities and were plagued by power struggles between the old elite and national-democratic or nationalist challengers. In addition, some of the successor states were themselves challenged by secessionist movements. This unprecedented case of state collapse constitutes the background crucial for understanding the internal wars that followed.

Between 1989 and 1993, there were three instances of organized violence in Georgia. The first, the violent ethno-political conflict over the breakaway region of South Ossetia, began in November 1989, escalated in January 1991, and then flared up again in June 1992. In July 1992, a Russian-Georgian-Ossetian peacekeeping mission was deployed to South Ossetia. The second war was the violent struggle for national power between rival political groups in Tbilisi. The violence began in December 1991 and ended in November 1993, and was triggered by the violent overthrow of President Zviad Gamsakhurdia by a coalition of opposition politicians and entrepreneurs of violence.[2] In the capital city of Tbilisi, this conflict lasted only a couple of weeks and ended with the expulsion of Gamsakhurdia in January 1992. Even after Eduard Shevardnadze's return to power in March, however, in western Georgia the ousted president's followers mounted military resistance to the new government, which lasted until November 1993. The third case of organized violence was the war over the breakaway Autonomous Republic of Abkhazia. It began in August 1992 and ended in September 1993 with the defeat of Georgian troops. The conflicts over South Ossetia and Abkhazia remain formally unresolved up to the present day. In both cases, the secessionist entities have asserted themselves militarily, but have failed to gain international recognition.

This chapter analyzes these three wars in Georgia, beginning with the chain of events that led from mass mobilization in 1988 to the wars in

---

[2] By "entrepreneurs of violence," we mean actors who mix the activity of warring with the pursuit of personal, material profit. Often, the latter becomes the driving force behind the activities of entrepreneurs of violence.

South Ossetia, the war over political power in Tbilisi, and the war in Abkhazia. The focus is on the spiral of ethno-national mobilization within Georgia. The second section discusses four clusters of factors that account for the organization of violence in Georgia: (1) the mechanism of Soviet ethno-federalism, (2) the internal fragmentation of the post-communist elite, (3) entrepreneurship of violence, and (4) the regional neighborhood. The third and last section puts these findings in contemporary perspective by examining the structural changes that have taken place in Georgia since 1993 and asks what this means for Georgian and regional security today.

THE SPIRAL OF NATIONAL MOBILIZATION

The course and the logic of events in Georgia cannot be understood without taking into account the specific institutions of the Soviet ethno-federal system that served as the stage on which this drama evolved. As Ghia Nodia details in his contribution to this volume, the Soviet Union was an asymmetric federation consisting of territorial units with different statuses. On the first level were the fifteen union republics, then came the autonomous republics, and then the autonomous regions. The Georgian drama resulted from the disintegration of this ethno-federal structure, where each level of governance was ordered hierarchically—with the union center (Moscow) at the top, the union republic of Georgia in the middle, and finally, the autonomous republic of Abkhazia and the autonomous region of South Ossetia at the bottom. Over the course of these events, the hierarchical links became increasingly loose, and secessionist pressures at lower levels gathered strength. The emergence of a sovereign Georgia was paralleled by the growing determination of forces in South Ossetia and Abkhazia to achieve their own sovereignty.

During the early years of *perestroika*, Georgia was a relatively peaceful republic, ruled by an ethnically homogenous Georgian *nomenklatura* that was organized into closely-knit patronage networks and skilled in exploiting the lucrative opportunities offered by the Georgian shadow economy. A Georgian nationalist discourse opposing Soviet assimilationist policies had been present sporadically since the 1970s, but a real opposition movement had not existed. It was not until the beginning of 1988 that an oppositional nationalist discourse similar to what existed in the Baltic states or Armenia—a discourse representing religious, cultural, and political concerns—established itself in Georgia. The first group with an explicitly separatist program was the National Democratic Party founded by Giorgi Chanturia. The nationalist tide soon grew stronger and developed variations on a general theme, such as Georgian victimization, the distortion of Georgia's national history, the prohibition of a national memory, and the imposition of Russian-Soviet foreign rule. Even the pro-Communist Rustaveli Society appropriated the main elements of the nationalist discourse (short of the demand for independence).[3] From the beginning of 1989 onward, however, it was the radical Georgian nationalists who dominated the public sphere—discursively, but also physically, with demonstrations and hunger strikes in the center of Tbilisi.

The national mobilization in Abkhazia mirrors the national movement in Georgia. In 1989, Abkhazia was an autonomous republic (ASSR) within Georgia. It had 525,000 inhabitants, of whom 45.7 percent were Georgians, 14.3 percent Russians, and 14.6 percent Armenians. The Abkhazians made up 17.8 percent of the population.[4] The Abkhazian-Adyghean language group belongs to the northern Caucasian linguistic family, akin to the Chechen-Dagestanian group and not related to the Kartvelian family of languages of which Georgian is a member. There are both Orthodox and Muslim believers among the Abkhazian population. The relationship between Georgians and Abkhazians had not been free of tension during the Soviet period. The severe policies of repression under Stalin, Abkhazians' fear of Georgians' demographic and political dominance, and the competition for resources between Tbilisi and Sukhumi (mainly over transfers from Moscow, but also over cadre positions in Abkhazia and control of lucrative segments of the shadow economy) had caused constant political friction. As long as Soviet rule was firmly established in the region, however, this friction had not led to violent conflict between the local Abkhazian and Georgian populations.

---

[3] Jürgen Gerber, *Georgien: Nationale Opposition und kommunistische Herrschaft seit 1965* (Baden-Baden: Nomos, 1997).

[4] This data comes from the 1989 USSR population census, the final and most comprehensive population census of the former Soviet Union ever conducted. See *Itogi vsesoyuznoi perepisi naseleniya 1989 goda* (Minneapolis, MN: East View Publications, 1989). These figures need to be taken with caution, since this census is less than accurate and not free of political manipulation. Demography is a hotly disputed issue between Georgians and Abkhazians.

In 1957, 1967, and 1977, Abkhazian cultural movements and parts of the intelligentsia (and some high-ranking Communist Party functionaries in 1977) requested that Moscow integrate Abkhazia into the territory of the Russian Soviet Federated Socialist Republic. The Soviet leadership turned down the Abkhazians' request each time, but compensated them by putting together a packet of concessions and increased regional investment. These compensatory measures led to the Abkhazians gaining disproportionate access to resources and to key political positions. This was particularly true at the end of the 1980s, when Tbilisi was losing its grip over local Abkhazian affairs. In 1990, 67 percent of the ministers of the Abkhazian government were Abkhazian.[5] As economic control went hand-in-hand with administrative power in the Soviet system, Abkhazians controlled most of the local economy.

The public sphere created in Abkhazia by *perestroika* in 1988 was immediately dominated by two diametrically opposed discourses about past injustices. The Abkhazians warned of the dramatic shifting of the demographic proportions in their republic. Primarily due to the immigration (including a government-led resettlement) of Megrelian (western Georgian) peasants to Abkhazia during the Soviet period, the proportion of Georgians in the autonomous republic had risen from 28 percent in 1914 to 45.5 percent in 1989, thus heightening competition over scarce land.[6] Abkhazians also complained that per capita investment in Abkhazia was only 40 percent of the level of investment in the rest of Georgia. This was factually correct, but wrongly interpreted as ethnic discrimination—since Georgians were the largest ethnic group in Abkhazia and would thus be the main victims of a discriminatory policy. Furthermore, Abkhazia, the "Soviet Riviera," was without a doubt one of the wealthiest regions of the Soviet Union and enjoyed a far higher standard of living than the rest of Georgia.

---

[5] See http://freedomhouse.org/survey99/relterr/abkhazia.html.

[6] Much of this population movement was instigated by the Soviet authorities for political reasons. See Georgi M. Derluguian, "The Tale of Two Resorts: Abkhazia and Ajaria Before and Since the Soviet Collapse," in Beverly Crawford and Ronnie D. Lipschutz, eds., *The Myth of 'Ethnic Conflict': Politics, Economics, and Cultural Violence* (Berkeley, CA: International and Area Studies, University of California Press, 1998), pp. 261–292 at p. 267, http://repositories.cdlib.org/cgi/viewcontent.cgi?article=1064& context=uciaspubs/research.

The Georgian population in Abkhazia, meanwhile, complained about the disproportionate allocation of key positions in Abkhazia. In particular, control over the distribution of land was important, since produce from the Abkhazian agricultural sector, including tea, tobacco, wine, and citrus fruits brought huge profits on the Soviet market. The Georgians in Tbilisi accused Abkhazians of having special connections to patrons in Moscow and regarded the Abkhazian national movement as an existential threat to Georgian independence.

In June 1988, fifty-eight Abkhazian Communists sent a letter to the Nineteenth Party Conference in Moscow demanding the uncoupling of Abkhazia from the Georgian SSR. This demand awakened Georgian fears of a repetition of the "Karabakh Scenario," where an autonomous entity in one former Soviet republic sought to be integrated into another. A mass demonstration in Abkhazia took place in March 1989 near Sukhumi at Lykhny, a place that is significant in Abkhazian history and mythology due to its "holy" tree and the fact that it was the historical residence of Abkhazian rulers. Twenty thousand people, including Abkhazian members of the Communist elite, signed the so-called Declaration of Lykhny, calling for the promotion of Abkhazia to the status of a union republic, which implied secession from Georgia. The declaration was published in Abkhazian newspapers on March 24. In July 1989, the first cases of intercommunal violence occurred. Sixteen people died and hundreds were injured.[7] However, neither the Abkhazians nor the Georgians yet had an organized capacity for violence.

The Georgian national movement reacted to Abkhazian mobilization with a new call of its own. Throughout the country, mass demonstrations took place, which mixed anti-Communist with anti-Abkhazian slogans. The anti-Abkhazian mood strengthened, especially among the Georgian community in Abkhazia. The news of a mass demonstration of Abkhazians—at which, again, the secession of Abkhazia from Georgia had been demanded—led in March 1989 to one of the largest protests in Tbilisi's history. The Georgian Communist leadership, fearing a loss of control over the situation in the capital, asked Soviet troops to move in against the demonstrators. On the morning of the April 9, the army violently broke up the demonstration. Hundreds were wounded and nine-

---

[7] Ronald G. Suny, *The Making of the Georgian Nation* (Bloomington, IN: Indiana University Press, 1994), p. 323.

teen people were killed. The consequence of this bloodbath was predictable: the Georgian national movement was radicalized, and the Georgian Communist regime lost legitimacy.

Moscow reacted as it had some months earlier during the Karabakh crisis by replacing local officials. In this case it sacked Georgian Communist Party chief, Jumber Patiashvili, and substituted the chairman of the Georgian KGB, Givi Gumbaridze. The shock of the events of April 9, however, was so great that the new Communist leadership adopted the main demands of the nationalist opposition. Far-reaching concessions were made to the national movement. First, the leaders of the movement—Zviad Gamsakhurdia, Merab Kostava, and Giorgi Chanturia—were freed from jail. In August 1989, the Communist-dominated Georgian Supreme Soviet passed a language law that made the use of Georgian mandatory in the public sector throughout the republic, a move that was badly received in Abkhazia (where the majority of the non-Georgian population does not know Georgian) and South Ossetia.

In September 1989, Gumbaridze demanded before the plenum of the Central Committee in Moscow that Georgia be allowed to regulate its own internal ethnic matters and suggested that it even be allowed to form its own armed forces for this purpose. In November, the Georgian Supreme Soviet proclaimed that it would not recognize Soviet law that contradicted Georgian interests. It declared Georgia's sovereignty in March 1990, thereby nullifying all treaties concluded by the Soviet government since 1921. Gumbaridze announced that it was the aim of the party to restore Georgian independence. The new Communist Party leader's increasingly nationalistic rhetoric had a fatal signal effect for those minorities that had regional autonomy within Soviet Georgia (namely, the Ossetians and the Abkhazians) and added to their fears of Georgian dominance.

A second hotspot to emerge was South Ossetia. An autonomous region within Georgia, South Ossetia had a population of just over 100,000, of which 66.2 percent was Ossetian and 29 percent Georgian.[8] Around half of all families in South Ossetia were of mixed Georgian and Ossetian origin.[9] The Ossetian language belongs to the northeastern

---

[8] See *Itogi vsesoyuznoi perepisi naseleniya 1989 goda.*
[9] Alexei Zverev, "Ethnic Conflicts in the Caucasus 1988–1994," in Bruno Coppieters, ed., *Contested Borders in the Caucasus* (Brussels: VUB Press, 1996), p. 39, http://poli.vub.ac.be/publi/ContBorders/eng/ch0103.htm.

group of Iranian languages. The majority of the Ossetians are Orthodox Christians, while a minority are Sunni Muslims. Between 1918 and 1921, Menshevik-ruled Georgia violently suppressed the Bolshevik revolt of the Ossetians. This event has played a role in the Ossetian discourse on the wrongs suffered throughout the group's history. In general, however, relations between Tbilisi and Tskhinvali, as well as relations between the Georgians and the Ossetians living in South Ossetia, were mostly free of severe tension until the end of 1988. But in 1989, problems between these two groups began to increase. It then became clear that South Ossetia was taking the same path as Abkhazia, one aiming at secession from an increasingly nationalistic Georgia. It wanted to be unified with North Ossetia, an autonomous republic situated in the Russian Federation.

During this time, the war of laws escalated: The Ossetians countered the Georgian language law that the Georgian Supreme Soviet had passed in August 1989 by making Ossetian the official language in South Ossetia. In November 1989, the South Ossetian Regional Soviet, the area's highest legislative organ, appealed to the Georgian Supreme Soviet and the Supreme Soviet of the Soviet Union to raise the status of South Ossetia from autonomous region (AO) to autonomous republic (ASSR). This appeal contained nothing unconstitutional and was not exceptional during the latter years of *perestroika* when all AOs and ASSRs strove to have their status raised. Nevertheless, Georgian Communists and the national opposition perceived South Ossetia's request as a step toward secession and a threat to the goal of Georgian independence.

The Georgian national movement, whose most popular leader was now Zviad Gamsakhurdia, made use of the increasing tensions with South Ossetia. On November 23, 1989, in reaction to the decision of the South Ossetian legislature to upgrade the area's status to that of a sovereign republic, 30,000 Georgian demonstrators were mobilized and bussed to a protest demonstration in Tskhinvali, the capital of South Ossetia. Upon entering the city, the demonstrators were obstructed by Soviet security forces. Clashes followed, primarily benefiting Gamsakhurdia, who had demonstrated that he was capable of mobilizing 30,000 people and able to force his agenda on the Georgian Communist Party leadership. In reaction to this demonstration by the Georgian nationalists, the leadership of the group Ademon Nykhas began to form the first militia groups in South Ossetia.[10] The Georgian population in South

---

[10] Ademon Nykhas ("The People's Assembly") was the South Ossetian popular

Ossetia began moving its transportable possessions to safety and preparing to flee should it prove necessary.

In March 1990, the Georgian Supreme Soviet legalized all banned opposition parties and completed its split with Moscow by declaring Georgia to be an annexed and occupied state. In reaction to these unmistakable steps toward Georgian independence from the Soviet Union, the Abkhazians in turn reacted with unmistakable steps toward independence from Georgia. Most significantly, the Abkhazian Supreme Soviet unilaterally proclaimed Abkhazia to be a sovereign union republic and petitioned Moscow to be incorporated into the Soviet Union as a union republic. These steps were declared invalid by the Georgian Supreme Soviet.

In August 1990, in preparation for the first free parliamentary elections in Georgia, the Georgian Supreme Soviet passed an electoral law forbidding the participation of groups that were only active on the regional level, essentially excluding any Ossetian party from participating in the elections. The regional South Ossetian Soviet reacted by proclaiming a Democratic Soviet Republic of South Ossetia on September 20, 1990, and asked Moscow to allow it to accede to the Soviet Union. On December 9, elections were conducted in South Ossetia. The newly elected Georgian parliament, in which Gamsakhurdia's supporters formed a majority, declared the South Ossetian elections to be invalid and suspended the autonomous status of the region. A state of emergency was imposed on South Ossetia, and Interior Ministry security forces were posted to Tskhinvali.

On January 5, 1991, a 5,000-strong Georgian military formation, comprised of local militias and members of the recently created Georgian National Guard, entered Tskhinvali, looting and attacking the civilian population. The South Ossetian militias resisted fiercely, and at the end of January, the Georgian troops withdrew, took up position on the heights around the city, and enforced a blockade, which lasted until the Russian-Georgian-Ossetian peacekeeping mission came to South Ossetia in July 1992.

The war over South Ossetia was the first war in Georgia and indirectly paved the way for the two wars to come. It saw the introduction of militias within Georgia, groups that escaped the control of the state that had to a great extent sponsored their emergence. The next wars in Georgia

---

movement created as a political platform for advancing the claim for more autonomy.

were the civil war (starting in December 1991) and the war over Abkhazia (starting in August 1992). In each of these wars, militias played the
dominant role.

The first free Georgian parliamentary elections on October 28, 1990,
ended in victory for Gamsakhurdia. The new government left no doubt
that its aim was full independence for Georgia. Gamsakhurdia's victory,
however, did not obscure the fact that the victors were unable to unite a
hopelessly divided national movement. Both the National Democratic
Party and the National Independence Party had boycotted the elections
to the Supreme Soviet and had instead held alternative elections to their
own parliament, the National Congress, on September 30, 1990. The
elections to the Supreme Soviet brought a new stratum of Georgian society into power, a stratum that was viewed by the *nomenklatura* and the
urban intelligentsia as poorly trained, poorly educated, and incapable of
governing the country—a judgment confirmed by this first parliament's
track record.

By the fall of 1990, Georgia was falling apart. Two out of three
autonomous entities, South Ossetia and Abkhazia, were largely outside
of Tbilisi's control. The Georgian national movement was deeply divided,
and paramilitary "pro-fatherland" groups were operating largely
unchecked. On April 9, 1991, exactly two years after Soviet troops violently suppressed the April demonstrations in Tbilisi, the Georgian parliament declared Georgia's independence, and on May 26, Gamsakhurdia
was elected president with over 86 percent of the vote. The non-Georgian population of Abkhazia and South Ossetia boycotted this election.

Gamsakhurdia lasted less than a year in office. The starting point of
the Georgian civil war was the August 1991 putsch in Moscow. Gamsakhurdia, surprised by these events, declared that he was neutral in relation to the struggle for power in the Soviet Union and complied with the
Soviet military commander's demand to integrate the Georgian National
Guard into the structure of the Soviet Interior Ministry. The leader of the
National Guard, Tengiz Kitovani, however, resisted this order, which
would have meant the dissolution of "his" guard and withdrew with his
troops from Tbilisi in September 1991, leaving the president without an
effective military force.

This meant Gamsakhurdia did not have a sufficient basis to secure his
regime. Although he managed to destroy the now-alienated Mkhedrioni
in February 1991, in August Kitovani and his ally, Prime Minister Tengiz

Sigua, defected. This left Gamsakhurdia with very few armed men on whom he could rely. Kitovani and Sigua moved against the isolated and increasingly erratic Gamsakhurdia, whose vehement anti-Soviet and nationalist politics could not hide the fact that the Georgian state was falling apart and remained internationally isolated. As soon as he was liberated from prison in the last days of December 1991, Jaba Ioseliani reconfigured the Mkhedrioni and joined the insurgents as well.

On December 22, 1991, approximately 500 National Guard soldiers entered Tbilisi and, after a short siege of the parliamentary building, drove the elected president into exile. On January 6, 1992, Gamsakhurdia fled to Armenia, and the opposition claimed victory. The civil war was, however, by no means over. The deposed president mounted military resistance from his home region in western Georgia against the new authorities in Tbilisi.

With the flight of Gamsakhurdia from Tbilisi, the stage was set for a new and substantial actor. The new interim authorities—Ioseliani (leader of the Mkhedrioni), Kitovani (head of the National Guard), as well as former Prime Minister Sigua (who was fired by Gamsakhurdia in August 1991)—called Eduard Shevardnadze back to Georgia. Shevardnadze, who had served as Soviet foreign minister during Gorbachev's most innovative phase, commanded a high reputation internationally and within Georgia, and was widely seen as a senior statesman who could lead Georgia out of civil war. After his return on March 7, 1992, Shevardnadze was named chairman of a transitional government, the so-called State Council, and entrusted with the task of leading the country out of civil war. This task was, in view of the circumstances, extremely complex: in South Ossetia, the war could no longer be won; the conflict with Abkhazia threatened to re-escalate at any moment; the deposed President Gamsakhurdia was operating with units loyal to him in western Georgia. In addition, Russia, as the successor state to the Soviet Union, put Georgia under pressure to join the newly formed Commonwealth of Independent States (CIS) and agree to a Russian military presence in the country. Shevardnadze's only (and very unreliable) backing at this time was his coalition with the entrepreneurs of violence, Ioseliani and Kitovani. In the conflict with South Ossetia, Russia now became a central factor. Political pressure from Moscow, in the form of thinly veiled military support for the Ossetians and threatening gestures, such as sporadic helicopter attacks on Georgian villages, forced Shevardnadze to agree to a cease-fire.

In July 1992, a Russian-Georgian-Ossetian peacekeeping force under Russian leadership began monitoring a negotiated cease-fire.

Simultaneous with the de-escalation in South Ossetia, a new increase in violence took place in Abkhazia. For several years, the Georgian-Abkhazian conflict had been chiefly a war of laws (issued by the respective parliaments) and of competing elections (where only one of the parties participated).[11] On August 25, 1990, the Abkhazian Supreme Soviet proclaimed Abkhazia to be a union republic within the Soviet Union. This decision was immediately declared invalid by the Georgian Supreme Soviet. One serious attempt at reaching a compromise was made in August 1991, when Gamsakhurdia reached a power-sharing deal with the Abkhazian leadership in the form of an electoral code whereby electoral districts would be demarcated according to ethnic lines, effectively giving each group a quota of seats in the new 65-seat Abkhazian parliament. Thus, the Georgian population (representing 45.7 percent of the population of Abkhazia in 1989) would receive 26 seats, the Abkhazians (17.8 percent) would receive 28 seats, while the other groups (primarily Armenians [14.6 percent] and Russians [14.3 percent]) would receive the remaining 11 seats. A two-thirds majority was required to make decisions on constitutional issues, thus preventing either of the main groups from pushing through constitutional amendments without the consent of the other.[12] On September 29, 1991, elections were held to the Abkhazian Supreme Soviet on the basis of this law, with a second round of voting held on October 13 and December 1. In the long run, however, the 1991 agreement would not be honored.

One of the reasons why this agreement failed was the collapse of the Gamsakhurdia government, which had several major repercussions. First, because the new Shevardnadze administration was doing everything it could to delegitimize Gamsakhurdia, it was reluctant to lend active sup-

---

[11] Human Rights Watch, "Georgia/Abkhazia: Violation of the Laws of War and Russia's Role in the Conflict," March 1, 1995, http://www.hrw.org/reports/1995/Georgia2.htm.

[12] See Ghia Nodia, "The Conflict in Abkhazia: National Projects and Political Circumstances," in Bruno Coppieters, Ghia Nodia, and Yuri Anchabadze, eds., *Georgians and Abkhazians: The Search for a Peace Settlement* (Koeln: Bundesinstitut für Ostwissenschaftliche und Internationale Studien, 1998), pp. 14–48, http://poli.vub.ac.be./publi/Georgians/chp0201.html; Revaz Gachechiladze, *The New Georgia: Space, Society, Politics* (London: Routledge, 1995), p. 41 and p. 84.

port to a power-sharing arrangement forged by him. Second, in response to criticism from Gamsakhurdia's supporters that Shevardnadze's government was "Moscow's puppet," the new government sought to portray itself as an even stauncher defender of national interests than Gamsakhurdia. For this reason, it was tempting for the government to portray the 1991 agreement as a "betrayal of the national interest." Finally, the Abkhazian leadership saw a window of opportunity in the breakdown of authority and legitimacy in Georgia, and on July 23, 1992, members of the Abkhazian Supreme Soviet, without attempting to secure a two-thirds majority in accordance with the power-sharing compromise agreement of August 1991, passed a law reinstating the draft 1925 Abkhazian Constitution adopted by the All-Abkhazian Congress of Soviets that declared Abkhazia to be a sovereign state.

In 1992, troops supporting Gamsakhurdia kidnapped the Georgian minister of the interior and a parliamentary deputy, and were said to have brought their hostages to the district of Gali within Abkhazia. Whatever the truth of this allegation, Georgian troops took it as a justification for entering Abkhazia. On August 14, 1992, the Georgian National Guard moved into Abkhazia and then occupied Sukhumi, igniting the long-simmering Abkhazian conflict. The Abkhazians, supported by volunteers from the Northern Caucasus as well as Russian forces stationed in the area, rapidly organized a much stronger military resistance than the Georgians had expected. At the time, Gamsakhurdia's forces in western Georgia were waging their own military campaign. Georgian forces, therefore, were threatened with the prospect of a war on two fronts, in which they risked being encircled by the Abkhazians in the north and Gamsakhurdia's forces in the south. This, in fact, materialized a year later. In September 1993, Gamsakhurdia's units attacked Georgian forces in western Georgia, and the Abkhazians, thanks to Russian support, won back Sukhumi. The Georgian population in Abkhazia fled.

After his defeat, a deeply humiliated Shevardnadze was forced to appeal to Russia for military help against Gamsakhurdia. Within two weeks, Russian troops had put an end to the military operations conducted by Gamsakhurdia's troops. In repayment, Georgia was forced to end its opposition to the CIS by becoming a full member and to sign a series of security cooperation agreements. In June 1994, the Abkhazian and Georgian authorities agreed to the deployment of Russian peacekeepers between Abkhazia and the rest of Georgia. Tbilisi also entered into negotiations with Moscow on the future of the Russian bases located in Vaziani, Gudauta, Akhalkalaki, and Batumi.

While the war in Abkhazia was still going on, a new Georgian parliament was elected on October 11, 1992. At the same time, a direct election for the chairman of parliament took place, an election for which Shevardnadze stood unopposed. He won 96 percent of the vote on a 74 percent turnout. On November 6, 1992, the new parliament ratified the Law on State Power—making Shevardnadze chief executive, supreme commander of the armed forces, and head of state. Shevardnadze became president after the new constitution was ratified on August 24, 1995, and elections to the post were held on November 5, 1995. Shevardnadze won 74 percent of the vote in 1995 according to official figures.

These elections gave Shevardnadze the democratic and constitutional legitimacy that he had lacked during his assumption of power. After his failure to re-establish control over South Ossetia and Abkhazia, Shevardnadze faced off against Ioseliani and Kitovani, the leaders who had called him back to Georgia in 1992 in the expectation that they would be able to control him with their paramilitary groups. Shevardnadze first neutralized the National Guard under Kitovani and gradually integrated it into the state structure. In May 1993, Shevardnadze dismissed Kitovani as minister of defense and in February 1994 Kitovani's protégé, Giorgi Karkarashvili, resigned and was replaced by a Shevardnadze loyalist, Vardiko Nadibaidze. In January 1995, in a last desperate bid for power, Kitovani (with the support of Tengiz Sigua) led a motley force of some 700 lightly armed supporters in a bid to retake Abkhazia. They were stopped by Georgian police and arrested. Meanwhile, in the autumn of 1993 Shevardnadze still had to rely on Ioseliani and his Mkhedrioni to defeat the forces loyal to ousted President Gamsakhurdia. Only in early 1995 did Shevardnadze order his Interior Ministry troops to take on the Mkhedrioni units. In fact, Ioseliani's deputy and the former Georgian minister of internal affairs, Temur Khachishvili, remained deputy minister of state security until the middle of 1995. Not until after the August 1995 assassination attempt against Shevardnadze were Ioseliani and Khachishvili arrested.

This short overview of events makes it clear that the first five years of the Georgian post-Soviet transformation were devastating. Between 1988 and 1993, there were two secessionist wars, both of which the Georgian state lost, and a violent contest for power in Tbilisi. The next section offers an explanation of this course of events.

The story of the ethno-national mobilization of the Georgians, Abkhazians, and Ossetians highlights three relevant issues. First, the mobilization of the three groups was an interdependent process in which each action produced a counteraction. Organized inter-communal violence was only the end of the spiral. For a long period, the competition of the ethno-national discourses remained purely a war of words. This was followed by a war of laws: from 1989 onward, many of the nationalist positions were turned into laws and proclamations by the revitalized Soviet legislatures, in which each authority claimed to be sovereign. The confrontation between ethnic communities in Abkhazia itself only turned violent through an external intervention.

Second, it is notable that nationalist agendas were very rapidly adopted by the Communist *nomenklatura* in Georgia, South Ossetia, and Abkhazia, and then imported into the political institutions of the Soviet system. In all three polities, the Soviet legislatures passed laws legitimizing national sovereignty or independence. Since the Communist authorities quickly put the mobilizing potential of party and state institutions at the disposal of the nationalist challengers, the mobilization was greatly facilitated.

Third, organized violence occurred much later than nationalist mobilization. In the case of South Ossetia, organized violence emerged because Gamsakhurdia exploited nationalist sentiments to stabilize his power base—unleashing his newly formed National Guard, which was essentially a private militia run by a profit-seeking commander. He was then unable to control these paramilitary groups. In the other Georgian wars, the escalation of organized violence also originated with paramilitary groups acting outside state control.

THE MECHANISM OF SOVIET ETHNO-FEDERALISM

The process of mobilization described in the previous section was decisively shaped by the institutions of the Soviet federal system. Ossetians and Abkhazians are not the only, nor even the largest, national minorities in Georgia. In 1989, 8 percent of Georgia's population was Armenian and 5.7 percent Azerbaijani. The largest number of both groups lived in relatively compact areas of settlement in southern Georgia, on the borders with Armenia and Azerbaijan. This constellation of factors corresponds to the "triadic situation" that Rogers Brubaker identifies as par-

ticularly burdened with risk.[13] Ethno-political conflicts are more likely
when a minority group with a compact settlement pattern in a nationalizing state has a "big ethnic brother" in a neighboring state. How explosive these constellations can be was demonstrated by the wars in Croatia
and especially Bosnia-Herzegovina. The Armenians and Azerbaijanis
living in Georgia did not mobilize, and in contrast to the Ossetians and
Abkhazians, demonstrated no separatist tendencies. The difference owed
decisively to the fact that the Abkhazians and Ossetians had their own
autonomy, and were equipped with political institutions and symbols
that facilitated mobilization and secession. Armenians and Azerbaijanis,
meanwhile, were not in autonomous regions or republics within Georgia.
South Ossetia and Abkhazia, therefore, turned out to be powerful
examples of the potentially subversive mechanism of Soviet ethno-
federalism.[14]

   Three factors explain why Soviet ethno-federalism facilitated mobilization and separatism in the autonomous regions. First and most important, the substantial privileges enjoyed by the titular nations of the
autonomous regions in the Soviet Union were threatened by Georgian
moves toward independence. This was especially clear in the case of
Abkhazia. As a result of dramatic demographic shifts in the Soviet period,
the Abkhazians made up only 17.8 percent of the entire population of
Abkhazia in 1989, while the Georgians comprised 45.7 percent. But the
Abkhazian elite at that time had disproportionate access to political and
economic resources, because they held the key bureaucratic positions.[15]
Moscow's increasing weakness, together with the gradual destabilization
of political control and property rights, threatened this system, particularly the privileged position of the Abkhazians.

---

[13] Rogers Brubaker, *Nationalism Reframed: Nationhood and the National Question in the New Europe* (Cambridge: Cambridge University Press, 1996), pp.
   55–76.

[14] An additional explanation of the non-mobilization of the Armenians in Georgia draws on Armenians' self-policing capacities. The political leaders of Armenia proper, together with the leaders of the Armenian community in Georgia,
   were able to contain the community's mobilization. Any such mobilization was
   seen as clearly undesirable by Armenia, which was already engaged in the conflict over Nagorno-Karabakh. This explanation is not often mentioned in the
   literature, but decision makers in the region have repeatedly put it forward in
   conversations with the author (July 2002).

[15] Derluguian, "The Tale of Two Resorts," p. 262.

Consequently, both groups mobilized in response to the new circumstances. The Georgians, hoping that they could take advantage of their position of relative majority, had the goal of abolishing the system of disproportional access to resources for the Abkhazians. The Abkhazians, who hoped for support from Moscow, sought to maintain the status quo or even to improve their political position. From this perspective, it was predictable that the Abkhazians would campaign for their autonomous republic to be directly subordinated to the Soviet Union. The demand for independence arose when the Soviet Union perished, depriving Abkhazians of this potential umbrella. For the Georgian national movement, on the other hand, the Abkhazians' loyalty to Moscow, inspired initially by simple economic interests, proved that they were the servants of the Soviet empire. In this way, a conflict over resources was ethnically reinterpreted and harnessed to aid mobilization.

Second, mobilization for separatism was favored by the fact that groups within autonomous entities, in contrast to national groups without their own territory, had political institutions that elites could exploit. In Abkhazia and South Ossetia, the national movements quickly gained ascendance in the context of a general crisis of the Soviet political system. In both entities, there was a fierce competition between national elites for control over the local state structures. Communist officials participated in the rallies in Abkhazia and South Ossetia, putting their state and party resources at the disposal of their own national movements. Similarly, both the Ossetian and the Abkhazian elites embodied a "personal union" of the national intelligentsia and Communist officeholders. In both cases, the separatist activities soon shifted to the legislative bodies (soviets). Both the South Ossetian as well as the Abkhazian soviets turned repeatedly to Moscow with the request to be directly subordinated to the Soviet center. Both legislatures initially followed Soviet procedures, thus gaining a certain degree of formal legitimacy that was difficult for the government in Tbilisi to contest, particularly when Georgia had itself ceased to play by Soviet rules.

Third, the Soviet central government encouraged the separatist aspirations of the autonomous entities within the various union republics—sometimes deliberately, sometimes involuntarily. The principle of divide and rule had been a core element of Soviet nationality policy since the Stalin era. In some cases, the autonomous units in the union republics were then used as a counterbalance to nationalist stirrings of the titular nation of a union republic. The titular nations of subordinated autonomies particularly profited from this arrangement, gaining disproportionate access to resources, at least as long as their loyalty to Moscow was not questioned. In the late *perestroika* period, Moscow reverted to this procedure and largely supported both South Ossetia and Abkhazia against Georgia politically, and, after the outbreak of hostilities, militarily as well. The Georgian side, struggling to explain away its two military defeats, often exaggerated this assistance. But South Ossetia and Abkhazia, prior to the outbreak of war, also almost certainly overestimated Moscow's real levers of influence. Distorted assessments doubtless did shape the separatist agendas in South Ossetia and Abkhazia.

THE INTERNAL FRAGMENTATION OF THE POSTCOMMUNIST ELITE

Along with the spirals of ethno-national mobilization and the enabling institutions of Soviet ethno-federalism, internal divisions among the new Georgian elites also paved the way for organized violence by preventing the consolidation of newly won independence.[16] There are important institutional reasons for the weakness of the state and the internal divisions among those in power—reasons that apply throughout the Caucasus, but especially in Georgia.

The weakness of the Georgian state had not arisen solely as a product of the postcommunist transition, but arose even earlier as an institutional legacy of the Soviet Union. Clientelism and patronage networks in the Caucasus and Central Asia were among the most effective informal institutions during the Soviet period, and they retained their function after the collapse of the Soviet Union.[17] In a study on the South Caucasus, Gerald Easter has shown how the Soviet state from Stalin's time had sought to secure its rule by incorporating local patronage networks.[18]

---

[16] Jones, "Georgia: A Failed Democratic Transition," pp. 288–310.

[17] Pavel K. Baev, "Civil Wars in Georgia: Corruption Breeds Violence," in Jan Koehler and Christoph Zürcher, eds., *Potentials of Dis/Order: Explaining Conflict and Stability in the Caucasus and in the Former Yugoslavia* (Manchester: Manchester University Press, 2003), pp. 127–144; Zürcher, Koehler, and Baev, "Internal Violence in the Caucasus"; Derluguian, "The Tale of Two Resorts," pp. 261–292.

[18] Gerald Easter, "Personal Networks and Post-Revolutionary State-Building: Soviet Russia Reexamined," *World Politics*, vol. 48 (1996), pp. 551–578.

The resulting weakness of socialist statehood was offset by personalized clientelist rule. The gigantic machinery of the Soviet redistributional economy proved to be fertile soil in which patronage networks thrived. It is by no means surprising that these networks survived the collapse of the Soviet Union.

Georgia's new nationalists were never able to replace well-entrenched patronage networks based on personal trust with a more modern, impersonal state bureaucracy.[19] In Georgia, the nationalist surge that brought Gamsakhurdia to power got tangled up in these finely spun and strongly anchored networks, which continued to control the allocation of resources. In addition, influential patronage networks, old cadres, and the urban intelligentsia were not represented in the legislature, which as a result was left without sufficient political backing. The inexperienced parliament was thus never in a position to halt the erosion of the state. In particular, it was not able to mobilize the economic and political resources of the old cadres and patrons.

President Gamsakhurdia and his new parliament fell back on ethnonational mobilization as a means of retaining power, and this had disastrous consequences. Nationalism was Gamsakhurdia's only resource. He had achieved power thanks to pressure from the streets and because of national-patriotic emotions. In the fall 1990 elections, he and his Round Table/Free Georgia coalition won 155 out of 250 seats. Nationalist mobilization had thus led to electoral victory, but did not create state unity.

Internal division and unconsolidated statehood in Georgia were directly linked to the escalation of organized violence in all three of the country's postcommunist conflicts. First, the war in South Ossetia followed directly from the patriotic mobilization by Gamsakhurdia, which had brought him to power in the first place. This mobilization secured him a large majority during the 1991 presidential election, but did not lead to victory in the war with South Ossetia. Wars cannot be fought or won with nationalist rhetoric alone.

The second war episode, the coup against Gamsakhurdia, was also a consequence of division and state weakness. Despite Gamsakhurdia's victory in the presidential elections, politics in Georgia remained dominated

---

[19] This is the central thesis of Barbara Christophe, "Bringing Culture Back into a Concept of Rationality: State–Society Relations and Conflict in Post-Socialist Transcaucasia," in Koehler and Zürcher, *Potentials of Dis/Order,* 193–207.

by personal rivalries, especially within the national movement. Gamsakhurdia was personally poorly suited to unite an already divided national movement. He had the capacity to make enemies very quickly and surrounded himself with people whose only qualification was often their personal loyalty.[20] Under these circumstances, it was not surprising that the national movement, itself constantly threatened by personal rivalries, could not develop any cohesion. Gamsakhurdia did not subordinate the engineers of violence and the defection of the National Guard paved the way for his overthrow.

Finally, the start of the war in Abkhazia in August 1992 was also a direct consequence of internal division and unconsolidated statehood after Shevardnadze's return to Georgia. Under the particular circumstances of that time, the National Guard's move on Abkhazia was to a very large extent the action of a private army out for plunder.[21]

The reasons for Gamsakhurdia's failure are discernible, if one examines how Shevardnadze slowly and skillfully—and despite the loss of control over a great part of Georgia's territory—strengthened his power base from 1992 to 1995 and pieced Georgian statehood back together. Shevardnadze's great personal prestige, his capacity to tap not inconsiderable funds in the West, as well as his talent as a mediator allowed him to forge a viable coalition, which included former cadres, members of influential patronage networks, and former parts of the national movement. After the Georgian defeat in Abkhazia, he bowed to considerable pressure from Moscow and brought Georgia into the CIS. As a reward, Moscow helped him to put down the rebellion of Gamsakhurdia's supporters. Shevardnadze then isolated the two most important entrepreneurs of violence—Kitovani and Ioseliani.

Nationalism as a means of consolidating statehood did not work in Georgia or anywhere else in the post-Soviet space, except in the Baltic states and Armenia, the latter of which consolidated its statehood by means of a war-nationalism fed by very real threat scenarios. In Chechnya, on the other hand, the Chechens' national mobilization failed to consolidate statehood, but resulted in a state of anarchy that eventually

---

[20] Suzanne Goldenberg, *Pride of Small Nations: The Caucasus and Post-Soviet Disorder* (London: Zed Books, 1994), p. 92.
[21] Zürcher, Koehler, and Baev, "Internal Violence in the Caucasus"; Baev, "Civil Wars in Georgia," pp. 127–145.

paved the way for the disastrous Russian military campaign of 1994. And in Azerbaijan, the national democrats failed in the end to consolidate their position.

WEAK STATEHOOD AND ENTREPRENEURSHIP OF VIOLENCE[22]

In much of the organized violence in Georgia during the postcommunist transition, private entrepreneurs of violence used fragments of the state to stir violence. Most of these figures had earlier been co-opted into state positions by an elite in need of muscle to pursue their political ends. The blurring of state-sponsored and private violence was a highly characteristic feature of the Georgian wars. Thus, one needs to understand what might be called a double process of "privatizing the state" and "turning private business into a state agency."

The two largest organized groups in Georgia that had the capacity to use force were the Mkhedrioni ("knights") and the National Guard. The Mkhedrioni was a loose union of criminal groups and juvenile gangs from Tbilisi, created in 1989 by Jaba Ioseliani, a former patron of the Soviet underworld. It funded its activities from criminal dealings, including extortion and racketeering. In 1992, it also gained control over lucrative sectors of the economy, such as the gasoline trade.[23] The Mkhedrioni saw itself as a patriotic society for the protection of Georgia, and its members often played with patriotic and religious symbols. Many displayed a large amulet with a portrait of Saint George on their chests. Essentially, the Mkhedrioni was the weapons-bearing arm of successful businessmen-patriots who put their private army at the service of the state when it was waging war against secessionist minorities.

The National Guard was formed in November 1990 and was supposed to become the core of a Georgian army. Since the Georgian state did not yet exist, the recruitment and maintenance of the troops was carried out almost exclusively by private individuals. The guard was financed through an almost nonexistent state budget as well as through contribu-

---

[22] This section draws largely on Zürcher, Koehler, and Baev, "Internal Violence in the Caucasus."

[23] Georgii Nizharadze, "The Institutional Framework of Caucasian and Central Asian Transitional Societies: Georgia, Abkhazia, and South-Ossetia," *The Economics of Political and Common Violence* (Tbilisi: World Bank Development Economic Research Group, 2002), typescript.

tions from successful black-market entrepreneurs. Kitovani, a close supporter and friend of Gamsakhurdia, was simultaneously appointed commander of the guard and minister of defense. He possessed neither military training nor experience, but proved himself to be a very effective
fundraiser.

Both the National Guard and the Mkhedrioni's weapons came from
the Soviet (and later Russian) army—in effect from the army of the state
said by the Georgian nationalists to be deliberately torpedoing Georgia's
independence. In July 1992, these paramilitary groups secured fifty tanks
from Soviet arsenals at a point when the Soviet military was rapidly dis-
solving.[24] A month after acquiring these tanks, Kitovani embarked on his
Abkhazian campaign.

Neither group was under the control of the state. Ioseliani's Mkhedrioni opposed President Gamsakhurdia from the time it was established;
but even the National Guard resisted incorporation into the state structure and refused to pledge loyalty to the president. Gamsakhurdia's
doom was sealed in the fall of 1991 when Kitovani and the National
Guard turned against him. The battle for power in Tbilisi ended quickly
with Gamsakhurdia's expulsion. Altogether no more than 500 fighters
participated in the battle, evidence that this violent episode of the civil
war was more a *coup d'état* by a paramilitary organization. After the successful coup, both organizations staked out their interests: the Mkhedrioni retained control over the gasoline and tobacco trade, while the
National Guard increasingly dominated the arms trade.

Shevardnadze, who was in desperate need of allies upon his return
to Georgia in March 1992, promoted the Mkhedrioni to the status of a
security force under the Ministry of the Interior and equipped it with
weapons from Soviet holdings. One of its leaders, Temur Khachishvili,
became minister of the interior. The leader of the National Guard, Kito-

---

[24] On May 15, 1992, the Republic of Azerbaijan, the Republic of Armenia, the
Republic of Belarus, the Republic of Kazakhstan, the Republic of Moldova, the
Russian Federation, Ukraine, and the Republic of Georgia, as successor states
of the Soviet Union, signed the so-called Tashkent Treaty, which stipulated
that signatories would build their own armed forces under their respective
national ministries and heads of state, thereby respecting the ceilings on conventional arms that the Conventional Forces Europe (CFE) Treaty had fore-
seen. Under this treaty, some 100 tanks and 200 armored combat vehicles
were transferred from the Soviet army to Georgia, which ignored the condition
requiring non-use of these arms in domestic conflicts.

vani, also remained minister of defense. Shevardnadze entrusted the Mkhedrioni with the task of organizing the war against Gamsakhurdia's supporters in western Georgia. It took on the form of a looting campaign, in which weekend fighters, attracted by Ioseliani and the Mkhedrioni's televised appeals for volunteers, joined in the plundering. The volunteers usually formed small groups from the same neighborhood and then obtained automatic weapons from the enlistment offices of the Mkhedrioni. This part of the civil war in western Georgia was much bloodier than the coup in Tbilisi. Up to 3,000 fighters were engaged on each side, and nearly 2,000 people are estimated to have died.

In South Ossetia, the systematic organization of violent capacities began in early 1990. By the end of 1990, the Ossetians had between 4,000 and 5,000 men at their disposal, the majority of whom were part-time fighters.[25] They obtained most of their weapons from the Soviet helicopter regiment stationed in Tskhinvali. The majority of the soldiers and officers serving in the regiment were actually Ossetians and a considerable number of them took part in the fighting. The Ossetian side of the war was financed to a considerable extent by donations from North Ossetia, an autonomous republic situated in the Russian Federation that is wealthier than South Ossetia.[26] At the height of hostilities, several hundred volunteers from North Ossetia were fighting against the Georgians.

The war in South Ossetia was conducted on both sides by undisciplined paramilitary groups that were lacking unitary command structures, and only light weapons were employed in the fighting. The Ossetians recruited exclusively from the local population, while the Georgian troops were mainly from the local Georgian communities in South Ossetia. Initially, there were Interior Ministry troops and fighters from the National Guard on the Georgian side. Finally, the paramilitary units of various "patriotic" organizations took part in the war. The White Falcons, the Merab Kostava Society, the Mkhedrioni, and the Georgian National Front sent groups consisting mostly of undisciplined weekend warriors, who conducted frequent attacks on the civilian population and took hostages. There are few and contradictory data on the number of victims in the South Ossetia conflict. Georgian sources speak of between

---

[25] Nizharadze, "The Institutional Framework of Caucasian and Central Asian Transitional Societies."

[26] Zürcher, Koehler, and Baev, "Internal Violence in the Caucasus."

500 and 600 victims on both sides.[27] Around 12,000 Georgians (out of approximately 30,000 Georgians living in South Ossetia) left the region in several waves between 1990 and 1992. At the same time, approximately 30,000 Ossetians living in Georgia left for North Ossetia in response to Gamsakhurdia's nationalist urgings.

In August 1992, Kitovani's National Guard started its military campaign in Abkhazia. Shevardnadze rallied to it from the beginning. Five thousand Georgian National Guard soldiers invaded Abkhazia, while a further 1,000 soldiers landed in the port of Gagra with the intent of cutting off the road connection to Russia. The Abkhazian government fled to Gudauta and called for a general mobilization. The Abkhazian National Guard, at this point around 1,000 strong and mostly equipped with light weapons, took up defensive positions along the Gumista River near the Russian air base. The Abkhazians gained support from volunteers from the North Caucasus. Hundreds of volunteer fighters arrived, trickling through the mountain passes in small groups. Most of their weapons were from Chechnya. Instrumental in the recruitment of these volunteer fighters was the Confederation of Mountain Peoples of the Caucasus. This was a pan-nationalist movement founded in August 1989 by activists from Adyghea and Karachai-Cherkessia (both autonomous regions in the North Caucasus within the Russian Federation) and Abkhazia. In the early 1990s, the Confederation of Mountain Peoples of the Caucasus evolved into an insurgent political movement seeking independence for the states of the North Caucasus. While independence from Russia remained an elusive goal, the confederation was nonetheless able to build up a volunteer armed force that proved to be of some importance during the war in Abkhazia. Later, in 1994, parts of this force became the core of the Chechen resistance against Russia.[28]

The numerically disadvantaged Abkhazians found further support from the Russian army. Officially, Russia was endeavoring to find a peaceful settlement in Abkhazia and denied any involvement in the war. But its policy of divide and rule included military support to both sides in the conflict, which, over the course of the conflict, increasingly favored the

---

[27] Nizharadze, "The Institutional Framework of Caucasian and Central Asian Transitional Societies." Other sources speak of 3,000 casualties on the Ossetian side (see www.geocities.com/vienna/strasse/5262/South.html).

[28] The organization changed its name in October 1992 and became the Confederation of the Peoples of the Caucasus (CPC).

Abkhazians. The Abkhazian National Guard received weaponry from a battalion of Russian forces stationed in Sukhumi, and some volunteer training camps were under the leadership of Russian instructors.[29] Furthermore, Russia supported the Abkhazians logistically, as well as with occasional air strikes carried out from an airbase in Abkhazia. Over the course of the year, while the fighting strength of the Abkhazians constantly increased thanks to reinforcements from the North Caucasus and Russia, on the Georgian side the opposite was true. The Georgian army of fighters and plunderers started to fall apart. On September 27, 1993, the Abkhazian fighters drove the last of the Georgian troops out of Sukhumi and a few days later were in control of the entire territory of Abkhazia. The remaining Georgian population in Abkhazia, totaling around 200,000 people, fled the region.

Organized violence is always fueled by a mix of motivation and opportunity. Paul Collier and Anke Hoeffler, in their seminal study on greed and grievances, argue that greed (i.e., profit-seeking by entrepreneurs of violence) and opportunity (such as the availability of cheap weapons, a perceived weakness in an opponent, the expectation of decisive support from a third party, etc.) often provide a better explanation for the emergence of violence than grievances (such as economic or political discrimination).[30] In the case of Georgia, the discourse of grievance (oppression, economic discrimination, and so on) employed by all of the nationalizing communities alone has little explanatory power. All instances of internal violence can, to a very large extent, be attributed to the actions of profit-seeking paramilitary forces. Access to cheap and readily available Soviet weapons facilitated the actions of these groups. Gamsakhurdia used such forces to consolidate his political position, but the weakness of the Georgian state then left him unable to control or constrain their actions. There are, however, marked differences among the mobilizations of Georgian, Ossetian, and Abkhazian forces. Whereas the Georgian militias—the Mkhedrioni and the National

---

[29] Nizharadze, "The Institutional Framework of Caucasian and Central Asian Transitional Societies."

[30] Paul Collier and Anke Hoeffler, "Greed and Grievance in Civil War," (Washington, DC: The World Bank Group, October 2001), http://econ.worldbank.org/programs/conflict/library/doc?id=12205; James D. Fearon and David. D. Laitin, "Ethnicity, Insurgency, and Civil War" (paper presented at the 2001 Annual Meeting of the American Political Science Association, San Francisco, CA, August 30–September 2, 2001), http://www.stanford.edu/group/ethnic/workingpapers/apsa011.pdf.

Guard—were to a very significant extent driven by the presence of private entrepreneurs of violence, the cases of the Abkhazian and Ossetian militias are different. The Mkhedrioni, ostensibly created to defend Georgia from Soviet oppression (particularly after the violence in Tbilisi on April 9, 1989), turned very quickly into a profit-oriented criminal organization, which legitimated its activities and recruiting by claiming patriotic motives. By 1992–1993, the main aim of the various groups calling themselves Mkhedrioni was to loot and plunder, and it was not even clear whether all members of these groups were still loyal to Ioseliani.

The National Guard had a different origin from that of the Mkhedrioni. It was created "from above" and for political aims. Still, it also taxed the shadow economy and controlled a lucrative arms trade. Many fighters motivated by the opportunity to loot joined its operations. In particular, the campaign against Abkhazia was clearly driven by the National Guard's economic motives, including a desire to control key sectors of the region's shadow economy.

One of the most remarkable features of the war was the rapid exhaustion of Abkhazia's resource base. As the violence escalated, the Abkhazian tourist industry was destroyed beyond repair, the transportation infrastructure was paralyzed, and local agriculture was deprived of its markets. The cost efficiency of hostilities diminished month by month and, in the process, so did the sustainability of the paramilitary organizations. Shevardnadze then skillfully exploited the erosion of these organizations' resource base in order to eliminate the warlords from the political arena.

In the case of the Ossetian and Abkhazian fighters, the use of military force was not mainly motivated by private profit, but by the perceived threat to the status quo posed by an independent and nationalistic Georgia. The fear of future discrimination, fueled by the nationalist tide in Georgia, made it easier for local nationalists to organize their own violence. Once the Georgian militias entered their territories, Ossetians and Abkhazians saw their fears confirmed, and organized violence ceased to be an option and became a necessity.

THE NEIGHBORHOOD

There are several external factors that may influence the dynamic of conflict within a country. Among the three most prominent are diaspora support for rebel movements, a conflict-prone geostrategic location, and the interference of other states.[31]All of these factors played a role in Georgia between 1988 and 1993, although their impact is often overestimated.

Diaspora groups and ethnic kin groups certainly helped to sustain the secessionist wars of Abkhazia and South Ossetia. The Ossetians received substantial financial assistance and (more importantly) supplies and manpower from their ethnic kin across the High Caucasian Mountain Range in North Ossetia.[32] The Abkhazian fighters were helped by fighting units of North Caucasian volunteers and received further support from the Abkhazian diaspora in Turkey. Among the most prominent and indeed effective of these units was the so-called Abkhazian Battalion of Chechen rebel leader Shamil Basaev. Basaev and his approximately 300 fighters—who later became the most formidable of the Chechen secessionist forces—actually gained their first combat experience in Abkhazia fighting the Georgians.

Georgia is commonly thought to be cursed with an unfortunate geopolitical location at the intersection of rival powers and with a difficult geomorphologic situation. The rivalry between the Persian, Ottoman, and the Tsarist empires and the Soviet form of political modernization have left a deep imprint on the sociopolitical and cultural landscape of the Caucasus. One of the most relevant of these legacies is a belated and weakly institutionalized statehood. In addition, mountainous terrain has made it difficult for both local elites and colonial powers to establish reliable administrations in many parts of the Caucasus. Thus, it cannot be denied that geopolitics and geomorphology have had an impact on the *longue durée* of Caucasian history. However, when it comes to the short, turbulent, and conflict-prone period between the crumbling of the Soviet empire and the establishment of a newly independent Georgia, both factors were of minor significance. Instead, that period was dominated by the very clear primacy of domestic policies, and events were shaped by local institutional structures and their interaction with the center in Moscow. None of the political actors normally thought to have an interest in the South Caucasus—Turkey, Iran, Armenia, Azerbaijan, the United States, and the European Union—significantly influenced Georgian domestic conflicts between 1988 and 1993.

---

[31] Collier and Hoeffler, "Greed and Grievance in Civil War"; Fearon and Laitin, "Ethnicity, Insurgency, and Civil War."

[32] Zürcher, Koehler, and Baev, "Internal Violence in the Caucasus."

Two qualifications, however, apply. First, as Mark Beissinger's seminal study convincingly shows, events in the Soviet successor states were interdependent and linked by what may be called the "demonstration effect of successful nationalist mobilization."[33] Publics and elites in all the Soviet republics closely monitored the efforts of other national movements, and every wave of mobilization that went unpunished by Moscow added energy to other national movements. In that sense, the spiral of ethnonational mobilization was not only fueled within Georgia by the rival movements of Georgians, Ossetians, and Abkhazians, but also by the national movements among the Balts and the Armenians.

The second exception is obviously the Soviet Union and—after its dissolution—Russia. It would be wrong to deny the influence of Moscow on the events in Georgia, but it is equally wrong to attribute all of Georgia's misfortunes to a malicious, well-planned imperial policy. In fact, from at least the summer of 1990 onward, Moscow was not capable of formulating a coordinated policy, let alone implementing one, due to the country's accelerating economic collapse and the ongoing power struggles in the Kremlin. In the Caucasus, poorly planned and executed operations to "restore" peace multiplied, such as the action taken against demonstrators at Yerevan Airport in July 1988, or in Tbilisi on April 9, 1989, or the bloody Sunday in Baku in January 1990. In the final analysis, these operations served only to speed the erosion of the Soviet monopoly of violence and the collapse of statehood, and to impart momentum to the national movements. All this in turn added fuel to the conflicts within Georgia.

Most important, in its struggle against the secessionist union republics, the Soviet central government sought a tactical alliance with national movements in autonomous regions and republics. In April 1990, the Supreme Soviet passed a law that stipulated that if a union republic seceded from the Soviet Union, the autonomous regions and autonomous republics of the seceding union republic would have the right to remain in the Soviet Union (after a referendum was held). This law was clearly meant to block the potential secession of union republics. It could not prevent the implosion of the Soviet Union, however. What it did was instead to provide incentives for the autonomous regions and

---

[33] Mark R. Beissinger, *Nationalist Mobilization and the Collapse of the Soviet State* (Cambridge: Cambridge University Press, 2002).

republics to push for their own independence from union republics. South Ossetia and Abkhazia are prominent examples. This law, therefore, was a clear (albeit misguided) signal to national movements in the autonomous entities within Georgia saying that should Georgia leave the union, then Moscow would adopt the autonomous entities within Georgia.

In sum, the collapse of Soviet hierarchies was the decisive factor effecting a dramatic change in the incentive structures of actors. In the final analysis, this more than anything else explains the organization of violence in the three Georgian cases. The weakness of Soviet structures made possible the initial emergence of a Georgian national movement, which quickly assumed a dominant position. In contrast to Azerbaijan and Chechnya, but similar to Armenia and the Baltic states, the Communist *nomenklatura* in Georgia rapidly embraced the political (although not the ideological) agenda of the national movements and put state institutions at their service. The increasing and recognizable weakness of the Soviet Union lessened the costs of establishing Georgian independence. Beginning in early 1990, the achievement of full sovereignty had become the stated aim of national movements and the *nomenklatura* of this union republic.

This development in turn added incentives for South Ossetia and Abkhazia to secede. The Georgian ethno-national mobilization caused the titular nations of the autonomous entities to fear (with justification) that their privileged access to resources would be endangered in an independent Georgia. Mobilizational obstacles to a secessionist policy were lessened by the political institutions that the Abkhazians and the Ossetians had at their disposal, in contrast to the Armenians and Azerbaijanis living in Georgia. In the autonomous entities, the Communist officeholders of each national community could and did put their state and party resources at the service of the national cause. In particular, the supreme soviets, little more than symbolic representative bodies until 1988, turned into a locus of genuine political power.

The radical nationalist discourse, the state's loss of its monopoly over violence, as well as the clear tendency of a rump Georgian state to employ private entrepreneurs of violence all created fertile soil for the emergence of paramilitary groups with obvious criminal–economic interests. The new elite around Gamsakhurdia did not succeed in consolidating either the regime or the state, and this greatly facilitated the work of the entrepreneurs of violence.

NEW TROUBLES AFTER THE TIME OF TROUBLES?

Soviet ethno-federalism no longer exercises its destructive energy, but it has left open wounds. After a decade of stalled negotiations, a solution to the Ossetian and Abkhazian conflicts is not yet in sight. In September 2003, Abkhazia celebrated the tenth anniversary of the victory in its "war of independence"—a "victory" that came at the price of heavy political and economic dependence on Russia and international isolation. Most Abkhazians have applied for Russian citizenship, which is widely perceived as a viable gateway to some social and political security. Violence erupts periodically, and dozens of Russian peacekeeping troops, Abkhazian officials, and civilians from the different national communities have been killed since the end of war.

The Abkhazian leadership greeted Mikheil Saakashvili's arrival in power in Georgia by putting the army on alert. At present, Moscow controls the situation in Abkhazia through its military presence and its economic and political support—none of which can be matched by Georgia. Criminal paramilitary groups still had a major impact on political and economic life in the border region at the end of the Shevardnadze regime. Some of these gangs remained closely linked to the so-called partisan groups, such as the White Legion (led by Zurab Samushia), the Forest Brothers (led by Davit Shengelia), and another group led by Ruzgen Gogokhia.[34] While ostensibly fighting the Abkhazian government in Sukhumi, they often vied with one another for control of contraband gasoline, cigarettes, and hazelnuts. After coming to power in November 2003, Saakashvili ordered a crackdown against these groups.

Compared to Abkhazia, the situation in South Ossetia seems more fluid. Like Abkhazia, this tiny quasi-state has become a hub for informal trade, mainly in alcohol and tobacco. Its political elite is centered around one or two powerful political clans that exploit what is a quasi-private free economic zone. During the escalation of the conflict in 2004, trade with the rest of Georgia remained extensive, although it was heavily "taxed" every step of the way between Tskhinvali and Tbilisi by formal and informal authorities.

In contrast to the situation in Abkhazia, Georgia under Shevardnadze and South Ossetia did take practical steps to mend their relationship after

---

[34] International Crisis Group, "Georgia: What Now?" *Europe Report* no. 151, December 3, 2003; www.reliefweb.int/library/documents/2003/icg-geo-3dec.pdf.

1992. Nonetheless, a final settlement to the conflict remained out of reach. Indeed, it was never clear what a political settlement would look like: what status, short of full independence, South Ossetia would have accepted and how much sovereignty Georgia was prepared to cede. In the last years of Shevardnadze's rule, all negotiations on the final status of South Ossetia were effectively stalled.

President Saakashvili's saber rattling policy has caused new tensions in 2004. He made it plain that South Ossetia is high on his agenda. After his success in Ajara, where Saakashvili brought down the local potentate, Aslan Abashidze, it was widely expected that Saakashvili would try to reintegrate South Ossetia into Georgia. In May 2004, Georgia closed the huge and famous Ergneti Market in South Ossetia, where all sorts of goods were traded, most of them smuggled from Russia. Some analysts estimate that the Ergneti Market, essentially an illicit free economic zone, had yielded as much as $35 million annually, a substantial portion of which ended up in the hands of the South Ossetian political elite around President Eduard Kokoiti.[35] The decision to close the market was a clear signal that Georgia would no longer accept the status quo. In addition, Georgia reinforced roadblocks in South Ossetia in July 2004, seeking to establish a Georgian-Russian border control on the Roki Pass in order to reduce the importation of untaxed goods into Georgia. Saakashvili's new government has also tried to change the power balance in the region through an energetic campaign that simultaneously attempted to win the trust of the Ossetian population and militarily intimidate its separatist leadership, but this led to a military showdown in the region and a political crisis in relations with Russia.

In short, both South Ossetia and Abkhazia remain unresolved conflicts. A solution still seems distant, given that Georgia has little to offer to the breakaway entities politically or economically, and is too weak militarily to alter the situation by force. Furthermore, Russia has an interest in maintaining the status quo and in keeping its position as the veto player in the region.

The task faced by the second generation of reformers may be no less difficult than the one posed during the great transition from Soviet

---

[35] M. Alkhazashvili, "South Ossetia's Reliance on Contraband," *The Messenger*, July 15, 2004, http://www.messenger.com.ge/issues/0655_july_15,2004/economy_0655_1.htm.

Georgia to independent Georgia. It is, however, a very different task. During the time of troubles, rival groups fought for power within a state that was largely nonexistent. Today, the troika of Mikheil Saakashvili and his colleagues are working to replace a deeply entrenched and corrupt state system, but there is no guarantee they will succeed. In short, Gamsakhurdia fought with competing politicians—and lost. Saakashvili is fighting a deeply corrupt, but highly institutionalized system—and he may lose as well. His most dangerous enemy is not a political leader or a political party, but rather what might be called the "Shevardnadze System."

Shevardnadze succeeded in piecing the Georgian state back together in a rough manner. However, it came at a price. His recipe against elite fragmentation was to tolerate a deeply corrupt system combined with the rotation of personnel. Because this system is now so thoroughly entrenched, it has become much more than the unfortunate consequence of weakly developed statehood. Rather, it represents a kind of alternative form of statehood. It has developed to the point that it has replaced the forms of normal statehood, such as impersonal bureaucracies that provide real public goods. Changing that system will require more than just ostentatiously jailing a couple of corrupt officials. The whole political system must be built anew and virtually from scratch. It is a difficult road, and one of the main dangers is that the new elite will try to rally support by means of ethno-national mobilization. Recent history, particularly in Georgia, underscores the immense risk such a strategy entails.

CHAPTER 3

Georgian Defense Policy and Military Reform

DAVID DARCHIASHVILI

eorgia's defense posture and, in particular, the fate of military reform depend heavily on the dynamics within the political system in which they unfold. Neither can be understood, elaborated, or successfully conducted if divorced from the country's overall social and political development. Put succinctly, without the establishment of good governance practices, an effective defense system, a coherent security policy, and healthy civil–military relations are impossible. This is true for all countries, but this proposition is especially poignant in Georgia.

Money also matters. Georgia remains a poor state with limited revenues, which restrains reform in all areas, but particularly in the defense and security spheres. Force restructuring, whether downsizing, modernizing, or creating an effective means of control, requires resources. A military should not be allowed to engage in business activity—least of all in illicit commerce—but to avoid this, the state must be able to provide its officers and soldiers with adequate salaries and living conditions. The Georgian state has not done this for most of its first dozen years of independence.

In addition, the ideological and sociopolitical orientations of Georgia as a whole have direct implications for security and defense policies. First, national security policy and the defense posture sustaining it flow from perceived national interests and threats, which returns us to the theme of national stereotypes and values. Values define the threats that a national security policy is expected to contain. National interests and threat perceptions—which directly or indirectly derive from societal values—influence the inner structure, personnel policy, and patterns of relations within the national security sector. Second, the choice of strategic friends and allies for any country depends heavily on the nature of that country's value system. Compatible values are as crucial as pragmatic economic interests or common geostrategic views in determining the cooperative arrangements a country hopes to build.

At this point, the basic value system of Georgian society, the definition of security threats facing the country (the underpinning for reform of the security sector), and the level of national expertise in the security sphere do not meet a Western standard or match the practices of the Euro-Atlantic community that Georgia wishes to join. State- and nation-building will therefore remain at the top of the country's political agenda for years to come.

In the first decade of its independence, Georgia deteriorated into a weak (or even a failing) state. Whatever Georgia's pretensions, its political practices and its style of management were hardly compatible with modern Western standards. State- and nation-building were too often understood in nineteenth-century terms with stress on nationalist poetry, mythological images of historical heroes, as well as on the values and symbols of the Orthodox Church. Georgians and the country's national minorities failed to create a common national identity. Exclusive ethnicities were often considered to be even more important than individual economic well-being.[1] As a result, a contradictory mixture of liberal-democratic and ethno-nationalist projects came to characterize President Eduard Shevardnadze's regime. It was also heavily shaped by the traditions of the Communist *nomenklatura*. Consequently, reforms were slow and indecisive.

Shevardnadze's regime condemned corruption and xenophobia, but only rhetorically. These two phenomena were too often understood as a peculiar feature of Georgian culture. The working group tasked in 2000 by President Shevardnadze with drafting a Georgian anti-corruption strategy stated: "Corruption has become the way of life in certain areas. Corrupt thinking so broadly embraces public perception that we have to be extremely cautious while drawing a line between the roots of national originality and corrupt customary practices."[2] Anti-corruption recom-

---

[1] Theodor Hanf and Ghia Nodia, *Georgia Lurching to Democracy* (Baden-Baden: Nomos Verlagsgesellschaft, 2000), pp. 92–102.

[2] National Anti-corruption Strategy Group, *Saqatvelos erovnuli antikorufciuli programis dziritadi mimartulebebi* privately published, October 31, 2000), p. 9. (The group was created by the president.)

mendations remained on paper only, having little relation to the real pattern of interaction among governmental officials, businesspeople, criminals, and the corrupt pyramids they formed. This purely rhetorical criticism was part of the regime's contradictory approach—balancing between reform-minded young politicians and officers on the one hand and former Communist *nomenklatura* on the other. In Shevardnadze's last years, the state even failed to constrain the use of force in disputes between religious believers. For example, Vasili Mkalavishvili, a defrocked priest from the Orthodox Church who led violent attacks on religious minorities, went unpunished.

Not surprisingly, defense policy and the process of military reform reflected these distortions within Georgian society. Defense and security policies were characterized by a constantly shifting foreign policy, inadequate funding for defense, and rampant corruption. Clear strategic guidelines were never articulated, not even a general national security concept. Integration into the Euro-Atlantic space was frequently declared as Georgia's top foreign policy priority,[3] but Georgia's political elite also considered pro-Russian strategic choices. Civil–military relations were undemocratic. Inadequate funding was compounded by the misuse of the scarce resources that did exist. Salaries for security and military agencies were in serious arrears, and most military and paramilitary structures had not been effectively integrated or placed under adequate civilian management. Existing legislation was progressive, but not coherent or detailed. In general, the "power" ministries suffered widespread popular mistrust.

Eventually, all of these failings contributed to Shevardnadze's downfall in November 2003. Georgia's new leadership under President Mikheil Saakashvili has shown an unprecedented resolve to break with the corrupt practices of the past and to fight organized crime. Westernized intellectuals that have come to the fore in Georgia recognize the importance of globalization and are using a postmodern political discourse that does not favor nationalism, the idea of unitary states, or the traditional exclusiveness of state actors in the international arena. The new leadership has proclaimed a crusade against corruption and embezzlement, and detained a number of former high-ranking state officials.

---

[3] At the end of the 1990s, Shevardnadze famously stated that by 2005, Georgia would be at NATO's door. See *Svobodnaia Gruziia,* October 26, 1999.

In January 2005, Mkalavishvili, the vigilante priest, was sentenced to six years in prison.[4]

Yet, not everything about Georgia's new direction has conformed to the regime's stated intention to speed the country's integration into the Euro-Atlantic community.[5] The new elite still struggles to balance widely popular traditional nationalist sentiments with liberal and democratic imperatives. Along with espousing the ideas of multiculturalism, decentralization, integration into the community of nations, and cooperative security, the new leadership clings to notions of centralism and is reluctant to delegate governmental responsibility down to regional and local bodies. To succeed, the new regime will need to find a way of transcending reform's dependence on the will of individual leaders and create a broad base of support for good governance, including in the sphere of defense.

The new Georgian leadership has been clear about the necessity of fighting corruption and organized crime. It has supported the idea of creating new reform groups and citizens' advisory councils within the security and defense agencies. Some of these groups have started drafting practical recommendations, giving anti-corruption policies that were never implemented under Shevardnadze a second chance. But more needs to be done to articulate the kind of laws and strategic discourse that should govern security agencies, the way these agencies should be structured, and last but not least, their code of conduct and missions.

Georgia's unsolved ethnic conflicts also create an obstacle to defense reform. These conflicts and the potential for renewed armed clashes are not the best environment for restructuring Georgia's military. Indeed, within months of assuming power, the new leadership found itself caught up in escalating tensions over South Ossetia, leading to the deployment of additional Interior Ministry troops to the conflict zone and hampering reforms planned by the new interior minister.

---

[4] IWPR Caucasus Reporting Service, no. 272, February 3, 2005, http://www.iwpr.net/home_index_new.html.

[5] This course has been proclaimed since the very beginning of modern Georgian statehood. The first president, Zviad Gamsakhurdia, outlined in his presidential program that Georgian defense doctrine would be oriented toward the support of the European security system. This corresponded with his idea of turning Georgia into a bridge between East and West. See *Sakartvelos Respublika,* no. 253, December 27, 1991.

This chapter analyzes the failure of Georgia's defense and security policies and the challenges confronting the new leadership.[6] It is divided into four parts. The first part explores the various stages in the history of building the Georgian Army, from the late 1980s until the Rose Revolution of 2003. This section lays out the systemic shortcomings of the process and explains a series of dramatic events that shook political–military relations. In the second section, the problem of civilian control over the armed forces—including the relationship between the executive and legislative branches of the government, the question of the defense budget, and the corruption among the military—is analyzed. The third section addresses the challenge of developing a national security concept. This chapter concludes with a fourth section analyzing new trends in defense policy and military reform after the Rose Revolution.

ARMED FORCES IN GEORGIA: A HISTORICAL OVERVIEW

Despite its long history, Georgia has had little experience with the formation of regular armed forces. In the brief period of independence after the

---

[6] The present chapter is based on previous research on security issues and civil–military relations in Georgia. See David Darchiashvili, "Georgia: The Search for the State Security," Caucasus Working Papers (Stanford, CA: Center for International Security and Cooperation, 1997), http://cisac.stanford.edu/publications/10255/; David Darchiashvili, "Trends of Strategic Thinking in Georgia: Achievements, Problems, and Prospects," in Gary K. Bertsch, Cassady Craft, Scott A. Jones, and Michael Beck, eds., *Crossroads and Conflict: Security and Foreign Policy in the Caucasus and Central Asia* (Routledge: New York, 2000), pp. 66–74; David Darchiashvili and Tamara Pataraia, "Return to Europe? Some Aspects of the Security Orientation of Georgia," *Österreichische Militarische Zeitschrift*, no. 1 (2001), pp. 43–55; See also my book, published in Georgian, on Georgian national security and civil–military relations in Georgia in the period 1990–2000: *Politikosebi, jariskacebi, moqalaqeni: saqartvelos erovnuli usaprtkhoebisa da samkhedro-samokhalakho urtiertobebis analizi* (Tbilisi: Tbilisis sakhelmtsipo universitetis gamomcemloba, 2000), http://www.cipdd.org/en/archive.shtml?lang=eng&detail=1&id=3; David Darchiashvili, "Power Structures in Georgia," International Institute for Democracy and Electoral Assistance, Discussion Paper no. 5 (Printinfo: Yerevan, Armenia, 2003); David Darchiashvili, "Georgian Security Problems and Policies," in Dov Lynch, ed., *The South Caucasus, A Challenge for the EU*, Chaillot Papers, no. 65 (December 2003), p.107–128, http://www.iss-eu.org/public/content/chaile.html; I was also the chief editor of *The Army and Society in Georgia* from 1996 to 2000. Issues for the period 1998–2001 can be found at http://www.cipdd.org/en/publication.shtml?cat_id=6.

Bolshevik Revolution (1918–1921), Georgia did mount a military with 20,000 to 25,000 regular troops and a militia-like Popular Guard. At the time, Georgia had a sizable corps of professional officers of noble descent who had served in the tsar's armies. Mistrust between these officers and the new social democratic government prevented the country from over-coming the many obstacles to fashioning an effective military, and the Georgian Army was poorly disciplined, poorly fed, and poorly equipped. This whole experiment only lasted until 1921, when the Georgian troops were overrun by invading Bolshevik military forces.

On several occasions after Sovietization, Moscow allowed the creation of national military units. These units, however, were hardly an adequate substitute for a real national army. Any movement in this direction com-pletely stopped in 1956 when Nikita Khrushchev banned all national units in the Soviet Army.

The initial stage in the creation of a new Georgian military began with the rise of the Georgian independence movement and the collapse of the Soviet Union. The first Georgian units created by anti-Soviet polit-ical groups to deal with emerging internal ethnic conflicts came into exis-tence at the end of the 1980s and operated outside of the law at the time. By the end of 1990, when the first multiparty elections brought Zviad Gamsakhurdia's Round Table bloc to power, these units claimed to have about 6,000 fighters.[7] This figure, however, is almost certainly exagger-ated, since in all armed operations to that point, scarcely more than few hundred troops had been involved. These units were organized and com-manded by Georgian officers who had served in the Soviet military, civil-ian activists, and individuals with a criminal past.

Under these circumstances, the subordination of these units to politi-cal authority went largely unaddressed. Since these units did not have a legal status, the question of Soviet control was irrelevant. The anti-Soviet political leaders might have constituted an alternative political authority, but they were in constant disagreement among themselves. As a result, no unified command structure existed. The units themselves were mostly autonomous entities with mixed political–military missions that obeyed only their immediate commander. In some instances, they were affiliated

---

[7] *Vooruzheniie i voienizirovaniie formirovaniia v SSSR* (Moskva: Rossiisko–Amerikanskii centr mezhdunarodnyh i vioenno-politicheskih issledovanii, 1991), pp. 8–9.

with anti-Soviet political organizations that were as numerous as the armed units were. The strongest of these units, the Mkhedrioni, was loyal only to its founder, Jaba Ioseliani, a professor of art and a well-known criminal. Comprised mostly of young urban toughs or the offspring of the intelligentsia, the Mkhedrioni hated Gamsakhurdia, who by 1990 was emerging as the most popular anti-Soviet national leader. They despised his authoritarian style; his populist nationalism, which was not popular in criminal circles; and his heavy reliance on people from the provinces and Tbilisi's outlying areas, who the Mkhedrioni viewed as socially and cultur-ally alien. They also resented his public apology and betrayal of other dissi-dents when he had been arrested for anti-Soviet activities in the 1970s.

Ioseliani found common ground with the last Georgian Communist leader, Givi Gumbaridze, who himself was moving closer to the growing national movement. As a result, Ioseliani and the Mkhedrioni were allowed to register the so-called Rescue Corps as an alternative military service institution, one intended to assist the government in dealing with natural disasters. Then there was the armed wing of the Merab Kostava Society led by Vaja Adamia, a Gamsakhurdia loyalist. Two other organi-zations—the Legion of Georgian Falcons and Imedi, the military wing of the Popular Front—maintained relative neutrality in the Gamsakhurdia–Ioseliani rivalry. Frequently, however, sub-groups within these various organizations switched allegiances. For example, a part of Imedi later joined the Mkhedrioni, while Ghia Kharkharashvili, who was initially affiliated with the Mkhedrioni, later formed a separate unit called "White Eagle."[8] Most of the military operations conducted by these units occurred during the first clashes between Georgian nationalists and eth-nic minorities. From a military perspective, these units were small-scale and disorganized, and required only small numbers of fighters.

After the first multiparty elections in October 1990 and the victory of the anti-Communist Round Table, a new stage in the construction of the Georgian military began. The new government created the National Guard. Its name, mission, and subordination to the Ministry of Interior reflected its paramilitary nature. It was to be responsible for protecting public order and the integrity of the state.[9] Its gendarmerie-like guise

---

[8] All these data were collected through personal interviews with former fighters as well as politicians during the 1995–1999 period.

[9] *Sakartvelos Uzenaesi Sabchos Utskebani*, no. 12, 1990.

served two purposes. First, because Georgia remained a part of the Soviet Union, the new elite hesitated to take steps implying full independence and risk a sharp reaction from Moscow. Creating a police agency seemed less provocative than forming a national army. Second, the threats facing the Georgian government at that time were inchoate separatist movements in the autonomous regions of South Ossetia and Abkhazia. To combat these movements, paramilitary forces were adequate. Meanwhile, external defense remained the responsibility of the central Soviet government.[10]

That said, it was clear that Georgian leaders saw the National Guard as the nucleus of a future national army. They had made explicit their intention to achieve national independence sooner or later, and in this context described the guardsmen as defenders of the homeland, a claim given practical form in the National Guard's staffing and training procedures. The National Guard operated on the basis of two-year compulsory service. All paramilitary units formed earlier were required to join the National Guard or disband. In spring 1991, the guard comprised 12,000 men. Young men accepted conscription with enthusiasm, which would hardly have happened if the society viewed the guard as simply a police agency. Many Soviet officers of Georgian origin joined the National Guard. Units such as White Eagle and Imedi were incorporated into it. The Mkhedrioni, which refused to reconcile with Gamsakhurdia's government, was banned and many of its members were imprisoned.

Meanwhile large units of the Soviet Army were still positioned in Georgia. Under certain conditions, they probably could have played a role in the foundation of a national army, as happened in Ukraine and Belarus. In Georgia, however, this was impossible. First, the number of Georgian officers in Soviet units was minimal, largely because the prestige of a military career among Georgians had drastically declined in the last years of the Soviet Union. Out of several hundred cadets in the Tbilisi Artillery School (the only military school in Soviet Georgia) in 1978–1979, only about twenty were Georgians.[11] According to one Georgian general, at the time of the collapse of the Soviet Union, Georgians were seventy-second among Soviet nationalities in terms of the number of officers per 1,000 citizens. Partly for this reason, but also

---

[10] *Akhali Sakartvelo,* November 15, 1990.

[11] Former graduates from the Tbilisi Artillery School, interview with the author, December 1996.

because of the increasingly ethnic-nationalist mood in Georgian society, Soviet troops were perceived as occupational forces. One of the main demands of Gamsakhurdia's government was their withdrawal, and, indeed, they were then slowly withdrawn, a process that stopped in 1993, leaving 15,000 to 25,000 former Soviet troops in Georgia, which were converted into the Group of Russian Forces in the Transcaucasus.

The third stage in the reconstruction of the Georgian Army started after the April 1991 declaration of independence and Gamsakhurdia's election to the presidency. Once his position had been elevated from parliamentary chairman to president, Gamsakhurdia attempted to get rid of the influential civil–military barons and to establish personal control over the armed forces. A presidential decree of August 19, 1991, reduced the status of the National Guard to the level of a police unit and abolished the position of commander of the guard. In acting he responded to the order of the short-lived State Committee for Emergency Situation (GKChP), during the attempted putsch in Moscow in August 1991, to abolish non-Soviet armed formations. In part, Gamsakhurdia was motivated by a genuine fear of Moscow's retribution if he did not act (behavior that undermined Gamsakhurdia's popularity in Georgian nationalist circles), but he also saw the order as a good excuse to get rid of the independent leadership of the National Guard. After the *coup d'état* in Moscow failed and Russia itself moved toward independence, Gamsakhurdia ordered the creation of the Ministry of Defense on September 9, 1991. The guard was restored to its previous status, but subordinated directly to the president, while the Ministry of Defense was given responsibility for its logistical support.[12] At the same time, new troops under the Ministry of Interior relieved the guard of its policing function.

This shift in Gamsakhurdia's state-building strategy has to be understood in the particular context of the time. The transitional period from Soviet rule to independence had ended, and Soviet laws and structures had ceased to apply in Georgia. But the process of state- and army-building did not go smoothly, ending in an armed uprising and Gamsakhurdia's ouster. One of the many reasons for this turn of events was Gamsakhurdia's failure in the military field. The leadership's vacillation in handling the National Guard issue contributed significantly to the instability of the military reform process. The guardsmen never forgave the

---

[12] Major-General Guram Nikolaishvili, interview with author, October 1996.

president for the August 19 decree where he had downgraded their status, and this helped trigger the armed uprising in winter 1991.

There are other factors behind the chaotic pattern of civil–military relations in Georgia. To begin with, a number of paramilitary units were never integrated into the National Guard. The Merab Kostava Society, which was allied with Gamsakhurdia, remained armed and autonomous. Its leader, Vaja Adamia, became chairman of the parliamentary Commission for Defense, Security, Law, and Order. Adamia combined the positions of party leader, unit commander, and legislator. The same can be said about Tengiz Kitovani. He was simultaneously a parliamentary deputy, head of the governmental Commission on Defense, and commander of the National Guard. Kitovani's position made the guard's subordination to the Ministry of Interior a mere formality. He cultivated personal loyalty among guard officers, who themselves were mostly former civilian volunteers unattuned to professional military ethics. Thus, under the guise of formal labels, the old clan or feudal spirit lingered within Georgia's armed forces. Professed loyalty to the nation never turned into a loyalty to the state's institutions.

The dismissal of Adamia and Kitovani in August 1991 united these two warlords who had initially disliked one another against Gamsakhurdia. In December 1991, after armed fighting between their followers and Gamsakhurdia's supporters in the capital, they were joined by a reconstituted Mkhedrioni. To further complicate the picture, all sides sought to enlist Russian military support—some at a high political level, others at the level of commanders of locally deployed Soviet troops. Not surprisingly, Russian sympathies, although cautious, were on the side of the rebels; Gamsakhurdia's nationalistic rhetoric had not served him well in relations with Russia.

The period from 1992 to 1993 represented the fourth stage in Georgia's efforts to build a military. It was the most chaotic and conflict-laden period in modern Georgian history. As a result, the armed forces developed on an ad hoc basis, again without conceptual guidance.[13] On paper, things seemed more or less organized, although susceptible to frequent changes. After Gamsakhurdia's ouster in January 1992, the Military Council assumed the role of supreme authority, but only briefly. It was

---

[13] Richard Wolff, "The Armed Forces of Georgia–An Update," *Jane's Intelligence Review, Europe*, vol. 6, no. 12 (December 1994), pp. 559–561.

superseded a few months later by the State Council under Eduard Shevardnadze, who had recently been invited back from Russia. Shevardnadze
started the organization of the Ministry of Defense from scratch. Troops
were to be organized along the lines of army corps, and the first real army
formation, the Eleventh Army Brigade, came into existence in April 1992.
That summer, Russian military authorities transferred the bulk of conventional weapons from Georgian-based Soviet caches to the new Georgian
Ministry of Defense. In the same year, the Border Guard was established,
and the National Guard was renamed the "Rapid Reaction Corps" and
placed under the Defense Ministry. The Interior Ministry was left with
control of the interior troops. In 1993, the government set about dealing
with the Mkhedrioni by attempting to revive the idea of an independent
Rescue Corps into which some of the Mkhedrioni would be integrated,
whereas others were to be brought into the armed forces.

In reality, however, both the National Guard and the Mkhedrioni
retained their independence. Ioseliani, who became a member of Parliament and deputy chairman of the National Council for Security and
Defense[14] in the fall of 1992, remained the unchallenged commander of
the Mkhedrioni. Ghia Kharkharashvili, who gradually replaced Kitovani
as the National Guard's commander, became the only person whom the
guardsmen would obey. In May 1993, Kharkharashvili took Kitovani's
place as minister of defense when Shevardnadze moved against the latter.
Kharkharashvili did take an interest in integrating the armed forces. New
regulations announced in May 1993 did not refer to the Rapid Reaction
Corps or the National Guard; battalions from these forces were integrated into the Eleventh Army Brigade; and the formation of the First
and the Second Army Corps accelerated. The Mkhedrioni, however,
remained separate from this process.

During the conflict in Abkhazia from late 1992 into 1993, little
actual progress occurred toward altering the composition and command
structure of the Georgian armed forces. Battalions in reality comprised
not more than a few dozen men. In some cases, the men themselves
elected their commanders. Most of these men could hardly tell to which
corps or any other umbrella formation they belonged. Some units even
consisted of so-called brotherhoods, drawn from various Tbilisi street

---

[14] It changed its name into National Security Council in 1995, with the adoption
of the new constitution.

gangs. Sometimes they had a formal title, sometimes not. Soldiers as well as junior officers would come and go from the front line whenever they chose. In some instances, they would shift from one unit to another. The defense minister himself occasionally acted as a battalion commander. Despite the fact that the National Guard had been dropped from the May 1993 regulations, one of the senior commanders of the guard has recalled that it never ceased to exist.[15] In October 1993, Shevardnadze ordered its formal re-establishment.

The military commanders were actually warlords who were indifferent to civilian leadership. Parliamentary control over the military was nonexistent or on paper only. As a minister of defense, Kitovani dared on several occasions to challenge Shevardnadze on defense matters, suggesting that the head of the state should be responsible only for foreign policy. At one press conference, Kitovani declared that neither Shevardnadze nor the Parliament, but rather the "people" and the army, should decide who the defense minister should be.

In addition to semi-autonomous units, there were armed groups that were openly opposed to Shevardnadze and loyal to the ousted President Gamsakhurdia. On various occasions, they managed to seize control over parts of western Georgia, effectively cutting off communications between Tbilisi and its forces deployed in Abkhazia. Over the same period, Ajaran leader Aslan Abashidze had set about creating his own militia units.

But Shevardnadze, unlike Gamsakhurdia, was able to maintain shaky control over the complex and fractured political and military environment in Georgia. His main tool was his personal influence, since almost all actors believed that only he was able to deliver international support. He also applied the old method of divide and rule, never going after all the warlord challengers at one time. On occasion, Shevardnadze even tried to reach an understanding with Gamsakhurdia's supporters. But gradually, he managed to get rid of Kitovani, Ioseliani, and other lesser known leaders of armed groups. He made good use of foreign assistance and the kind of international support that Gamsakhurdia never had to achieve this objective and to consolidate his power in the process.

The period from 1994 to 1995 appeared to be decisive for the consolidation of Shevardnadze's personal position. It constituted a fifth stage

---

[15] Major Koba Liklikadze, former head of the press center of the Georgian Ministry of Defense, interview with the author, September 27, 1999.

in the history of the creation of Georgia's armed forces. After the Georgian defeat in Abkhazia in September 1993, Shevardnadze agreed to join the Commonwealth of Independent States (CIS) in October and legalized the presence of the Russian troops on Georgian soil. He made this move in order to obtain Russian support against Gamsakhurdia's supporters, who had used the defeat in Abkhazia to establish control in parts of western Georgia. Georgia's key ministries—the Ministry of Interior, Ministry of Security, and Ministry of Defense—were placed under the command of people favored by Moscow. This policy facilitated the elimination of various semi-legal armed units and military leaders whose nationalist excesses and anarchic behavior threatened central authority.

The new security minister, General Igor Giorgadze, emerged as a particularly strong figure, and consequently became an object of Shevardnadze's suspicions. Giorgadze was allegedly heavily involved in illegal arms and cigarette smuggling through his Russian connections. Russian security and military leaders trusted him far more than they trusted Shevardnadze, who was seen as responsible for the destruction of the Soviet empire.

The conflict between Shevardnadze and Giorgadze came into the open in 1995. At the time, Georgia was already recovering from armed turmoil. Georgians looked forward to peace and the prospect of economic improvement, particularly as the West appeared to be developing an interest in the country. As it turned out, Giorgadze lacked the capacity to challenge Shevardnadze politically or through the use of force. After years of warlord domination, the Georgian population would not accept a ruler in uniform. Giorgadze did not command an overwhelming military force either. His Special Assault Brigade built with Russian help in 1994 could not have prevailed against the collective strength of the other so-called power agencies,[16] whose leaders had their own ambitions. As in the past, Shevardnadze had been continuing his policy of multiplying armed agencies and balancing one against the other. In 1995, these policies had fully paid off. These various agencies were becoming more insti-

---

16 "Power agencies" is the literary translation of the Russian expression *silovyie struktury*. This expression is used in a number of post-Soviet countries and refers to the army, the police, security forces, border guards, and some other forces that have never been properly and completely separated. For more on this topic, see the English-language journal *Power Institutions in Post-Soviet Societies*, http://www.pipss.org/.

tutionalized and disciplined than they had been during the civil and ethnic conflicts of 1992–1993. Under these circumstances, Moscow was unable to back any new coup—it would have been clearly unacceptable to the Georgian public and to the Western community. For Russia, the better part of wisdom was to maintain some degree of cooperation with Shevardnadze himself.

After an attempted assassination of Shevardnadze in August 1995, an event that was never well investigated, the Georgian president accused Giorgadze and Ioseliani, the military figures most dangerous to his personal power, of complicity. The police disarmed and disbanded the Mkhedrioni, which left Ioseliani increasingly isolated. In September 1995, Giorgadze fled from a Russian military base in Georgia to Moscow, giving credence to accusations of his personal involvement in the assassination attempt (and that of Russia as well). At the same time, Giorgadze's flight and the jailing of Ioseliani opened the way for further defense and security reform. Shevardnadze could now move the construction of the army in a direction of his choosing. No other politician or military chief around him had the power or influence to defy his will.

The period from 1995 to the spring of 1998 may be considered a sixth stage in the army-building process. Until spring 1998, Vardiko Nadibaidze, a Russian general of Georgian origin who formerly served as a deputy commander of Russian troops based in Georgia, led the Georgian armed forces. When he was appointed in 1994, the Georgian Army supposedly had approximately fifty detachments of different size and mission totaling 49,000 men.[17] But conscription at that time[18] occurred only occasionally and on a very small scale, meaning the army and National Guard units were mostly made up of volunteers. Many enlisted officers and soldiers rarely showed up in their units. Out of the 49,000 troops said to be under Georgian command, only a few thousand were present in their barracks at any one time.

Under Nadibaidze, the size of the army was reduced and the conscription system made more orderly. Many of the unprofessional officers left the army, which was now commanded increasingly by older generals with years of Soviet military experience. In 1996, the new system

---

[17] *Sarke,* October 18, 1995.

[18] Conscription was governed by the Law on Defense and Universal Compulsory Military Service adopted in 1992. In practice, however, the legislation had little force.

assumed a more or less complete form. The army corps system had been abolished, because it was considered an unnecessary bureaucratic layer between brigades and the high command. The armed forces under the Ministry of Defense, now numbering 30,000 men, was divided into seven motor-rifle brigades, a mixed naval brigade, air defense and air force units, and several separate battalions. The National Guard remained a department of the Defense Ministry and maintained its status as one of the infantry brigades.[19]

The Ministry of Defense forces, however, were not the government's only military resources. In 1994, the Border Guard was separated from the Ministry of Defense. In the same year, Shevardnadze organized the Special State Protection Service. In 1995, the Special Assault Brigade of the Security Ministry was transferred to the Ministry of Interior. In total, according to the annual legislative account of military forces in 1997, these combined structures were estimated to include 42,000 men and officers.

The law specifying the size of the military was not the only new legislation. The constitution adopted in 1995 affected military reform, particularly civilian control over the armed forces. Under the new constitution, Georgia moved toward a presidential system, in which the president was to be the supreme commander of all military forces. After the 1995 parliamentary and presidential elections, the government introduced new laws on defense and compulsory military service, state secrets, parliamentary oversight, and a general administrative code. All of this laid the groundwork for not only civilian, but also democratic control over the military. For example, the Group of Trust created in 1998 consisted of three members of Parliament who were charged with monitoring all secret military and security programs.

A seventh stage in the recent history of Georgia's armed forces started in 1998. As former Minister of Security Djemal Gakhokidze noted, it was then that the Georgian government unambiguously chose a Western orientation for Georgian security and foreign policies.[20] In the same year, the Council of Europe decided to accept Georgia's bid for membership, and Western oil companies, as well as the U.S. and Turkish governments,

---

[19] Staff members of the parliamentary Committee on Defense and Security, interviews with the author, October 1996.

[20] *Akhali Taoba*, October 19, 1999.

finally agreed to build a large oil pipeline through Georgian territory. Encouraged by the increased Western interest in Georgia, and realizing that cooperation with Russia was not bringing the breakaway territories back, President Shevardnadze decided to withdraw from the CIS Collective Security Treaty in order to pressure Moscow on the issue of military bases and to affirm Georgia's desire to join NATO.

Despite the doubts later raised about the level of commitment to this new orientation, the shift did force Georgia to confront the need to adapt its military posture to Western standards. In April 1998, Nadibaidze was dismissed as minister of defense. Davit Tevzadze, a former commander of a paramilitary unit, replaced him. During the same period, Revaz Adamia, chairman of the parliamentary Committee on Defense and Security, convinced the president to create the International Security Advisory Board (ISAB), a conscious imitation of similar institutions in the Baltic countries. In 1999, the ISAB produced a set of recommendations that included the reduction of the armed forces, the elimination of parallel structures, the need for a formal national security concept and a White Paper on defense, and the appointment of a civilian minister of defense. Simultaneously, U.S. experts began helping the Georgian Defense Ministry set up the Defense Resource Management Office and draft a defense budget meeting Western standards. But the government failed to implement these reforms.

The global war on terror launched by the United States after September 11, 2001, has had an interesting side effect on the Georgian armed forces. In consultation with reform-minded Georgian military and political leaders, the United States launched the Georgia Train and Equip Program (GTEP). As a result, by the end of 2003, the Georgian Army had acquired four professional battalions trained for anti-terrorist and counterinsurgency warfare. It was the last, and probably one of the most tangible, of the Shevardnadze government's inconsistent steps toward military reform.

Tbilisi failed to establish full control over the armed forces stationed on its territory. Apart from Abkhazia and South Ossetia, whose armed forces are not under the control of Georgian authorities, the leadership in Ajara continued to build its own combat units until spring 2004. At the time of the Rose Revolution, Ajaran leader Aslan Abashidze's military reportedly had roughly twenty tanks and armored vehicles, as well as helicopters and coastal cutters. He also controlled special units, whose total number can be estimated at 500 to 1,000 men. Shevardnadze was never able to check Abashidze's activities or his collaboration with Russian commanders stationed at the military base in Batumi. Furthermore, Tbilisi failed to reach an agreement with Moscow about the remaining two Russian bases that were supposed to be closed according to the agreement between both countries at the Organization for Security and Cooperation in Europe (OSCE) Summit in Istanbul in November 1999. In the beginning of 2004, between 3,000 and 6,000 Russian troops were still based at the Batumi and Akhalkalaki bases. Guerilla and criminal groups in the western part of the country (adjacent to the Abkhazian conflict zone) and in the Pankisi Gorge constituted a third group of militarized forces outside the control of the Georgian government. In 2002, under both U.S. and Russian pressure, Georgian law enforcement agencies finally undertook a special operation in the gorge. Chechen armed units reportedly left the gorge to avoid engaging Georgian forces.[21]

As a summary judgment, one can say that after 1994, Shevardnadze's regime had made progress in keeping men with guns off the streets. In addition, the Georgian armed forces acquired greater discipline. But it failed, particularly during the years leading up to the Rose Revolution, to implement the necessary reforms. It did not manage to build an effective defense establishment or to introduce a genuine system of democratic civilian control and oversight. Georgia became increasingly perceived as a weak, if not failing, state.

The following two sections will focus on two important challenges for military reform that the Shevardnadze administration failed to address adequately. The first is civilian control over the military and the second the development of a defense and security strategy.

CIVILIAN CONTROL OVER THE MILITARY

"I understand what the police is for," Shevardnadze once told one of his advisors, "and how they conduct their daily business. But these military [officials], what are they thinking while in their barracks?"[22] This remark revealed Shevardnadze's deep suspicion toward the military and his neg-

---

[21] On the question of Russian bases in Georgia and the conflict with Russia concerning Chechen troops in the Pankisi Gorge, see the contributions of Jaba Devdariani and Oksana Antonenko in this volume.

[22] A former high-ranking Georgian public servant made these remarks in a confidential interview with the author, February 2003.

lect of the question of democratic civil–military relations. Civilian control over the military in Georgia by 1995 remained, to use Samuel Huntington's term, "subjective."[23] The actual line of political and legal subordination of the armed forces was not clear. Different parts of the government as well as different political factions competed to control and guide the military, and they did so in ways that exploited the military for their own political or personal advantage. The ambiguity over the ultimate power in defense matters stemmed largely from the 1995 Constitution. According to this document, the Parliament was responsible for defining the main directions of internal and foreign policy, while the president was charged with guiding these policies.[24] In the Georgian language, the meaning of "defining" and "guiding" cannot easily be distinguished, and this ambiguity allowed personality, charisma, and personal influence to prevail over institutional frameworks. Or, to take another example, Article 98 of the Georgian Constitution mandated that the structure of the armed forces be defined by the president, but that its size be set by the Parliament. As a result, if the president and the Parliament disagreed over the composition of the army, there was no easy resolution. Nor did it make sense that the president was supposed to structure the forces, but with no assurance that the Parliament would supply the men and arms that would be needed.

Moreover, in some instances, legislation passed by the Parliament contradicted the Georgian Constitution. Article 78 of the constitution, for example, prohibited any merger of the armed forces, security forces, and police. But the 1997 Law on Defense made Ministry of Interior troops part of the "military forces." Similarly, according to the Law on Interior Troops, their commander was responsible for coordinating the actions of local police during an emergency situation.[25] The issue of state secrecy also illustrated a contradiction in Georgia's laws. The relatively liberal General Administrative Code only allowed the classification of information touching on operational plans, actual operations, and their

---

[23] Samuel P. Huntington, *The Soldier and the State: The Theory and Politics of Civil–Military Relations* (New York: Vintage Books, 1964), pp. 162–192. Huntington is referring to situations when different political bodies have parallel oversight roles, leaving an opening for the military to insert itself into the political bargaining.

[24] Constitution of Georgia, articles 48, 69.

[25] Law on Interior Troops, April 30, 1998.

participants. But the list of state secrets accompanying the law under the same name prohibited the disclosure of information on the development and organization of the armed forces and on the creation of armed detachments, as well as on the quantity of troops, weapons, and their distribution among military units.[26]

The list of contradictions goes further. If implemented, some laws would have created gridlock between the president and the Parliament, while others would have left very little room for transparency and democratic accountability. Informed parliamentary debates on defense spending would have been made impossible by the laws on state secrecy. In fact, however, such debates, however unprofessional, did take place, albeit with restricted information. Deputies did not have details on specific items in the budget, let alone on the unreported income the military earned and spent off the state budget. Symptomatically, the chairman of the Defense and Security Committee, who also headed the parliamentary Group of Trust that was cleared for access to top state secrets, complained in March 2000 that he was denied adequate information on the Ministry of Defense's finances.[27]

In each of these respects, the law was violated. Politicians, journalists, and nongovernmental organization (NGO) representatives had no trouble visiting military units and asking about numbers and structure, since few officers observed the restricted secrets list. On the other hand, the Ministry of Defense ignored its legal obligation to provide the Group of Trust with accurate budget information on appropriation and spending. Thus, the Defense Ministry sold unused property, earning extra-budgetary funds, but neither the sums involved nor a detailed breakdown of their expenditure were supplied to the Parliament. The root of the problem, of course, was the corruption widely present in the Defense Ministry and elsewhere in Shevardnadze's government. Shevardnadze, however, could only have had a general idea of the scale of the problem. Sometimes the Chamber of Control, which was responsible for auditing budgetary outflows, would check Defense Ministry spending and report the improper use of hundreds of thousands dollars. In 1999, for example, the ministry met only 66 percent of required salary payments, while overspending on

---

[26] *Sakartvelos Respublika,* February 4, 1997.
[27] Defense and Security Committee of the Georgian Parliament seminar on civil–military relations, March 21, 2000.

business trips by 42 percent.[28] No one was sanctioned, because defense officials blamed the treasury for failing to provide funds for exercises and business trips abroad in a timely fashion. Or they simply complained that the treasury failed to transfer allotted monies to the Defense Ministry, forcing it to reorient available funds for other, more urgent purposes.

Unauthorized defense expenditures, however, were only one aspect of the financial problems in the defense sector. Even after Georgia's defeat in Abkhazia in 1993, the war economy, with its criminal dimension, largely survived. Guerillas and criminals in the zones of conflict continued to extort and smuggle, often with the help of law enforcement authorities. After 1995, the regular troops had less chance to participate in such activities, but they found other illegal means of earning money. During government hearings in September 2001, the secretary of the Anti-corruption Policy Coordination Council stated that all "power structures" had become heavily involved in various forms of corruption and the creation of patronage systems based on it.[29] For once, Shevardnadze felt compelled to address the issue of widespread corruption throughout the government and the elite's sense of untouchability.

Yet action did not go much beyond the level of declarations. The highest officials within the Ministry of Defense continued to cut illegal deals with commercial firms responsible for supplying the army. During Nadibaidze's period as defense minister (1994–1998), it was common for the army to sign supply contracts with organizations where relatives of key generals were employed. Defense officials sought funding for ammunition and arms already in their inventory. Nor was the Ministry of Finance clean. For any significant budgetary appropriation to the Ministry of Defense, Finance Ministry officials expected and received kickbacks.[30]

Davit Tevzadze, who was appointed minister of defense in spring 1998, attempted at the outset to follow Western advice in attacking corruption, but without great success. During Tevzadze's tenure from 1998 through 2003, the earlier practices continued. The Ministry of Defense continued to purchase ammunition from Russian military bases without

---

[28] Saqartvelos kontrolis palatis angarishi 1999 wlis saxelmtsipo biujetis shesrulebis shesaxeb (Tbilisi: unpublished version from the Parliamentary Research Department, 2000), pp 44–45.

[29] *Sakartvelos Respublika,* September 6, 2001.

[30] Georgian Ministry of Defense officials, confidential interviews with the author, 1998–2004.

documentation or transparency. The transactions may have saved money, but there was no control over cash flows. On more than one occasion, Georgian officers were caught reselling weapons illegally. The old practice of officers letting conscripts return home in exchange for bribes persisted. Military units continued to count so-called dead souls in justifying funding requests for food and clothing. Nikoloz Janjgava, a commander of ground forces who was appointed in spring 2001 and dismissed soon afterwards, later declared that instead of the 20,000 troops registered by the Ministry of Defense, fewer than 10,000 existed in reality.[31] At times, officers and soldiers worked as bodyguards in nightclubs as one way of meeting needs when they were not paid for months on end. As one of Tevzadze's colleagues explained after the minister's dismissal in 2004, black cashboxes were needed to feed soldiers.[32]

Corruption of this sort grew worse because of the mishandling of the general state budget. In 2000, the Ministry of Defense was originally budgeted to receive 42 million lari ($21 million), but within months an already inadequate budget allocation was slashed. Under these financial pressures, Western efforts to assist with security sector reform in Georgia did not have much of a chance. As one foreign expert put it, since budgetary parameters were constantly changing, it was unclear what missions the government meant the army to undertake, making future defense planning impossible.[33]

Shevardnadze himself offered only window dressing in the struggle against corruption. Personal loyalty to the president remained the criterion by which punishments and rewards were doled out to both uniformed and civilian functionaries. Loyalty networks based on corruption, however, inevitably fell short, not least because they could not incorporate all officers. Toward the end of his rule, Shevardnadze suddenly faced the problem of troop loyalty. In May 2001, a National Guard battalion revolted over poor service conditions and was joined by a group of criminals and former servicemen. Encircled by loyal units, the rebels soon relented, but only after intensive negotiations that involved the president. None of them, however, was punished, apparently because Shevardnadze

---

[31] Colonel Nikoloz Janjgava, interview with the author, June 2001.

[32] Ministry of Defense official, confidential interview with the author, February 2004.

[33] An official of the German armed forces, interview with the author, August 2000.

calculated that given rising public frustration over the absence of socioeconomic progress, he needed to treat men-in-arms gingerly.

Many of the essential details in military and security policy were defined by executive order, undermining the Parliament's ability to play its role in helping to shape the country's national security posture. Only the president reserved the right to make changes in the annual budget. Parliament's choice was to agree to his proposed figures or reject the draft budget completely. The Parliament offered only weak resistance, as Shevardnadze could always count on the support of a majority of its members. But even if the Parliament would have mounted a challenge, it could not have reversed the president's course. By Georgian law, in the case of a deadlock between the executive and the legislative branches, the government could use the figures from the previous year's budget. This formally undermined the Parliament's budgetary oversight over the defense sector, the principal tool of parliamentary control in any democracy.

Parliament's weakness was especially evident during the adoption of the 2002 budget.[34] In this instance, the Ministry of Defense had attempted to write a proper program budget with separately identified figures for specific large structural components. For the first time, the official defense portion of the draft budget was divided into three parts in accordance with NATO standards: personnel, readiness, and investments. Despite these improvements, the draft budget failed to address key questions: What was the rationale for distributing funding? What would likely be the financial effect of the proposed downsizing of the army? The Defense Committee of the Parliament supported the draft, viewing it as a step forward in the budgeting process. The Ministry of Defense, however, had failed to coordinate its budget proposal with the Ministry of Finance, which wanted to reduce the Defense Ministry's request from 71 to 38 million lari. The Parliament hesitated to accept the smaller figure, and the Ministry of Defense refused to recalculate its request. Ultimately, in January 2002 the Parliament did adopt a state budget with cuts in defense, but it did so without further review. Neither the Ministry of Finance nor the Ministry of Defense provided an explanation for how the funding should be allocated to meet NATO budgetary standards. Once again, the Parliament had passed up an opportunity to strengthen a key mechanism of civilian control over the military.

---

[34] In Georgia, the fiscal year coincides with the calendar year.

Moreover, parliamentary oversight over defense, security, and interior was weak. The constitution and parliamentary regulations guaranteed the accountability of the ministers of defense, security, and interior to the Parliament, but did not establish parliamentary oversight over autonomous armed agencies, such as the Special State Protection Service and the Border Guards. Their heads were appointed and dismissed by the president without legislative consent. Furthermore, there was no legal provision for a vote of no-confidence against the president or any minister. A high-ranking public servant could in theory be impeached for violating the constitution or committing a felony, but the consent of the Supreme Court was needed to bring charges.

Nor could Parliament exercise control over the National Security Council (NSC). According to the relevant legislation of 1996, the council was defined as an "advisory" body to the president on security issues. As such, it was free from parliamentary accountability. In reality, the council, and particularly its staff, exceeded its advisory function and played an influential role in coordinating various military and paramilitary agencies as well as personnel policy. Under Shevardnadze, defense and security policies were decided by an inner circle close to the president; the president substituted high-level fiat for interagency cooperation; and not only Parliament, but even ministries grew less relevant in setting and implementing national security policy.

In autumn 2001, the Parliament amended the Law on Defense to require the General Staff under the Ministry of Defense to coordinate all armed agencies during emergency and martial situations, as had often been recommended by foreign experts. The amendment, however, said nothing about the scope and procedures of such a coordination; nor did it address the relation of the General Staff to the autonomous armed agencies in times of peace. In January 2002, the minister of defense still openly complained of a lack of coordination among the various agencies, noting that it occurred only on an ad hoc basis during a crisis and without any kind of preliminary planning or legal clarification of responsibilities. Shevardnadze and officials in the National Security Council, however, appeared in no hurry to remedy this situation.[35]

---

[35] As one of the foreign experts said in spring 2000, "It seems the National Security Council is not quite ready to consolidate its military structures. This is regrettable." Confidential interview with the author, spring 2000.

IN SEARCH OF A NATIONAL SECURITY STRATEGY

In order to succeed, military reform must be based on well-articulated national interests and a strategy by which they are to be pursued. All of this, in turn, requires a well-developed policy planning process. Shevardnadze never openly opposed the development of a national security concept, but failed to deliver. As early as 1996, he had ordered the creation of a state commission to develop such a concept. In 1997, Parliament adopted a resolution on military doctrine, based on a document written largely by the minister of defense and modified by the parliamentary Committee on Defense and Security. But this document did not generate the kind of basic strategic thinking required for effective military reform. The 1997 military doctrine adopted by Parliament simply repeated language from the Russian military doctrine issued four years earlier. It touted the need to cooperate with all states, but did not define Georgia's national interests or the threats the country faced. Almost nothing was said about strategic partners, and it avoided the contentious issue of the Russian military presence. The document objected loosely to the militarization of neighboring territories, but was unspecific. Because it borrowed almost literally from Russian documents, one might have thought the reference to militarization was in regard to NATO enlargement. If so, it seemed to contradict Georgia's growing cooperation with NATO in the Partnership for Peace Program. Regrettably, the Parliament paid little attention to this document, and it had little chance of serving as a strategic guideline for military reform.

In 1999, the National Security Council acknowledged that it was a priority to follow the recommendations of the ISAB and formulate a national security concept. During the period from 1996 to 1999, a number of drafts had appeared. Some of them had been worked out under the state commission's auspices; others were written within the walls of Parliament or in government agencies. Together they offered an insight into the security discourse in Georgia. Most emphasized the problems of state-building, the challenge of separatism, the interference of external players in domestic affairs, corruption, social inequality, the risk of regional conflict, Georgia's military inferiority, and possible ecological catastrophes. Some of these draft documents invoked the prevalence of ethnic identity over citizenship in the broader public's attitudes, the low prestige of law enforcement agencies, and the violation of human rights by representatives of those agencies. Many of them emphasized the need to protect human rights, to achieve civilian control over the military, to foster political pluralism, and to strengthen local self-government. They also urged the peaceful solution of Georgia's frozen ethnic conflicts.

Most of these projects, however, were marred by eclecticism, contradictory statements, broad generalizations, and the avoidance of sensitive issues. Some drafts stressed the importance of human rights and integration into the democratic community of nations, but one could also find warnings about the dangers of globalization and individualism. Other projects referred to "the social responsibility of the family." Most of the projects added education and culture to the security mix, but had little to say about Russia's military presence or its interference in Georgia's domestic affairs, even though these latter issues dominated public discussion.

In summer 1999, after the National Security Council accepted the ISAB's recommendations, the state commission prepared a new draft document. This one had several advantages. Georgia's preferred strategic orientation was made clearer: Georgia, it affirmed, intended to join the key institutions of Euro-Atlantic community. In this spirit, to the extent education figured in security calculations, the document indicated that the country's educational system should promote values relevant to Georgia's Western-oriented aspirations. Still, the new draft also suffered from vague, but troubling, generalizations, like the reference to the "necessity to build a social and political system appropriate to cultural peculiarities." While covering as broad a spectrum of public life as possible, this document failed to elaborate the concrete threats confronting the country, although its authors recognized the need to do so. As with previous efforts in Georgia, and unlike comparable documents in Europe and the United States, it made no effort to lay out systematically either threats to national interests or a strategy for addressing them.

It was becoming increasingly obvious that Georgia needed a basic document articulating a national security concept, not least if the country hoped to deepen its cooperation with the West. The ISAB, together with various international expert groups, regularly urged the government to develop such a document, but Shevardnadze's regime was slow to act. The absence of a strategic concept not only impeded the development of a coherent security policy, but hampered the development of civil–military relations along democratic lines and the coordination among various security agencies. By 2000, high-ranking military leaders—like Minister of Defense Tevzadze and the head of the Border Guard, General Valeri

Chkeidze—were openly underscoring how much the absence of strategic guidelines was undermining the things they wished to accomplish.

At this point, the ISAB grew tired of waiting and drafted its own document in cooperation with the Ministry of Foreign Affairs. When publicly issued, it was entitled, "Georgia and the World: Vision and Strategy for the Future."[36] In the document, the authors were more explicit about Georgia's intention to join NATO and to deepen cooperation with the EU. They also stressed the importance of the closure of Russian bases and expressed skepticism over the effectiveness of the Russian-led Commonwealth of Independent States (CIS). For the first time, a draft strategic concept gave concrete attention to defense missions, suggesting that the armed forces should be better integrated in order to constitute a deterrent force capable of defeating an attack by modest-sized forces, controlling small-scale cross-border infiltrations, coping with terrorist attacks, helping the authorities to restore law and order in extreme situations, providing humanitarian and disaster relief, and participating in international peacekeeping missions.

Although a document of this kind cannot be expected to explore the details of defense policy, this effort had something of the character of a wish list. It touched only superficially on threat assessment. Even if a document enlisting the assistance of foreign experts was unlikely to articulate Georgia's precise concerns about neighbors, any realistic security concept needed to deal more directly and thoroughly with the security challenges facing the country. However, the principal deficiency of the "Vision and Strategy for the Future" had more to do with its status than its content. It was not discussed in many of the relevant governmental agencies before its publication; its contents were not widely publicized in Georgia; and no leader, including the president, bothered to mention the document in a public announcement or speech. In fact, key figures within the government refused to embrace the document as the country's national security concept, noting that the National Security Council was still preparing such a document.

In 2002, the Ministry of Defense produced a White Paper[37] of its own, although with a relatively modest purpose. Written in response to

---

[36] The document was made available on the NATO website, http://www.nato. int/pfp/ge/d001010.htm.

[37] Unpublished document.

ISAB exhortation, it simply summarized the organization of the armed forces, emphasized civilian supremacy in military matters, underscored the importance of cooperating with NATO, and expressed a wish to make the army stronger. It attempted to say something about the armed forces' missions, but without a precise picture of the security challenges facing the country or the articulation of a broader strategy, this effort did not go far. Given the unresolved disagreement between the Ministry of Defense and the Ministry of Finance on defense spending, there was little the White Paper could contribute here. Nor did it comment on the problem of coordinating with other armed agencies. Basically it was a document written without serious consultation with other governmental institutions. The rumor was that it had been written by one or two mid-level Defense Ministry functionaries, largely without the involvement of key departments in the ministry itself.

By the middle of 2003, the National Security Council had prepared its own draft. Some ideas from the earlier ISAB text made their way into the new paper, but it differed in other respects, and the differences were not always for the better. The NSC document[38] covered too many themes, many of them inappropriate for a national security concept. For example, the authors laid stress on the need to develop the "traditional fields" of industry and agriculture. The text was vague about the concrete missions of the military. It did underscore Georgia's intention to join NATO, but the chapters devoted to foreign relations, and especially Georgia's role on the regional level, provided no real assessment of the challenges the country faced or how they might be addressed. The concept paper was surprisingly undiplomatic on the subject of relations with Russia. In addition, democratization and human rights issues were ignored. Instead, the document noted the chance the Georgian nation had to build a state corresponding to its spiritual preferences and cultural distinctiveness. It then laid out a series of ambitious goals without considering their feasibility. For example, it declared that the share of the shadow economy in GDP was to be cut by 15 to 20 percent, but gave no idea of how this might be achieved or whether it would significantly affect the defense budget. In the end, the NSC paper did not clearly identify the country's security priorities, provide a coherent risk analysis, or set out an appropriate range of strategic options. The chapter on

---

[38] Unpublished document.

"Risks to Georgia's Security" drew no distinction between risks, threats, and challenges.

This was the last national security project developed by Shevardnadze's government. Like the others that came before, it was never adopted. By the time it appeared, Shevardnadze's regime was already in deep crisis. In his defense and security policies, Shevardnadze vacillated between the various contending forces, focusing not on policy concepts but simply on his personal political survival. By the end of his rule, he had grown ambivalent toward the United States and the EU. He found it ever more difficult to tolerate harsh criticism from a burgeoning democratic opposition, especially because U.S. and other Western leaders appeared increasingly to identify with his critics. By late 2002, Georgian anger over Russia's reluctance to withdraw its military bases appeared to soften. At the ministerial meeting of the OSCE in Lisbon in December 2002, the Georgian delegation seemed inclined toward further compromises with Russia concerning the dates of their closure. According to a high-ranking OSCE official, a lack of transparency and consistency weakened the Georgian position on the disputed bases.[39] This shift of policies happened at a time when some major Western companies who had heavily invested in Georgia were reducing their activities or were even leaving the country,[40] and when Russian state-owned firms began to appear in strategic sectors of the Georgian economy.

During the Shevardnadze period, Georgia suffered from a vicious circle: the weakness and disorder in developing and managing the military impeded the formulation of a coherent strategic vision, but the absence of a national security concept delayed and burdened the process of military reform. In Shevardnadze's last years, defense restructuring fell considerably short of the ISAB's recommendations. The army was downsized, but there were still 20,000 troops on the state budget—6,000 to 7,000 more than the ISAB had said Georgia could afford. The Special Assault Brigade was integrated into the Interior Ministry, contrary to the ISAB's urging that this ministry should be relieved of military missions. The Border Guard also retained a military function, despite the ISAB's recommendation that it be converted into a law enforcement agency.

---

[39] OSCE official, confidential interview with the author, January 2003.
[40] Such as the American energy company AES that had created the newly privatized electricity company AES-Telasi.

Shevardnadze appeared unable to break out of this dilemma for three reasons. First, he had built a corrupt network with parallel lines of control in order to manage the political environment. The transparency of a clear national security concept would have endangered this system. Second, his wavering between the West and Russia made it difficult to settle on a security strategy or to coordinate military reform with security policy. On the one hand, he feared Russia's opposition should he turn firmly toward the West. On the other hand, he placed too many hopes on Russia assisting him to restore Georgia's territorial integrity. Third, Shevardnadze did not seriously adhere to democratic values, as demonstrated by his toleration of corruption in politics and the special fiscal, economic, and political privileges that he accorded the Orthodox Church. He seems to have desired integration into Europe for instrumental rather than intrinsic ideological reasons. In late 1999, he stated that the issue of Georgia's orientation toward either the West or Russia was unimportant—what mattered was which side would provide what.[41]

Pragmatism of this sort was a recipe for ineffectiveness. Any state, however small or weak, must make clear commitments to its allies and benefactors. Only then can it expect long-lasting and mutually beneficial cooperation. Shevardnadze did not manage to accomplish this with either the West or Russia. In the process, he failed to satisfy the basic needs of the Georgian citizens on whom the country's defense forces would depend. As a result, when the people rose against him in 2003, the military and police establishments that he had nurtured refused to protect him. It was a further consequence of Georgia's distorted and undemocratic civil–military relations. The Army and paramilitary forces by and large did not respect an aging head of the state, much like the rest of society and for many of the same reasons. Because of a corrupt, clientelist, and ineffective command and control system in Georgia's military and security institutions, an unpopular leadership could not rely on unanimous or unambiguous obedience in critical situations. In contrast, opposition leaders might well have been able to strike deals with some of the more energetic and Western-oriented officers. If Shevardnadze had decided to use force, the outcome would have been very unclear and his personal fate might have been much more tragic.

----

41 *Evropa,* December 25–31, 1999, pp. 107–128.

MILITARY REFORM AFTER THE ROSE REVOLUTION

The post-Shevardnadze era has only just begun, and it is not easy to judge how far the changes in defense and security policy will go. Some of the new leadership's first declarations and initiatives, however, opened the possibility of positive advances. These opportunities are further bolstered by the new wave of security assistance extended by the United States and the EU.

To begin with what are promising first steps: on several occasions, President Mikheil Saakashvili has stressed that security issues, including refurbishing the army, will be a policy priority, and he has backed his pledge with increased funding. In addition, the new government has created, with the assistance of private and foreign donations, a separate fund intended to raise the salaries of senior public officials, including those in the Ministry of Defense. And the government has begun repairing tanks, armored vehicles, helicopters, and other military hardware that had badly deteriorated by the end of 2003.

Military restructuring, carried out with U.S. and British technical assistance, has received a new impetus. Upon returning from the United States in early 2004, Saakashvili was able to report that the Americans would not only continue previous material and technical assistance, but would help to form a full-size infantry brigade of 5,000 soldiers trained to NATO standards. According to current plans, the Georgian armed forces will consist of four full-sized brigades. As for the defense budget, in 2005 it exceeded 300 million lari, which is almost ten times more than in Shevardnadze's last years.

Two other important changes took place in the Ministry of Defense during the first months of the new regime. In March 2004, Saakashvili approved interim regulations for the ministry that will closely resemble those of NATO countries. The reorganization of the ministry, as well as the delineation of functions between its civilian and military staffs, has been entrusted to Cubic, a private U.S. consulting firm hired by the Pentagon, and to a team from the British Ministry of Defense. Part of the process already includes a restructuring of the National Guard and fully integrating its combat units into the army. The National Guard itself will only consist of training centers for reserve forces.

Saakashvili has also appointed a civilian minister of defense and an unprecedented number of civilians to key leadership posts in the ministry. At the same time, he has retired many of the generals who either resisted reforms or lacked the knowledge and skill to carry them out. Younger officers and civil servants trained in Western institutions now have a far more prominent role in carrying out military reform.

Moreover, reform has now reached other armed agencies and the government has begun integrating parallel structures. Georgia's State Department of Frontier Protection has been made a part of the Ministry of Interior, laying the groundwork for transforming this agency into a law enforcement structure. The Ministry of Interior's troops are to transfer heavy armament to the Ministry of Defense and turn themselves into something closer to a gendarmerie. Within the Ministry of Interior, a reform agency has been created to carry out this change and others intended to bring policing in Georgia closer to Western standards. Similarly, the Coastal Protection Forces, once a part of the Department of Frontier Protection, and the Defense Ministry's Naval Defense Forces have been instructed to work out plans for their integration.

The last and the most serious structural changes in the security sector have been amendments to the Law on the Structure, Responsibilities, and Rules of Activity of the Government of Georgia adopted by the Parliament in December 2004. They mandated the merger of the Ministry of Security with a reorganized Ministry of Interior into a single Ministry of Police and Public Safety. That process is now underway. An independent foreign intelligence agency, directly subordinated to the president, is also being created.

All of these measures are expected to improve the interoperability of Georgian forces with NATO, while also improving their management and effectiveness. Through integration and downsizing, financial savings are also anticipated. To increase transparency and accountability and to promote sound civil–military relations, negotiations between the government and the NGO community on the establishment of public oversight boards within the law enforcement, security, and defense agencies began in 2004.

Beyond the reform of military and paramilitary forces, Saakashvili has confirmed Georgia's intention to join NATO, which he has said he hopes will take no more than a few years. He has expressed similar sentiments about Georgia's goal to be admitted to the EU. In April 2004, a newly created Georgian interagency team drafted a NATO Individual Partnership Action Plan (IPAP), which has been largely approved by the relevant NATO agencies.[42] The new post-revolutionary version of the IPAP

---

[42] One of the authors of this document, representing the Secretariat of the

explains the logic of the above-mentioned reforms in the military field and requests concrete technical assistance in order to reach NATO standards. At the same time, the IPAP confirms Georgia's commitment to Euro-Atlantic integration, regional cooperation, respect for democracy, human rights, a market economy, and the peaceful resolution of ethnic conflicts. Thus, the IPAP has begun to address a number of issues crucial to a national security concept.

At the same time, Saakashvili has declared a crusade against organized crime and corruption, and has followed through with greater vigor than either of his predecessors. The unwillingness to touch high-ranking public officials and organized crime bosses characteristic of the Shevardnadze era has been abandoned by the new leadership. The former chief of the state railway service, Akaki Chkhaidze, has been arrested. So has Giorgi Kenchadze, a former member of Parliament well-known for his contacts with the criminal world. And the authorities have moved against the Aprasidze criminal gang that, from its base in the village of Etseri in Svaneti province, had terrorized the local population and organized criminal activity throughout Georgia.

None of these changes, however, is yet irreversible, and there remain important deficiencies in the security and defense spheres. First, control over the military remains insufficiently democratic and has too much duplication. In February 2004, the new leadership, with near unanimous parliamentary consent, amended the constitution to create the post of prime minister and to allow the president the right to dissolve Parliament when the executive and legislative branches are deadlocked. Some have argued that as a result, the legislative branch has grown weaker in exercising civilian democratic control over the military. At a minimum, even if one disagrees on this score, it is evident that the problems stemming from the blurring of functions among the key political bodies in the security and defense field have not ended. For example, the Parliament now has the right to vote no-confidence in individual ministers or the entire

---

National Security Council of Georgia, confirmed this in an interview with the author in April 2004. Although the Shevardnadze administration promised to create such a document, his government never delivered. On the eve of the November 2003 revolution, it finally produced the first version of an IPAP, but NATO experts regarded it as window dressing. Source: A representative of the Georgian Ministry of Foreign Affairs, interview with the author, December 2003.

cabinet, albeit at the risk of being dissolved. The creation of the prime minister's post appears to have led to dual lines of authority. The principal ministries are supervised by the prime minister, but the president retains the right to dismiss the ministers of defense as well as of police and public safety without the prime minister's consent. At the same time, the president remains the supreme commander of the armed forces and chairs the National Security Council. On extraordinary occasions, he even chairs the cabinet of ministers. This overlap risks recreating the problem of "subjective" civilian control referred to earlier in this chapter.

Moreover, leadership in the Ministry of Defense has been subject to unusual and potentially disturbing volatility. In February 2005, the fourth minister of defense since the Rose Revolution requested all directors of the General Staff, including its chief, to resign. The chief of the General Staff, also the fourth since the revolution, was replaced by Levan Nikoleishvili. Two things about these events are unfortunate. First, they reflect serious leadership instability both in the Ministry of Defense and more generally in political circles. Second, the request of the minister was probably illegal, since he is not entitled to urge the chief of the General Staff to resign. Legally the chief is appointed and dismissed by the president himself. Thus, a mix of revolutionary chaos and quasi-legality persists in Georgian defense policy.

In spring 2005, NATO undertook the first assessment of Georgia's performance under the Individual Partnership Action Plan. As the process remains largely classified, not much is publicly known. The government states that NATO experts are quite impressed with ongoing army restructuring and increased combat capability. However, according to some confidential sources, the experts did question the rationality and planning procedures for procuring military hardware.

Under these circumstances, it is important that the role of the NSC be clearly defined. This process began in 2004, and as a promising first step, the secretary of the National Security Council, Vano Merabishvili, turned to NGOs for advice and to the civilian expert community for help in drawing up a national security concept, but this lasted only so long.[43] His successor, Gela Bejuashvili, chose to work without much involvement from civil society or academic circles. Before this work can

---

[43] Representatives of the National Security Council Secretariat, interview with the author, April 2004.

be completed, however, the president, the prime minister, and the leadership of the ruling National Movement-Democrats need to answer the following questions: How is the issue of the Russian military presence in Georgia to be solved? How does the Georgian government plan to resolve the problem of the separated territories? How does the government propose to achieve energy security, deal with extreme poverty, and defeat corruption, organized crime, and the religious as well as ethnic intolerance still plaguing Georgia's social and political life? How are the resources necessary for dealing with these and other security issues to be generated? What missions are to be assigned to the security and defense agencies? Without clarification of Russian–Georgian relations in the field of defense or of the role of the Georgian armed forces in restoring the territorial integrity of the country, and without socioeconomic and cultural modernization and the elimination of favoritism and government corruption, military reform—even under the guidance of the best foreign experts—will remain stillborn. Currently, corrupt networks in the army as well as in the police and other security-related agencies seem to have been seriously damaged, but they have scarcely been eliminated, and any loophole in the reform design will open the way to their revival.[44]

Georgia does not face the threat of large-scale aggression anytime soon. Russian politicians, however frustrated with Georgia's tilt toward NATO, have no reason to contemplate broad military intervention—not when they can employ alternative forms of economic and diplomatic pressure and they have the opportunity to manipulate Georgia's tense internal ethnic relations. Thus, it makes no sense, even if it were possible, for Georgia to try to build a large conventional military force. What the country needs is a light regular force able to control mountainous borders, a naval defense to control the maritime border, and paramilitary forces that can be used against organized criminal groups. A part of these forces can also be trained and used for international peacekeeping missions, an important way for a small country such as Georgia to contribute to international stability and security. For more remote or hypothetical large-scale threats on Georgia's borders, it would make sense to enhance the existing reserve force. Because of the short-term obligatory training

---

[44] Representatives of the Georgian Ministry of Defense, interview with the author, April 2004.

that the reserves provide, this would have the additional benefit of aiding nation-building in Georgia's multiethnic setting.

If corruption is curbed and the system of management optimized, Georgia, even with its modest resources, can maintain a professional force of 15,000 to 20,000 soldiers along with a conscript reserve component. All of this, however, brings us back to the challenge of addressing Georgia's fundamental internal problems, including the legacy of distorted civil–military relations left by prior leaderships. If the new leadership is steadfast and effective in dealing with these problems, Georgia can begin to enjoy greater, albeit relative, security based on a more adequate and reliable defense establishment.

CHAPTER 4

Georgia and Russia: The Troubled Road to Accommodation

JABA DEVDARIANI

In January 2004, Georgia's newly elected President Mikheil Saakashvili urged that relations with Russia start from a clean slate. Once again, the troubled coexistence of these two neighboring states has arrived at a moment of choice. A lack of trust and a sense of insecurity have marked Russia's relations with many post-Soviet states, especially the Baltics, but also with Georgia's neighbor, Azerbaijan. None, however, match the decade of verbal skirmishing between Russia and Georgia, jousting that occasionally has bordered on armed incidents. Why have Russian–Georgian relations been so full of tension, arguably more so than any other of Russia's post-Soviet relationships?

Healthy relations between neighbors with a checkered history of coexistence can only come through increased self-confidence, but the fallout from the Soviet collapse left both Russia and Georgia with very little confidence to spare. Both countries went through an identity crisis in the 1990s. Georgia's ruling elite consolidated its power by seeking a clean break from the dominant power, the Russian Federation. Since the late eighteenth century, "Georgianness" has meant linguistic, territorial, and religious separation from the Russian Empire. With the disintegration of the Soviet Union, grievances that had accumulated since the time of the Russian Empire led Georgian elites to perceive their interests as utterly incompatible with those of Russia. For the Russian elite, the loss of control over the South Caucasus was serious enough; witnessing the zealous efforts of Georgian nationalists to distance themselves from Russia added insult to injury.

In this context of fear and mutual mistrust, pressing security concerns have not been addressed constructively. Georgia cast Russia as a primary security threat, while Russia was suspicious of Georgia's interest in NATO and its growing ties with Russia's historical rival, Turkey. Personal rivalries also blocked channels of communication. Weak governments in Moscow and especially in Tbilisi sought to strengthen themselves by waging a war of words against the other side. Successive Georgian elections were run and won by attacking Moscow for its sins, both real and imagined. The Georgian government's inability to deliver both economically and politically tempted it to boost popularity at home by framing the Russian threat starkly. This same weakness, however, prevented Georgia from insulating itself from the more aggressive elements in the Russian polity and made it easier for Russia to influence Georgia's internal politics.

All of these developments have left little room for pragmatism and cooperation between Georgia and Russia. Yet two factors are now helping to increase the levels of confidence and pushing the two countries closer together. One has been the gradual change of leadership. A new generation has come to power in both countries, with less of a need to legitimize itself at the other's expense and less of a grudge against the other side. More importantly, regional and international players—state, non-state, and commercial—have begun to play an increasing role in the South Caucasus. Oil and hydrocarbon transit routes have raised the revenues and also the stakes of the game for all actors, most of whom want to see stability in the region. There also are common problems that are better solved through cooperation. The threat of international terrorism has prompted a reassessment of security. The financial flows from Georgian citizens working in Russia and the growth of Russia's energy interests in Georgia draw these two governments further together. Both Moscow and Tbilisi are now trying to improve their communication with each other. For the moment, however, divisive factors remain at least as strong as those that unite, and this blocks tangible progress.

This chapter begins by examining the reasons behind the conflict between Russia and Georgia, focusing on two levels of confrontation: the countries' simultaneous identity crises of the early 1990s and the search for security in the mid- to late 1990s. The middle section of the chapter explores the new pragmatism in bilateral relations. The chapter concludes with the two countries' recent attempts to find common ground.

IN SEARCH OF IDENTITY

Much of the current tension between Russia and Georgia has its roots in the late 1980s, when both countries struggled to find new identities during the period leading up to the collapse of the Soviet Union. During the troubled and complex process of reinventing themselves, Georgians and Russians sought identities that were in essential respects juxtaposed. The tension was greatest in the early years through 1994, but the degree of mutual mistrust and the accompanying harsh (albeit sometimes inconsistent) language on both sides never fully subsided. Value-related conflicts such as this one are difficult to resolve, because, as Jeffrey Rubin notes, they "may be settled if one can persuade the other to change his or her mind, but will not be settled through the give and take of negotiations."[1] This also makes it hard to account for the conflict in pragmatic political terms, because events that should have had a negligible impact on "normal" interstate relations, such as an odd television news report or a particular book, gain disproportionate attention when seen through the prism of conflicting values and agendas.

The anthropological concept of "collective identity" helps to explain this phenomenon. "Collective identity" refers to shared concepts of social reality or an "[all] encompassing frame of reference that guides social action."[2] The identities of both the Russian and the Georgian "nations" derive from their common history as a part of first imperial Russia and then the Soviet Union. But each has given a very different meaning to this identity. Identity is a narrative or a myth that guides and defines social action and is embodied in history, art, literature, and social practices. In this sense, one can speak of the "master myth" as the broadest part of the symbolic universe that a society uses to define threats to its existence, as well as appropriate responses.[3] While master myths need to be enduring in order to help create and sustain identities, they are also regularly remade. Dramatic changes, such as the collapse of the Soviet

---

[1] Jeffrey Z. Rubin, "Models of Conflict Management," *Journal of Social Studies,* vol. 50, no. 1 (1994), pp. 33–45.

[2] Peter L. Berger and Thomas Luckmann, *The Social Construction of Reality: A Treatise in the Sociology of Knowledge* (New York: Anchor Books, 1967), p. 62.

[3] Berger and Luckmann, *The Social Construction of Reality,* p. 62; Margaret R. Somers and Gloria D. Gibson, "Dark Thoughts about the Self," in Craig Callhoun, ed., *Social Theory and the Politics of Identity* (Oxford: Blackwell, 1994), p. 67.

Union, often lead to a redefinition of history and a redesigning of the master myth.[4]

Modern Georgia's national identity has been shaped around the idea of independence from Russia. Hence, Russia dominates the Georgian national consciousness and carries a symbolic significance in Georgian politics no matter what it does.[5] Interpreting Georgian history in terms of opposition to the Russian Empire creates an emotional inertia that Manuel Castells calls a "resistance identity." This is the self-awareness that forms when an alien discourse is imposed and when sovereignty over the public realm and institutions is limited or lost. Under these conditions, societies create deviant, parallel, and autonomous social interactions and institutions—the "trenches of resistance and survival" that differentiate their collective "us" from an oppressive "them" in ethno-linguistic, religious, or other ways.[6]

Caught between the Ottoman and Persian empires, Georgia's political and physical existence was threatened in the late eighteenth century. When the Georgian elite failed to attract the attention of the European powers, they asked for Russian protection. At this juncture, Georgia's identity, which was based on Orthodox Christianity, facilitated this choice. For many decades, the Georgian aristocracy had fought alongside Russian troops to pacify unruly tribes in the Northern Caucasus. Georgian generals in the Russian army had played a significant role in quelling the first Chechen rebellion, led by the legendary Imam Shamil. Simultaneously, through Russian poetry, arts, and education, Georgian aristocrats gained access to contemporary European culture and values.

But while the cultural affinity with Russia proved resilient, the political alliance faltered. From the early decades of imperial Russian governance in Georgia, there were rumblings among the commoners that periodically escalated into spontaneous rebellions. The Georgian feudal system was milder, and people resented the extremely harsh oppression characteristic of Russian rule, including corporal punishment. The young

---

[4] Somers and Gibson, "Dark Thoughts about the Self," p. 67. Also, Manuel Castells, *The Power of Identity* (Malden, MA: Blackwell, 1997), p. 31.

[5] Gia Tarkhan-Mouravi, "The Georgian–Abkhazian Conflict in a Regional Context," in Bruno Coppieters, Ghia Nodia, and Yuri Anchabadze, eds., *Georgia and Abkhazia, The Search for a Settlement* (Cologne: Sonderveröffentlichung des BIOst, 1998), pp. 90–112, http://poli.vub.ac.be.

[6] Castells, *The Power of Identity*, p. 8.

Georgian aristocrats who acquired European ideals of freedom and liberalism in Russian universities challenged their fathers' readiness to seek the protection of the Russian imperial crown. Georgian literature in the nineteenth century revolved around the conflict between fathers and sons, and ended with the victory of the latter. By the end of the nineteenth century, a young aristocracy, through arts, literature, and journalism, shifted the Georgian sense of national identity to the idea of "betrayal" by Russia, whose imperial policies had forced the annexation of the Georgian kingdom and the abolition of the royal dynasty.

The short-lived Democratic Republic of Georgia in 1918 sought legitimacy in this discourse. When Soviet Russian troops invaded in 1921, Russia became in the eyes of Georgian nationalists an unreliable and scheming partner set on undermining the Georgian nation and state. Although the Georgian aristocracy was decimated in the mid-1920s, new generations of Georgian writers in the 1930s, 1950s, and 1970s drew inspiration from the nineteenth-century notion of "Georgianness" as opposition to an imperial oppressor. Thus, the Georgian master myth crystallized around a resistance identity.[7]

Georgian attitudes toward Russia hardened as the result of traumatic experiences during the Soviet period, such as in 1956 when Soviet troops fired on demonstrators in Tbilisi protesting Nikita Khrushchev's anti-Stalin campaign (since they saw this campaign as an assault on "Georgianness"). A similar episode occurred on April 9, 1989, when Soviet interior troops violently disbanded a peaceful rally in Tbilisi and killed twenty protesters, mostly young women. This event led to a surge in pro-independence sentiment and nationwide indignation.

Ridding Georgia of the oppressive Russian "other" served as the all-embracing goal of the independence movement in the late 1980s. Its leaders spoke constantly of fighting for "full independence," but never defined the term and seemed to be responding to a simple impulse to be free of the hated oppressor. Suspicion of Russia bordered on paranoia: the Georgian press, for example, contended that Russia's televised weather forecasts for Tbilisi were a manifestation of imperial thinking ("Why don't they leave us alone?"), or that the earthquakes that rocked various parts of Georgia in the 1990s were engineered by Russia at secret underground laboratories.

---

[7] For an in-depth review of the issue, see Irakli Chkonia, "Remaking the Identity Master Myth in Georgia: The Intellectual and Social History of Discourse of Modern Georgian Nationalism," unpublished manuscript.

At the same time, real threats to Georgia's security were wrongly interpreted or dismissed on the assumption that without Russian meddling, the dissent voiced by the country's ethnic minority communities—most notably by Ossetians and Abkhazians—would resolve itself automatically.[8] Economic issues were considered secondary and easy to handle once independence was achieved. With the country's natural riches (tea and mineral water were frequently mentioned) returned to their rightful owners, they supposedly would create the basis for national prosperity.

Independence suddenly seemed to be a feasible goal after Mikhail Gorbachev began dismantling some of the most stifling Soviet institutions. While Georgian society now envisaged the prospect of liberation, the Russian elite found it much harder to turn its back on the past. Russia's collective identity remained bound up with the country's imperial "great power" and cold-war-superpower status. This identity set Russia politically apart from Europe, notwithstanding the cultural affinity the Russian elite shares with it. During the Soviet era, the master myth made the Soviet Union the military and ideological counterweight to the capitalist West. According to Boris Dubin, the key components of Soviet identity from the 1930s onward consisted of the "mission" (counterbalance to an imperialist West), *derzhava* ("self" as a great power, uniting diverse nationalities), and "border" (a physical separation of "self" from "others").[9] These concepts dated back to the Russian Empire, but under Stalin's rule, the messianic "divine mission" became entwined with a militarized and highly centralized state waging a global contest against the "capitalist West."[10]

Gorbachev attempted to shed the ideology of counterbalancing the West and instead sought to integrate the Soviet Union with the West by making the Soviet economy and political institutions compatible with those of the capitalist powers. His assault on a master myth that retained its popular legitimacy, however, prejudiced reform "from above" and helped to trigger a backlash that expressed itself in the August 1991

---

[8] In his contribution to this volume, Ghia Nodia argues that Georgia's ethnic communities had grounds to feel threatened by the definition of the Georgian nation in ethnically exclusive terms.

[9] Boris Dubin, "Counterweight: Symbolism of the West in Contemporary Russia," *Pro et Contra*, vol. 8, no. 3 (2004), p. 24.

[10] Dubin, "Counterweight," p. 24.

Moscow putsch. Nor were Soviet state institutions able to accommodate the pluralism essential to democratic reforms. As a result, the Soviet Union collapsed. Paradoxically, in an attempt to reform its mission, Russia lost its "self"—the *derzhava* uniting many different nationalities, crowned with superpower status.

Thus, the real crisis of Russia's identity started with the demise of the Soviet Union. Initially (i.e., 1990–1993), Boris Yeltsin's administration continued attempts to integrate with the West. The new Russian elite claimed that ending the Soviet Union was an act of "self-liberation." An independent, Western-oriented Russia, it was expected, would shift to a market economy and swiftly achieve prosperity. Liberal reformers, led by Yegor Gaidar, viewed the former Soviet republics as an economic burden. If Russia did not have to pay for economically backward provinces, it could boost growth, catch up with the Western states, and rebuild its status as a great power in the process. The ideology of economic liberalism, however, failed to catch on, and the distorted privatization of public assets, which enriched a well-connected few, turned the public against reform. In the end, the new narrative could not replace the traditional master myth.

Russian authors are divided on the causes of this failure. Some say the notion of economic prosperity based on individual effort contradicts the traditional Russian "myth" of collectivist unity and the primacy of spiritual development over material gain. Others argue that integration with the West diverged too much from the master myth of Russia as the counterweight to the West. Opinion surveys in 1996 revealed that 20 percent of Russians believed their country should replicate the Soviet way of life, 47 percent preferred "traditional Russian" ways, and only 11 percent preferred Western ways. In 1997, 51 percent of Russians surveyed viewed the West as "an adversary of Russia" trying "to solve its own problems at Russia's expense and by harming Russian interests."[11]

In the absence of the new master myth, Russia relapsed into its pre-Soviet past in search of a new basis for statehood, a process not unlike that in many Eastern European states.[12] Unlike most Eastern European states, however, Soviet Russia between the two World Wars maintained

---

[11] Dubin, "Counterweight," p. 27.
[12] Dmitri Trenin, "Identity and Integration: Russia and the West in the 21st Century," *Pro et Contra*, vol. 8, no. 3 (2004), p. 11.

the basic characteristics of a territorial empire and did not consolidate into a nation-state or a capitalist democracy. Hence, the symbolism of empire (and within it, the *derzhavnik* rhetoric) was preserved and, after the Soviet collapse, revived. A major break with Russia's Euro-integrationist course coincided with the start of the Chechen war in 1994, leading the West to abandon hopes for a rapid democratization and economic liberalization of Russia.

The master myths of the new Georgia and the new Russia were obviously in conflict. Georgia greeted the Soviet collapse as opening the way to independence. Russia was the "other" against which Georgia defined itself in a nearly paranoid, passion-driven fixation on achieving full and complete separation. On the other side, Russia's elite, for the most part, rued the collapse of Soviet power, viewing it as imperiling core components of the state's identity. Most traumatically, the death of communist ideology and the collapse of a centrally planned economy left Russia without its self-defining identity that served as a counterbalance to the capitalist West. Georgia constituted only a negligible element in the original Russian master myth, but clashing identities in the post-Soviet era put Georgia and the Caucasus back on the Russian mind.

Russia's conquest of the Caucasus and expansion toward warm-water ports, "bringing enlightenment to savages," has been an integral part of the Russian imperial narrative. This idea weaves its way through the works of major Russian literary figures, such as Pushkin, Lermontov, and Tolstoy. Georgia's rigid and aggressive self-conception denigrated this narrative. Georgia denied being a part of *derzhava,* because it did not share the mission of countering the West nor even align itself with Russia in this confrontation. Worse, Georgian president Zviad Gamsakhurdia's romantic nationalist notions led him not only to embrace the cultural and historical unity of the South Caucasus and North Caucasus, but even to challenge Russia's imperial reach. Fanciful as these ideas may have been, Russians readily exaggerated the danger they represented.[13] Talk of "pan-Caucasian" movements caused even greater consternation in Russia, because any real progress in this direction would give an economic and political advantage to Turkey, its historical rival in the region.

---

[13] Liz Fuller, "New Geopolitical Alliances on Russia's Southern Rim," *RFE/RL Newsline,* April 16, 1997, http://www.rferl.org/newsline/1997/04/160497.asp.

Diverging strategic visions and ideological incompatibilities did not exclude some forms of practical cooperation between the Yeltsin and Gamsakhurdia governments. However, the deeper identity conflicts echoing through Georgian domestic politics undermined any real progress in this direction. Confrontation with Russia was central to Georgia's domestic politics. Gamsakhurdia's preoccupation with resisting Russia obscured the real tasks of nation-building. For example, he was fixated on the influence Moscow could exert within the country through its security services and former Communist Party cadre. Georgia's professional elite and intelligentsia who gravitated toward Russia culturally and through their professional ties were stigmatized as "collaborators."[14] This witch-hunt diverted the government from vital economic and social problems. It also stripped Gamsakhurdia of many of the bureaucracy's most capable administrators and led to a simmering internal confrontation between the politically appointed ministers and their *nomenklatura* subordinates. The alienation of the elite contributed significantly to the downfall of his government.[15]

Similarly, Gamsakhurdia and his administration perceived Abkhazia and South Ossetia as simply tools for Russian pressure directed against Georgian independence. As a result, the concerns of local elites in these areas were not taken into consideration, and channels of communication remained blocked. In the absence of a dialogue, tensions spiraled into violent clashes. By refusing to see how its own quest for independence challenged the identities of the Abkhazians and Ossetians, Georgia failed to create a more integrated national identity.[16]

To some extent, of course, Gamsakhurdia's anti-Russian posture had a functional aspect. He meant to use Georgians' fear of an external enemy to consolidate power and promote a common national identity. Exploiting an enemy image, however, proved insufficient as a tool for pushing the country forward. Thus, while Georgian society may have moved toward a consensus on what Ghia Nodia calls the "national

---

[14] Both Gamsakhurdia in Georgia and Abulfaz Elchibey in Azerbaijan tried to distance themselves from "Red Intelligentsia," although it proved to be impossible and had the effect of "elite alienation" (with revolutionary results).

[15] On the effect of the alienation of the Soviet elite on the Gamsakhurdia government, see Jaba Devdariani, "Georgia: Rise and Fall of Façade Democracy," *Demokratizatsiya*, vol. 12, no. 1 (winter 2003), pp. 87–91.

[16] See Ghia Nodia's chapter in this volume.

project"—namely, to become a nation-state based on the principles of European liberal democracy—this only specified *what* Georgia wanted to become, not *how* it was to be achieved.[17] The Georgian elite was so consumed by its "resistance identity" that it failed to articulate what Manuel Castells calls a "project identity," that is, a myth for a better future—"a project of a different life, perhaps on the basis of an oppressed identity, but expanding toward the transformation of society."[18] Sadly, while Georgians professed cultural, value-based affinity with Europe, the country also lacked a democratic, capitalist experience that might have underpinned the national project. In 1991, a newly independent Georgia inherited only the aspiration for (and not the experience of) a European identity from the social-democratic Georgian Republic of 1918. Three years of statehood from 1918 to 1921 was insufficient to create the viable institutions of a functioning democracy.[19]

Gamsakhurdia's successor, Eduard Shevardnadze, was equally unable to define a popular development project for Georgia. He also resorted to conspiracy theories, using the "Russian factor" as a smokescreen to cover his regime's inefficiencies and wrongdoing.[20] Compared to Gamsakhurdia, Shevardnadze initially seemed to many in Georgia to be a pro-Russian politician. He came to power in 1992 pledging to improve relations with Russia. During the Abkhazian war, he distinguished between "two Russias"—an "imperial Russia" represented by the military and a "democratic Russia" represented by President Yeltsin. But as his government weakened in the late 1990s, Shevardnadze increasingly used Russia as a scapegoat to excuse his own failures. In truth, however, Georgia's own internal deficiencies—particularly the weakness of the Georgian state and its inability to shape resilient, inclusive institutions—led to a severe economic collapse and two bloody secessionist conflicts that resulted in the loss of control over 15 percent of the country's territory.

It is harder to establish the motivation behind Russia's actions in the Caucasus in the early 1990s. A widespread public perception in Georgia

---

[17] See Ghia Nodia's chapter in this volume.

[18] Castells, *The Power of Identity*, p. 8.

[19] This was different in the Baltic states (after which Georgia frequently modeled its struggle for independence). The Baltics had functional states from 1918 to 1939 and thus possessed a living memory of democratic institutions, including through people that had lived in an independent state.

[20] Tarkhan-Mouravi, "The Georgian–Abkhazian Conflict in a Regional Context," pp. 90–112.

is that Russia worked to prevent the consolidation of nationalist regimes in Georgia and Azerbaijan by using its military and political leverage to aid political (often armed) opposition in these two countries. Yet, there is no clear evidence that the return to power of Communist figureheads like Heydar Aliev in Azerbaijan and Shevardnadze in Georgia was engineered in Moscow. The nationalist leaderships in both countries faced domestic political problems of their own, problems that were sufficient to topple them. True, the armed anti-Gamsakhurdia opposition was allowed to use Soviet army weapons caches, which convinced part of the Georgian public that Russia had plotted the regime change. It is more likely that Russian military commanders, cut loose from political control in the chaos accompanying the dissolution of the Soviet Union in December 1991, acted on their own.

In the Abkhazian case, the Russian military is known to have provided Abkhazian military elements with munitions, intelligence, and even direct military support. Were these actions the result of a conscious Kremlin policy or simply a side effect of general policy confusion in Russia? This question still cannot be answered conclusively. One can only speculate about plausible reasons why the Russian military might have been acting against Georgian interests and why Russian authorities did nothing to restrain them. As noted earlier, Westward-looking Russian liberalism had an economic face. Privatization unfolded in close cooperation with the International Monetary Fund and the World Bank. In foreign policy, Russia completed its military withdrawal from Eastern Europe and recognized the independence of the Baltic states. These steps, however, faced strong domestic resistance in Russia, and, amid the country's own identity crisis, Russians felt a need to define the state in terms of *derzhava*. As early as fall 1992, Foreign Minister Andrei Kozyrev in a mock speech at the Conference on Security and Cooperation in Europe (CSCE) ministerial council session in Stockholm voiced popular opinion when he said the former Soviet republics are in effect a post-imperial space where Russia has to defend its interests by all available means.[21] While Kozyrev dismissed his speech as a ploy to underscore the threat posed by hard-liners, the formal security and foreign policy doctrines adopted by Russia in 1993 already contained the notion of the "near abroad." The concepts

---

[21] Roland Dannreuther, *Russian Perceptions of the Atlantic Alliance: Final Report for the NATO Fellowship* (Brussels and Edinburgh: 1997), p.11, http://www.nato.int/acad/fellow/95-97/dannreut.pdf.

underlying these documents came close to the ideas ridiculed in Kozyrev's Stockholm theatrics.[22]

Russia, of course, had no chance of restoring its prior imperial rule over the post-Soviet space. Hence, these emotional cravings for a "historical" role were aimed at exerting hegemonic influence over the foreign policy of weaker states.[23] By the mid-1990s, the significance of the "near abroad" formula (if not always its precise meaning) had become clearer. Russia viewed these new states as foreign, but in a special way that kept them within a "virtual" *derzhava* border over which a hegemonic master presided. The "near abroad" meant different things to different Russians and thus a coherent policy never followed. The hawkish defense establishment was deployed in the field, closest to the area of perceived Russian interests. In the absence of clear guidelines, these people interpreted the concept of the "near abroad" as they chose, and, thus, exerted the largest influence on Yeltsin's policy in the South Caucasus.

The military became the representative of Russia's interests in the Caucasus—an outcome that, while unplanned, was written into the logic of events. Entrusting the Caucasus to the military has been a traditional Russian pattern since the time of the Russian Empire. Russia has long stressed the strategic importance of the region. Simply from a practical perspective, the military had a strong presence because the forces of the former Transcaucasian Military District (now the Group of Russian Troops in Transcaucasus) remained stationed throughout the region even after the Soviet Union collapsed as a political entity. The military also enjoyed personal relationships with key leaders in South Caucasus governments.[24] Thus, negotiators during the conflicts in Georgia and between

---

[22] John J. Maresca, "Russia's 'Near Abroad'—A Dilemma for the West," in Hans-Georg Ehrhart, Anna Kreikemeyer, and Andrei V. Zagorski, eds., *Crisis Management in the CIS: Whither Russia?* (Baden Baden: Nomos Verlagsgesellschaft, 1995), pp.192–193; Yuri E. Fedorov, "Foreign Policy-Making in the Russian Federation and Local Conflicts in the CIS," in Ehrhart, Kreikemeyer, and Zagorski, *Crisis Management in the CIS*, p.122 and pp.126–127.

[23] Rajan Menon, "The Security Environment in the South Caucasus and Central Asia," in Rajan Menon, Yuri E. Fedorov, and Ghia Nodia, eds., *Russia, the Caucasus, and Central Asia, The 21st Century Security Environment* (New York: East West Institute, M.E. Shape Inc., 1999), p. 9.

[24] Dmitri Trenin, "Russia's Security Policies and Interests in the Caucasus Region," in Bruno Coppieters, ed., *Contested Borders in the Caucasus* (Brussels: VUB University Press, 1996), p. 98.

Azerbaijan and Armenia came from the Russian Ministry of Defense. Russian generals in the conflict areas also regularly made statements on behalf of Russia. In fact, Russia's Minister of Defense Pavel Grachev personally brokered several agreements between the Georgian and Abkhazian sides, as well as in Nagorno-Karabakh as a special envoy of President Yeltsin. The military's role had both symbolic and practical weight. Some analysts maintain that historically the Russian military has defined Russian statehood, and, hence, in times when civil authority is in disarray, its relative weight naturally grows.[25] The role of the military as a protector of the Russian state identity seems to be welcomed by the society at large, which sees the army as a "basic, model institution" based on order and vertical hierarchy.[26]

Russia's choice of the military as the institutional interlocutor, however, was rather unfortunate for Georgia, scarcely putting those who already perceived Russia as a militarist bully at ease. To make matters worse, Russian army officials frequently chose to speak in aggressive, unconciliatory terms, exuding a combination of Soviet and imperial arrogance. As political control over the military weakened following the Soviet demise, it should be no surprise that individual commanders, even at the highest levels, sanctioned arms sales and acted on their own discretion in regional conflicts. Nor were they free of self-serving motives, because considerable money was to be made selling arms.[27]

The territorial integrity of a multi-ethnic Russia was also threatened in the early to mid-1990s, and nowhere was this more true than in the North Caucasus. The Kremlin faced the task of stabilizing inter-ethnic rivalries between ethnically non-Russian peoples and republics of the North Caucasus (Chechnya, Dagestan, Ingushetia, and North Ossetia). Simultaneously, Moscow was trying to neutralize ethnically Russian right-wing radicals (Cossacks in Northern Caucasus) who enjoyed the support of a powerful military and the Communist lobby in the parliament. The Yeltsin regime struggled to find a balance, and the balance struck was not always helpful. For example, Russian volunteers in the Abkhazia conflict (both secessionist Chechens and *derzhavnik* Cossacks)

---

[25] Alexander Golts, "Main Obstacle to Military Reform—Russian Militarism," *Pro et Contra*, vol. 8, no. 3 (2004), p. 56.

[26] Dubin, "Counterweight," p. 30.

[27] Both journalists and officials noted arms sales to the Chechen rebels from the North Caucasus military stockpiles during the first Chechen campaign.

posed no direct threat to Russia. On the contrary, their marauding might have been a factor helping to quell Russia's internal strife by letting the steam out of the North Caucasus.[28]

During this period, there were few constraints on Russian actors. The conflicts in South Ossetia or Abkhazia did not receive much attention in the West. Georgian authorities also hesitated to speak out. Despite occasional protests from the Georgian Parliament, Russia's participation in the Abkhazian conflict was for the most part only weakly condemned, and the government continued to acquiesce in Russia's role as the peace broker. When the South Ossetian and Abkhazian conflicts subsided, the international community demurred from deploying a peacekeeping force to these areas, leaving little formal reason to challenge the Kremlin's readiness to mediate the conflicts. Russia has jealously guarded its peacekeeping mandate in Georgia, trying to restrict international involvement beyond the UN's rather limited observation mandate in Abkhazia and the mandate of the Organization for Security and Cooperation in Europe (OSCE) in South Ossetia. Russia has worked to create a situation in which "no international body, except the CIS [Commonwealth of Independent States], can carry out effective peacekeeping operations . . . more than that, no peacekeeping operation within the CIS will be a success without Russia participating in it."[29]

After its defeat in Abkhazia, the Georgian state was on the verge of disintegration. In the minds of many Georgians, Russia had incited and sustained the secessionist conflicts in Abkhazia and South Ossetia. Shevardnadze said as much following the fall of Sukhumi to Abkhazian forces, when he confessed that "Russia brought Georgia to its knees."[30]

---

[28] Involvement of the Chechen and Circassian mercenaries, as well as right-wing Cossacks, in Abkhazian conflicts through the Caucasian People's Confederation (CPC) has been widely acknowledged (see "Human Rights Watch Report: Georgia 1995," http://www.hrw.org/reports/1995/Georgia2.htm). It was argued that this involvement had prevented Chechen–Russian clashes in the early 1990s. At the same time, the participation of mercenaries was popular with radical Russian politicians and military officers, who eased pressure on the troubled Yeltsin administration. Some allusions to this line of argument can be seen in Tarkhan-Mouravi, "Georgians and Abkhazians: The Search for a Peace Settlement," pp. 90–112.

[29] Emilia Krivchikova, "Peacekeeping Operations on the Territory of the Former Soviet Union," in Ehrhart, Kreikemeyer, and Zagorski, *Crisis Management in the CIS*, p. 162.

[30] This widely known quote was made on Georgian TV. Reference to it can be

Georgia felt it had no choice but to accept Russian troops as peacekeepers in both South Ossetia and Abkhazia. In effect, however, these forces' primary objective was to secure the borders of the secessionist territories, virtually underwriting their de facto independence. But at the same time, Russia's dreams of renewed grandeur ran into trouble in the North Caucasus. Rather than expanding its influence, Russia faced a dangerous conflict in Chechnya. Moreover, as a result of the conflicts in the South Caucasus, Russia's southern underbelly was painfully exposed to uncontrolled migration flows, unruly secessionist regimes, and criminal activity.

IN SEARCH OF SECURITY

Security considerations predominated as Russia waged the first Chechen war, an unpopular war both at home and abroad. The conflict dashed hopes for Russia's swift integration into Europe and exposed the values gap between Europe and Russia. While the war weakened the Russian government by empowering business tycoons and power-hungry regional elites, Georgia remained in chaos. Numerous armed gangs controlled business and politics, and the state continued to sell assets accumulated during the Soviet period just to make ends meet. Bread shortages became common, natural gas was not supplied to families for cooking or heating, and the supply of electricity was erratic. In both countries, the deterioration threatened the very core of national consciousness. Security issues now dominated as both societies operated in a survival mode. *Realpolitik* considerations displaced all others from 1994 to 1999.

Georgia's security agenda was two-pronged: first, to prevent the complete disintegration of the state, and second, to balance what Georgia saw as its primary external threat—Russia. To achieve the first aim, Tbilisi made previously unthinkable concessions to Russia: Georgia entered the CIS; Shevardnadze fully supported Russia's campaign in Chechnya; an active-duty Russian officer, Vardiko Nadibaidze, was appointed Georgia's minister of defense; and a cadre loyal to Russia took posts in the security establishment. Simultaneously, in order to achieve a degree of internal stability, Shevardnadze cracked down on criminal gangs, eventually outlawing the notorious Mkhedrioni militia and jailing the two most influen-

---

found at http://www.philipjohnston.com/centraleurope/chron/
fsu/1993sep.htm.

tial warlords, Jaba Ioseliani and Tengiz Kitovani. As the police and security forces grew in strength, several high-profile operations were conducted against criminal gangs in various Georgian provinces. Zviad Gamsakhurdia's supporters were ruthlessly suppressed in western Georgia. In 1995, Shevardnadze created the Citizens' Union of Georgia (CUG), which became the ruling party in the 1996 general elections. Young MPs from the CUG, led by the Speaker Zurab Zhvania, stirred Western hopes for a more rapid democratization. A new national currency was introduced in 1996 and achieved exchange rate stability, a welcome change from triple-digit inflation in 1993. After several years of sharp decline, double-digit GDP growth was recorded in 1996–97.

In foreign policy, Shevardnadze sought Western security guarantees, but a response only came with the gradual growth of Western interest in Caspian Sea oil. Untapped oil and gas reserves in the Caspian basin created tangible economic interests for Western powers. By 1998, more than a dozen Western oil companies were present in the Caspian region—providing Azerbaijan alone with contracts totaling more than $28 billion.[31] The South Caucasus attracted U.S. attention when transportation projects for bringing Azerbaijani (and potentially Central Asian) oil to European markets took on greater importance. Two projects—the smaller-scale Baku–Supsa Pipeline and the main export Baku–Tbilisi–Ceyhan Pipeline—were launched. Shevardnadze endorsed the concept of a "Great Silk Road" of transportation links between Asia and Europe that crossed the Southern Caucasus. As the conflicts in Abkhazia, South Ossetia, and Chechnya severed Georgia's transportation lines with Russia, Turkey became Georgia's main trading partner.

Russia saw the South Caucasus through the prism of its own internal and external security concerns. Many Russian analysts would have agreed with the view of Dmitri Trenin that "Transcaucasia is inseparably linked with the Northern Caucasus, which is an integral part of the Russian Federation."[32] Indeed, the independence of the South Caucasus republics did generate several security challenges. Russia's border with these new states had only had administrative status within the Soviet Union, and

---

[31] Glen E. Howard, "NATO and the Caucasus: The Caspian Axis," in Stephen J. Blank, ed., *NATO after Enlargement: New Challenges, New Missions, New Forces* (Carlisle, PA: Strategic Studies Institute, U.S. Army War College, 1998), p. 157.

[32] Trenin, "Russia's Security Policies and Interests in the Caucasus Region," p. 91.

thus turned porous when the country dissolved. This exposed Russia to waves of refugees from South Ossetia, Abkhazia, and, to a lesser extent, Nagorno-Karabakh.

Before 1995, Russia's ability to project power into the Caucasus was hindered primarily by its own internal conflicts; after 1995, Russian influence was increasingly challenged by Western powers. Western observers began speaking of a new "Great Game" over oil in the Caspian and the Caucasus. "This is the region both the West and East have their eyes on," wrote one commentator in the British *Guardian* in 2001.[33] The notion of a strategic contest in the Caucasus entered the minds of both Russian and Western analysts and reporters, influencing policy papers and decision-making. As Glen Howard noted in 1998, "With the end of the Cold War, the Caucasus is once again at the forefront of world geopolitics as Caspian oil transforms NATO's eastern flank."[34] Whether Brussels or Washington precisely shared this view or not, it did capture a chain of thought linking control over energy resources with a struggle for power characteristic of a *realpolitik* discourse.

Russia, for its part, was still playing a political game by old cold war rules. The infancy of Russian foreign policy, marked by the emotional drive to "reintegrate into a family of civilized nations," was gone. The ideology of counterbalancing was rekindled in Foreign Minister Kozyrev's second term and then assumed full force when he was replaced by a cold-war security specialist, Yevgeny Primakov, in January 1996. Russian policy now sought to check the strategic advance of the United States and advocated a multipolar world in place of a U.S.-dominated unipolar version. The Russian government portrayed the United States not as an "enemy," but a partner, yet one with which it intended to compete for international influence. In fact, while many in the Russian military viewed the United States as an enemy, the U.S. side did not see the new Russia as capable of competing with the United States on a global scale. Still, Yeltsin's administration tried to establish the CIS as a strong security and political alliance. Moscow also proposed strengthening the security component of the OSCE, where Russia has a political veto. In addition, it attempted to balance NATO and U.S. actions in the Balkans

---

[33] Richard Norton-Taylor, "The New Great Game," *The Guardian,* March 5, 2001, http://www.guardian.co.uk/Archive/Article/0,4273,4146099,00.html.
[34] Howard, "NATO and the Caucasus," p. 152.

and, especially during Primakov's tenure, to act as a mediator between the United States and so-called rogue states.[35] Russia's security cooperation with Iran added a further source of tension with the United States.[36]

The South Caucasus was but a small part of this greater scheme, and Georgia was only one element in a broader contest between the United States and Russia. The U.S. *National Security Strategy* of 1998 argued for the full integration of key areas of the CIS into Western economic and political structures.[37] In contrast, Russia's 2000 foreign policy concept put a priority on "ensuring the compatibility of bi- and multilateral cooperation with member states of the CIS with the national security tasks [of Russia]."[38] Russia considered NATO expansion, including the Partnership for Peace (PfP) Program, to be an encroachment on Russian power. Thus, Georgia's increased participation in PfP and planned economic projects with Turkey and the European Union (EU) were seen as extensions of a perceived Western policy to encircle Russia by unfriendly security and economic alliances.

In 1999, Russia's Foreign Minister Igor Ivanov outlined Russian policies in terms that were strikingly reminiscent of cold war terminology. This was a time when Russia's attempts to seek security parity with the United States were increasingly frustrated, and Ivanov's comments captured contemporary Russian fears:

> The question often raised in Moscow is whether Kosovo and Chechnya are links in a chain of steps toward the creation of a one-dimensional, NATO-centered world. Is Chechnya being used as a smokescreen for preparing NATO to assume the role of a world policeman, for undermining the fundamental components of strategic stability and reversing the disarmament process? Has the anti-Russian campaign over Chechnya been launched to force Russia out of the Caucasus, and then out of

---

[35] Allen C. Lynch, "The Realism of Russia's Foreign Policy," *Europe–Asia Studies*, vol. 53, no. 1 (2001), pp.15–23.

[36] Patrick G. Moore, "Russia to Sell Iran More Arms," *RFE/RL Newsline*, March 13, 2001, http://www.rferl.org/newsline/2001/03/130301.asp.

[37] William J. Clinton, *A National Security Strategy for a New Century* (Washington, DC: The White House, October 1998), pp. 37–40.

[38] *Kontseptsiya Vneshnei Politiki Rossiiskoi*, Ministry of Foreign Affairs of Russia Online, http://www.ln.mid.ru/ns-osndoc.nsf/0e9272befa34209743256 c630042d1aa/fd86620b371b0cf7432569fb004872a7. This document was approved by President Vladimir Putin on June 28, 2000.

Central Asia? And these are by no means the only concerns that have arisen in Russian public opinion with respect to the actions—or, sometimes the lack of actions—of our Western partners.[39]

By the end of the 1990s, it was clear that Russia had set tasks for itself that it would be unable to achieve. For instance, it had failed to curtail the first wave of NATO expansion in 1999. In fact, further NATO expansion, including the Baltic states, was planned. In the same year, Russia's "counterweight" strategy did not succeed in Kosovo. In addition, the first Iraq war had limited Russia's role in the Middle East. Due to its economic weakness and constant internal haggling, the CIS never gained the clout of the Soviet Union.

In Georgia and the South Caucasus, however, Russia retained a security advantage throughout the 1990s. By 1994, in holding the keys to a resolution of the "frozen" ethnic conflicts, Russia had essentially realized a *Pax Russica* in the region. To institutionalize this dominance, the Russians worked to undercut international participation in the OSCE's Minsk Group, an international body mandated to find a solution to the Nagorno-Karabakh problem.[40] Russia made similar efforts at the UN and OSCE to prevent "internationalization" of the peacekeeping operation in Abkhazia beyond the UN/OSCE observer mission.[41] Nonetheless, the Western presence in the Caucasus, which was small at the beginning of the 1990s, continued to grow. In 1999, the Baku–Supsa Pipeline became operational, and Georgia entered the Council of Europe, reviving the hopes for Georgia's European "national project."

At the same time, Russia's failure in the first Chechen campaign exposed the internal weakness of its administration and military. Its ineptitude in this internal crisis underscored how overstretched it had become in its unstable southern regions. Western analysts argued that the weakening of Russia's security presence and the need to address internal deficiencies would induce its "strategic retreat" from the South Caucasus, especially with regard to its military presence.[42] The decision to close two

---

[39] Igor Ivanov, "West's Hypocrisy over Chechnya," *Financial Times*, November 16, 1999, p. 19.

[40] Maresca, "Russia's 'Near Abroad,'" p. 194.

[41] Reportedly, Russia traded its vote on U.S. involvement in Haiti for U.S. abstention from involving international peacekeepers in Abkhazia (see Maresca, "Russia's 'Near Abroad,'" p. 197).

[42] Pavel K. Baev, *Challenges and Options in the Caucasus and Central Asia*

Russian military bases in Georgia and to negotiate the withdrawal from the remaining two was reached at the OSCE's meeting in Istanbul in November 1999. In Istanbul, Yeltsin's government, demoralized and weakened by a sequence of failures, yielded to U.S. pressure and committed itself to withdraw from Georgia.[43] In 1999, Russia also completed the withdrawal of all of its border troops from Georgia, thereby abandoning the former Soviet frontier with Turkey.

Between 1994 and 1999, Georgia did preserve its political integrity and even managed to establish a degree of long-awaited economic growth. Shevardnadze's success in curbing the chaos of the early 1990s was genuinely remarkable. It became increasingly apparent, however, that in Georgia's new order, the parliament's "Westernizing" influence was checked by patron-client networks where real power lay—networks tied to the top echelons of the political, security, and police establishment. By 1998, the economy had already begun to slow. Negotiations over Abkhazia and South Ossetia stagnated, while the autonomous region of Ajara developed into a quasi-independent fiefdom governed by a local leader who openly challenged the central authorities. The Shevardnadze regime's motto was "stability at any cost," but the government gradually lost popular appeal as basic social and political problems grew.

When Shevardnadze talked about his aspirations of "knocking very hard on the door" of NATO in 1999, he seemed to be addressing public opinion at home rather than articulating a feasible policy aim.[44] In the same year at NATO's Fiftieth Anniversary Summit, Georgia, Ukraine, Uzbekistan, Azerbaijan, and Moldova officially announced the creation of the GUUAM alliance, but the capacity of its members to implement long-term military-security arrangements rang hollow from the outset. Still, the announcement was sufficient to irritate Russian leaders who interpreted GUUAM as an unfriendly NATO-led alliance of states on Russia's vulner-

---

(Carlisle, PA: Strategic Studies Institute, U.S. Army War College, April 22, 1997), p. 17, http://www.carlisle.army.mil/ssi/pdffiles/00111.pdf.

[43] Stephen J. Blank, *U.S. Military Engagement with Transcaucasia and Central Asia* (Carlisle, PA: Strategic Studies Institute, U.S. Army War College, June 2000), p. 6, http://www.milnet.com/pentagon/Russia-2000-assessment-SSI.pdf.

[44] "World News: Georgia Plans to Seek NATO Membership FT Interview: Eduard Shevardnadze," *Financial Times*, October 25, 1999, http://globalarchive.ft.com/globalarchive/articles.html?id=991025016635&query=shevardnadze#docAnchor991025016635.

able southern border. Shevardnadze's policy of using regional (Turkish) or international (NATO and U.S.) forces to balance Russia coexisted with his occasional concessions and submissive remarks toward Moscow. This double-faced policy proved highly irksome to the Russian leadership, now deeply mistrustful of Shevardnadze. The policies he had helped to engineer while Soviet foreign minister made him popular in the West but equally unpopular in Russia.[45] Shevardnadze's presidency, especially after 1995, was marked by bitter personal relations between the Georgian leadership and its Russian counterpart, which in turn destroyed the chance of any real dialogue on shared security concerns.

In Georgia, the "national project" was largely intact at the end of the 1990s and aspirations toward Western-style democracy were reflected in the immense public support for Georgia's accession to the Council of Europe. Simultaneously, however, opposition to Shevardnadze's government for its inability to address the basic needs of citizens grew steadily, endangering the country's pro-European project. The chasm between Georgia's European aspirations and the grim domestic reality prompted the growth of fundamentalist movements challenging the "national project" and calling for a unique "Georgian" way to development. Their adherents argued that Georgian values expressed in Orthodox Christianity were in conflict with European values such as freedom of expression and protection of human rights. Significantly, however, in contrast with Russia, Soviet nostalgia did not resurface in Georgia. In all likelihood, a return to the past was deemed both undesirable, given the popular commitment to independence, and infeasible, given the violence and dramatic changes that separated modern Georgia from its Soviet past.

IN SEARCH OF PRAGMATISM

Since Putin's accession to the presidency in 2000, Russia has continued its quest for a greater international role, but has based this quest on a more realistic assessment of its current political, military, and economic capabilities. The notion of "counterbalancing" the West has shifted to seeking a mode of coexistence and interaction with it, but without actually integrat-

---

[45] These were years of rising nostalgia for the Soviet Union, when Stalin's rating among "the most distinguished persons of all times and peoples" rose to fourth place in public opinion surveys. Lenin, in second place, was the only Soviet figure to rank ahead of Stalin. See Dubin, "Counterweight," p. 26.

ing into it. This adjustment in policy was neither instant nor linear; it has been achieved through trial-and-error, as Russia's new leaders probed the degree of international tolerance for a more assertive Russia, particularly in its immediate neighborhood. The foreign policy and security doctrines drafted under the supervision of Putin while he was secretary of the Security Council and then prime minister continued to reflect a desire to position Russia as a global power—again, by "countering and diluting U.S. power" wherever possible.[46] Once in the presidency, however, Putin departed from this rigid policy line, especially after 2001. Instead of countering and diluting its cold-war rival's power on a global scale, Russia has engaged foreign powers differently in various parts of the world and remained more competitive in the areas neighboring Russia.

Following Russia's strategic retreats during the Yeltsin era, some expected his young and energetic successor to concentrate on "soft power"—that is, on economic expansion and competition with Western companies over pipeline projects.[47] These expectations have been only partially on the mark. Putin has reinforced the eclectic mix of Soviet and imperial symbols, but rather than focus on external challengers, he has chosen to focus on threats at home. He brought the squabbling regional leaders to heel and made the once-potent Federation Council, the upper house of the parliament, fully dependent on the presidency. As part of the process of consolidating power, he promoted cadre members from the security services (his political base) into the highest public offices. He forced influential financial and business tycoons, the so-called oligarchs, to demonstrate their loyalty or be driven into exile. Private media outlets that once belonged to these oligarchs were suppressed. Former or current Kremlin functionaries acquired control over key energy companies, including Gazprom, ITERA (Gazprom's affiliate controlling its CIS energy assets), and RAO Unified Energy Systems (UES), providing the government with crucial financial flows. To the extent that Putin invoked an external enemy, it was Islamic terrorism linked to Russia's second Chechen campaign, an enemy that he has used to justify his tough internal policies. The Chechen war gave Putin unprecedented political sup-

---

[46] Ariel Cohen, "The Russia Bush Faces," *The Heritage Foundation Online*, March 12, 2001, http://www.heritage.org/Press/Commentary/ed031201.cfm; Ariel Cohen, "Russia and Eurasia," *Issues 2000* (Washington, DC: Heritage Foundation, 2000), p. 703.

[47] Baev, *Challenges and Options in the Caucasus and Central Asia*, p. 5.

port within Russia and helped to neutralize homegrown criticism of human rights abuses. In the post-September 11 context, international criticism of Russia's Chechen operation has also subsided.

As a result, Putin's Russia approached a self-image compatible with its master myth to a degree that was never achieved under Yeltsin. Strict order at home was enforced by the powerful, but "benevolent" supreme ruler; the military–security establishment dominated the state administration, while the country fought an "enlightened" battle against the "backward" Caucasus. One of Putin's major successes has been to invoke the imagery of "Islamic terrorism" to justify Russian military operation in Chechnya.[48] With respect to Georgia, Russian analysts commonly described the country as a "failing state."[49]

Putin's Russia is not (and does not aim to become) European in the sense of emulating Europe's political institutions, civil rights, and rule of law. It attempts to present itself as a strong and governable state, able to understand Western rules, and willing to exploit the economic benefits of ties with the West. The far-flung outer frontiers of the global Soviet empire have been abandoned; military bases have been closed in Cuba (Lurdes) and Vietnam (Kamran), and a peacekeeping contingent in Bosnia-Herzegovina and Kosovo was completely withdrawn in 2003. Relations with former client regimes in Libya, Syria, and Cuba have been sidelined. In addition, Putin has rallied behind U.S. military operations in Afghanistan.

Steven Blank describes this new policy as a "paradoxical pattern of combining the confrontation with the West . . . with an attempt to gain a foothold at the influential international clubs (like G-8)."[50] In fact, however, the paradox is an illusion. Confrontation with the West has ceased to

---

[48] Dmitri Trenin, *The Forgotten War: Chechnya and Russia's Future,* Policy Brief no. 28 (Washington, DC: Carnegie Endowment for International Peace, November 2003), http://www.ceip.org/files/pdf/Policybrief28.pdf.

[49] The Russian scholar Aleksei Malashenko went so far as to argue that Moscow could discount "as hypothetical the chance of democratization of the Post-Soviet societies of Central Asia and Caucasus." Thus, he claimed, "'De-modernization' of the region could be halted only by continued projection of the Russian cultural influence that "contributed to modernization [of the Central Asian and Caucasian societies] and became the tool for their communication with . . . European culture." See Aleksei Malashenko, "Post-Soviet States of the South and the Interests of Moscow," *Pro et Contra,* vol. 5, no. 3 (2000), p. 43.

[50] Blank, *U.S. Military Engagement with Transcaucasia and Central Asia,* p. 6.

be global and has been transferred to Russia's immediate neighborhood, including the South Caucasus. Even here Putin has avoided a head-on conflict with the West, preferring to exploit the numerous vulnerabilities of the South Caucasus states. At times, Russian officials still claim an imperial "right" to pursue their interests in the "near abroad" as they choose. But more often, Russia has committed itself to general international principles, such as the territorial integrity of states (including that of former Soviet republics) and then sought to expand its influence via subtler, more practical means. Thus, it has capitalized on the tactical achievements of the 1990s, such as the special relationships it established with the de facto states of Abkhazia and South Ossetia in Georgia. In this fashion, Putin sought to create a new normative regime for the South Caucasus, superficially compatible with international law, but tilted toward exploiting ad hoc post-Soviet arrangements. Russia's claims of a special role in the "near abroad" were frequently framed in a language acceptable to the West. In other words, a *derzhavnik* discourse was twisted to fit Western ideas in order to justify the need for Russian stewardship in the South Caucasus.

Georgia figured high on the Russian agenda, in part because of the parallel between Georgia's breakaway regions and Chechnya. Given the similarity between the challenge Chechnya poses for Russia's territorial integrity and that Abkhazia and South Ossetia pose for Georgia, one might have expected Russia to have a sympathetic approach toward Georgia's situation. Indeed, President Shevardnadze repeatedly tried to nudge his Russian counterparts in that direction, but without success. In dealing with Georgia, Russian decision-makers had several options: (1) to help Georgia become stronger; (2) to try to coerce the Georgian government into following Russian wishes; and (3) to share the burden of managing instability in the region with the Georgian national government and/or other international actors. Alas, the weakness of the Georgian authorities and the unpredictability of their actions under Shevardnadze tilted the scales toward the second option.

Russian officials requested the use of Georgian territory to launch military attacks on Chechnya and demanded permission to deploy Russian special forces in areas of Georgia where fleeing Chechens had sought refuge.[51] At the same time, Russian military aircraft began what would

---

[51] Valerii Rokotov, "Eshche odin faktor vliyaniya," *Nezavisimaya gazeta*, January 16, 2001, http://ng.ru/cis/2001-01-16/5_factor.html.

be repeated violations of Georgian airspace, launched air-to-surface missiles, and mined gorges in northern Georgia.[52]

In November 2000, Russian pressure on Georgia culminated in Moscow's unilateral decision to introduce a visa regime for Georgia starting in December 2000, the first such decision in the CIS. In addition, Russia introduced a "simplified"—in effect a visa-free—regime for the residents of Abkhazia and South Ossetia.[53] From 2000 on, it also accepted applications from Abkhazian and South Ossetian residents for Russian citizenship, further strengthening its links with these entities.[54] Through the winter of 2000, Russian gas suppliers repeatedly cut off gas deliveries to Georgia in what the international media treated as an effort to use Russia's energy monopoly as leverage in the political disputes between the two countries.[55] The speculation was given official credence on January 19, 2001, when the European Union's external affairs commissioner severely criticized Russia for using gas supplies as a means of political pressure.[56]

The list of Russian–Georgian incidents during this period is long. Pavel Baev suggests that some of the apparent pressure tactics may "have [had] little if anything to do with Russia's attempt to subdue Georgia." For instance, energy cutoffs may have been the result of internal haggling between Gazprom and ITERA or the consequence of a new business plan that placed emphasis on cost-efficiency and earnings.[57] It is particularly

---

[52] Liz Fuller, "Unknown Fighters Again Violate Georgian Air Space," *RFE/RL Newsline*, August 23, 1999, http://www.rferl.org/newsline/1999/08/2-TCA/tca-230899.asp.

[53] Armen Hanbabyan, "Vvedeniye vizovogo rezhima neizbezhno," *Nezavisimaya gazeta*, November 10, 2000, http://ng.ru/cis/2000-11-10/1_vises.html.

[54] This was done with little respect for the principle of territorial integrity. Officially, Moscow argued that Abkhazia and South Ossetia residents were left without citizenship and Russia granted them citizenship as a successor state to the Soviet Union. However, the political undertone is apparent: some of the long-time residents of Russia, such as Meskhetian Turks in Krasnodar (who were also stateless persons), were refused citizenship by Russia.

[55] Michael Lelyveld, "Western Press Accuses Moscow of Using Energy as a Cudgel," *RFE/RL Newsline*, January 1, 2001, http://www.rferl.org/nca/features/2001/01/05012001104106.asp.

[56] Andrew Jack, "Russia Warned over Attitude to Georgia," *Financial Times*, January 19, 2001.

[57] Pavel Baev, *Russia Refocuses Its Policies in the Southern Caucasus* (Cambridge,

difficult to discern Russia's responsibility in these conflicts when Shevardnadze, threatened by opposition from within, used Russia as a scapegoat
to mobilize domestic support for his administration. He and his supporters did so directly (by appealing to the emotionally charged symbolism of
the mid-1990s and calling on the nation to stand united against the
threat) and indirectly (by implying that only he could secure the involvement of Europe and the United States on Georgia's behalf). In fact, however, the Georgian government grew particularly weak during this period.
The 2000 presidential elections were judged by international observers as
a step back in the democratic process. Public confidence was at record
low levels, and the protest vote grew as modest economic growth failed
to trickle down to the majority of citizens. Political crises within Shevardnadze's own Citizens' Union of Georgia Party became commonplace.

Nonetheless, Shevardnadze's tactic of exploiting the Russian threat to
rally international support did work to a certain extent, at least for a
while. Seeing the weakness of Georgia, as well as the willingness of Russia
to pressure Tbilisi, the European powers and the United States drew a
redline against Russia's direct interference in Georgia's affairs. The new
Bush administration was quick to criticize Russia's "near abroad" policies. In March 2001, Secretary of State Colin Powell reassured the Georgian foreign minister of U.S. support and explicitly condemned Russian
pressure.[58] During this period, Georgia held its first political consultations at NATO headquarters, and in June 2001, it hosted military exercises within the framework of NATO's Partnership for Peace Program.[59]

TESTING GROUND: THE PANKISI CASE

Russian–Georgian relations since 1999 have been significantly influenced
by the issue of Georgia's Pankisi Gorge and its direct links to the problem
of Chechnya. Developments in and around Pankisi are a good example of
the way the security confrontation between Russia and Georgia touches
upon core national interests for both countries. Despite a dangerous esca-

---

MA: Harvard University Caspian Studies Program, 2001), p. 11.

[58] Liz Fuller, "U.S. Assures Georgia of Support," *RFE/RL Newsline,* March 21,
2001, http://www.rferl.org/newsline/2001/03/210301.asp.

[59] Liz Fuller, "Georgia Consults NATO, EU," *RFE/RL Newsline,* April 2, 2001,
http://www.rferl.org/newsline/2001/04/020401.asp.

Map 4. The Pankisi Gorge

Central Intelligence Agency map, courtesy of the Central Intelligence Agency, The World Factbook 2005, http://www.cia.gov/cia/publications/factbook/geos/gg.html.

lation in tension between Russia and Georgia in the years after 1999, the involvement of international actors has helped to promote a pragmatic outcome. The Pankisi crisis that started in 1999 and culminated in 2001 contributed to a substantial policy revision in Georgia, which in turn played its part in the eventual collapse of the Shevardnadze government.

Russian officials had attempted to secure the Georgian side of the Chechen border since late 1999. As early as August 1999, when the fighting in Chechnya expanded to Dagestan, Yeltsin asked Shevardnadze for consent to fly missions against Chechnya from Russian military bases in Georgia. Shevardnadze refused. In the first months of the second Chechen war, about 7,000 Chechens crossed the mountain passes from Chechnya to Georgia in the face of advancing of Russian troops. Confronting this influx of refugees, Georgia granted them refugee status *prima facie*, meaning that all entering Chechens were legally regarded as refugees without extensive background or documentation checks, which was in compliance with Georgia's international commitments under the 1951 UN Convention on the Status of Refugees and its 1967 protocol. Almost immediately, Russia launched a massive diplomatic and public relations campaign, arguing that thousands of Chechen guerrillas had set up "terrorist" training camps in Pankisi and were using the region as a base from which to infiltrate Chechnya.

Initially, the Georgian government vigorously denied these accusations and invoked its international legal obligation to shelter refugees.
Soon, however, a surge of crime and kidnapping associated with Pankisi
gave the Russian claims more credibility. It also further undermined the
popularity of the Georgian government. The weakness and negligence on
the part of the government had allowed Pankisi to become a refuge for
all sorts of criminals, including former combatants. The Georgian
government had failed to control the region even before the arrival of
Chechen refugees. In fact, because of the region's complex ethno-
political history, customary law had long prevailed over official legal
institutions in Pankisi.[60] The resulting lack of law enforcement created a
conducive environment for sheltering criminal and other armed elements.

The arrival of the Chechen refugees simply put a spotlight on Pankisi
and exposed the lawlessness of the region to the Georgian and international public. Pankisi presented a severe security dilemma to the Georgian
authorities. A political consensus existed within Georgia that armed escalation in Pankisi could be fatal to the country, which was already fragmented by secession, political instability, and economic stagnation. The
weakness of the armed forces prevented the government from formulating tasks and implementing military operations. As a result, the government only made a feeble attempt to seal off the gorge. A police check-
point at the entrance to the gorge not only failed to stop crime, but, as
investigative media reports argued at the time and official sources confirmed later, itself became a conduit for drug trafficking.

In the course of these events, Russian diplomatic and military pressure
on Georgia to take action grew in intensity. It developed in noticeable
waves, peaking immediately after the arrival of Chechen refugees in 2000,
the beginning of 2001, the fall of 2001, and the summer of 2002. The
logic of Russian pressure was simple: Russia's Defense Minister Sergei
Ivanov and Chief of Staff Anatoli Kvashnin argued that since Georgian law
enforcement agencies were incapable of restoring order in Pankisi, Russian
military involvement was needed to put an end to this "center of terrorism."[61] Georgian society strongly resented the military dimension of

---

[60] Jaba Devdariani and Blanka Hancilova, "Georgia's Pankisi Gorge: Russian,
U.S., and European Connections," CEPS Policy Brief no. 23 (Brussels: Centre
for European Policy Studies, June 2002).

[61] Ian Traynor, "Russia Angry at U.S. War Plan for Georgia," *The Guardian*,

Russian pressure. According to Radio Liberty's military analyst, Koba Lik-likadze, there were at least twenty-five cases of Russian violations of Geor-gian airspace in the period after the second military campaign in Chechnya began in fall 1999 up until August 2002.[62] In all cases save one, Russia denied its responsibility. On the other hand, Shevardnadze's confused statements—first denying a Chechen presence in Pankisi, then speaking about one of the Chechen commanders as a "fine, educated man," only to later plead for a crackdown on terrorists—convinced an already skeptical Georgian public that the government, indeed, had something to hide.

This is not to say that the official Georgian view that Russia was using Pankisi as a lever of influence on Georgia was without any basis. Nor were Georgian officials wrong in claiming that Russia's failure in Chech-nya would only be made worse by intervening in Georgia. Surely, the weight that Russian politicians attached to Pankisi did not compare to the quagmire they faced in Chechnya itself. Some Russian experts even challenged the causal link between Pankisi and Chechnya advanced by Russian officials, arguing instead that Pankisi represented the spillover of failures in the Chechen campaign, and thus was a consequence rather than the cause of the failure of the Russian military to put an end to the Chechen imbroglio.[63] But Georgia showed no sign of being capable of addressing the Pankisi issue, underscoring that the general stagnation occurring under Shevardnadze now bordered on the edge of state failure.

The need for urgent action became apparent after the events of Sep-tember 11, which gave Pankisi an international twist. The terrorist attacks in New York presented the Russian leadership with a clear chance to gain international approval for its actions in Chechnya and possible interven-tion in Georgia. In his first televised reaction soon after the attacks, Presi-dent Putin expressed his determination to crack down on "terrorist hide-outs" near Russia's borders, implicitly asking the United States for a green light in Pankisi.

An increasingly unpopular Georgian government was now pressured by the international community to uproot terrorism and under fire from

---

February 22, 2002, http://www.guardian.co.uk/international/story/ 0,3604,654020,00.html.

[62] Koba Liklikadze, interview with Rustavi-2 TV, August 29, 2002.

[63] Oleg Kusov, Radio Liberty observer, interview with *Ekho Moskvy*, August 26, 2002, http://www.echo.msk.ru/guests/5754/.

its own disgruntled citizens who were angry over the high-profile kidnappings traced to Pankisi. The government admitted the presence of Chechen guerrillas in Pankisi in October 2001, reportedly after Shevardnadze had been pressed to adopt a "zero-tolerance policy" toward terrorism during his visit to Washington.[64] Shevardnadze's inconsistent handling of the Pankisi issue, opening the way for Russian pressure and humiliation, contributed to his plunging popularity. By autumn 2001, it stood at a record low of 6 percent. His failed policies at home forced the president to fire his government, following popular protests in October 2001 against governmental pressure on an independent television station. His ruling Citizens' Union of Georgia was on the brink of collapse. Under these circumstances, Georgians feared that an embattled Shevardnadze would seek Russia's support in order to preserve his presidency and that in return he would concede on the Pankisi issue.

The weakness of the Georgian government constituted one of the main reasons for the abnormal state of relations between the two countries. Russian leaders vacillated between assuming that Georgia would give shelter to Chechen militants simply because it sympathized with the Chechen cause (and wanted to annoy Russia) and worrying that Georgia was too weak to act effectively. Western leaders also mistrusted Shevardnadze's unpredictable swings, the contradictory declarations of Georgia's security, defense, and interior ministers concerning the presence of Chechen field commanders on Georgian territory, and allegations in the Georgian media that the Georgian Ministry of Interior had tried to "ship" Chechen militias to Abkhazia in 2000 simply confirmed Russian perceptions.[65]

Under pressure from all sides, the Georgian political elite's distrust of Russia prevailed. It saw the West (and the United States in particular) as the only hope for protecting the country from the spillover of the Chechen conflict into Georgia. The Georgian government exploited the shifting international context to advance its own security interests by playing the classical *realpolitik* game of balancing between Russia and the United States. Beginning in late 1999, OSCE observers were stationed in Georgia

---

[64] Zeyno Baran, *Georgia Update*, March 4, 2002, p. 3, http://www.csis.org/ruseura/georgia/gaupdate_0203.htm.

[65] The latter allegation appears to have some basis. In June 2004, the Saakashvili government ordered an investigation into the 2000 raid of Chechen rebels into Abkhazia. Meanwhile, State Minister Giorgi Khaindrava has confirmed the role of the Shevardnadze administration in these events.

to monitor the Chechen section of the border. While their testimony questioned Russia's accusations of massive guerrilla movements, a dramatic turn occurred in February 2002, when Philip Remler, the U.S. chargé d'affaires in Tbilisi, referred to the possible presence of "persons linked to al-Qaeda" in the Pankisi Gorge. The story figured prominently on the front pages of U.S. newspapers, and the alleged presence of international terrorists almost immediately became the basis for a decision to substantially upgrade U.S. military assistance to Georgia. This took the form of the $64 million Georgia Train and Equip Program (GTEP), aimed at providing anti-terrorism capabilities to the impoverished and underpaid Georgian troops. In the framework of GTEP, around 200 U.S. military officers were sent to Georgia to provide training to Georgian border guards and rapid deployment forces. The GTEP was officially launched in March 2002.

Juergen Schmid speculates that the timing of the program suggests that the U.S. decision was not influenced by any new information about the presence of terrorists linked to al-Qaeda, but rather had to do with the need to prevent possible unilateral Russian involvement in Pankisi.[66] In the end, it seems likely that the United States was both wary of allowing trigger-happy Russian generals to venture into Pankisi and concerned that Georgian military weakness would allow Pankisi to remain a comfortable terrorist haven.

The dispatching of U.S. military personnel to Georgia stirred a fury in Russian political circles. Many Russian politicians, still faithful to the "counterweight" ideology, alleged that the United States had covert plans to push Russia out of the Caucasus. A military supplement to *Nezavisimaya gazeta* went as far as to suggest that Washington was planning its own military incursion into Chechnya.[67] The official response from President Putin, however, was more measured. Whether or not the new U.S. assistance program was discussed with the Kremlin in advance is unclear. Putin nonetheless displayed his new pragmatic approach toward Georgia: If U.S. involvement would rid Russia of the security problem, the burden-sharing was welcomed. Still, the assistance program did not mean that the Pankisi issue was solved, and Russian political pressure

---

[66] Juergen Schmid, "Krieg gegen den Terrorismus im Südkaukasus? Die USA entsenden Militärberater nach Georgien," *SWP Brennpunkte*, http://old.swp-berlin.org/produkte/bparchiv/zentralasien6druck.htm.

[67] Vadim Soloviov, "GI's Go To Caucasus," *Nezavisimoye voyennoye obozreniye*, August 30, 2002.

continued. Irritation over the U.S. assistance program seemed to encourage aggressiveness in Russian military circles.

Initially, Russia reached for political levers. On August 8, 2002, Russian negotiators failed to appear for a discussion of the framework agreement on friendly relations with Georgia. According to the official explanation, the Russian experts were "not ready" to discuss the details. Georgian officials, however, assumed that the Russian denial was a device to convince Tbilisi of the need for "joint" military action in Pankisi.[68] Reaching a settlement on a framework agreement was a key issue for the Georgian government. It had been one of Shevardnadze's major foreign policy goals, because the issue was closely tied to the question of Russia's withdrawal from military bases in Georgia and improved protection for the rights of some 200,000 Georgian citizens working in Russia.

At the same time, Russia's military pressure became more pronounced and dangerous. In April 2002, Russian and Georgian military forces verged on engagement during a standoff in Abkhazia's Kodori Gorge, when Russian paratroopers moved unexpectedly into the Georgian-controlled area.[69] From July 29 through August 2002, five cases of Georgian airspace violation were recorded near the Russian–Georgian borders adjacent to Chechnya and Abkhazia. On at least three occasions, Russian jets or gunship helicopters opened fire on Georgian territory. Major-General Vasily Prizemlyn, the Russian commander of the joint peacekeeping forces in South Ossetia, unilaterally went beyond his area of responsibility on August 22 by having his troops build trenches and checkpoints on Georgian territory.[70] At dawn the next day, three Russian warplanes bombed Georgian territory adjacent to the Chechen sector of the Russian border, leaving one civilian dead and at least seven injured. Despite statements by Georgian officials and by OSCE observers confirming this incident, Russia denied that its military had participated in the attacks. Minister of Defense Ivanov called the attack "a step in the right direction," suggesting that the Georgians had bombed the villages themselves in a crackdown on Chechen guerrillas.[71] The situation appeared to balance precariously on the brink of an open military confrontation.

---

[68] *Civil Georgia*, August 8, 2002, http://www.civil.ge.
[69] *Civil Georgia*, April 12, 2002, http://www.civil.ge.
[70] *Civil Georgia*, August 22, 2002, http://www.civil.ge.
[71] *Civil Georgia*, August 23, 2002, http://www.civil.ge.

At this point, the pressures coming from many sides produced their effect. The combined arm-twisting of the United States and Russia, as well as domestic intolerance for the continued lawlessness in Pankisi, induced Georgian decision-makers to launch an anti-criminal operation on August 25, 2002. Some 1,000 servicemen from the interior and state security ministries went into the gorge, while some 1,500 Ministry of Defense soldiers backed up the operation. In the background, GTEP entered its third phase during which Georgian troops, attired in newly supplied American uniforms, engaged in actual field training. Georgia's commitment of a major part of its one capable force to this operation was a risky decision. The relative success the mission achieved, however, may have helped to change Georgian politics, drawing the country ever closer to the United States and mitigating some of Russia's security fears.

During the August–September 2002 police–military operation in Pankisi, up to a dozen criminals were detained by the law enforcement agencies. Police control was restored in all of Pankisi's villages and settlements, and more than ten checkpoints were established by the interior troops. Moscow's aggressive stance and the dreaded possibility of direct Russian military involvement seem to have made the ethnic Kists (Georgian citizens of Chechen descent) and Chechen refugees more accommodating to the Georgian military presence. Georgia's special services also used some "creative" tactics. The new minister of security, Valeri Khaburdzania, said in January 2003 that Georgian agents had "convinced" the Chechen guerrilla commanders to leave the gorge.[72] Arguably, Chechen militants preferred leaving their families and relatives in the safety of Georgia, with the chance of future emigration, rather than risk another of Russia's notorious "sweep operations" into Pankisi itself.

As a result of the Pankisi operation, Georgians recovered a long-lost confidence in their own military capabilities, thanks in part to assistance from the United States. Most of the armed Chechen groups believed to be present in the area left the gorge. Pro-Western sentiment was strengthened and so too was the readiness of most political parties to adopt a tougher stance toward Russia. Parliament called for the cancellation of Georgia's membership to the Commonwealth of Independent

---

[72] Valeri Khaburdzania, "Georgia's Key Security Concerns: Pankisi and Abkhazia," Discussion at the Nixon Center, Washington DC, January 30, 2003, http://www.civil.ge/eng/article.php?id=3163.

States and for the withdrawal of all Russian troops from Georgia. Even parties that generally support Russia, such as the Socialist Party, backed the government's actions and called for a joint investigation into the bombing incident. To adopt a pro-Russian position at that particular juncture would have been political suicide for any Georgian party.

Indeed, regaining control over the gorge without major violence and without angering the local population did represent a genuine success for the Georgian government. Russia, however, was not satisfied, and demanded the detention of all Chechens who could potentially constitute a threat to the Russian Federation.[73] In September 2002, Putin took a page from the book of recent U.S. policy and, on the first anniversary of the New York attacks, ordered the development of the plans for "preemptive" aerial and land strikes on Pankisi directed at eliminating the "terrorists." It meant in effect planning an attack on the territory of Georgia. Putin asked the United Nations to recognize Russia's right to self-defense in the face of terrorism under UN Security Council Resolution 1378 and Article 51 of the UN Charter.

While this threat was taken seriously in Georgia and elsewhere, Russian observers were puzzled by Putin's behavior. Some suggested that his attitude was the result of a miscalculation. Perhaps he expected President Bush to make a stronger defense of the unilateral right to preemptive strikes against terrorist threats in his address to the UN a year after September 11. Defense analyst Pavel Felgenhauer argued that Moscow was merely bluffing. Others saw Russia's Georgia policy as a reflection of its interest in Caspian pipelines or as a contrived distraction from its failures in Chechnya.

Russian pressure had the effect of testing the limits of international tolerance for the Kremlin's unilateral actions in Georgia. In response to Russia's threats, the United States praised Georgia's role in the anti-terrorism coalition. The U.S. State Department, the European Union, and the OSCE also expressed their concern over the possible spillover of the Chechen conflict into Georgia. Following the 2002 showdown, Georgia felt more confident of its ability to tackle the Pankisi issue independently, while the United States consistently affirmed the right of the Georgian

---

[73] Jaba Devdariani, "Georgian Security Operation Proceeds in Pankisi Gorge," *Eurasia Insight*, September 3, 2002, http://www.eurasianet.org/departments/insight/articles/eav090302a.shtml.

government to deal with the gorge without Russian interference.[74] It was made clear, in effect, that Russia would not be allowed to copy the U.S. strategy of "preemptive strikes."

Having secured U.S. military assistance and with Pankisi pacified, Georgia may have emerged as a short-term winner from the crisis. Georgia's use of the United States as a big brother to counter the Russian threat, however, added to popular stereotypes and mutual mistrust on both sides. For Russians, Georgia emerged as a weak, unpredictable neighbor and a "traitor" that was willing to open the region to powers hostile to Moscow. For Georgians, Russia was seen more than ever as an aggressive, unfriendly neighbor with hegemonic aspirations. To many Georgians' alarm, in an express poll taken by the Russian radio station *Ekho Moskvy* during the height of tension over Pankisi on August 26, 2002, a stunning 58 percent of the Russians surveyed said Moscow should not apologize for the bombing raids in Georgia, even if they turned out to be true. The results were all the more striking because a high proportion of *Ekho Moskvy* listeners are liberal Muscovites.

The crisis also demonstrated the precariousness of Georgia's balancing game. As long as Georgia remained a weak state, U.S. intervention could bring about only a modest easing of Russian pressure, not a long-term normalization of Georgian–Russian relations. In the Pankisi Gorge confrontation, Russia's behavior could be checked by the international community and the U.S. military presence in Georgia. At the same time, however, Moscow extended citizenship to residents from Abkhazia and South Ossetia and in the winter of 2001 restored railway communications with Abkhazia, presenting Tbilisi with new and complex challenges that could only be resolved with Moscow's cooperation.

Shevardnadze's political demise in November 2003 occurred not simply because of rigged elections, but also because the opposition responded to a popular demand for a stronger and more assertive Georgia. Moreover, consistent with the Georgian master myth, Georgians liked to think that the bloodless Rose Revolution was an example of a civilized European way of solving an acute political crisis.[75] The new government readily exploited this sentiment, and even Moscow seemed

---

[74] *Statement of the White House Press Secretary,* August 24, 2002.
[75] This is indeed a questionable assertion, but understandable if one compares the Rose Revolution to the bloody coup in Tbilisi in the winter of 1991.

ready to recognize that a stronger Georgia was in its interests. Such, at least, appeared to be the implication of the role that Igor Ivanov, the Russian foreign minister, played in facilitating Shevardnadze's resignation.[76]

After his landslide victory in the January 2004 Georgian presidential elections, Mikheil Saakashvili underscored his willingness to repair relations with Russia. During his inaugural speech, he said he was "extending a hand of friendship" toward Russia, adding that he was "neither pro-Russian, nor pro-American, but pro-Georgian." Saakashvili made it clear, however, that his government would remain firm in demanding the closure of the two remaining Russian military bases—in Batumi and Akhalkalaki. But he indicated a willingness to "divorce" the most contentious issues from the broader relationship and to seek a compromise on those issues. "We acknowledge Russia's [security] interests in the region," he said, "but these can be served better by means other than the bases."[77] He also offered to open the door to Russian investors in the energy sector and port infrastructure, and to replace the military bases with a joint anti-terrorist center.

So far, Russia has adopted a wait-and-see tactic, an indication that it remains skeptical of Saakashvili's ability to resolve Georgia's problems and restore effective governance. Shevardnadze's government was an unreliable and weak partner, easy to throw off track and intimidated by its own internal frailty. When Saakashvili took on the Ajaran strongman, Aslan Abashidze, in April 2004, Russia initially (albeit half-heartedly) backed Abashidze. But once Saakashvili's forces started to gain the advantage, Russia sent a senior figure from the armed forces to the Batumi base to ensure that the local command, known to be sympathetic to Abashidze, stayed out of the fray. In the end, Igor Ivanov arranged Abashidze's evacuation to Moscow, after the latter received security guarantees from Saakashvili. This episode offered compelling evidence that if Georgia is strong and seizes the initiative, Russia will not challenge it. It raises the possibility that if the Georgian government manages to sustain the pace of reform and preserve public support, Russia may be willing to deal more even-handedly with a stronger Georgia.

---

[76] Ivanov denied, however, he was aware of Shevardnadze's plans to resign.
[77] Mikheil Saakashvili, *President Mikheil Saakashvili's Inauguration Speech*, January 25, 2004.

For the legacy of mistrust between the two countries to be overcome, however, Russian policy must shift, and the Georgian leadership must continue to gain self-confidence. Opinion is divided on Putin's willingness (or ability) to alter Russia's foreign policy toward Georgia. In the December 2003 parliamentary elections, Putin's supporters secured absolute control over the Duma, presumably allowing him to do what he wants in relations with Georgia. Still, voices embracing a nationalist approach, such as the Communists, Vladimir Zhirinovsky's Liberal Democrats, and Rodina remain active in parliament and able to agitate public opinion. Thus, it may not be as easy as it first appears for Putin to set a course of reform, because it risks alienating segments of the political establishment and popular sentiment.[78]

Observers are divided on Russia's preferred policies toward Saakashvili's administration. Ariel Cohen quotes a senior U.S. diplomat in Moscow who predicts that a "reservoir of imperial nostalgia" in Russia will lead to a "more muscular approach" toward Central Asia and the Caucasus.[79] Aleksei Malashenko, a researcher at the Carnegie Moscow Center, has argued that "two-thirds of the [Kremlin's] position would be based on reason and willingness to cooperate," while "one-third is . . . an imperial attitude."[80] Sergei Karaganov of the Council on Foreign and Defense Policy has asserted that "[Russia] should start offering [Georgians] a carrot. If need be, we can always use the stick."[81] But the "carrot" Georgia asks for—Russian support in restoring Georgian sovereignty over Abkhazia and South Ossetia—may be tough to deliver.

Based on past experience, Russian policymakers more naturally think of the stick before the carrot; and learning to appreciate the utility of carrots may take more time. In addition, obvious stumbling blocks remain in the way of a more pragmatic Russian–Georgian relationship—in particular, the problems surrounding Russia's peacekeeping role in South Ossetia and Abkhazia and the unresolved issue of Russian military bases in Georgia.

---

[78] Ariel Cohen, "U.S. Officials Warily Monitor Russian Policy Debate on Caucasus," *Eurasia Insight*, January 9, 2004, http://www.eurasianet.org/departments/insight/articles/eav010904b_pr.shtml.

[79] Cohen, "U.S. Officials Warily Monitor Russian Policy Debate on Caucasus."

[80] Igor Torbakov, "Russian Policy Makers Struggle to Respond to Political Changes in Georgia," *Eurasia Insight*, January 8, 2004, http://www.eurasianet.org/departments/insight/articles/eav010804_pr.shtml.

[81] Torbakov, "Russian Policy Makers Struggle to Respond to Political Changes in Georgia."

The new Georgian authorities have learned in Pankisi and in ousting both Shevardnadze and Abashidze that Russia does not always have the resources to back up its own threats. But this insight can lead to errors, as in summer 2004, when the Saakashvili administration tried to reintegrate South Ossetia by a combination of humanitarian, political, and military pressure. Russian armed volunteers and military assistance poured in, leading to Georgian casualties and bringing the new administration to the brink of large-scale hostilities. The Georgian government backed down, and was left to ponder its longer-term political settlement options.

In contrast with Shevardnadze, however, Saakashvili tries to stay proactive, putting the ball in Russia's court. There are signs that Putin's administration has suffered a loss of confidence at home. The West's skepticism also increased in the wake of the Yukos affair and in response to signs that Putin is veering toward authoritarianism. Saakashvili calculates that he can induce Putin to overreact and to make political mistakes. Thereby, as long as Georgia adheres to Western values and political style, he hopes to attract Western support in settling the pressing issues of Russian military bases and the frozen conflicts in Abkhazia and South Ossetia.

THE RUSSIAN MILITARY PRESENCE IN GEORGIA

The new Georgian leadership is trying to identify the areas where pragmatic cooperation with Russia is possible, and trying to determine if Russia will cooperate voluntarily or only in response to pressure. This new policy direction was most evident regarding the Russian military bases. Russia's military presence in Georgia has had two main forms: the military bases it has occupied since Soviet times and the deployment of peacekeeping forces in Abkhazia and South Ossetia. Georgia has pressed for Russia to withdraw from the military bases. Its official position regarding the peacekeepers has been more ambiguous. When power initially passed from Shevardnadze to Saakashvili, Georgia downplayed the base issue, treating the Russian presence as symbolically but not practically significant. In late 2004 and in 2005, the base issue again moved to the forefront of Georgia's agenda with Russia, reflecting Tbilisi's frustration when trying to find a common language with the Kremlin.

Russian withdrawal from Georgian military bases became central to the Russian–Georgian relationship after the 1999 Istanbul OSCE Summit, where Yeltsin's government agreed to close the Vaziani and Gudauta bases by July 2001 and to negotiate the withdrawal from the remaining two bases of Batumi and Akhalkalaki. The Vaziani base near Tbilisi was closed by July 1, 2001, and on November 9, 2001, the Russian Foreign Ministry announced the Gudauta base had been shut down as well. Gudauta is located in Abkhazia and had reportedly been used by the Abkhazian rebels and Russian troops during the 1992–94 conflict against Georgian military forces. Observers were not allowed to monitor the withdrawal from this base in Abkhazia, and according to Georgian reports in 2001, only 300 out of some 1,100 Russian servicemen were withdrawn at that time.[82] The rest were transferred to Russia's peace-keeping battalion, and the physical infrastructure of the base was placed under the control of the peacekeeping force.[83] In June 2002, OSCE military experts were finally allowed to inspect the base, and they confirmed the withdrawal of Russian arms and personnel.[84] Georgia, however, wants the base under permanent international monitoring.

By January 2004, negotiations on withdrawal from the Batumi and Akhalkalaki bases had made no headway through eight rounds of talks. Russia now demanded a withdrawal period of eleven years and, according to the Georgian foreign minister, Tedo Japaridze, financial compensation of $500 million.[85] The bases have been neuralgic for Georgia for symbolic as well as practical reasons, not least because they remind people of their Soviet origin and, worse, create a Russian military presence that is seen by the Georgian government as subversive in sensitive geographic areas. The Akhalkalaki base is located in an area populated almost entirely by ethnic Armenians, many of whom are employed on the base. The local population is opposed to Russian withdrawal from the base, not only because they want to keep their jobs, but also because of Armenia's his-

---

82 *Statement by the Ministry of Foreign Affairs of Georgia*, November 21, 2001, http://www.bits.de/NRANEU/docs/GeorgiaMFA211101.htm.

83 "Russian–Georgian Contradictions Worsen," *Russian Military Analysis*, issue 68 (June 2001), http://www.wps.ru/en/products/pp/military/2001/06/15.html.

84 Liz Fuller, "OSCE Says Russian Withdrawal from Georgian Base Complete," *RFE/RL News Digest*, June 17, 2002, http://www.eurasianet.org/resource/georgia/hypermail/200206/0036.shtml.

85 Giorgi Sepashvili, "U.S. Backs Georgia in Hard Talks Concerning Russian Military Bases," *Civil Georgia*, January 15, 2004, http://www.civil.ge/eng/print.php?id=6023. Japaridze reported this in January 2004.

torical grievances with Turkey. Unlike Georgians, they fear any increase of Turkish influence, even if it is under NATO auspices. In addition, the base in Batumi had served as a prop for Abashidze as he fashioned his local fiefdom in Ajara.

Georgia's new leaders (no less than their predecessors) worry that Russia, so long as it retains the bases, has the ability to feed trouble in Georgia's separatist regions. In an interview with *Time* in January 2004, Saakashvili said that the bases serve more "to bolster imperial self-confidence than Russian security." He added, "The Russians have interests like safeguarding their southern borders, making them terrorist-proof. We have the same interests."[86] To address these concerns, Georgia's Foreign Minister Salome Zourabichvili proposed establishing a joint Russian–Georgian anti-terrorist center in exchange for Russia's withdrawal from the military bases.[87]

When the base talks resumed in June 2004, however, little had changed. The Russian military confirmed that while withdrawal had been agreed to in principle, adequate facilities would first have to be available back home in order to receive the troops. Defense Minister Sergei Ivanov stated that he did not intend to "throw men and equipment into an empty field, as happened [with the troops from] East Germany."[88] But, as the Russian analyst Pavel Felgenhauer noted, most of the troops in Batumi and Akhalkalaki, including the officers, are local inhabitants. This would mean that the bases in Georgia could be closed in several months. The "withdrawal" would only entail the relocation of several officer families and quantities of military hardware.[89]

To Georgians, it appeared that Russia wanted to use the base issue to shape prevailing norms in the post-Soviet space. While Russia may not aim at reviving the Soviet Union as such or some kind of supranational union, it does intend to create a favorable context for its extended economic and political interests. In this game, Putin seems willing to aban-

---

[86] Paul Quinn-Judge, "10 Questions for Mikheil Saakashvili," *Time*, January 19, 2004, p. 19.

[87] "Russia, Georgia Discussed Joint Anti-Terrorism Center," *Civil Georgia*, June 24, 2004, http://www.civil.ge/eng/article.php?id=7195.

[88] Sepashvili, "U.S. Backs Georgia in Hard Talks Concerning Russian Military Bases."

[89] Pavel Felgenhauer, "Motives in Georgia are Base," *The Moscow Times*, January 13, 2004.

don some of the burdensome commitments accepted by Yeltsin.[90] At the OSCE Summit in Maastricht in December 2003, Russia asserted that it had no obligation to withdraw its troops from Georgia or Moldova. Pressed by the United States and Europe, the Russian Foreign Ministry responded that at the 1999 Istanbul OSCE meeting it had only expressed an "intention" to withdraw from the bases, provided (unspecified) "necessary conditions" were met. At the Porto OSCE meeting at the end of 2002, the United States, eager to secure Russian support over Iraq, signed on to this interpretation. An indifferent EU also failed to press Russia to fulfill its commitments.[91] On the eve of the NATO Istanbul Summit in June 2004, the Russian Duma ratified the modified Conventional Forces in Europe (CFE) Treaty, but again, Foreign Minister Sergei Lavrov stated "there is no legal linkage" between the withdrawal from the bases and the CFE.[92] NATO's Secretary-General Jaap de Hoop Scheffer disagreed, however, confirming that both issues were linked. The fulfillment of the commitments from the 1999 Istanbul OSCE Summit was a precondition for the ratification of the CFE by NATO's new members, something Russia very much wanted.[93]

By 2005, hopes for progress in Georgia's relations with Russia had been dashed. Russia refused to back away from its support for Georgia's secessionist provinces and allowed Russian volunteers to aid secessionists during the escalation of the conflict in South Ossetia in summer 2004. Russia also interfered in the marathon presidential election in Abkhazia, hoping to install its own protégé. It vetoed the OSCE Border Monitoring Mission on the Russian–Georgian border in December 2004 and maintained that Chechen guerillas continued to infiltrate Russia from Georgian territory. Although Tbilisi awarded several large privatization deals to Russian companies, improved economic relations failed to produce a political détente.

---

[90] Trenin, "Identity and Integration: Russia and the West in the 21st Century," p. 17.

[91] Vladimir Socor, "OSCE, R.I.P.," *IASPS Policy Briefings: Geostrategic Perspectives on Eurasia* no. 47 (Washington, DC: Institute for Advanced Strategic and Political Studies, January 1, 2004), p. 5.

[92] Gennadiy Sisoyev, "Ministr otrabotal na vysshem urovne," *Kommersant Daily*, June 30, 2004.

[93] "Press Conference by NATO Secretary-General after the NATO-Russia Council," NATO News Release, June 28, 2004, http://www.nato.int/docu/speech/2004/s040628i.htm.

As a result, in January 2005 the new round of talks on the bases collapsed.[94] After the February visit of Russian Foreign Minister Sergei Lavrov to Georgia failed to bring progress, the Georgian Parliament—with the qualified support of the Foreign Ministry—initiated a resolution instructing the government to outlaw the Russian presence in Georgia, and seek forceful removal of the troops by January 2006, unless a schedule of withdrawal had been negotiated by mid-May 2005.

Foreign Minister Salome Zourabichvili articulated the new tougher policy in an interview with a Russian news agency.[95] She insisted that Georgia is committed to European values of human rights and standards of state conduct, and it is for Russia to demonstrate its commitment to the same.

The new leadership's position seems clear: if Russia agrees to play by international rules and renounces its attempt to have a special sway over the country, then Georgia will take steps to accommodate Russian security interests. However, in contrast to the Shevardnadze government, it has no intention of cutting a secret deal, and, if Russian pressure continues, Georgia will use the full force of international law and turn to international forums to mobilize pressure on Russia and to expose it as a pariah state.

There are echoes of this policy in the decision of the Georgian Parliament, taken unanimously on March 10, 2005, that instructed the Georgian government to blockade the Russian bases in Georgia, cease issuing visas to Russian military personnel, and cut off utilities to the bases unless Russia agrees to a "reasonable" timeline for withdrawal.[96] The decision also partially circumvents Russia's apparent attempt to renege on its 1999 commitments. If the parliament's decision is implemented, it would not depend on agreements regulating the Russian presence, but on the sovereign right of Georgia not to have foreign troops stationed on its soil. Evidently the issue of the bases was also raised at the highest level by the U.S. and European leadership in their talks with Russia.

Georgia's toughened stance has appeared to bear fruit. While the parliamentary resolution was still under deliberation, the deputy chief

---

[94] "Russian Foreign Minister Visits Georgia", *Civil Georgia*, February 17, 2005, http://www.civil.ge/eng/article.php?id=9106.

[95] "Rossiya Pered Viborom," Regnum News Agency, December 25, 2004, http://www.regnum.ru/news/382323.html.

[96] "Parliament Sets a Deadline for Withdrawal of the Russian Military Bases," *Civil Georgia*, March 10, 2005, http://www.civil.ge/eng/article.php?id=9310.

of staff of the Russian Defense Ministry, in an unsuccessful attempt to prevent its passage, said that Russia would accept a three- to four-year period for withdrawal, half the time requested by the Russian delegation only a month earlier. Two rounds of negotiations took place in March and April 2005, at which Russia officially confirmed its willingness to work within the three- to four-year time limit. Yet these talks did not bring a breakthrough on the issue, because Georgia insisted that no troop training should be conducted or reinforcements sent to the bases during this period.[97] Despite the growing pessimism of many, at the last minute on May 30 the foreign ministers of the two sides did reach an agreement pledging Russia to withdraw from the remaining military bases by the end of 2008, largely on Georgian terms.[98] On its side, Russia demanded Georgia's written commitment not to station NATO bases on its soil.

The decision to elevate the withdrawal of Russian military bases to the forefront of Georgia's agenda indicates that the Saakashvili administration is running out of options and patience. The Putin administration, however, resents this pressure and is tempted to mount a counteroffensive, deterred only by the difficulty it would have justifying harsher measures before the international community.

POSSIBLE OPPORTUNITIES: THE ECONOMIC DIMENSION

Since the late 1990s, Russia's economic expansion into Georgia, especially through energy projects, has been overshadowed by two political concerns: (1) that Russia would use its economic leverage to apply political pressure, and (2) that Shevardnadze would enter into non-transparent and economically unjustified contracts to boost his weak presidency. Tbilisi's balancing act between Russia and the West depended on the country's participation in U.S.-backed energy projects, such as the Baku–Tbilisi–Ceyhan Pipeline, which were expected to diversify Georgia's energy supplies and reduce dependence on Russia. From 1992 on, however, the Georgian government has never been able to assure the basic gas and electricity needs of either the population or industry. Frequent blackouts

---

[97] *Civil Georgia*, April 18, 2005, http://www.civil.ge.
[98] Joint Declaration of the Foreign Ministers of the Russian Federation and Georgia, May 30, 2005, http://www.civil.ge/eng/detail.php?id=10009.

further mobilized the public against the government, especially since millions of dollars in Western aid had been wasted or misappropriated.

Two deals that were negotiated in 2003—a crucial election year for Shevardnadze—proved to be very controversial. On August 11, 2003, the Georgian government announced that under a contract between the U.S. company AES and Russia's Unified Energy Systems (RAO-UES), the Russian company would acquire 75 percent of the shares of the Tbilisi electricity distribution network, two 600-megawatt power plants, power lines carrying electricity to Turkey and Armenia, as well as the rights to manage two hydroelectric power plants. The deal seemed to have major political implications, because AES had been the largest U.S. investor in Georgia ($240 million), and it occurred soon after Shevardnadze's government had signed up to a "strategic partnership" with Gazprom. As part of this deal, the Russian conglomerate committed itself to multimillion-dollar upgrades in gas pipelines from Russia to Armenia and Turkey. These upgrades were to energize Georgia's anemic economy and secure deliveries of reliable, relatively cheap gas for Georgia in the months leading up to the November parliamentary elections.

The Bush administration took a dim view of this deal with Gazprom. Ambassador Steven Mann, the senior advisor for Caspian Basin energy diplomacy, was urgently dispatched to Georgia, where he cautioned that the Gazprom agreement could "significantly weaken Georgia's position along East-West energy transportation routes." Washington worried that the Gazprom initiative would compete with a pipeline project, led by Anglo-American conglomerate BP and Norway's Statoil, to deliver gas from Azerbaijan's Shah Deniz field to Erzerum, at the Georgian–Turkish border.[99]

Shevardnadze argued that these deals, especially the RAO-UES one, were guided by purely economic considerations and would have a positive economic effect. He maintained that "the sale [of the Tbilisi electricity network] has become possible only after the U.S. company AES modernized the entire electricity network, thus, creating a precondition for the entry of the Russian company." But both Georgian analysts and Ambassador Mann argued the deals had been "insufficiently trans-

---

[99] Jaba Devdariani, "Potential Deal with Russian Gas Conglomerate Sparks Controversy in Georgia," *Eurasia Insight*, June 6, 2003, http://www.eurasianet.org/departments/business/articles/eav060603.shtml.

parent."[100] The main U.S. fear was not over Georgia's purchase of gas or electricity from Russia, but that Russian control over Georgia's strategic power grid and the main gas pipeline would hamper future U.S.-backed projects.[101] Both the Georgian opposition and the U.S. government were concerned not only by the potential growth of Russian influence, but also by the willingness of the weak and corrupt Shevardnadze government to cut shady deals to secure re-election.

Georgia's mistrust of Russian motives had been influenced by the past perception that when ITERA turned off the gas tap in Georgia, it was acting to increase Russia's political influence. The Kremlin's influence over major energy companies only reinforced Georgia's apprehension. Gazprom had long been under government sway. RAO-UES was headed by Anatoli Chubais, who had defended the notion of a Russian "liberal empire." Chubais saw Russia as a "natural and unique leader" of the CIS, which meant that it needed to "beef up, increase, and strengthen its leadership position in this part of the globe."[102] Unlike more traditional views of Russia's imperial vocation, Chubais's idea was that Russia should become a liberalizing force in Eurasia. However, the fact that the Russian business elite thinks in terms of empire, even a liberal one, stirs unease in Georgia and causes many to view the motives of Russian companies with suspicion.

The Georgian government acknowledges the need to open the country's markets to international competition. Even taking into account the vast shadow economy, the extent of Georgia's economic collapse has been staggering. Under these circumstances, Russian companies could provide needed investment and reliable services. However, the risk that Russia could emerge as a monopoly provider of natural gas in Georgia, allowing it to create barriers to entry for potential competitors, is still present. Thus, seeking diversification of energy supply is a logical direction for Georgia to take.

---

[100] Zeyno Baran, "Deals Give Russian Companies Influence over Georgia's Energy Infrastructure," *Eurasia Insight*, August 18, 2003, http://www.eurasianet.org/departments/business/articles/eav081803.shtml.

[101] The only existing alternative gas pipeline from Iran through Azerbaijan has not been used since the Soviet era and needs rehabilitation. Also, gas produced in Iran is more expensive than gas produced in Russia.

[102] Igor Torbakov, "Russian Policymakers Air Notion of 'Liberal Empire' in Caucasus, Central Asia," *Eurasia Insight*, October 27, 2003, http://www.eurasianet.org/departments/insight/articles/eav102703.shtml.

On the economic front, the Saakashvili government announced its intention to cut taxes further and to create other favorable conditions for investment. Russian companies have been specifically invited to participate in the new investment projects. The government has announced the privatization of state-held assets that were previously designated as "strategically significant" and thus not for sale. These include hydroelectric plants and shares in the seaports of Batumi and Poti. Tbilisi has also hosted a conference for major business figures close to the Kremlin, a delegation led by Putin's key economy minister, German Gref. These efforts succeeded. Russia's EvrazHolding won a privatization bid for the Chiatura Manganese Plant in January 2005 for $132 million.[103] Also in January, the Russian state-owned Vneshtorgbank purchased 51 percent of the shares of the United Georgian Bank, which seemed to indicate a long-term Russian interest in the Georgian market.[104]

Saakashvili's appointment of a well-known Russian businessman of Georgian origin, Kakha Bendukidze, as the country's economy minister was a key element in this new economic policy. Bendukidze professes a liberal economic policy aimed at the large-scale privatization of state assets.[105] While some observers saw Bendukidze's appointment as a sign of openness toward Russian business interests, one can also argue that his intimate knowledge of arcane Russian business practices allows him to protect Georgia's economic interests.

Georgian permanent and seasonal workers in Russia constitute another critical aspect of the countries' economic relationship. According to Georgia's State Department of Statistics, 205,000 Georgians were working in Russia in October 2002. Unofficial data suggest that the figure may be as large as 500,000, with many (if not most) employed illegally for meager wages. The flow of Georgian seasonal workers is largest toward Russia, but some also go to the United States, Greece, and Germany. Remittances to Georgia from workers abroad are estimated to be $480 million to $500 million per year, which amounts to 20 percent of Georgia's annual GDP

---

[103] *Civil Georgia*, January 19, 2005, http://www.civil.ge/eng/article.php?id=8833.

[104] *Civil Georgia*, January 18, 2005, http://www.civil.ge/eng/article.php?id=8830.

[105] In December 2004 Bendukidze became State Minister for Structural Reforms, but he continued to exercise considerable influence over national economic policy.

and is an important source of daily support to much of the population.[106] Thus, economic ties with Russia are extremely significant. In fact, the legalization of employment of Georgian workers would allow the Georgian government to better protect the rights of Georgians in Russia and to better monitor the financial flows involved.

In short, the economic dimension of the Russian–Georgian relationship offers the best prospect for cooperation, provided that security-related anxieties over economic ties can be overcome. This process will not be easy. Georgia's new leaders stress the importance of creating an environment of free competition with transparent rules, while Russia is pressing for preferential treatment. Putin's government has lately emphasized the development of the Eurasian Economic Cooperation Organization (EvrazES) and the creation of a Single Economic Space (OEP), in effect, a Russian-dominated free-trade area. Georgia has no desire to join either enterprise, and, unlike Russia, is already a member of the World Trade Organization (WTO), which obliges it to offer most–favored nation treatment to all WTO members. This gives Georgian leaders room for maneuver and an opportunity to pursue European rules of trade by synchronizing Georgian legislation with EU standards. For Georgia to fashion an economic regime that avoids granting Russian investors undue advantage, the country will need other foreign companies to invest, which of course requires that the country be made attractive to these investors by curbing corruption, improving infrastructure, and passing progressive legislation.

OUTLOOK FOR THE FUTURE

Relations between Georgia and Russia have long been troubled by mistrust, which can easily be triggered on both sides. For Shevardnadze's Georgia, dealings with Russia formed something of a development dilemma: The country needed to strengthen itself internally to be able to withstand external pressures from Russia, but also in order to act as a reliable partner. On the other hand, internal strength, as many Georgians

---

[106] *Labour Migration from Georgia* (Tbilisi: International Organization for Migration/Association for Economic Education, 2003). This research focused on 630 families who had members working in Russia. It was conducted in four Georgian regions (provinces).

believe, cannot be mustered without finding solutions to Abkhazia and South Ossetia, and this requires a constructive Russian role.

This argument, however, is not only circular; its logic is deeply flawed, even perverse. It posits Russia as both a source of weakness and the ultimate savior, and diverts attention from Georgia's own responsibility for addressing its most painful problems. This dead-end logic suggests that Abkhazia, South Ossetia, Russian military bases, and economic aspects of relations with Russia represent one giant knot of problems, all of which have to be resolved simultaneously. Saakashvili seems ready to move away from this logic by separating the knot into individual threads, articulating those issues on which Georgia's position is non-negotiable and then seeking a compromise with Russia on remaining issues.

For instance, Saakashvili says the Russian military bases in Batumi and Akhalkalaki have to be closed. After they are closed, the creation of the joint anti-terrorism centers can be negotiated. The talks on Abkhazian and South Ossetian issues are separated from the discussion on military bases. Tbilisi also tries to build regular personal communication with Russia's Security Council, presidential administration, and key ministries. Saakashvili hopes that in the long run, he will be able to build trust with his Russian counterparts and gradually overcome the stumbling blocks through compromise.

As a foundation for rapprochement, the Georgian government believes that Georgia and Russia must recognize that trouble within the Caucasian states—including secessionism, regime instability, and a fragmented and non-transparent political landscape—is likely to destabilize the region, which is against the interests of both states.

This approach can be productive, as Russia has the advantage of an intimate knowledge of the South Caucasus, and it could capitalize on this if it wished to promote stability in Georgia as a way of enhancing its own security. Currently though, Russia and Georgia tend to disagree on the rules of interaction. Georgia is a small state, and it seeks external guarantees that will compensate for Russia's incomparably larger economic resources and political muscle. Thus, Georgia prefers the European normative space as a foundation for its dealings with Moscow. Russia seems to prefer a bilateral or a CIS-based normative regime, which almost certainly falls short of European standards for both human rights and trade. Importantly, it also leaves the Georgian government feeling vulnerable to possible Russian bullying and with no international intermediary on which it can rely.

Georgia's recent conflicts with Russia over the military bases and the peacekeeping regime in South Ossetia can be seen within this context. In the South Ossetian case, Georgia can claim to be acting in accordance with international norms. Saakashvili's government insists on the right of sovereign control over national borders. Moscow, on the other hand, is opting for the (albeit shaky) status quo, which is more favorable to Russia.

Hence, the vicious cycle between Russia and Georgia continues: Saakashvili's government seeks to strengthen Georgia internally, and, on some level, the Russians seem to want to deal with a stronger Georgia. Current relations, including the Russian role in Georgia's secessionist areas, however, make it difficult to achieve a stronger Georgia as long as borders remain unprotected and criminal activity flourishes across them. Moreover, secessionist leaders have no incentive to negotiate with Tbilisi. As a result, Georgia risks remaining weakened, and, ironically, a less reliable partner for Russia.

More broadly, Saakashvili and his young colleagues are Western-educated and have few ties to the Soviet old-boy network. Saakashvili also relies on his own national electorate and does not need to look toward Moscow for validation. The new, young generation of Georgian politicians has its base of power within the country; and they see their careers tied to Georgia itself or possibly to the West, but no longer to Moscow. The broader Georgian public counts on eventual inclusion in Western economic, political, and security mechanisms as a guarantee of prosperity. In 1994, Shevardnadze argued on the floor of the Georgian Parliament that joining the CIS would bring "grain and eggs." A decade later, it is clear that foreign goods from many sources flow into the Georgian market irrespective of the country's political alignment.

It is no longer obvious that popular disenchantment over the corruption and inefficiency in post-Soviet economic transitions leads inevitably to a tilt back toward Russia or a growth in pro-Russian sentiment. In Moldova, for example, the electoral victory of the Communist Party in 2001 that was seen as a retreat into the past by a frustrated public turns out not to have been so.[107] The country's Communist president, Vladimir Voronin, recently replaced his pro-Russian foreign minister with the one

---

[107] Dan Wisniewski and Zsolt-Istvan Mato, "Moldovan Communists Win Absolute Majority," *RFE/RL Newsline,* February 26, 2001, http://www.rferl.org/newsline/2001/02/260201.asp.

who believes that there is "no alternative to integration into Europe."[108] He also won the elections on a starkly anti-Russian ticket and moved closer to reviving the alliance with Georgia and Ukraine in pursuing NATO and EU membership.

A "wait-and-see" policy toward Georgia's new leadership is not a reasonable option for Moscow. Such a policy carries too much of an echo of earlier policy predicated on the assumption that given sufficient time, Shevardnadze would stumble, providing Russia with an opening (and an advantage in its competition with the United States). A destabilization of Georgia would have detrimental consequences for Russia's security interests. Russia would be wiser to seek a positive role in Georgia and to look for ways of reducing the mistrust between the two countries.

As for the West, Shevardnadze's vacillation between Russia and the United States impeded the country's integration into Western institutions such as NATO and the EU, despite the importance this objective has in Georgia's "national project." Not only must Georgia pursue a steadier course in pursuit of integration, but, as a first step, it must make existing arrangements work, such as NATO's Partnership for Peace Program and the Partnership and Cooperation Agreement with the EU. The effort to draw closer to the EU would appear to be particularly important, because Russian objections to this initiative are likely to be less intense. One encouraging development in this respect has been the EU's decision to include the South Caucasus in its new European Neighborhood Policy (ENP). But Georgia's new policy of forcing Russia to make hard decisions can also prove dangerous. The 2004 escalation in South Ossetia showed how dangerous a severe confrontation with Russia could be.

Can Russia and Georgia achieve a new relationship, as Saakashvili has urged? The prospect depends most heavily on Georgia's ability to reform. The new government's search for more pragmatic approaches puts its policies toward Russia in more of a tactical than a strategic perspective. Georgia's major strategic challenge is to restore vitality to a debilitated political structure and depressed economy. This will permit Georgia's participation in the politics and economics of the post-Soviet space.

Russia's ideological transition is still in progress. The strength of nationalist forces reduces Putin's room for maneuver on the issues at

---

[108] Natalya Prihodko, "Kishinev izbavlyayetsya ot pro-Rossiiski nastroennyh ministrov," *Nezavisimaya gazeta*, February 6, 2004, http://www.ng.ru/cis/2004-02-06/5_kishinev.html.

the core of the Georgian–Russian relationship. Thus, Georgia's wish list should be divided into those goals where a bilateral consensus can be reached and those requiring a prod from the international community before Russia is likely to move. Withdrawal from the military bases has been and recasting the Russian peacekeeping role is likely to remain in the latter category. Russia has sent mixed signals on the military bases. Pressure from Washington, coupled with its cautious willingness to help finance the withdrawal, illustrates well what is needed. Unfortunately, after the fall 2004 tragedy in Beslan, Putin's government seems to be less self-confident and, as a result, more likely to perceive any challenge as a threat and to respond to it aggressively. In relations with Georgia, Putin has personally activated contacts with the leaders of Abkhazia and South Ossetia, even meeting with both of them in Sochi on April 5, 2005, the same day that Putin had scheduled talks with Javier Solana. Putin even convinced the EU's High Representative to meet these two leaders.[109] While some took this as a sign that Russia sought to play a more constructive role in settlement, it could also be read as a desire to annex these areas. Where the truth lay remained unclear.

As for the problems of Abkhazia and South Ossetia, the Georgian government needs to build direct links with the de facto leadership in these territories and to end the practice of talking over their heads to Moscow. At the same time, a joint approach to conflict resolution with Russia is possible. For example, Moscow has indicated a willingness to open a railway link with Georgia via Abkhazia, and this opportunity should be pursued. In addressing the issue of peacekeeping, Georgia should attempt to work through the European Union to complement the UN, perhaps using the experience of the EU police monitoring mission in Bosnia-Herzegovina to strengthen a joint Georgian–Abkhazian administration in the Gali region. So, in sum, after a difficult initial decade, relations between Georgia and Russia still have the prospect of taking a more constructive course. This will only happen, however, if Georgia accepts its own responsibility for overcoming internal weaknesses and pursues the difficult road of reform.

---

[109] Vladimir Socor, "EU Policy in Disarray in Georgia and Moldova," *Eurasia Daily Monitor,* April 15, 2005, http://jamestown.org/edm/article.php?volume_id=407&issue_id=3301&article_id=236959

CHAPTER 5

Frozen Uncertainty: Russia and the Conflict over Abkhazia

OKSANA ANTONENKO

The demise of the Soviet Union ignited a series of local conflicts that, after an initial violent phase, settled into political deadlock and remain unresolved more than a decade later. Two of these conflicts—in Abkhazia and South Ossetia—erupted in the former Georgian Soviet Socialist Republic during its uneasy transformation into a newly independent state. The conflict in Abkhazia, which took place from 1992 to 1993, was one of the bloodiest post-Soviet conflicts, producing thousands of casualties and the displacement of about 250,000 people (most them ethnic Georgians).[1] It has also undermined the economic prospects for one of the most well-known resort areas on the Black Sea. The cease-fire agreement in May 1994 has not led to an agreement

---

[1] The figure 250,000 is often used by experts and officials. However it is disputed. Officially Georgia has 262,217 registered internally displaced persons (IDPs), of whom 11,987 are from the conflict in South Ossetia and the rest from Abkhazia. But most observers doubt these figures. Many who initially did go to Georgia have moved on: the 2002 census in Georgia revealed that the country has lost around a million people to emigration over the last decade, and people originally from Abkhazia can be assumed to be among them. Georgia's new President Mikheil Saakashvili stunned supporters and critics alike with a recent announcement that he wanted a complete recount of the number of people displaced by the 1992–1993 war in Abkhazia. Saakashvili told a cabinet meeting on April 5, 2004 that "the current number of refugees—260,000— is grossly inflated,"("Georgia's Refugee Recount," IWPR Report, April 28, 2004). In August 2004, 216,947 identity cards were issued to IDPs by the Ministry of Refugees and Integration. However, this figure only covers IDPs and does not cover refugees who left for Russia and other countries.

settling Abkhazia's political status; instead, Abkhazia has emerged as a de facto state outside Tbilisi's control, albeit still formally recognized by the international community and by Russia as part of Georgia.

The initial stage of state-building in post-Soviet Georgia as a whole has been nationalistic in its political rhetoric and ideology, lawless in its means, and often justified on the basis of historic grievances (and myths).[2] All of these factors played a particularly important role in starting the Georgian–Abkhazian conflict, which despite economic and geopolitical rationales, evolved into an ethno-political conflict that divided the multinational society of prewar Abkhazia into two camps. Mobilization took place on the basis of ethnic identity, with a majority among ethnic minorities (Russians, Armenians, Greeks) fighting on the side of the Abkhazians.

Georgians see this conflict as one of the key obstacles to realizing their aim of building a strong, united, and viable Georgian state. This was true for the first Georgian president, Zviad Gamsakhurdia. It was true for his successor, Eduard Shevardnadze, during whose leadership the war occurred and whose government failed to re-establish control over Abkhazia by military means. The new Georgian president, Mikheil Saakashvili, also sees "reunification" of the Georgian lands as one of the key priorities for his presidency. Like his predecessors, President Saakashvili is prepared to grant Abkhazia broad autonomy, but not international sovereignty.

For Abkhazians, the conflict symbolizes a struggle for national survival and the imperative of preserving their national identity. Following the demise of the Soviet Union, the Abkhazian elite saw the rise of nationalism in Georgia as both a threat to their survival and an historic opportunity to build first a nation and then a state for themselves. The war ended in September 1993 with the withdrawal of Georgian troops and a massive depopulation of Abkhazia's Georgian residents (45 percent of the prewar population).[3] So far, no state has recognized Abkhazia as

---

[2] For analysis about the role of historic myths in Georgian–Abkhazian conflict, see Victor Shnirelman, *Voiny pamiati: Mify identichnost' i politika v Zakavkaz'e* (Moskva: Akademkniga, 2003), pp. 259–461.

[3] According to the last Soviet census of 1989, Abkhazia had a population of 525,000, of which 45 percent, or 239,000 people, were ethnic Georgians. Almost all the Georgians fled Abkhazia by October 1993 when the war ended.

an independent entity. Its population—which at present also includes Georgian, Russian, Greek, and Armenian communities—remains economically isolated and is largely relying on a subsistence economy. Nonetheless, it has succeeded in developing de facto state institutions, including a parliament, presidency, and military force. Since the 1999 referendum on independence, Abkhazian authorities have insisted that they are determined to build a sovereign state and that recognition of their independence is only a matter of time.

Given that the positions of the Georgian and Abkhazian parties remain polarized with no prospect of a political settlement, attention is increasingly focused on the role of third parties. Russia is particularly important in this respect. It has played a dominant, if often controversial, role throughout all stages of the conflict. Georgians blame Russia for conspiring to initiate the conflict, then for keeping the conflict "frozen," and finally for openly supporting Abkhazian separatist aspirations with all but formal recognition. Tbilisi strives to include military personnel from other states in the Russian peacekeeping force stationed in Abkhazia and to subsume Moscow's political role as mediator more clearly under the UN negotiation process.

Abkhazians also have a number of grievances against Russia for its military support of Georgia in the initial stages of the conflict. However, they now see Russia as the key guarantor of their security. Since 1999, the Abkhazian Parliament several times appealed to Moscow to establish associated relations between Abkhazia and Russia by the inclusion of Abkhazia into the Russian Federation as a "freely associated state," a status that would preserve Abkhazian sovereignty. Finally, the international community, although wary of Russia's increasingly unilateralist efforts in its diplomacy vis-à-vis the Georgian–Abkhazian conflict and conscious of its uneasy relations with Tbilisi, still views Russia's engagement in the political process as essential if any lasting peace and political settlement is to be achieved.

What is Russia's position on the Abkhazia conflict? How high is it on Russia's political agenda? Does Russia have a strategy toward the Georgian–Abkhazian conflict or does it merely react to events in the region?

Tens of thousands of them were resettled in makeshift accommodations in a string of Georgian towns and cities. See http://www.reliefweb.int/rw/RWB.NSF/db900SID/ACOS-64D87Q?OpenDocument.

To what extent is Russia really pulling the strings with Sukhumi? To what extent is Russia's cooperation with Abkhazia a mere by-product of the tensions in its relations with Tbilisi? What are the key interest groups shaping Russia's policy, and how has their influence been transformed under President Vladimir Putin?

This chapter offers answers to these questions by analyzing key factors that define Russia's policy toward the Georgian–Abkhazian conflict, focusing specifically on the 2000–2004 period under President Vladimir Putin. My objective is threefold: first, to describe the evolution of Russian policy; second, to highlight the complexity of policymaking and its implementation by focusing on different powerful interest groups within Russia. My interest is in which forces generate the primary motivations behind Russian policy and which constrain its effectiveness. The third objective is to place Russia's policy in Abkhazia within the context of its relations with other key actors in the conflict. All three dimensions should provide clues as to how Russia's policy might evolve when confronting the double challenge of leadership change in Georgia and Abkhazia.

RUSSIA'S INVOLVEMENT IN THE CONFLICT

Ten years after the May 1994 agreement on a cease-fire and on the deployment of a Commonwealth of Independent States (CIS) peacekeeping force to Abkhazia, no comprehensive analysis that has been published on Russia's role in the Georgian–Abkhazian military conflict has incorporated Russian archives or the memoirs of key players. A number of published accounts, however, suggest that from 1992 to 1994, the Russian armed forces and security services provided direct and indirect political and, more importantly, military assistance to both Georgian and Abkhazian sides of the conflict.[4] Some Georgian sources go as far as claiming that Russian security services planned and then provoked all of the seces-

---

[4] For an analysis of Russia's involvement, see Stanislav Lakoba, *Abkhazia de fakto ili Gruziia de iure?* (Sapporo, Japan: Hokkaido University Slavic Research Center 2001), http://src-h.slav.hokudai.ac.jp/publictn/lakova/lakova-contents.html; Alexei Zverev, "Ethnic Conflicts in the Caucasus," in Bruno Coppieters ed., *Contested Borders in the Caucasus* (Brussels: VUB Press, 1996), pp. 51–60, http://poli.vub.ac.be./publi/ContBorders/eng/; Svetlana Chervonnaya, *Abkhazia 1992: Post-Kommunisticheskaya Vandeja* (Moskva: Mosgorpechat, 1993).

sionist conflicts in the Caucasus, including the Georgian–Abkhazian conflict, in order to undermine Georgia's prospects for statehood.[5] Abkhazian commentators, on the other hand, downplay Russian involvement, emphasizing instead the role of volunteers and criticizing the transfer of ex-Soviet military assets by Russia to the Georgian National Guard prior to its initial attack on Abkhazia on August 14, 1992. Russian sources usually avoid detailed accounts of the war, focusing instead on the confusion in Russian policymaking at the time of the Soviet Union's breakup and blaming local military commanders for their financially motivated role during the war.[6] In the end, it remains difficult to judge whether or not Russia's involvement in Abkhazia from 1992 to 1993 was part of a conscious Kremlin strategy, but there is little doubt that the Abkhazian–Georgian conflict has become and remains an important instrument of its policy since.

Russia's role during the 1992–1993 war, both in reality and in popular myth, has evolved into the key obstacle to normal relations between Georgia and Russia. Russia's perceived part in Georgia's defeat in Abkhazia shaped a whole generation of Georgian politicians and citizens. Abkhazian expert Yuri Anchabadze writes that, "The view still prevails in Georgia that all political shocks that the republic has suffered in recent years, including the conflict in Abkhazia, have been inspired by some third force," which usually means Russia.[7]

Even today, the history of the conflict still has a significant impact on how Russia defines its interests and strategies vis-à-vis the Georgian–Abkhazian conflict and how it is viewed by both Abkhazians and Georgians. The impact is visible on a number of levels. First, the conflict has been so

---

[5] See, for example, Gia Tarkhan-Mouravi, "The Georgian–Abkhazian Conflict in a Regional Context," in Bruno Coppieters, Ghia Nodia, and Yuri Anchabadze eds., *Georgians and Abkhazians: The Search for a Peace Settlement,* (Köln: Bundesinstitut für Ostwissenschaftliche und Internationale Studien, 1998), pp. 90–112, also on http://poli.vub.ac.be/; or see Svetlana Chervonnaya, *Conflict in the Caucasus: Georgia, Abkhazia and the Russian Shadow* (Glastonbury: Gothic Image Publications, 1994).

[6] See Dmitrii Danilov, "Russia's Role," *Accord,* issue 7 (September 1999), pp. 42–49, http://www.c-r.org/accord/geor-ab/accord7/index.shtml.

[7] Yuri Anchabadze, "Georgia and Abkhazia: The Hard Road to Agreement," in Coppieters, Nodia, and Anchabadze, eds., *Georgians and Abkhazians,* pp. 80–89, also on http://poli.vub.ac.be/.

violent and had such a major effect on Russia itself, particularly its North Caucasus region, that since the cease-fire agreement was signed in 1994, Russian policy has been primarily focused on preventing any prospects for its resumption. No doubt the fear of a new war has constrained Russian policy, particularly in the period immediately after the conflict when more political progress could have been achieved.

Second, Russia's involvement on both sides of the conflict has undermined both Georgian and Abkhazian trust toward Russia as an impartial and reliable mediator. Instead, Russia has been and continues to be perceived as a party to the conflict. Moreover, Russia's assistance to both sides contributed to a widespread belief, in both Georgia and Abkhazia, that the conflict had been either plotted by Moscow or was carried out in Russia's interests. This is particularly visible in Georgia, where Russia's involvement is now perceived as the main reason Georgia "lost Abkhazia." Eduard Shevardnadze went as far as to suggest that Russia's support for Abkhazia during the conflict became the main spoiler for Georgian–Russian relations throughout the entire decade. Abkhazians, who are forced to rely on Russia's help, also tend to mistrust Russia's patronage, seeking (unlike South Ossetia) only associated relations with Russia rather than being fully integrated with and subordinated to it.

Third, the involvement of volunteers from the North Caucasus, of the Russian military, and of Russian politicians in the Abkhazian conflict has made it, more than any other separatist conflict in the post-Soviet space, an important issue in Russian domestic politics, which it remains to this day. Moreover, because of the links between Abkhazian and Chechen elites in 1991–1992 and later during the Abkhazian conflict itself, Russian policy toward the Georgian–Abkhazian conflict has been influenced by the situation in Chechnya.

Given these consequences, it is important to provide a brief overview of Russia's official policy on Abkhazia and the actions of different groups acting on Russia's behalf or perceived to be doing so. An involved exploration of Russia's involvement is appropriate because from 1991 to 1993, Russia did not have a consistent policy toward the Caucasus as a whole or toward the Georgian–Abkhazian conflict specifically.[8] Its policy was

---

[8] On Russian policies in the Caucasus, see Dmitri Trenin, "Russia's Security Interests and Policies in the Caucasus Region," in Coppieters ed., *Contested Borders in the Caucasus*, pp. 91–102, http://poli.vub.ac.be/.

shaped by many groups who later became important political actors in the post-conflict period.

Russia initially divided its loyalties between the two parties in the Georgia–Abkhazia conflict. Some among the Russian political elite were proponents of a unified Georgia while others were supporters of a pro-Moscow Abkhazia, de facto independent from Georgia. However, these loyalties did not remain static throughout the conflict; as violence persisted, more and more Russian actors were drawn to support the Abkhazian side in the conflict. The group supporting a unified Georgia included those in the Russian government who had established personal links with Eduard Shevardnadze when he was the Soviet minister of foreign affairs and those who were opposed to the Abkhazian secessionist aspirations for fear that they would result in challenges to Russia's own territorial integrity in the North Caucasus. Russia's President Boris Yeltsin and Foreign Minister Andrei Kozyrev (as well as other key Ministry of Foreign Affairs officials) were part of this group. Some Abkhazian sources go as far as to claim that Yeltsin provided political backing to Shevardnadze's plan to use force against Abkhazia.[9] After the start of the conflict in August 1992, the Russian Foreign Ministry sent a letter to the Georgian Foreign Ministry in which it expressed support for Georgia "fighting against terrorists"—support motivated by Russia's own swelling problems in Chechnya.

As for the Russian military establishment, there were significant differences in attitudes and loyalties regarding the Abkhazia conflict. Ministry of Defense officials in Moscow originally backed Georgia's actions, while commanders on the ground in Abkhazia almost from the start of the conflict were inclined to support the Abkhazian side either passively by not facilitating Georgia's actions or later more actively by providing direct assistance to the Abkhazian forces.

Russia's Minister of Defense Pavel Grachev remained a close friend of General Tengiz Kitovani, the Georgian Minister of Defense and commander of the National Guard from May 1992 to May 1993. Before the

---

[9] Stanislav Lakoba argues that during the Dagomis Summit on June 24, 1992, when the "Agreements on Principles of Settlement of the Georgian–Ossetian Conflict" were signed by the head of Georgia's State Council, Eduard Shevardnadze received President Yeltsin's backing for Georgia's military action against Abkhazia. See Lakoba, p. 10.

beginning of the war in August 1992, Grachev was helpful in transferring Soviet equipment and heavy weapons from the Russian Transcaucasian Military District to Georgian armed forces, which gave them unquestionable military superiority over the Abkhazian fighters. Georgian troops received tanks, artillery systems, helicopters, and light weapons.[10] On August 14, 1992, between 2,000 and 5,000 Georgian troops moved into Abkhazia and entered Sukhumi, while another 1,000 troops landed in Gagra and blocked Abkhazia's border with Russia. Grachev originally tried to restrain Russian military commanders on the ground in Abkhazia from providing assistance to the Abkhazian side, and some Abkhazian reports even indicate that tacit support was given to the Georgians, although these claims could not be verified.[11]

The Abkhazian side received significant support from volunteers from the North Caucasus, including ethnic groups related to the Abkhazians, such as the Adygheans and Circassians. By the end of September 1992, over 1,000 volunteers had arrived from the North Caucasus to support the Abkhazian fighters.[12] The Confederation of Mountainous Peoples of the Caucasus (later the Confederation of Peoples of the Caucasus) that was striving for sovereignty of the North Caucasus republics from Russia played a key role in mobilizing thousands of volunteers to fight in Abkhazia. Regional elites who initially resisted such mobilization had to acquiesce or be excluded from the political process, dominated from 1991 to 1993 by ethnic revival and mobilization. Georgian and Russian analysts claim that parts of the Russian security services and the military recruited and trained fighters from the North Caucasus, including Shamil Basaev, to take part in the Abkhazian–Georgian conflict.[13] Basaev was later appointed as deputy defense minister of Abkhazia.

---

[10] In March 1993, during the conflict, Russian troops transferred thirty-four military cantonments with equipment to Georgia. See Zverev, p. 53.

[11] According to Abkhazian sources, Russian troops took part in the initial assault on Abkhazia. For example, Russian ships were used by Georgian troops during their initial deployment to the city of Gagra. See Lakoba, p. 35.

[12] Pavel Baev, Jan Koehler, Christoph Zürcher, *Internal Violence in the Caucasus: Study Prepared for The World Bank Development Economic Research Group (DECRG)* (Washington, DC: The World Bank, 2002).

[13] After 1994, Shamil Basaev became one of the most famous Chechen warlords fighting against Russian troops in Chechnya. According to Colonel Stanislav Lunev: "[Basaev] received special training and, during the war of indepen-

The Russian military also gave substantial support to the Abkhazian side. This was mostly done on the regional level or by the military command of the Transcaucasian Military District and there is speculation, but so far no hard evidence, that such assistance was ordered from Moscow. Local units in Abkhazia offered various forms of support to the rebels, including personnel, weapons, information, and other services. But the question of who authorized such activities remains in dispute. According to Alexei Zverev, Grachev gave a strict order not to take part in either side of the conflict.[14] Others argue that at that time, military commanders on the ground acted independently and without orders—often motivated by financial gain or by personal sympathies formed in the course of the conflict.[15] According to General Alexander Lebed, many orders at that time were delivered in phone calls to avoid responsibility at the highest political level.[16]

By September 1992, when it became clear that Georgian plans for a *blitzkrieg* had failed and the conflict was transformed into a protracted and brutal war, Russian policy changed, and Abkhazian troops increasingly became beneficiaries of Russia's military assistance.[17] The shift could be primarily explained by the fact that political forces in Moscow had lost control over the situation in the dynamically developing conflict, while Russian military forces and volunteers in Abkhazia had become the key players who defined Russia's policy by their actions. Abkhazian fighters were supplied with armaments by the Russian 643rd Anti-aircraft Missile Regiment and a

---

dence in Abkhazia in 1992–1993, and became commander of the special 'Chechen Battalion.'" Colonel Stanislev Lunev, "Chechen Terrorists in Dagestan—Made in Russia," August 26, 1999, http://www.newsmax.com.

[14] Zverev, p. 53.

[15] Yevgeny Primakov writes in his memoirs, "I know that Russian leadership, first of all the President, never sanctioned Russian military involvement—direct or indirect—on either side of the [Georgian–Abkhazian] conflict... However, it is a known fact that Georgian positions were attacked from the air by "unidentified" aircraft—which [the] Abkhaz did not have. I do not exclude that these actions were perpetrated by a group of corrupt Russian military [personnel], who represented [a] small group and clearly their actions could not have influenced the outcome of the conflict." See Yevgeny Primakov, *Gody v Bolshoi Politike* (Moskva: Kollektsiia Sovershenno Sekretno, 1999), p. 417.

[16] Alexander Goltz, "Armiia Rossii: 11 Poteriannykh let" (Moskva: Zakharov, 2004), p. 151.

[17] Lakoba, p. 21.

supply unit based in Gudauta. The Russian units' weaponry before the war consisted of a thousand sub-machine guns, eighteen machine guns, half a million rounds of ammunition, and several armored personnel carriers.[18] How much of this was transferred or sold to the Abkhazian side, however, remains unknown. Moreover, views differ on the extent to which Russian troops stationed in Gudauta were under the direct command of the Russian Ministry of Defense or acted independently.[19]

In either case, the scale of assistance was significant. According to Zverev, the fact that more than 100,000 mines were used in the conflict zone, when before the war there were no mine depots in Abkhazia, indicated the scale of Russia's assistance. Mikhail Demianov stated in interview on Georgian television that weapons were transferred to the Abkhazian side free of charge.[20] Stanislav Lakoba, on the other hand, argues that Abkhazians purchased (and were not given) most of the mines, small weapons, and even some heavy weapons they used in the conflict from Russian troops. In February 1993, Russian military planes bombed Georgian positions. On March 19, 1993, Georgian forces shot down a SU-27 fighter jet flown by a Russian pilot. This episode was confirmed by UN military observers and later acknowledged by the Russian side, which claimed that the sortie aimed to protect Russian facilities.[21] And in March 1993, *Izvestia* reported that Abkhazian forces had received extensive help from Russian military advisers and listed the armaments supplied.[22]

---

[18] Evgeny Kozhokin, "Georgia–Abkhazia" in Jeremy R. Azrael and Emil A. Payin eds., *U.S. and Russian Policymaking with Respect to the Use of Force* (Santa Monica, CA: Rand Corporation, 1996), quoted by Robert Seely in *Russo–Chechen Conflict 1800–2000: A Deadly Embrace* (London: Frank Cass, 2001), p. 192.

[19] The Human Rights Watch Report "War or Peace? Human Rights and Russian Military Involvement in the 'Near Abroad'" provides the following assessment: "It is difficult to determine at what level permission, if not orders, have been given...what is clear is that the Russian government has failed to investigate, let alone prosecute, any reported cases of criminal behaviour, suggesting high-level complicity." See http://www.hrw.org/reports/1993/russia/.

[20] "War or Peace?" p. 5

[21] *Krasnaya Zvezda*, March 23, 1993, p. 1.

[22] "Abkhazskiie Voiska Shturmuiut Sukhumi: Shevardnadze obvinyaet Rossiiu v Agressii," *Izvestiia*, March 17, 1993, quoted by Seely, p. 193. The list included seventy-two tanks, a Russian landing force battalion, twenty armored personnel carriers (APCs), Grad rockets, Uragan rocket launchers, and twelve artillery pieces, with Russian officers commanding ten of the crews.

Furthermore, thousands of volunteers and mercenaries from the North Caucasus regions, organized by the Confederation of the Peoples of the Caucasus, provided important military assistance for the Abkhazian forces. To a large extent, the presence of North Caucasus volunteers, which according to Abkhazian sources constituted around 10 percent of all Abkhazian forces, was more important and decisive for the Abkhazian side than any Russian military technical assistance.[23] North Caucasus volunteers received key positions in the Abkhazian forces, including chief of staff, deputy minister of defense, and head of the naval staff.

Regardless of the character of Russian military involvement in the Georgian–Abkhazian conflict, there is no documentary evidence to suggest that the conflict itself had been planned and executed by Moscow. Still, this claim is often heard among representatives of the Georgian political elite. Moreover, some question still exists whether Russia's involvement had a decisive impact on the dynamics of the conflict.[24] Such a Russo-centric interpretation of Georgia's defeat disregards the unprecedented mobilization among the Abkhazian population who feared for their national survival and thus had a much stronger motivation to fight than many Georgian fighters. In addition, it exaggerates the extent to which the Abkhazians needed external support to prevail, given how poorly organized, disciplined, and trained Georgian forces were, notwithstanding the assistance they had received from the Russian regional military command before the war. Moreover, those who blame Russia for the conflict tend to deny the existence of indigenous Abkhazian forces, interests, and motivations. Ghia Nodia wrote in 1996 that Abkhazians "were seen not as fighting for their own rights, but as siding with 'them,' the Russians, against 'us,' the Georgians."[25] Yuri Anch-

---

[23] Lakoba, p. 19

[24] Some Georgian sources claim, however, that Russia's involvement could have been decisive. Jaba Devdariani in comments to the author cited Georgian claims that Abkhazian forces resumed the assault on Sukhumi after the Sochi agreements using heavy artillery, that was supposed to be withdrawn from the engagement line with the artillery gun locks (*zatvor*) placed under Russian command for safe keeping. If we assume that the Russian commanders did hand back the artillery before the assault on Sukhumi, then they could have had a decisive impact on a crucial episode of the war.

[25] Ghia Nodia, "Political Turmoil in Georgia and the Ethnic Policies of Zviad Gamsakhurdia," in Coppieters, ed., *Contested Borders in the Caucasus*, p. 84.

abadze noted that "persistent efforts to make Russia the sole culprit cloak a desire by the Georgian side to justify its defeat in the war" and reduce "the possibility of the Georgians properly assessing their own role and the errors which led to an escalation in the tragic events on 1992–1993."[26]

END OF MILITARY CONFLICT AND RUSSIAN DOMESTIC DEBATES

Russia's major political success during the conflict included an agreement signed by the Georgian and Abkhazian sides in Sochi on July 27, 1993. The agreement provided for a cease-fire and the demilitarization of Abkhazia. In accordance with the Sochi Agreement, the Georgian side started to withdraw its forces and some of the displaced population returned to their homes. Russia's Defense Minister Grachev proposed deploying two brigades of the Russian military into Abkhazia to disarm both sides of the conflict. Georgia, however, refused and according to Yevgeny Primakov, it later regretted this decision.[27] In contrast, the Georgian expert Paata Zakareishvili—who attended negotiations in Sochi, Pitsunda, and Gudauta mediated by Russia's representative Sergei Shoigu—claims that the Russian side always took a clearly pro-Abkhazian position and applied great pressure on the Georgian side.[28] Shoigu pushed for deploying Russian military authorities (*kommendanty*) in Sukhumi and other large towns, but the Georgian negotiator, Zhuli Shartava, rejected this proposal.[29]

On September 27, 1993, Abkhazian forces recaptured Sukhumi from Georgian troops. Shevardnadze himself had to be evacuated from Sukhumi hours before Abkhazian troops seized control of the city. The Georgian president then protested to Moscow over the violation of the Sochi Agreement by the Abkhazian forces, but received no response. In

---

[26] Anchabadze, pp. 86–87.

[27] Primakov, p. 417.

[28] Shoigu's links with Abkhazian officials continued after the conflict. For example, he appointed Nodar Khazhba, who represented the Abkhazian side at negotiations in Sochi, to a senior position in his Ministry of Emergencies, where Khazhba served until 2004 when he was sent back to Abkhazia to represent Russia's interests as interim prime minister of Abkhazia during the 2004 disputed elections.

[29] Paata Zakareishvili, "Bylo li oruzhie v meshkah s mukoi?" *Rezonansi*, October 9, 2004.

fact, events in Sukhumi coincided with a major political crisis in Moscow—the standoff between President Yeltsin and the Supreme Soviet, when the government resorted to force against rebel parliamentarians barricaded inside the "White House."

As a result, Georgian calls for Russian assistance during the final fight for Sukhumi remained unanswered. The only response from Moscow came in the form of Russian economic sanctions applied against Abkhazia on September 20. Georgian sources maintain that Russian troops were heavily involved in supporting the Abkhazian offensive to recapture Sukhumi. Some even claim that Russian troops stormed Sukhumi ahead of the Abkhazian forces. According to Abkhazian reports, however, Russian assistance was limited only to the fact that Grachev refused to use Russian troops to stop the Abkhazian offensive.[30] Lakoba argues that if such an order to use force had been given, this would have led to a fight between Russian and Abkhazian/North Caucasian forces who were unlikely to have withdrawn even under pressure from Moscow.[31] By September 30, following the flight of Georgian forces and civilians, Abkhazian forces reached the Inguri River separating Abkhazia and Georgia's Samegrelo (Megrelia) region.

Georgia was shocked by the defeat and hoped to reverse the result by appealing both to Moscow and to the international community. On October 9, 1993, after months of pressure from Moscow, Georgia finally joined the Commonwealth of Independent States (CIS), seeing it as a last resort to reverse the new status quo in Abkhazia by gaining Russia's support. Russia, however, provided assistance to Shevardnadze only in the Georgian government's civil war with Zviad Gamsakhurdia and not against Abkhazia. After Gamsakhurdia's return to Georgia from Chechnya, the Zviadists had gradually seized much of western Georgia, threatening to advance to Tbilisi and reinstate Gamsakhurdia as head of state. Following the October CIS agreement, Russian forces took control of the main roads and provided critical assistance to pro-Shevardnadze forces in crushing the revolt. Gamsakhurdia himself died in western Georgia on December 31, 1993.

In the meantime, no progress was achieved in resolving the situation in Abkhazia. In October–November 1993, Moscow applied pressure on

---

[30] Zverev, p. 54.
[31] Lakoba, p. 31.

both Abkhazia and Georgia to discourage them from restarting the conflict. The political dialogue, however, remained deadlocked after meetings in Geneva and Moscow. A breakthrough did come in Moscow on April 4, 1994, when both sides finally signed the Declaration on Measures for a Political Settlement of the Georgian–Abkhazian Conflict. The declaration was signed by both Georgian and Abkhazian representatives in the presence of officials from Russia and the Conference on Security and Cooperation in Europe (CSCE) as well as representatives of the UN secretary-general. Both sides also signed an agreement on the voluntary return of refugees and internally displaced persons (IDPs), with the exception of those involved in war crimes.[32]

While Russian mediators were working on the Moscow agreement, President Yeltsin and his military were trying to secure Russia's strategic interests directly with the Shevardnadze government in Tbilisi, a government significantly weakened by its recent defeat in Abkhazia. On February 3, 1994, Yeltsin visited Tbilisi and signed a Friendship, Good Neighborly Relations, and Cooperation Treaty with Georgia. At the same time, Defense Minister Pavel Grachev and Georgia's Prime Minister Otar Patsatsia concluded a protocol allowing Russia to establish three military bases in Georgia for a twenty-five year period.[33] These were at Vaziani, Akhalkalaki, and Batumi, with branches in Gudauta and Sukhumi. In return, Moscow agreed to provide Georgia with technical military assistance and reaffirmed Russia's support for Georgia's territorial integrity.

On February 17, 1994, the State Duma Committee on CIS Affairs and Relations with Compatriots Abroad held special hearings on the two agreements, during which Yeltsin was criticized for signing an agreement with one side of an ongoing conflict. The hearings highlighted a number of the lawmakers' key concerns. They objected that Russia had recognized Georgian territorial integrity without any guarantees on the status of Abkhazia and South Ossetia. They argued that this one-sided approach could lead the Abkhazian and South Ossetians sides to lose trust in Russia and undermine its prospects of playing a mediating role acceptable to both sides of the conflict.

---

[32] Both documents are published in Jonathan Cohen, ed., "A Question of Sovereignty: The Georgia–Abkhazia Peace Process," *Accord*, issue 7 (September 1999), pp. 66–69, http://www.c-r.org/accord/geor-ab/accord7/index.shtml.
[33] Zverev, p. 9.

Second, the deputies were particularly alarmed over Article 3 of the agreement providing for Russian assistance in creating Georgia's armed forces, including the supply of equipment, weapons, and military technology. A special declaration by the State Duma Committee on CIS Affairs on February 3, 1994 (the day the treaty was signed), asserted that this clause "could dangerously destabilize the situation in the Caucasus, in Georgia, and in Russia itself." The transfer of weapons to Georgia, it was said, could be viewed as Russian encouragement to Georgian authorities to use force to restore control over Abkhazia and South Ossetia. Lawmakers also contested the Defense Ministry's claims that Russian military assistance and training would increase Russian military influence in Georgia. Finally, they feared that Georgia in its weak and divided state would not be able to ensure that Russian military equipment and technology were not transferred to third parties, specifically citing the case of Nagorno-Karabakh.

This was scarcely the end of their objections. They saw Russia's commitment to close its borders to prevent volunteers from the North Caucasus entering Abkhazia and South Ossetia in the event of renewed hostilities as encouraging Tbilisi's use of force. They criticized the UN's growing role in the Abkhazian conflict as a challenge to the role of the CIS. And they also raised concerns over the Grachev–Patsatsia protocol on Russian military bases in Georgia and the ability of Georgia to ensure the functioning of Russian bases in Abkhazia, a territory not within its control.

The February 1994 Duma declarations represented a turning point in the Russian domestic political debate on policy toward Abkhazia. Prior to 1994 the Russian government could conduct its policy toward Georgia and Abkhazia without political opposition, except for the protests of regional elites in the North Caucasus who had little political influence. Therefore, during the Abkhazian war, policy was dominated by largely pro-Georgian political elites in Moscow, including Yeltsin himself, and a divided military that provided assistance to both Georgia and Abkhazia. After 1994, the government came under increasing pressure from the State Duma, which had emerged as a powerful protagonist of the Abkhazian cause. It retained this role throughout the 1990s, particularly as the government lost interest in the Georgian–Abkhazian conflict. The parliament, therefore, became the principal force shaping Russian public and elite opinion. And, as a result, public opinion shifted in favor of closer relations with Abkhazia and away from an "unfriendly" Georgia.

Faced with the Duma's opposition, Yeltsin decided not to submit the Friendship, Good Neighborly Relations, and Cooperation Treaty for ratification until the conflicts in Abkhazia and South Ossetia had been settled. Consequently, the State Duma never ratified the treaty. Had it been ratified in 1994, it might well have altered the course of Georgian—Russian relations and the outcome in Abkhazia.

In the absence of a legal framework, the Russian government still went ahead with the military bases, creating a major source of tension in Georgian–Russian relations five years later. Whether Moscow fulfilled its commitment to Georgia on military assistance remains unknown, although some transfers of equipment did occur along with limited training of Georgian officers. Contrary to Duma recommendations, the Russian government did accept a UN mediating role and the deployment of a UN observer mission in the zone of conflict. Almost from the start, however, Moscow sought to marginalize the UN and promote itself as the main mediator between Tbilisi and Sukhumi. To accomplish this, it relied on the presence of Russian peacekeepers under CIS mandate and on its special relations with Sukhumi, which prospered notwithstanding a formal embargo, not least because powerful interest groups saw a "neither war nor peace" scenario in Abkhazia as fertile ground for realizing their economic interests and political ambitions.

RUSSIAN PEACEKEEPERS AND THE UN

Georgia and Abkhazia signed an agreement on a cease-fire and separation of forces in Moscow on May 14, 1994.[34] The agreement was concluded under the auspices of the UN with facilitation by the Russian Federation. It provided for the deployment of CIS forces to monitor its implementation.[35] On June 9, 1994, President Yeltsin signed a decree on the participation of the Russian armed forces in the CIS peacekeeping operation in the Georgian–Abkhazian conflict area. On June 21, the Russian peacekeeping force (CISPKF), the only troops actively involved in the CIS mission, were deployed to two security zones (*zony bezopasnosti*)—

---

[34] Cohen, ed., pp. 69–70.
[35] Since 1994, only Russian forces have been part of this peacekeeping force under the CIS mandate.

"North" (the lower part of the Kodori Gorge) and "South" (along the Inguri River).

At the same time, the UN Observer Mission in Georgia (UNOMIG), deployed in the conflict area since August 1993 to monitor temporary cease-fires, was now assigned the task of monitoring the implementation of the Moscow Agreement and observing the operations of the CISPKF. Between 1994 and 2004, over 30,000 Russian forces took part in the CISPKF. Ninety-seven of them were killed and 251 wounded while carrying out their duties. Today, the Russian contingent in the CISPKF comprises 1,700 troops. In 2004, UNOMIG included 114 military observers from twenty-three different countries.[36]

CISPKF security zones are over 85 kilometers long and 24 kilometers wide, stretching over both sides of the cease-fire line, and include twenty-two observer posts and four checkpoints. In addition, Russian peacekeepers regularly patrol the lower part of the Kodori Gorge jointly with UN observers, monitor the upper Kodori Gorge region by air, and control any movement of heavy weapons in the demilitarized zone. The mandate of Russian peacekeeping forces, unmodified since 1994 despite continued criticism from the Georgian side, includes the implementation of the cease-fire and preventing the resumption of armed conflict. The peacekeeping forces, however, do not have a direct mandate to carry out police operations in the Gali region where they are deployed.

In summer 1994, Russian officials pressed the Abkhazian side to accept the return of large groups of Georgian IDPs to Abkhazia, primarily to the Gali region. Peacekeepers were prepared to guarantee their security, although the Abkhazian side claimed that this was outside of their mandate and insisted on a gradual return. The Abkhazian authorities even threatened to contest Russian peacekeeping forces assisting the return of a large group of Georgian IDPs. On September 14, 1994, the Abkhazian forces entered the security zone, forcing the Russian peacekeepers to retreat.[37] Such incidents demonstrated Moscow's limited power to change Abkhazian policy when the Abkhazians viewed their

---

[36] See http://www.unomig.org; the total costs of UNOMIG operations up to October 2003 amounted to $1.5 billion. *Report of the Secretary-General to Security Council,* 17/10/03, S/2003/1019, p. 7. The cost of the CIS peacekeeping operations up to 2003 was $490 million. See *The Military Balance, 2003–2004* (London: The International Institute for Strategic Studies, 2003).

[37] Lakoba, p. 37.

own vital interests to be at stake. Disagreements over the pace and scale of refugee return provoked tensions in relations between Moscow and Sukhumi. Clearly Moscow could have threatened to use force, but this would have certainly provoked a resumption of conflict, violating the Russian government's overriding priority of preserving the September 1993 cease-fire.

Therefore, soon after the deployment of the CISPKF, the Georgian government realized that the Russian authorities would not put enough pressure on the Abkhazian side to force compliance with the April agreements on the return of IDPs. Instead, the role of Russian peacekeepers was fast transformed from one of helping to promote gradual reintegration between the Georgian and the Abkhazian communities into one of keeping them apart.[38] This is the main reason why Georgia has continuously sought ways to internationalize the peacekeeping effort. These initiatives, however, have proven unsuccessful.

Just months after Russia deployed its peacekeeping forces in Abkhazia, the Russian military, with Yeltsin's blessing, launched a military assault against the separatist regime of Djokhar Dudaev in Chechnya, dragging Russia into an unexpectedly protracted violent conflict for which it was poorly prepared. The war in Chechnya made it increasingly difficult for Russian politicians to support separatist regimes in neighboring states. Developments in this first Chechen war moved Georgian and Russian national interests closer together. Remembering the previous active participation by Chechens in the war on the side of Abkhazian troops, President Shevardnadze readily supported the Russian military campaign against Chechen separatism. Meanwhile, Moscow agreed to Georgia's demands to introduce a more comprehensive blockade on Abkhazia, after having relaxed the initial blockade of Abkhazia in December 1993 with a limited opening of the Psou River border crossing.

In December 1994, Russia once again closed its border with Abkhazia at the Psou River, the only land access for Abkhazian residents to the outside world. In addition to its land and sea blockade of Abkhazia, Russia disconnected Abkhazia's phone lines and refused to recognize Soviet passports from people with Abkhazian resident status.[39] Later,

---

[38] Dov Lynch, "Managing Separatist States: A Eurasian Case Study," *EU-ISS Occasional Papers*, no. 32, (November 2001), p. 17.
[39] Lakoba, p. 38.

Russia endorsed a decision adopted by the CIS heads of state on January 31, 1996, to institute an economic and arms embargo against Abkhazia.[40] This policy of isolating Abkhazia lasted until 1999, when Moscow reopened its border with Abkhazia, and facilitated cross-border trade and travel. The sanction policies (often referred to as trade restrictions) failed to push the Abkhazian leadership toward practical concessions. The blockade did not compel Sukhumi to seek closer links with Georgia or change its position on the question of its political status; on the contrary, it contributed to a hardening of the Abkhazian position.

Since the beginning of the conflict, Russia has taken part in various efforts to promote a political dialogue between the Georgian and Abkhazian leaderships. The UN-led process became the main vehicle for such a dialogue. In 1997, a Coordinating Council was established, chaired by the special representative of the UN secretary-general, with Russia acting as facilitator. The Organization for Security and Cooperation in Europe (OSCE) and the Group of Friends of the UN Secretary-General (consisting of France, Germany, the United States, the United Kingdom, and Russia) were included as observers. The Coordinating Council established three working groups: one on security and the non-resumption of hostilities; one on the return of IDPs; and one on economic and social issues. Moreover, between 1997 and 1999, Moscow brokered a number of meetings between President Shevardnadze and President Vladislav Ardzinba, the leader of Abkhazia, as well as with other high-level representatives of the two sides. Moscow thought that such direct talks could produce a breakthrough. To this end, Moscow encouraged Tbilisi to accept a federative model and to offer Abkhazia special status within an asymmetric federation. At the same time, Moscow delivered a clear message to Sukhumi that it had no prospect of becoming either an independent state or a member of the Russian Federation. Still, no progress ensued, and the process was soon interrupted by a new crisis.

In May 1998, fighting broke out in the Gali region where many of the displaced Georgian population had returned and where Russian

---

[40] There has not been any independent assessment of whether the sanctions were indeed holding. According to fragmentary evidence, the sanctions regime was sabotaged by trafficking across the Russian–Georgian border by sea (using Turkish and Russian vessels) and especially through cross-border trade with Georgia proper, which even involved Abkhazian militias and so-called Georgian partisans in the Zugdidi region.

peacekeepers patrolled the line of separation between the sides along the Inguri River. The fighting was provoked by Georgian paramilitaries crossing the cease-fire line and Abkhazian forces then undertaking a security operation against them. In his memoirs, Yevgeny Primakov claims that Shevardnadze was not informed about the planned incursion, although the paramilitary groups involved in the campaigns, the White Legion and the Forest Brothers, were supported by Georgia's state structures.[41] Hundreds of people were killed, over 20,000 Georgians who had recently returned to their homes were once again displaced, and over 1,500 homes, many of them rebuilt under UN programs, were destroyed. Russian peacekeepers did not provide sufficient protection for the Georgian population, although they stopped both sides from bringing heavy weaponry into the security zone. According to the Russian side, this move helped to localize violence and to restore the cease-fire.[42]

The Russian response to the violence in Abkhazia fell short of enforcement. Russia's political leadership, once again following the over-riding objective of preventing a resumption of conflict and thus avoiding risks, had refused to allow Russian peacekeepers to intervene. Moreover, Primakov explained Russia's restraint and unwillingness to authorize the transformation of its peacekeeping mandate into police functions or some form of peace enforcement by the fact that such a mandate had to be authorized by the UN Security Council. The CIS could not do so. He further stated that such a change in the mandate would likely have resulted in a higher number of casualties among Russian peacekeepers (during the 1998 events, Russian troops sustained sixty casualties).[43] He also made clear that any change of mandate would not be politically acceptable to Russia's leadership or public opinion.

After the 1998 Gali incident, the Georgian government, outraged by the unwillingness of Russian peacekeepers to protect the Georgian civilian population, stepped up its calls for expanding the CISPKF mandate to guarantee the safe return of IDPs, and not only to the Gali region. Georgia also declared that if Russia refused to expand its mandate, its forces should be replaced by a new multinational peacekeeping force.

---

[41] Primakov, *Gody v Bolshoi Politike*, p. 414. At the time Primakov was Russian foreign minister.

[42] Primakov, *Gody v Bolshoi Politike*, p. 413.

[43] See Dmitry Danilov, "Role of Russia" in Cohen, ed., p. 55.

Ukraine was willing to participate, but only under a UN Security Council mandate and with outside funding for its contribution.[44] Given Russian opposition, however, neither the UN nor the OSCE cared to dispatch an alternative peacekeeping force. On July 16, 2003, the Georgian Parliament authorized the government to appeal to the Security Council to allow it to invoke Article 7 of the UN Charter against Abkhazia.[45] The Georgian leadership realized this would not be approved by the UN and did not act on the authorization.

Russia's increasingly assertive policy in the South Caucasus, its cooperation with Abkhazia, primarily by regional elites, and its reluctance to enforce the return of Georgian IDPs to Abkhazia caused increasing frustration in Tbilisi. Moreover, Shevardnadze accused Moscow of organizing two assassination attempts against him.[46] Russia, in turn, reacted angrily in July 1998 when five Russian peacekeepers were killed in the Gali sector by a booby trap, and Georgian politicians used this occasion to accuse peacekeepers of complacency in the deaths of Georgian civilians in Gali two months before. Georgia declared its intention to withdraw from the CIS Collective Security Treaty and began demanding that the Russian military bases be closed. In 1999, with broad international support, Tbilisi succeeded in securing a Russian commitment to close its bases as a precondition for a modification of the Conventional Forces in Europe (CFE) Treaty, a goal much sought by Russia in the wake of NATO enlargement. The Russian–Georgian joint statement on base closures was signed at the OSCE Summit in Istanbul in October. Georgia's closer ties with the United States and NATO, however, were perceived in Moscow as part of an attempt to push Russia out of the South Caucasus, a traditional sphere of Russian influence. As a result, commentary in the Russian press and statements in the Russian Parliament turned increasingly hostile to Georgia.

---

44 "The Georgian Ambassador Suggests Internationalizing the Abkhazia Peacekeeping Operation," *Interfax Military News Bulletin,* July 15, 2003, http://www.interfax.com.

45 "Georgian Parliament Wants UN to Use Force in Abkhazia," *Interfax Military News Bulletin,* July 16, 2003, www.interfax.com.

46 See http://encarta.msn.com/encyclopedia_761574966/Shevardnadze_Eduard_A.html.

YELTSIN'S LEGACY: COMPETING INTEREST GROUPS

After his re-election in 1996 and the end of the first Chechen war, Yeltsin was ill and out of action for long periods of time. He paid no attention to the Abkhazian conflict. It is interesting that in his memoirs covering the whole period from 1997 to 2000, he speaks a lot about the CIS but does not mention Abkhazia.[47] Russian policy appeared to be directed at "freezing" the status quo according the formula "neither war nor peace." Moscow continued to support Georgia's territorial integrity, while actively engaging with Abkhazia's unrecognized authorities.

From 1997 to 1999, Moscow's policy toward the Georgian–Abkhazian conflict was highly compartmentalized. Policies were delegated to a variety of competing interest groups, each pursuing its own line. The Foreign Ministry remained formally in charge of the political process, but in 1998, Boris Berezovsky, a powerful oligarch who later became the head of the Russian Security Council and then the secretary of the CIS, assumed the role of mediator. It was Berezovsky who brokered a meeting between Shevardnadze and Ardzinba in August 1997 in Tbilisi. His strategy included an economic policy designed to benefit Russia, while "helping to restore trust among the parties to the conflict." Berezovsky proposed building an oil pipeline through Abkhazia and reopening the railway to trade as well as a border crossing on the Psou River. Abkhazian leaders were interested, but the Georgian side refused to negotiate on economic projects that were not linked to progress on the return of IDPs. Russia's alternative proposal to seek agreement on a mechanism for IDP return was rejected by Tbilisi. As a result, no economic projects were implemented.

Therefore, the Russian business lobby failed to extract benefits from the political process, mainly because any major project required agreement from both sides. Still, regional elites took on an increasingly prominent role in Abkhazia, particularly in the economic field. They included Moscow's mayor, Yuri Luzhkov, leaders of the Republic of Tatarstan, regional officials from the North Caucasus, and others with national

---

[47] Even the 1998 events in Gali, which almost led to a resumption of the war, are not mentioned. See Boris Yeltsin, *Prezidentskii Marafon* (Moskva: Izdatelsvo AST, 2000). The only mention of Abkhazia is made in relation to Yeltsin's personal perception of Shevardnadze. He writes: "[Shevardnadze] always carried inside him the pain of tragedy in Abkhazia," p. 190.

ambitions. They actively developed ties with Abkhazia, ignoring the economic sanctions regime that by 1998 had been significantly eroded by cross-border trade. Abkhazia, for example, signed agreements with the Adyghean Republic, the Republic of Kabardino-Balkaria, the Republic of Tatarstan, Krasnodar Krai, Rostov Oblast, and the Republic of North Ossetia-Alania. These agreements, although not providing formal political or legal recognition for Abkhazian statehood, nonetheless helped Abkhazia circumvent the CIS blockade and break free from its isolation. Abkhazia's partners were regions and republics with real economic stakes in Abkhazia, and their leaderships' policies were publicly popular.

In addition to regional governments, political movements with strong political connections also played an important role in providing a vehicle for bypassing the embargo. The 1997 annual report of the Duma's Committee on CIS Affairs and Relations with Compatriots Abroad includes extensive information on different agreements signed by L.N. Smirnov, the secretary of the Duma-sponsored Compatriots Council, with the Abkahzian branch of the Congress of Russian Communities (an influential political organization in Russia). These agreements covered the export of mineral fertilizers, citrus fruits, and other agricultural produce from Abkhazia to Russia. The report also refers to a special decree by the Russian government (N1397) authorizing transportation of citrus fruits and other agricultural products from Abkhazia into the Russian Federation. While these ties remained limited and had an insignificant impact on the lives of an Abkhazian population struggling to survive the economic blockade, they did reinforce a pro-Abkhazian political lobby within the Russian government and among private interest groups operating an illegitimate but profitable trade through powerful Abkhazian groups. This was evident in a letter sent from the chairman of the State Duma Committee on CIS Affairs to the Russian Foreign Ministry. The letter calls on the Russian government to respond to the plight of Abkhazian residents, including Russian nationals, by softening travel and trade restrictions on the Abkhazian–Russian border. At the same time the letter also calls on the Abkhazian authorities to create conditions aiding Russians to acquire real estate in Abkhazia and to make investments in the Abkhazian economy.

Therefore, in addition to the neighboring Russian regions, the Russian Duma helped to preserve a minimum of cooperation with Abkhazia at a time when Moscow, following its defeat in the first Chechen war, displayed little interest in the Caucasus. In the years 1996–1999, the State Duma could play such a political role because of the weakness of the government and of the president himself. The Duma remained the place where key political debates on the Georgian–Abkhazian conflict took place. On April 8, 1997, the Committee on CIS Affairs and Relations with Compatriots Abroad held a closed hearing on Russia's policy toward the Transcaucasus region attended by representatives from key ministries including foreign affairs, defense, and the economic sphere. What came out of the session well illustrated the dilemmas Russia faced. The committee's statement stressed the importance of the region for Russia's national security and economic interests, and recognized that without a resolution to the conflicts in Abkhazia, South Ossetia, and Nagorno-Karabakh, there could be no peace in the region. Without that, Russia's long-term interests could not be realized. Thus, Russia should continue to play the key role in seeking an end to the Georgian–Abkhazian conflict, but this would be difficult to do when both parties to the conflict increasingly blamed Russia for the stalemate and were actively seeking support from other important external actors, including NATO.

The Duma committee's statement urged the Russian government to intensify its negotiating efforts and then warned that, if in the near future Russia failed to achieve a breakthrough, its role as the key mediator would be undermined. It reflected a dilemma that remains to this day. If Russia helps to resolve the conflict, it will lose its geopolitical monopoly in Abkhazia. But, if it fails to achieve progress and is seen as a weak status quo power, it could well end up marginalized by more dynamic actors willing to fill the void.

How should Russia proceed? Russian mediators, the Duma committee said, should pursue negotiations on the basis of equality for the two sides, seeking to postpone the hard issue of Abkhazia's political status while focusing first on the resumption of economic ties. Restrictions on border trade between Abkhazia and Russia should be lifted on the condition that Abkhazian authorities facilitate the return of refugees to Abkhazia. It also proposed that any future guarantees by Russian peacekeepers (the CISPKF) on behalf of returning Georgian refugees be linked to the resumption of rail traffic through Abkhazia and an easing of border restrictions between Georgia and Abkhazia. These principles became the basis for Russian policy throughout the late 1990s up to the Sochi agreements in March 2003. Therefore, during Yeltsin's second term, the State

Duma served as both a source and a driving force behind ideas that surfaced in government policy in this troubled region.

PUTIN'S POLICY: WAR IN CHECHNYA AND
RE-ENGAGEMENT WITH ABKHAZIA

On August 9, 1999, Yeltsin appointed Vladimir Putin as Russia's prime minister. Putin immediately took a tough line on Chechnya. Following a series of apartment building explosions in Moscow and Volgodonsk in August 2000, as well as armed incursions by Chechen warlords into the neighboring republic of Dagestan, Russia launched the second Chechen war.

Contrary to the first war, which brought Georgia and Russia closer together in dealing with Abkhazian separatism, the second war exacerbated the existing crisis in their bilateral relations. The reason was that the Georgian government, presumably motivated by already widespread resentment toward Moscow, failed to support the Russian war effort, and was even perceived in Moscow as sheltering Chechen warlords. This had an immediate impact on Russia's policies toward Abkhazia.

Between September and December 1999, thousands of refugees fleeing from heavy fighting in Chechnya crossed the mountain paths into Georgia's Pankisi Gorge, a region populated by Kists—an ethnic group related to the Chechens. Moscow claimed that in addition to refugee women and children, a number of fighters moved into Pankisi and established training centers there. Out of fear that the Chechen conflict might spread into its territory, Georgia refused Moscow's demands to allow Russian troops to carry out military operations against Chechen troops in the area. Moreover, the Georgian leadership refused to extradite thirteen Chechens whom Russia requested for prosecution at the end of October 2002. Russia in turn responded by several times violating Georgian airspace.[48] And in September 2002, Putin threatened to resort to a preemptive military strike against Chechens in Georgia, which he justified as exercising the right of self-defense.[49]

---

[48] Although these actions were denied by the Russian Ministry of Defense, they were confirmed by OSCE observers. OSCE Press Release, August 2, 2002, http://www.osce.org/news/show_news.php?id=2636.

[49] OSCE Press Release, September 13, 2002, http://www.osce.org/news/show_news.php?id=2724.

The deterioration in Russian–Georgian relations led to a reorientation of Russian policies toward Abkhazia. Following years of limited engagement, Putin moved to step up Russia's relations with Abkhazia. Moscow tacitly endorsed the presidential elections in Abkhazia and a referendum that led to a declaration of Abkhazian independence in October 1999. This declaration closed the door to political negotiations between Tbilisi and Sukhumi on a federative model. Although Moscow did not explicitly recognize the results of the 1999 referendum and officially continued to support Georgia's territorial integrity, it also expanded its relations with Sukhumi.

In 1999, Russia reopened its border with Abkhazia, thus lifting its earlier blockade. In December 2000, citing concerns over Chechen rebels crossing the border, Russia introduced a visa regime for Georgian citizens, while deliberately making an exception for residents of Abkhazia and South Ossetia. Georgia regarded the action as a de facto annexation of Georgian territory.[50]

Russian–Georgian tensions further intensified when Georgian security forces staged an incursion into the Abkhazian part of the Kodori Gorge. In September 2001, Chechen fighters under the command of Ruslan Gelayev, who had previously spent considerable time in the Pankisi Gorge, were transported by the Georgian Interior Ministry to the Kodori Gorge on the border between Georgia and Abkhazia. Gelayev intended to enter Chechnya through Abkhazia—although there is no contiguous border between the two areas and therefore their detour to Abkhazia appears to have been deliberate rather then accidental. The Georgian authorities may have hoped to destabilize Abkhazia. Gelayev, reportedly with support from Georgian paramilitary groups, staged a number of attacks in Kodori. These incidents seriously exacerbated Georgian–Abkhazian tensions and threatened to reignite the war. Russia backed the Abkhazian demand for a withdrawal of Georgian troops from the Kodori Gorge (UN observers confirmed that 350 Georgian troops had been deployed in Kodori). Moreover, Russia provided assistance to Abkhazia against this incursion, fearing that Gelayev's group would cross into Russian territory. Russian SU-25 aircraft, violating Georgian airspace, bombed the areas where clashes with Gelayev's troops had taken place.

---

[50] CSCE Hearing, September 24, 2002, http://www.csce.gov/witness.cfm?
briefing_id=232&testimony_id=326.

Russia even deployed a small number of troops in Kodori (which were only withdrawn in April 2002). The crisis continued for several months, until February 2002 when Georgian troops withdrew from Kodori. Joint patrols by Russian peacekeepers and UNOMIG observers in lower Kodori then resumed.

The events in Pankisi and Kodori played a key role in shaping Russia's policy toward the conflict. In the first years of Putin's presidency, relations with Georgia and Abkhazia moved much higher on Russia's political agenda. While relations with Georgia passed from crisis to crisis and were often on the verge of an open conflict, Moscow pursued a policy of active engagement with Abkhazia. Support for Abkhazia was further reinforced by Russia's declared "victory" in the second war in Chechnya. Although Russia's military campaign had failed to produce a comprehensive political solution in the breakaway Russian republic, the prospect of Chechnya's successful secession from Russia diminished. As a result, Russia was no longer concerned that its support for separatist regimes elsewhere would echo within Russia itself. In December 2003, Putin made the following statement regarding Russia's policy toward the Georgian–Abkhazian conflict:

> Until recently the task of preserving Russia's territorial integrity represented one of the most important tasks, but now the problem is mostly solved. Following these principles, we cannot deny our neighbours the right to preserve their territorial integrity. The two sides should come to agreement and Russia will guarantee these agreements. We follow with great interest the situation in the [separatist] republics. We support the territorial integrity of Georgia. We will take decisions that will not negatively affect the interests of people living in these territories.[51]

Putin's statement outlined three sets of Russian objectives that still apply: first, Moscow bases its policies toward Abkhazia on its own security interests, particularly in the North Caucasus. Therefore, the non-resumption of conflict in Abkhazia remained a primary objective. In this light, the renewal of economic ties with Abkhazia, by easing the living conditions of its population, is also seen as a guarantee of stability in the

---

[51] RosBusinessConsulting Information Agency, December 18, 2003, http://top.rbc.ru/arc.shtml?2003/12/18.

region. Second, Russia continues to support officially Georgia's territorial integrity, guaranteeing that Moscow will play the key role in brokering a Georgian–Abkhazian dialogue and, should there be a settlement, that Russia will be its main guarantor. Third, Russia does not see a contradiction between its support for the principle of Georgia's territorial integrity and Russia's increasing economic engagement and political involvement with the de facto authorities in Abkhazia.

In addition to political and economic motivations, geopolitics play a key role in providing a strategic rationale for Russia's policy. Concern over the growing U.S. and later European engagement in the South Caucasus rose during Putin's term in office. While he himself refrained from publicly linking Russia's policy on Abkhazia with broader geopolitical preoccupations, the Russian political elite, including parliamentarians as well as security and military officials, increasingly viewed Abkhazia as a sort of "buffer" zone between Russia and an increasingly Western-oriented Georgia.[52] Moreover, against the backdrop of deteriorating Georgian–Russian relations, Abkhazia and South Ossetia were seen as potential allies, places where Russia did not have to face a challenge from Europe and the United States.

WESTERN MILITARY ASSISTANCE

Russia's geopolitical worries grew with the appearance of U.S. military trainers in Georgia. Reacting to the deteriorating situation in Georgian–Russian relations, and with growing concerns that al-Qaeda would find a new refuge in the Pankisi region, the United States pledged direct military support to the Georgian army. The deployment of U.S. military instructors in Georgia under the Georgia Train and Equip Program

---

[52] An adviser to the Russian State Duma Committee on Security, G.K. Kolbaya, writes: "Geopolitical reality is such that Georgia, which enjoys the support of the international community, conducts a consistently anti-Russian policy… under these difficult circumstances Russia has few opportunities to influence the situation inside Georgia. Therefore the lack of Georgian control over Abkhazia is a great benefit…Abkhazia already plays the role of a buffer zone dividing Russia from a hostile Georgia demonstrated by the elimination of Georgian–Chechen paramilitaries in the Kodori Gorge. Strengthening of such role for Abkhazia is in the interests of Russia." See *Bezopasnost Rossii: Abkhazskii Rubezh* in G. N. Osipov, ed., *Reforming Russia: Realities and Prospects,* http://www.duma.gov.ru/search/kmpage/80200016/arc3/public/92.html.

(GTEP), with the aim of training over 2,000 Georgian servicemen at a cost of $64 million, stirred angry reactions among a variety of Russia's nationalist forces and among Russian *realpolitik* foreign policy experts.[53] GTEP was perceived as a direct threat to Russia, a symbol of declining Russian influence in the Caucasus, and by some even as a first step toward Western intervention in Chechnya.

Putin, who had recently accepted the establishment of U.S. military bases in Central Asia, found himself again attempting to moderate these reactions. He wanted to avoid an intemperate response that might threaten Russia's post-9/11 "anti-terrorist" coalition with the United States. During his visit to Kazakhstan, Putin issued statement, saying that GTEP "is no tragedy and it cannot be...Why should [U.S. forces] be in Central Asia and not in Georgia?" He added, "Every country, in particular Georgia, has the right to act to protect its security. Russia recognizes that right."[54]

While geopolitical concerns dominated Russian reactions to GTEP, a more legitimate concern was raised about its potential impact on the military balance between Georgia and its separatist regions. Despite explicit assurances from the U.S. and Georgian leaderships, no one could guarantee that with the Abkhazia political process in a deadlock, increased Georgian confidence and military strength would not encourage new attempts at a military solution. In March 2002, Abkhazia's President Ardzinba urged the United States and other Western states to recognize that providing military assistance to Georgia could lead to an escalation of the conflict with unpredictable consequences. On April 11, 2003, the Russian State Duma approved (by a vote of 351 to 1) a resolution condemning the Status of Forces Agreement between United States and Georgia, expressing concern that U.S.-trained troops might be used in future military operations against Abkhazia.

The Kremlin, however, continued to stress that U.S. military assistance to Georgia would not undermine Russia's relations with Washington. Although the Bush administration rejected any claim by Moscow to a veto over GTEP, it reported that it had informed the Russian government in advance about the program, and the situation in the South

---

[53] At the time the adherents of a Russian *realpolitik* prevailed over other schools of thought and received unrestricted access to the state-controlled media and press.

[54] "Putin: U.S. Deployment 'No Tragedy,'" *CNN News,* March 1, 2002, http://www.cnn.com/2002/WORLD/europe/03/01/georgia.putin/.

Caucasus was placed on the agenda of the Bush–Putin Moscow summit in May 2002. At this summit, the two presidents ritually reaffirmed their commitment to preserving Georgia's territorial integrity and their readiness to cooperate in promoting a settlement of the Georgian–Abkhazian conflict. Not surprisingly, this expression of a common interest in the stability of the South Caucasus did not lead to a common approach to the conflict. Clearly neither the United States nor Russia considered the Georgian–Abkhazian conflict crucial to their bilateral relationship.

DISPUTES CONCERNING PEACEKEEPING FORCES

Growing tensions in Georgian–Russian relations following the Pankisi and Kodori episodes prompted new disagreements over the extension of the Russian peacekeeping mandate in Abkhazia. In October 2002, the Georgian Parliament adopted a resolution calling for the withdrawal of Russian peacekeeping forces. Georgia, however, soon learned after consultations with the UN and the Group of Friends of the Secretary-General that it could not realistically expect an international force to replace Russian peacekeepers, particularly when after September 11 few foreign troops were available.[55] Shevardnadze regularly complained that the existing peacekeeping operation was not helping to bring about the resolution of the conflict, but was repeatedly discouraged by Western governments and international security institutions from seeking unilaterally to change the post-1994 status quo regarding the CIS peacekeeping operation.[56] Moreover, the UN even stated that the withdrawal of the CISPKF would be followed by the withdrawal of its own observers.[57]

---

[55] In January 2002, Shevardnadze stated in an interview to Georgian radio that after the terrorist attacks of September 11, all countries who take part in the settlement of the conflict in Abkhazia, including the United States, Russia, Germany, France, and the United Kingdom consider any demands regarding withdrawal of Russia peacekeeping troops from Abkhazia to be unjustifiable. See http://www.sakartvelo.info.

[56] On February 3, 2003, President Eduard Shevardnadze had to admit that "the Russian peacekeepers fail to cope with their duties and, regrettably the UN Security Council does not pay enough attention to this fact." See http://www.una.org.ge.

[57] The UN Security Council resolution on January 30 which has extended the mandate of the UN observers in the conflict zone, states that the decision on extension of the mandate shall be reconsidered if the decision regarding the

Thus, each semi-annual extension of the CISPKF mandate now seriously agitated Georgian–Russian relations. Russia complained that its peacekeeping troops were suspended in a legal vacuum. When the mandate expired in both December 2001 and December 2002, the Georgian side took weeks or even months to accept its extension. While Georgia was struggling to change the mandate, the Abkhazian side was determined to keep it unchanged and even threatened to reject any decisions taken without its agreement. The presence of CIS (Russian) peacekeepers remained essential for the stability of Abkhazia's de facto statehood. The mandate of the CISPKF imposed no pressure on the Abkhazian side to accept a large-scale return of Georgian IDPs, which would change both the demographic and the political balance within the country. For all these reasons, the Abkhazian authorities stressed that a change of the status quo would have severe consequences and declared that withdrawal of the peacekeeping force would inevitably lead to a resumption of the conflict.[58]

Russia has never explicitly opposed Georgia's appeals to the international community regarding the CISPKF, but neither has it ever indicated that it would seriously consider withdrawing its peacekeeping forces or accept their internationalization.[59] Such a move would weaken

---

CIS Peacekeepers' mandate could not be made before February 15, 2003. See "Abkhazia Situation Fragile," http://una.org.ge.

[58] In December 2001, the Foreign Minister of Abkhazia, Sergei Shamba, insisted on the extension of the mandate and emphasized that the Abkhazian side opposed a change of format and internationalization of the peacekeeping operation. See "Abkhazia prosit prodlit' mandat rossiiskikh mirotvortsev," http://www. gazeta.ru. In December 2002, the Abkhazian Ministry of Defense warned that if Russian peacekeepers were to leave Abkhazia, Abkhazian forces would advance to the Inguri River (statement by Gari Kubalba, deputy defense minister of Abkhazia). In December 2003, the prime minister of Abkhazia, Raul Khadzhinba, stated that there was no alternative to the Russian PKF and that it should remain in the zone of conflict until full normalization of relations between Georgia and Abkhazia. See http://www. kavkaz.memo.ru/newstext/news/id/619609.

[59] Although in July 2003, the Russian ambassador to Georgia, Vladimir Chkhikvishvili, stated in an interview that "Russia is ready to withdraw its forces at the first request from either side, and that a plan for such withdrawal has been already prepared." See "Abkhazskii tupik," *Vremia Novostei,* July 27, 2003.

Russia's geopolitical position and would be feared as encouraging NATO's involvement in the region, although NATO has never indicated any readiness to replace CIS peacekeeping forces. Moreover, Russia believes that the presence of its peacekeeping force in the zone of the Georgian–Abkhazian conflict serves its own security.[60] Finally, even those Russian analysts who were prepared to consider alternative options for maintaining peace in the region, such as Alexander Nikitin, the head of Center for Political and International Studies, argued that realistically Russia would remain the only provider of peacekeeping forces in the Abkhazian conflict zone for the foreseeable future. There was, indeed, no willingness among UN members to establish a separate a peacekeeping force under UN auspices and there were few prospects that the OSCE or, even more improbably, an ad hoc regional effort might have provided an alternative to the Russian operation.[61]

THE NEW ORGANIZATIONAL PATTERN IN RUSSIAN POLICIES ON ABKHAZIA

Under the first Putin government, Russia's policy toward the CIS in general and Abkhazia in particular became more coherent than under Yeltsin. With the re-centralization of executive power in Russia, the Duma's role in influencing policy on Abkhazia diminished. Responsibility shifted back to Russia's security and military establishment, supported by a more prominent role for the Foreign Ministry.

The Russian political and military leaderships shared a common concern over the impact of the Georgian–Abkhazian conflict on Russian security, particularly in the North Caucasus and Chechnya. Because security issues dominated the Georgian–Russian agenda under Putin, particularly during his second term, Minister of Defense Sergei Ivanov was one

---

[60] In June 2004, Deputy Chairman of the State Duma Defense Committee Gennady Gudkov stated that "Russian PKF has guaranteed peace in the conflict area over the past ten years at a price of its ninety-seven soldiers killed there. The fact that there is peace [in the zone of conflict] is due to Russian forces, and this peace also means peace in Russia because any new war in Abkhazia would lead to instability inside Russia itself," http://www.kavkaz.memo.ru/newstext/news/id/677572.html.

[61] See "Vtiagivaniie Rossii v voiennoie resheniie Abkhazskoy problemy ostaiotsia naibolee veroiatnym," http://www.abkhezati.ru/pages/3/315.html.

of the most frequent spokesmen on Russia's policies toward Georgia. Putin gave full support to the Russian military when they applied pressure on Georgia during the Pankisi and Kodori crises. As noted earlier, he even threatened to use military force preemptively against Chechen militants in Pankisi.

Yet, the Russian military no longer had the same degree of autonomy to act against Georgia or in Abkhazia as they had during and immediately after the Abkhazian war in the Yeltsin era. At times they had to accept and implement decisions with which they clearly disagreed, such as the removal of troops and weapons from the Gudauta military base in Abkhazia in July 2001 under the OSCE Istanbul agreements. Similarly, the military was compelled to mute its response to U.S. military cooperation with Georgia. For example, on July 11, 2003, after the Georgian government permitted U.S. AWACS aircraft to fly over Georgian territory, sparking sharp criticism in Russia, the Russian Ministry of Defense felt it necessary to deny claims that it intended to respond by deploying an S-300 air defense system in Abkhazia.[62]

That said, while the Russian military can no longer act independently, its shadow in Abkhazia is long. More than 1,700 Russian troops serve in the area as members of the CISPKF and as guards for the Gudauta military base. Many military commanders have acquired property and developed close personal ties with the local authorities. In June 2004, the former deputy commander of the Trans-Baikal Military District, General Anatoly Zaitsev, was appointed Abkhazia's deputy defense minister. The Russian military has also reportedly taken part in training Abkhazian forces.

Simultaneously, the role of Russia's Foreign Ministry in the Abkhazian conflict has increased during the Putin era. The Foreign Ministry has emerged as the central pillar for carrying out President Putin's strategic foreign policy decisions and has gained influence over CIS policy. This situation stands in a sharp contrast to the Yeltsin period, when the Foreign Ministry competed for influence with other actors, including economic elites and the Ministry of Defense. In no sphere was this more true than Russian policy in the CIS countries. The Foreign Ministry was more

---

[62] "Russia Not Planning to Deploy Air Defence Missile Systems in Abkhazia—Defence Ministry," *Interfax Military Information Bulletin*, July 15, 2003, http://www.interfax.com.

neutral on the Georgian–Abkhazian conflict than the Ministry of Defense or the economic ministries, because its personnel did not have a similar institutional or personal stake in Abkhazia.

In April 2002, Putin appointed Valery Loschinin, then deputy minister of foreign affairs, as special presidential representative on the Georgian–Abkhazian conflict. The Foreign Ministry, together with the president, played the key role in designing and implementing Russia's initiatives, as well as in coordinating with international institutions such as the UN, the OSCE, and the "Group of Friends." This new organizational pattern produced a more tightly coordinated policy, and it became easier to distinguish between official policy and the initiatives of individuals pursuing their separate interests. No Ministry of Foreign Affairs representative attended the tenth anniversary celebrations of the Abkhazian victory in the 1992–1993 war, although several Russian governors and members of the Duma did.

There is, however, a newly emerging trend that further colors Russian policy. Although still at an early stage, Putin appears interested in increasing Russian cooperation with NATO and other international undertakings such as the Black Sea Naval Cooperation Task Force (BLACK-SEAFOR) initiative, and this appears gradually to be changing attitudes within the Russian military. Moreover, UN observers in the zone of the Georgian–Abkhazian conflict, many of whom are military personnel from NATO countries, report that cooperation between UNOMIG and the CISPKF has been improving.

THE BODEN INITIATIVE

Despite increased coherence in Russian policies toward Abkhazia in the first years of Putin's administration, little progress was achieved in re-establishing a political dialogue between the parties to the conflict. On the contrary, the Kodori crisis in the fall of 2001 led, for all practical purposes, to a suspension of the Georgian–Abkhazian political dialogue and any development toward confidence-building measures under UN auspices. A few months later, in July 2002, the special representative of the secretary-general of the UN (UN SGSR), Dieter Boden, released a discussion paper entitled the "Basic Principles of the Division of Competences between Tbilisi and Sukhumi" (often referred to as the "Boden Document"). Its core premise was that Abkhazia should get the broadest autonomy and even recognition as a "sovereign entity" within Georgia compatible with the preservation of Georgia's territorial integrity.[63] Abkhazian authorities, however, refused to negotiate based on any document that did not contain a path to their independence. Russia had little enthusiasm for the Boden Document and only accepted it after sustained diplomatic efforts from the UN and the Western members of the "Group of Friends."[64] Its attitude can largely be explained by the burden the Russians would have had for selling it to the Abkhazian side.

After the formal endorsement of the document, Moscow stated that it made several attempts to persuade the Abkhazian side to embrace the initiative as a basis for negotiations with the Georgian government. These included high-level meetings with Abkhazian officials.[65] Western diplo-

---

[63] The Russian version of the Boden Document text has been published on http://www.cipdd.org (The Caucasus Institute for Peace, Democracy, and Development). For an analysis of the federal model proposed in this document see Bruno Coppieters, "The Georgian–Abkhaz Conflict," in Bruno Coppieters et al., *Europeanization and Conflict Resolution: Case Studies from the European Periphery* (Ghent: Academia Press, 2004), pp. 203–208; also published in the electronic *Journal on Ethnopolitics and Minority Issues in Europe*, http://www.ecmi.de/jemie/.

[64] Coppieters, "The Georgian–Abkhaz Conflict," pp. 203–208.

[65] On May 25 2002, Russian Foreign Minister, Igor Ivanov, met in Moscow with the Abkhazian de facto Prime-Minister Anri Jergenia and the de facto foreign minister, Sergei Shamba, in order to impress upon the Abkhazian side the need to move forward in the settlement process. See *Report of the Secretary-General on the situation in Abkhazia, Georgia,* July 10, 2002, http://www.un.org/Docs/sc/reports/2002/sgrep02.htm. In June, the Russian president's special representative on the Georgian–Abkhazian conflict, Valery Loschinin, traveled to Sukhumi to meet with representatives of Abkhazia's de facto government. In October 2002, the Russian side offered to facilitate a meeting between de facto Abkhazian Prime Minister, Anri Jergenia, and UN representatives at which the Abkhazian side would be acquainted with the substance and rationale behind the discussion paper. The meeting was scheduled for October 5, but it was cancelled because Mr. Jergenia rejected that paper and the participation in the meeting of the UN SGSR, Heidi Tagliavini, who had replaced Dieter Boden. See *Report of the Secretary-General on the Situation in Abkhazia, Georgia* October 14, 2002, http://www.un.org/Docs/sc/reports/2002/sgrep02.htm. On November 14, 2002, the Russian side again tried to arrange a meeting in Moscow of the Group of Friends and the UN SGSR with Abkhazian side in hopes of exchanging views on the principles underlying the UN discussion paper on division of competences. Again, the meeting was cancelled because of a rejection from the Abkhazian side.

mats and Georgian leaders, however, maintained that Moscow had not tried hard enough. In response, officials from the Russian Ministry of Foreign Affairs argued that Russian leverage was limited. Accepting the Boden Document would be political suicide for any Abkhazian politician. As a result, the Boden initiative, intended to stimulate negotiations, ended up becoming part of the problem rather than a means to move forward.[66] Russia's role in the failure is difficult to assess: if it had, in fact, pressed the Abkhazian side, then the failure suggested that Russia's influence over the Abkhazian side was vastly overestimated by Georgia and the international community. On the other hand, if it really had not made much of an effort, this implied that the Putin government was only interested in a settlement in which it could play the decisive role. It could also be that Russia was not interested in any quick move toward a political settlement for fear of renewed conflict and a destabilization of the North Caucasus or alternatively for fear of losing influence over Georgia and the South Caucasus.

While the UN-led political process was on hold after the Abkhazians refused to consider the Boden Document, Russia accelerated its engagement with Abkhazia. Following the adoption of a new Law on Citizenship by the Russian parliament in April 2002, Russian authorities in the Krasnodar region started to accept Abkhazian applications for Russian citizenship, a step actively encouraged by the Abkhazian authorities. By the end of 2002, over 50,000 Abkhazian residents had received Russian passports or Russian stamps in their old Soviet passports (later these passports were replaced by official Russian passports). On December 25, 2002, Russia reopened a rail link between Sochi and Sukhumi. In response to Georgian protests, Moscow claimed that this was a privately operated railroad over which it had no influence.

On January 28, 2003, during a CIS summit in Kyiv, Putin proposed to Shevardnadze to re-establish rail links between Sochi and Tbilisi via Abkhazia. Shevardnadze agreed to consider the proposal, but only on the condition that it was accompanied by the return of Georgian IDPs to Abkhazia, particularly to the Gali region.[67] Under these circumstances

---

[66] Jonathan Cohen, "Overview of the South Caucasus," presentation to the conference "The South Caucasus—A Challenge for Europe?" Heinrich Boell Foundation, Berlin, May 8–9, 2003.

[67] *Report of the Secretary-General on the Situation in Abkhazia,* Georgia, April 9, 2003, http://www.un.org/Docs/sc/reports/2002/sgrep02.htm.

and without Western support, the Georgian leadership decided to relaunch its diplomacy with Russia. In this new bilateral framework, Abkhazia was not included as an equal partner. It had to defer to the Russian lead and when the presence of its representatives was inconvenient, Moscow excluded them. The new framework was formalized when the Russian and Georgian presidents met in Sochi on March 6–7, 2003. Gennady Gagulia, the prime minister of Abkhazia, was invited for part of the meeting. At this meeting, Georgia and Russia agreed to modernize the Inguri hydropower station, servicing both the Abkhazian and Georgian sides. They also agreed to reopen the rail link between Sochi and Tbilisi (via Abkhazia) in parallel with the return of Georgian IDPs, initially into the Gali region. Three bilateral working groups were established to implement the previous decisions on energy projects, including on the rehabilitation of the Inguri hydroelectric power station; the return of refugees and IDPs; and on the reopening of railways between Sochi and Tbilisi.[68] The working groups were to be formally bilateral, thus underscoring Russia's support for Georgia's territorial integrity. The Abkhazian side, however, was included in the bilateral commissions and the UN representatives were also invited to attend some meetings.

At the Sochi Summit, the Georgian side also agreed to replace the complex and politically charged procedure involving a biannual renewal of the peacekeeping mandate with an indefinite extension or until one side of the conflict withdrew its consent. However, the procedure for terminating the mandate remains ambiguous. Even after one of the parties to the conflict requests it, the final decision must be approved by the CIS Council.

The Sochi meeting was a success for Russian diplomacy. It helped to restart the political dialogue between Abkhazia and Georgia, placed Moscow in the role of key mediator, created a foundation for pursuing Russia's economic interests in both Georgia and Abkhazia, and legitimated Russia's new engagement policy toward Abkhazia. During the ensuing press conference, Putin reiterated that Russian policy was based on "preserving Georgia's territorial integrity, while taking into account

---

[68] *Report of the Secretary-General on the Situation in Abkhazia,* Georgia, April 9, 2003, http://www.un.org/Docs/sc/reports/2002/sgrep02.htm.

the legitimate rights and interests of a multinational Abkhazia."[69] And he underscored that the "implementation of joint economic projects will diminish confrontation, promote the economic development of the region as a whole, and serve the interests of the people living there."

It would be far more difficult to describe the Sochi meeting as a success for Georgian diplomacy. Shevardnadze had agreed to an indefinite extension of the mandate of the Russian peacekeeping forces without receiving additional security guarantees. He had also failed to secure assurances that the return of displaced persons would actually occur.

For the Abkhazian side, the Sochi process was a step back from the previous negotiating format where it had had an equal role. The Sochi framework made Russia not an impartial mediator, but a party to the negotiations representing not only its own interests, but also those of the Abkhazian side, particularly as far as economic projects were concerned. At the same time, Abkhazia preserved a veto over any decisions on IDP return.

While the UN secretary-general officially welcomed the Sochi agreements, many observers and officials saw it as undercutting the Geneva process led by the "Group of Friends."[70] Indeed, the bilateral working groups established in Sochi directly paralleled the three UN commissions (on security issues, IDPs, and economic issues) established in Geneva the week prior to the Sochi meeting. The UN and Russia had competed for years for a leading position in the negotiation process, and the Sochi meeting had given Moscow the edge.

Still, Western diplomats and the Georgian government made a serious effort to link the Russian-led Sochi process to the UN Geneva process. The Abkhazian side, on the contrary, sought to use the Sochi meeting to lobby for a restart of the long dormant security dialogue under the Georgian–Abkhazian Coordinating Council.[71] Russia was also reluctant to

---

[69] President Vladimir Putin, press conference after the Sochi meeting, March 7, 2003.

[70] In his report to the Security Council on the situation in Abkhazia, the UN SGSR stated that, "New proposals by the Group of Friends as well as bilateral agreements between President Putin and President Shevardnadze have given fresh momentum to the efforts to reactivate the peace process." See *Report of the Secretary-General on the situation in Abkhazia*, Georgia, April 9, 2003.

[71] Abkhazia's de facto prime minister, Raul Khadzhinba, noted that the Sochi meeting "had favourably influenced the general atmosphere in Georgian–

link the Sochi process formally with the Geneva process or to engage the "Group of Friends" formally in the Sochi meeting or future meetings under the new format. Russia did agree to involve the UN by inviting representatives of UNOMIG and the Office of the United Nations High Commissioner for Refugees (UNHCR) to take part in the working groups on IDP return.

With Russia taking the lead in promoting economic initiatives and redressing the problem of IDPs, the UN and the Group of Friends were left to deal with security and political issues, including the most difficult one—the unresolved status of Abkhazia. The Abkhazian side continued to refuse to work within the framework of the Boden Document, but a partial revival of the Georgian–Abkhazian dialogue did follow the Sochi meeting. A number of meetings took place under various formats between March 2003 and March 2004.[72] Two meetings between Georgian and Abkhazian representatives were held in Gali under the chairmanship of UN SGSR Heidi Tagliavini. The first one occurred in October 2003 just before the Rose Revolution, and the second in January 2004. According to Abkhazia's foreign minister, Sergei Shamba, the security situation in the Gali region improved after the October meeting only to worsen following Saakashvili's election in January 2004.[73] The UN secretary-general reports, however, do not substantiate this claim. They indicate that security problems continued in October, November, and December. Only by summer had the security situation improved.[74]

Abkhaz settlement and helped to defuse tensions in relations between Tbilisi and Sukhumi. Under these conditions a possibility has emerged to resume meetings of the Georgian-Abkhaz Coordinating Council." See http://www.mid.ru for information about consultations between the Russian presidential envoy for Georgian–Abkhazian conflict, May 7, 2003.

[72] On July 15, after a long disruptive period, a joint Georgian–Abkhazian meeting took place in Sukhumi, chaired by the UN SGSR. The meeting discussed security guarantees against the resumption of conflict. Security guarantees were important for the implementation of economic projects as well as for the return of IDPs. On July 21–22, 2003, a special meeting on security guarantees was convened in Geneva with participation of representatives of the Georgian and Abkhazian sides with the "Group of Friends" and the UN SGSR.

[73] "Predvaritel'nye itogi gruzino-abkhazskoi vstrechi po voprosam bezopasnosti," http://www.kavkaz.memo.ru/news/id/625957.html.

[74] *Report of the Secretary-General on the situation in Abkhazia, Georgia,* July 14, 2004, http://www.un.org/Docs/sc/sgrep04.html.

The new Georgian government had made a significant contribution to this end by conducting a major anti-crime operation in Zugdidi in February 2004 and by withdrawing support for illegal partisan groups operating across the Inguri River and in Kodori.

On the Russian side, high expectations after the Sochi meeting were soon replaced by frustrations summarized by Russian experts as "Georgia's attempts to revise or sabotage the Sochi agreements."[75] Georgia, on the other hand, blamed Russia for the lack of progress on the IDP issue, saying Russian envoys had failed to persuade the Abkhazian authorities to accept Georgian demands on refugee return. Abkhazians insisted that the sides should first register those who had already returned to the Gali district. Moreover, Georgia started to raise new concerns over the railroad project linking Georgia with Abkhazia. The Abkhazians, in turn, blamed Tbilisi for the lack of progress on the issue of rehabilitation of the Inguri power station.

Shevardnadze claimed that during the Sochi meeting he and Putin discussed the creation of a joint Georgian–Abkhazian administration in the Gali district, but according to Russian sources, no decision had been reached. After the meeting, however, the Georgian authorities insisted on the establishment of "temporary transition authorities" under international oversight, first for Gali and then later for other parts of Abkhazia. They also refused to reopen the Tbilisi–Sukhumi–Sochi rail link until the IDPs had returned not only to Gali but to other parts of Abkhazia. As a result of these ongoing disputes over the nature of commitments made at the Sochi meeting, it soon became apparent that the agreements would not serve to relaunch the political dialogue as the UN SGSR had hoped. Instead, the Sochi agreements became a convenient instrument to justify future economic links between Russia and Abkhazia, lending them implied Georgian approval.

President Shevardnadze received a lot of criticism within Georgia for signing the Sochi agreements. After the Rose Revolution, the new Georgian authorities distanced themselves from these agreements and indicated that they did not intend to accept the bilateral format they had created. However, a number of working groups under the Sochi

---

[75] See Alexander Chepurin, "How to Strengthen Stability and Security in the Caucasus," *Journal of Social and Political Studies,* http://www.ca-c.org/online/2004/journal_eng/cac-02/07.cheeng.shtml.

process—particularly the working group on the return of refugees and internally displaced persons—continued to convene in 2004 with the participation of the UN SGSR, the UNHCR, and the commander of CIS peacekeeping forces. On the economic side, Russia began unilaterally to implement many of the projects that it had sought to legitimize through the Sochi process, including the reopened rail link between Sochi and Sukhumi and the expansion of cross-border trade.

ECONOMIC INTERESTS: TRADING IN ISOLATION

Russia's small scale cross-border trade conducted through the Psou border crossing supplies goods for Sukhumi markets as well as income for Abkhazian "shuttle traders." This is the only source of survival for many thousands of Abkhazia's residents. According to Dov Lynch, Abkhazia exists thanks to its favorable economic position on the Black Sea and at the border with Russia.[76]

For most of the 1990s, however, Abkhazia had no particular economic importance for Russia. The economic sanctions applied against Abkhazia by the CIS heads of state in 1996 did not significantly impinge on Russia's economic interests. Throughout 1990s Russia's economic involvement was limited to private individuals, including active or retired military officers and regional officials in the neighboring regions of Russia, who had acquired property in Abkhazia. Some of the latter were engaged in a small-scale cross-border trade, primarily in citrus fruit and other limited agricultural goods. Some Russian enterprises and government agencies that had "corporate" (*vedomstvennye*) resorts in Abkhazia before the war (including the Ministry of Defense and the Ministry of Atomic Energy) leased them from the Abkhazian authorities after the war in order to offer discounted vacations to their employees. Several southern regions in Russia, as noted earlier, had concluded economic cooperation agreements with Abkhazia in the fields of tourism (they also leased resorts) and trade (tobacco, wine products, citrus fruit, nuts, and so on). They also had small timber and construction projects in Abkhazia. The Rostov region, for example, concluded an agreement to use Abkhazia's ship repair facilities. Finally, criminal groups (Russian, Abkhazian, and Georgian) engaged in a wide range of smuggling activities via the territory of Abkhazia. According

---

[76] Lynch, p. 17.

to some studies, Abkhazia was a major route for illegal commerce as well as smuggling of weapons and drugs, although the actual volume of smuggling was arguably no greater than by alternative routes through South Ossetia or through Azerbaijan and Dagestan.[77]

Abkhazia has tried to use the prospect of economic benefits as leverage to generate support among Russian politicians, such as Moscow's Mayor Yuri Luzhkov, various southern governors, and patriotic forces within the State Duma, albeit these elements were already disposed to closer Russian–Abkhazian relations. But, as previously noted, their influence on Russia's Abkhazian policy has dramatically shrunk since Putin moved to rein in the power of oligarchs, regional governors, and parliament. Russia's economic lobbies, however, played an important role during the 2004 presidential elections in Abkhazia.

The Georgian government also sought to use economic interests as a way to gain influence over Moscow's policy toward Abkhazia, but without major success. After the Rose Revolution, the new Saakashvili government officially offered to consider a pipeline that would cross Abkhazia. Abkhazians, for their part, seized on Russia's interest in a reopened rail link, vowing to speed up its construction and to engage Russian workers. Saakashvili also tried negative leverage by threatening to confiscate property that Russian citizens in Abkhazia had acquired without the approval of Georgian authorities. The Georgian government had done this with some Russian property in Ajara after the regime of Aslan Abashidze collapsed. Neither economic carrots nor sticks, however, have had much effect in altering the Russian position.

In recent years, Russia has repeatedly insisted that economic sanctions against Abkhazia are counterproductive and simply generate a siege mentality, self-reliance, and resistance to serious negotiations.[78] Sanctions have not compelled the Abkhazian leadership to soften its demand for independence or enhanced stability and security in the area. Rather, they have left Abkhazia economically impoverished, isolated, and criminalized.

---

[77] Alexander Kukhianidze, *Organized Crime and Smuggling through Abkhazia and its Impact on Georgian-Abkhazian Conflict Resolution* (Tbilisi: Transnational Crime and Corruption Center, American University, Georgia Office, 2003).

[78] It is a view shared by some outside observers. See Cohen, "Overview of the South Caucasus."

Under Shevardnadze, Georgia refused to discuss the removal of
sanctions against Abkhazia, including the opening of railroads, without
achieving progress on political issues including IDP return. In July 2003,
Shevardnadze sent a public letter to Putin criticizing Moscow for ignoring the 1996 CIS commitment "forbid[ding] any unilateral economic
and political contacts with the Abkhazian de facto authorities without
agreement from the Georgian side."[79] After the Rose Revolution, however, initially Moscow was more hopeful. In a January 2004 interview
with *Rossiiskaia Gazeta*, Russia's presidential envoy to the Georgian–
Abkhazian conflict, Valery Loschinin, suggested that lifting economic
sanctions would "create favorable conditions for conflict resolution"
and then noted that Saakashvili had made statements saying that Tbilisi
would not seek to isolate Abkhazia.[80] These developments, Loschinin
said, encouraged the hope that Georgia's new government was ready
to reconsider the sanctions question. According to Loschinin, a mutual
understanding was reached in Sochi in March 2003 on lifting the ban
on state, economic, and other ties with Abkhazia. Later, however, the
Georgian leadership, he said, balked.[81]

There is little doubt that the 1996 sanctions against Abkhazia now
exist only on paper. Since the late 1990s, various levels of the Russian
government have allowed the travel limitations on tourism and the trade
embargo to erode. From 2000 to 2003, Russia's main contribution to
the Abkhazian economy came not from trade, but in the number of
Russian tourists traveling to Abkhazian resorts unimpeded by the Russian
authorities. The number reached 300,000 in summer 2003.[82] Saakashvili

---

[79] http://www.globalsecurity.org/military/library/news/2003/07/mil-
030721-rfel-121604.htm.
[80] "Russia Wants to Lift Sanctions on Abkhazia," http://www.civil.ge/eng/arti-
cle.php?id=6138.
[81] Interview in *Rossiiskaya Gazeta*, January 29, 2005, http://www.rg.ru/2004/
01/29/loshinin.html. No agreement was reached with the new authorities in
Tbilisi.
[82] In 2003, 300,000 tourists went to Abkhazia and, although these figures are far
from the estimated 3 million annual tourists before the war and much of the
money goes back to Russia (most hotels are owned by Russians), this created a
few seasonal jobs. See the European Commission's report, "Humanitarian Aid
for the Most Vulnerable People of Georgia," http://europa.eu.int/comm/
echo/pdf_files/ decisions/2004/dec_georgia_01000_en.pdf.

has strongly opposed the strengthening of these economic links between Russia and Abkhazia. In August 2004, he warned Russian tourists against traveling to Abkhazia and threatened to open fire on Russian ships bringing tourists form Sochi to Sukhumi.[83] His threat sparked a very public crisis in Georgian–Russian relations, which had a major impact on the perception of President Saakashvili among the Russian public and political elites. While the Russian Foreign Ministry vowed to protect its citizens (even though it did not specifically note that the majority of Abkhazian residents are also citizens of Russia), the flow of Russian tourists continued unabated throughout the summer.

Following the summer incidents, Saakashvili took a firm position against the lifting of sanctions. In September 2004, the CIS summit in Astana reaffirmed the need to implement all CIS decisions on Abkhazia, including the 1996 decision not to engage in any economic or political relations with the breakaway republic. At the time, Saakashvili publicly challenged President Putin at the press conference to guarantee that Russia would adhere to these decisions, not least because the rail link between Sochi and Sukhumi had been opened just one week before the CIS summit.[84]

Despite trade sanctions, by early 2004, the share of imports in the overall external trade turnover of Abkhazia stood at 75 percent, most of them from Russia.[85] Russia, however, is not Abkhazia's only trade partner. In the late 1990s, Russia started to lose its dominant trade position to Turkey, whose ships regularly enter Abkhazian ports. Turkey now ranks first among importers of Abkhazian timber, although Russia remains the primary market for Abkhazian agricultural products. According to some estimates, trade in timber and scrap metals accounts for the major part of Abkhazian export revenue, with timber accounting for 80 percent of government revenues.[86]

---

[83] "Georgian President Promises to Sink Russian Ships," *The Russia Journal,* August 4, 2004, http://www.russiajournal.com/news/cnews-article.shtml? nd=44913.

[84] Giorgi Sepashvili, "CIS Summit Reveals Rift in Russo–Georgian Relations," http://www.civil.ge/eng/print.php?id=7852.

[85] "Gosudarstvennyi tamozhennyi komitet Respubliki Abkhazia podvel itogi svoey raboty za pervoie polugodiie," July 15, 2004, http://www.kavkaz. memo.ru/newstext/news/id/684112.html.

[86] Kukhianidze, p. 5.

Under Putin, Abkhazia's economic significance has risen, largely because economics has become central to Russia's strategy throughout the CIS region. From this perspective, Russia has the following economic interests in Abkhazia: first, the hope of re-establishing the railway transit of Russian goods through Abkhazia to Armenia, Iran, Turkey, and to Georgia itself; second, exploring options for building an oil pipeline through Abkhazia to join the Baku–Tbilisi–Ceyhan (BTC) Pipeline, thus bypassing the Bosporus straits; third, rehabilitating the Inguri hydropower station and exporting its excess electricity to Russia, some of which already goes to Russia's southern regions; fourth, using the Abkhazian port of Sukhumi for Black Sea shipping (after the collapse of the Soviet Union, Russia retained only Novorossiisk as a major port on the Black Sea); and, fifth, expanding the Black Sea resort area for Russian investment. In the latter case, however, the Abkhazian authorities have not permitted large-scale privatization thus far, and foreigners cannot legally acquire property. Most Russian enterprises in Abkhazia lease resorts, but this prevents major investment in infrastructure.

Abkhazia's unresolved political status and uncertainty over property rights present major obstacles to the pursuit of these economic interests. While Moscow in theory could reach agreements with either the Abkhazian or the Georgian authorities allowing many projects to go forward, most of them require the involvement of both Georgia and Abkhazia to be feasible.

In the longer run, however, the question of reopening the railway through Abkhazia will have to be addressed. The railroad is essential in reducing the price of Russian exports and preserving Russia's economic interests in Armenia, a country still isolated by the Azerbaijani–Turkish blockade. It could also lower the costs of supplying Russian troops stationed in Armenia. Moreover, Russian companies are interested in taking part in the privatization of both the Georgian and Abkhazian railways.[87] The Abkhazians have considered inviting Russian railroad troops to assist in restoring the railroad, and this has caused concern on the Georgian side, which is not keen to see more Russian troops of any kind in the zone of conflict.[88] The Armenian government has indicated a readiness

[87] Interview with Vladimir Yakunin, vice president of "Russian Railroads" in "OAO 'RZHD,' hochet privatizirovat zheleznie dorogi Gruzii," June 16, 2004, http://www.kavkaz.memo.ru/newstext/news/id/675512.html.

[88] "Abkhazia predlozhila Rossiyskim voiskam vosstanovit' zheleznuiu dorogu," Interfax, December 22, 2003.

to finance the project and has pointed out its advantages to the Georgians. Armenia's Transport Minister Andranik Manukyan noted that the current rail transport route for Georgian cargo into Russia goes through the territory of Azerbaijan and is 700 kilometers longer than the Abkhazia route. According to Duma Deputy Alexander Gustov, Georgia loses nearly $300 million annually because this rail connection is missing.[89]

Such economic arguments have not persuaded Tbilisi to support the project. Rather, it views the rail link as a key bargaining chip with Moscow in its efforts to secure the return of Georgian IDPs. Initially, during Saakashvili's February 2004 visit to Moscow, it appeared that the Georgian authorities might be willing to reopen the railway as a confidence-building measure rather than as a precondition for a settlement. Within weeks, however, the Georgian president returned to his previous position. Still later, the Georgians tried to link the prospects of the railway project to overall progress in defining the status of Abkhazia.

By mid-2004, Russia's enthusiasm for the rail project had waned.[90] So had that of the Abkhazian side in the wake of escalating tensions growing out of the renewed confrontation between Georgian interior troops and South Ossetian forces in early summer 2004. Instead, on September 10, 2004, Russia and Abkhazia reopened the rail link between Sochi and Sukhumi. This rail connection plays a key role in economic ties and tourism, and ultimately represents a vehicle for greater integration between Abkhazia and Russia. Saakashvili, as well as members of the international community, criticized this action, saying it was a violation of Russia's commitment to preserving Georgia's territorial integrity. But from a humanitarian point-of-view, the rail link is badly needed by the residents of Abkhazia who have been living in isolation for over a decade. Georgia's refusal to engage in serious negotiations on the extended trans-Caucasus rail link has been a lost opportunity to demonstrate its humani-

---

[89] "Gruzziia ne schitaiet tselesoobraznym peredachu abkhazskogo uchastka Zakavkazskoy zheleznoy dorogi v kontsessiiu Armenii," May 29, 2004, http://www.kavkaz.memo.ru/newstext/news/id/669692.html.

[90] One well-known Russian expert, Sergei Karaganov, wrote, "Georgia de facto rejected the idea of rebuilding a railroad through Abkhazia, Georgia, and Armenia, which could have started to rebuild single economic space within Georgia." See Sergei Karaganov, "Proshchanie s Gruziei?" *Rossyiskaia Gazeta*, August 20, 2004.

tarian credentials in dealing with Abkhazia. This means that Georgia has failed to use the railway project as a tool for conflict resolution.

Russia's economic links with Abkhazia served not only as a carrot for Sukhumi, but also as a stick during Abkhazia's disputed presidential elections at the end of 2004. Moscow pushed for a rerun of the first election in September, and used its economic leverage—closing its border to Abkhazian traders and suspending transportation links—to pressure the original victor, Sergei Bagapsh, to accept a Moscow-brokered compromise diluting his power. Despite this move, after his second electoral victory in January 2005, Bagapsh went to Moscow and reaffirmed his intension to develop even closer cooperation with Russia in the economic field. He called for greater Russian investment, the development of tourism, and a closer coordination of Abkhazian economic legislation with that of Russia. His initiatives indicate that Russia will remain Abkhazia's key economic partner for the foreseeable future.

Still, economic links between Russia and Abkhazia will remain limited. The lack of political and economic guarantees for Russian investment means that Abkhazia is unlikely to attract the kind of Russian investment that Georgia did with its privatization tenders at the end of 2004. Indeed, as the presence of large Russian businesses in Georgia grows, the balance of economic interests among the Russian elite may well begin to change. If the Georgian economy improves, the Russian business community may have less interest in maintaining its monopoly over the Abkhazian economy. However, those economic interests that are already heavily invested in Abkhazia—regional elites and small-scale specialized traders—still have the ability to influence Kremlin policy, as was demonstrated by the high-level Russian involvement in the Abkhazian elections, discussed below.

In sum, despite potentially important Russian economic interests in Abkhazia, these interests are not likely to be realized as long as the underlying conflict between Georgia and Abkhazia goes unresolved. Russian interests remain limited, highly personalized, and concentrated on the Sochi region and parts of the North Caucasus. As such, they do not play a decisive role in shaping the Moscow's approach to the conflict at the moment. In the future, however, Abkhazia—regardless of its status—is likely to figure in Russia's broader economic calculations. Russia will remain a key economic partner for Abkhazia and guarantor of its economic survival.

ABKHAZIA IN RUSSIAN DOMESTIC POLITICS

Unlike economic factors, at least six domestic political considerations have had a clear role in shaping Russia's policy toward Abkhazia and the Georgian–Abkhazian conflict in general. First, Russian nationalist and patriotic forces have made the "protection of Abkhazia" one of their political priorities. Throughout the past ten years, members of the Russian State Duma have been the strongest voice on Abkhazia. Vladimir Zhirinovsky's Liberal Democratic Party and, more recently, the Rodina ("Motherland") Party have been active supporters of Abkhazian independence and the most frequent visitors to the region. Zhirinovsky rushed there in August 2004, at the time Saakashvili was threatening to use force to prevent Russian tourists from traveling to Abkhazia, and declared that Abkhazia would never be part of Georgia. Dmitri Rogozin, Rodina Party leader and chair of the Duma's International Affairs Commission, has publicly announced that his faction will promote full international recognition of Abkhazia.[91] He has also actively supported the campaign to register Abkhazian residents as Russian citizens and to secure Russian pensions for them. In addition, in May 2004, the Communist faction in the Russian State Duma weighed in with a statement calling on President Putin to demonstrate "clear and unambiguous support for Russian citizens residing in Abkhazia, including strict security guarantees."

Russian political parties have also used the Abkhazian issue as a rallying cause in their electoral campaigns, especially once many Abkhazian residents obtained Russian citizenship. The Russian People's *(Narodnaia)* Party, for example, included the leader of the Abkhazian People's Party—a Russian citizen—on its party list in the 2003 Duma elections. As a result, it received 21 percent of the votes cast Abkhazia, although elsewhere in the country it failed to pass the 5 percent level necessary for representation in the parliament.

Statements by individual Russian parliamentarians often cause an angry response from the Georgian elite and public. In contrast, official statements adopted by the State Duma as a rule reject radical proposals. In March 2002, for example, in reaction to the U.S. military presence in Georgia, some deputies proposed recognizing the sovereignty of Abk-

---

[91] "Dmitrii Rogozin: fraktsiia 'Rodina' budet sodeistvovat' mezhdunarodnomu priznaniiu Abkhazii," http://www.kavkaz.memo.ru/newstext/news/id/674872.html.

hazia, but the measure did not carry a majority. In May 2004, Konstantin Kosachev, the chairman of the Duma's International Affairs Committee, reaffirmed Russia's commitment to Georgia's territorial integrity and called on Georgia to use peaceful means in resolving the conflicts with Abkhazia and South Ossetia.

Second, Abkhazia's repeated appeals for associate status within Russia have figured in Russia's internal politics. With few prospects of international recognition and the Georgian government insisting on reunification "by any means," the Abkhazian elite sees some form of Russian protectorate as the main guarantee of its continued independence.[92] Abkhazian commentators often compare the Russian–Abkhazian relationship to that between the United States and Taiwan. Such association does not mean that Abkhazia (unlike South Ossetia) wants to join the Russian Federation as a constituent part. Abkhazia's version of association, as explained by Abkhazia's former foreign minister, Igor Akhba, only involves, as far as competences related to security are concerned, "closer cooperation in security and defense policy, border issues, customs union, and common currency."[93]

Zhirinovsky, for one, has responded positively by proposing that Abkhazia be allowed to join the Russian–Belarusian Union, theoretically a confederation preserving each country's sovereignty. But it is far from clear that this union will ever become a reality. In any event, Putin is reluctant to open the option of an associated relationship for fear that it will lead to similar demands from other de facto states, such as South Ossetia and Transnistria. At home, it would complicate his strenuous efforts to harmonize relations between the center and the regions by eliminating "special" arrangements. On March 11, 2005, the State Duma voted down a resolution, introduced by the Rodina faction, proposing associate membership in the CIS for "breakaway regions." Although the proposal did not pass, the vote was significant because it was the first time that such a resolution was actually put to a vote. As a result, so far Abkhazia's appeal has gone unanswered by Russia's leadership.

---

[92] The vice president of Abkhazia, Valery Arshba, stated, "We want to be Russia's protectorate as in 1810 so that it could help to preserve the [ethnic rights] of the Abkhaz people and prevent war." See *Interfax*, June 15, 2004, http://www.interfax.com.

[93] "Yuri Luzhkov pribyl v Abkhaziiu," August 5, 2004, *RosBusinessConsulting*, http://top.rbc.ru/index.shtml?/news/daythemes/2004/08/05/05151418_bod.shtml.

A third way that the Abkhazian problem intrudes into Russian domestic politics stems from the citizenship issue. From 1991 to 2001, any holder of a Soviet passport was almost automatically granted Russian citizenship under Russian law. But new legislation passed in October 2001 made the process far more complicated, despite heated objections from Communist Party deputies who lobbied to provide blanket citizenship for the residents of the unrecognized republics, particularly Abkhazia. Putin refused, emphasizing that Russia had no intention of interfering in others' conflicts or of taking measures that violated the sovereignty of a neighboring country.[94]

However, when the new legislation produced a wave of applications for citizenship from Abkhazians, most of whom had refused to apply for Georgian passports and therefore could no longer travel internationally, the Russians responded sympathetically.[95] The campaign was led by the Congress of Russian Communities of Compatriots in Abkhazia and the Society of Abkhazian Cossacks, the latter closely linked with Cossack organizations in the Krasnodar region of Russia. By August 2004, Abkhazia's de facto Vice President Valery Arshba claimed that 170,000 of 320,000 Abkhazian residents had become Russian citizens and that 70,000 more were awaiting approval. Whatever the precise number, it seemed likely that an absolute majority of Abkhazian residents had become Russian citizens.[96]

---

[94] "Zakon o grazhdanstve: uzhestocheniie pravil na fone voiny v Abkhazii," October 18, 2001, http://www.kavkaz.memo.ru/news/id/424551.html.

[95] Abkhazian politicians had appealed to the UN to issue them temporary UN travel documents (modeled on similar documents issued in Kosovo and East Timor). According to Tsiza Gumba, a member of the Abkhazian parliament, who made this proposal to the UN SGSR, the issuing of such documents could have prevented mass rush of applications for the Russian citizenship. See "OON mozhet vydat' grazhdanam Abkhazii vremennye dokumenty," January 16, 2004, http://www.kavkaz.memo.ru/newstext/news/id/625275.html. But the UN could not respond favorably to this request. The formal status of Kosovo and East Timor is very different than the one of Abkhazia. Doubtless many of the applicants for Russian citizenship were also motivated by a practical economic consideration: they would then be entitled to Russian pensions, which are considerably higher than those for Georgian citizens or Abkhazian residents.

[96] C.J. Chivers, "The Threat of Civil War is Turning the Abkhaz into Russians," *New York Times,* August 15, 2004 (http://www.sakartvelo.ru, in Russian translation).

The rush to extend citizenship to Abkhazian residents stirred not only Georgian anger, but also critical voices among Russian observers. In August 2004, when tensions between the new Georgian government and South Ossetia put Georgia and its separatist conflicts back on the front pages of Russian daily newspapers, Valentin Fedorov, the deputy director of the Institute of Europe, criticized Moscow for pursuing a policy toward Georgia that it would not have tolerated if applied to its own citizens. What would be Russia's attitude, he asked, if Japan were to issue passports to the majority of residents of the Kuril Islands, territory over which Tokyo refuses to recognize Russian sovereignty?[97] The new Georgian president, however, seems ready to reduce the urgency of the citizenship issue. He is known to be in favor of allowing dual citizenship in some cases, a step that might create a way around the current impasse.

Fourth, the tendency of Russian politicians, pundits, and media to frame the Abkhazian issue in terms of greater geopolitical stakes colors the domestic context of policy. The idea that Russia is losing influence in the Caucasus and being replaced by the United States and NATO—and that Georgia plays an important role in this trend—has become a matter of almost universal consensus across the entire Russian political elite. This increases the significance of unrecognized entities like Abkhazia that have few places to turn other than Russia. Zhirinovsky is not exceptional when he argues that, "For us Abkhazia is interesting because it wants to be with us," and then adds, "The closer Georgia comes to NATO membership, the faster Abkhazia becomes a part of Russia."[98] Stanislav Belkovsky, the president of the Institute for National Strategy, describes these "unrecognized states" as a Russian salient in the Caucasus, without which "Russia would have been pushed out of the Caucasus a long time ago."[99] Even more moderate voices often view Abkhazia as a "buffer state" between Russia and a potentially Western-dominated Georgia.[100]

---

[97] "Vmesto reshenya problem Gruzii Rossiya dolzhna ne dopustit' sobstvennogo raspada," August 11, 2004, http://www.sakartvelo.info.

[98] "Chem bystree Gruziia budet v NATO, tem bystree Abkhazia—v Rossii," http://www.sakartvelo.info/result_ar.php?key=58420.

[99] Radio Russia "Are We Going to See War in Georgia?" August 12, 2004.

[100] Karaganov, "Proshchanie s Gruziei?" Karaganov writes: "Russia will need buffer states if Georgia will continue the current policy which is leading it toward self-destruction." At the same time, growing democratic forces within Abkhazia resent the notion that they must reject Western values in order to obtain Russian support.

Abkhazian officials often use geopolitical arguments in order to obtain concessions from Moscow.

There are countervailing views within the Russian elite, and only a limited circle of experts who closely follow developments in Georgia and Abkhazia are deeply impassioned on the issue.[101] These people, however, tend to be anti-Georgian or, as in the case of politicians like Dmitri Rogozin and Konstantin Zatulin, strong nationalists who are harshly protective of the Russian diaspora anywhere.

The fifth intersection between Abkhazia and Russia's domestic politics concerns the role of regional political elites. A number of local leaders have sought to raise their political status by fashioning closer ties with Abkhazia. Much of this activity occurred in the mid-1990s, when, as noted earlier, several regions signed trade and cooperation agreements with Abkhazia. Following Putin's clampdown on the regional governors, however, they lost much of their autonomy in conducting their own separate foreign policies. As a result, few of them publicly flouted their support for Abkhazia any longer. Those who did included the governor of Krasnodar region, Alexander Tkachev, and Moscow's Mayor Yuri Luzhkov. Moscow continues to make (small) investments in Abkhazia. It has also provided humanitarian assistance, although this remains largely symbolic.

In contrast, the Krasnodar region bordering Abkhazia has maintained relatively intense economic and political ties, including cross-border trade and the importation of electricity. Krasnodar authorities have even made ostentatious political gestures, such as organizing a parade of 500 Cossacks in Sukhumi on May 24, 2004.

---

[101] For example, writing at the time of the summer 2004 on tensions between Moscow and Tbilisi, Vladislav Inozemtsev, from the Center for Post-Industrial Societies accuses Russia of taking sides in Georgia's internal conflict and sees its policy of "managed instability" in Abkhazia and South Ossetia as a mistake. Russia, he says, should instead provide guarantees for a federal treaty between Tbilisi and the separatist regions. See Vladislav Inozemtsev, "Saakashvili sleduiet zakliuchit' federativnyi dogovor s miatezhnymi liderami—pri garantiiah so storony Rossii," *Nezavisimaya Gazeta*, August 16, 2004. Boris Volkhonsky, another critic, condemns Russian elites for playing the nationalist card, which has created black holes for smuggling, lent tacit support to mercenaries, and used patriotic slogans vis-à-vis Georgia and by all these actions only propelled Russia into international isolation. See Boris Volkhonsky, "Tsena voprosa: tonal'nost zaiavlenii razdaiuschihsia v Moskve vyzyvaiet nedoumeniie," *Kommersant*, August 20, 2004.

Abkhazians also maintain friendly relations with a number of ethnically related peoples residing in the North Caucasus, particularly the Adygheans. In 1996, the Republic of Adyghea and Abkhazia signed a cooperation agreement.[102] Russian authorities, however, do not encourage these political links between Abkhazians and Adygheans, or with the Abkhazian diaspora in Turkey and other parts of Middle East, fearing further "imported" Islamization of North Caucasus communities through links with diasporas. While Abkhazia seeks closer ties with Russia, the Russian government worries that the national-territorial autonomy of ethnic republics in the North Caucasus has gone too far, creating concern over the fate of the Russian population in these republics. Various proposals have surfaced, some entailing the abolition of ethnic-territorial divisions within Russia's federal system altogether. Movement in this direction would have an inevitable impact on Russia's evolving policy toward Abkhazia.

Finally, divisions within Russian public opinion are also a part of the picture. During the July 2004 increase in Georgian–Russian tensions over events in South Ossetia, 47 percent of Russians believed that Russia should intervene if Georgia were to use force against Russian citizens in Abkhazia, while 38 percent believed that Russia should not. At the same time, 14 percent believed that Abkhazia should be part of Georgia, 32 percent thought that it should join Russia, and 29 percent thought that it should be independent. For South Ossetia, the corresponding numbers were 12 percent, 34 percent, and 30 percent.[103]

Russian attitudes toward Georgia improved after the Rose Revolution. In August 2002, only 26 percent of Russians had a positive attitude toward Georgia, 28 percent were neutral, and 39 percent had negative feelings. After the Rose Revolution, these figures changed dramatically. In January 2004, 41 percent expressed a positive attitude, 42 percent were neutral, and only 10 percent had negative feelings. By July 2004, these moved back toward their 2002 levels, with 29 percent holding a positive attitude, 40 percent neutral, and 22 percent negative.[104]

[102] "President Adygey i mer Moskvy otpravilis' v Abkhaziiu," *Regnum*, August 5, 2004, http://www.regnum.ru/forprint/303693.html.

[103] "Rossiiane o konfliktakh mezhdu Gruziey, Yuzhnoi Ossetiiey I Abkhaziiey," *Levada Tsentr*, July 30, 2004, http://www.levada.ru/press/2004073004.html.

[104] "Vokrug Abkhazskogo konflikta," *Baza Dannyh Fom*, August 10, 2002, http://bd.fom.ru/report/map/gg021707.

Between February and July 2004, the number of Russians who believed that Georgian–Russian relations could be improved under the new Georgian leadership declined from 30 percent to 13 percent. The number of people who believed that President Saakashvili would fail to achieve significant improvement of the situation in Georgia increased from 1 percent to 32 percent.[105]

In sum, these six instances of the way domestic politics affect Russian policy toward Georgia and the Abkhazian conflict are important, but scarcely uniform. Abkhazia plays a greater role in Russian domestic politics than other breakaway territories in the former Soviet Union, and it roils relations with Georgia more than other conflict areas affect Russia's relations with other neighbors. Yet, its impact does not push in only one direction, and, indeed, is often contradictory. This has become clear under Putin, who views many of these countervailing pressures as potential problems. From 2000 to 2003, he moved to rein in the nationalist opposition, to suppress the independent actions of regional leaders, and to overcome traditional geopolitical paranoia in favor of pragmatic relations with the West. He also discouraged ethnic mobilization in the North Caucasus by appointing *siloviki*—that is, representatives of the interior, defense, and security ministries—to positions of power in ethnic republics, while resisting calls for an assertive "protection" of Russian citizens in CIS states.

PRESIDENTIAL ELECTIONS IN ABKHAZIA:
LIMITS OF RUSSIA'S INFLUENCE

All the constraints and contradictions in Russia's policy toward Abkhazia were clearly demonstrated during the period of the disputed presidential elections in Abkhazia that took place in two stages on October 3, 2004, and on January 12, 2005. During the crisis that occurred between those two stages, Russia emerged as the main external force in Abkhazian affairs. Its involvement initially contributed to destabilizing the situation, but later helped to broker a political compromise between the two main presidential candidates by seeking to reconcile a dangerously divided Abkhazian society. Russia's policy regarding Abkhazian elections demonstrated how far it was willing to go in its attempts to control Abkhazia,

---

[105] Russian Polling Agency VsTIOM, Press release N 105, "Russians about Georgia and Situation in South Ossetia."

and, at the same time, highlighted the real constraints on its ability to exercise effective influence.

The presidential elections in Abkhazia were not recognized as legitimate by Georgia or the international community, including the UN and the OSCE.[106] Russia, in its capacity as facilitator of the peace process, should also have respected the provision of UN Resolution 1255, which deems such elections illegitimate. However, Russia had too many interests at stake, and Russian politicians not only stressed the importance of these elections but took a very active part in trying to shape their outcome. Indeed, the elections were important because they determined the transfer of power from the first postwar president of Abkhazia, Vladislav Ardzinba, to a new leader, who would be presiding for the next four years over important changes both within Abkhazia and potentially in its relations with Georgia, Russia, and the outside world.

President Ardzinba had been a convenient leader for Moscow because of his uncompromising attitude toward Georgia (colored by his role in the 1992–1993 war) and his long-standing ties to Moscow, including earlier ties with Yevgeny Primakov. Ardzinba, however, had been incapacitated by illness for a number of years, which opened the door to corruption and behind-the-scenes maneuvering by self-seeking Russian politicians and business elites. It was clear that Ardzinba's successor was unlikely to have the same connections to Moscow, and as a result could be more unpredictable in dealing with either Russia or Georgia. Consequently, Russian political elites were determined to ensure that a new successor with at least a minimum of loyalty to Moscow was elected and not someone likely to act against Russian economic interests (both legitimate and criminalized). Russian political consultants, however, failed to understand that despite his contribution to nation-building, Ardzinba and par-

---

[106] The UN Position was stipulated in the UN SG Report to the UN Security Council on October 18, 2004. In Resolution 1255 (1999), the Security Council considered unacceptable and illegitimate the holding of self-styled elections in Abkhazia, which took place in the absence of the majority of the population and the determination of the political status of the territory. UNOMIG has maintained this position. European Parliament Resolution (P6_TA(2004)0023) on Georgia adopted on October 14, 2004, rejected "the 'presidential elections' in Abkhazia as illegitimate" and called on "the Commission and Council to give their support to an intensification of the UN-led negotiation process in the Georgian–Abkhazian conflict."

ticularly the people around him had lost public support among the
impoverished Abkhazian population long ago. The people of Abkhazia
were looking for a new beginning. The plan to prolong Ardzinba's legacy
without Ardzinba did not have much chance of succeeding in a genuinely
representative poll.

Russia's strategy of assuring that a new pro-Moscow leader take over
from Ardzinba was far from subtle. In fact, it amounted to unprecedented
external interference in the electoral process during all its stages. This policy can be compared only with Russia's own "elections" of governors,
which under Putin depend almost entirely on decisions made in Moscow
and are simply "ratified" through manipulated elections. A similar strategy
was attempted in Abkhazia, but backfired. As presidential candidate Sergei
Bagapsh explained, "These were the first competitive elections and the
Abkhazian people wanted to decide by themselves about the future of
[their] republic. Therefore, the electorate voted against the pressure exercised from [Ardzinba's] authorities, against an information blockade, and
against black [public relations] in the Russian press."[107]

Even before the beginning of the official election campaign, Russian
politicians made no secret of their support for Raul Khadzhimba, who had
served as the last prime minister of Abkhazia under Ardzinba. In addition
to being a close associate of President Ardzinba, Khadzhimba fit the profile
of an "Abkhazian Putin," given his long career in the security services.
Khadzhimba was seen as a politician who would remain completely
dependent on Moscow. As a prime minister, he had established close links
with Moscow and was seen as likely to continue Ardzinba's economic and
political ties with Russia. But Khadzhimba's close relationship with Ardzinba meant that he enjoyed little public support within Abkhazian society.
For the public, the election was not a referendum on policy toward Russia
or Georgia, but a chance to vote on Ardzinba's record. However, Moscow
either failed to understand or deliberately ignored this fact. Moreover,
Moscow's political advisers underestimated the ability of Abkhazian society
(as well as Georgian IDPs who had returned to the Gali district) to mobilize behind an alternative candidate. Sergei Bagapsh, the head of the
regional electricity utility company Chernomorenergo, was this alternative.

---

[107] The quote is from an interview given by presidential candidate Sergei
Bagapsh to *Nezavisimaia Gazeta*. See "Samoprovozglashennyi Falstart,"
Nezavisimaia Gazeta, October 5, 2004.

Bagapsh was not on record calling for a significant change in Abkhazia's close ties with Russia or suggesting a reconsideration of Abkhazia's refusal to rejoin Georgia. However, because of his broad popular support, he promised to be a much more independent leader capable of defending the interests of the Abkhazian nation not only with Georgia, but also with Moscow. Moreover, for the elections, Bagapsh joined forces with Alexander Ankvab, a tough politician who represented a bigger danger for Moscow and Russian interests due to his strong commitment to fighting corruption and criminality. Russian political elites viewed a Bagapsh–Ankvab alliance as a threat, and were determined to ensure Khadzhimba's victory.

Putin personally met with Khadzhimba in Sochi during the run-up to the elections. While no explicit endorsement was issued at that meeting, which was clumsily presented as a meeting with veterans of World War II, there was no doubt of its symbolic meaning. Moscow's support for Khadzhimba did not stop at the top official level. Moscow used its economic power and its unique role as Abkhazia's only link to the outside world to offer practical rewards. Not only did it reopen the rail link between Sochi and Sukhumi, but regular bus service also resumed between the two cities on September 23. The Russian government claimed that it had not violated any international agreements by reopening rail and bus services with Abkhazia, but Georgia's Ambassador to the UN, Revaz Adamia, sent a formal letter to the UN Security Council calling the reopening of the railway link an "infringement upon [Georgia's] sovereignty and a violation of international law." Putin's "broken commitments" to synchronize economic projects with the return of IDPs, Adamia said, had damaged the UN-led peace process.[108]

Khadzhimba's candidacy was even more enthusiastically supported by traditional pro-Abkhazian interest groups in Russia—including nationalist politicians, businesses, North Caucasus peoples' organizations, and some regional politicians from southern Russia. Just days before the elections, a group of "Moscow activists"—including Vladimir Zhirinovsky, Deputy Prosecutor General Vladimir Kolesnikov, Deputy Speaker of the

---

[108] "Georgian Ambassador's Letter to the UN Security Council over Abkhazia," http://www.civil.ge/eng/detail.php?id=8202. The Russia defense can be found at "Organizovano Dvizheniie electropoezdov iz Sochi," http://www.kavkazweb.net/news/news.cgi?action=view&nid=01&yy=2004 &mm=9&dd=13&message_id=1095100970154196zbrjYiB7KCpmZ.

Russian State Duma Arthur Chilingarov, and popular Russian singers and artists—visited Sukhumi and spoke at a mass rally campaigning directly for Khadzhimba. Their statements went as far as issuing direct threats of cutting economic links with Abkhazia if Moscow's favored candidate was not elected.[109]

This public pressure produced the opposite of its intended effect. Instead of strengthening Khadzhimba's support, it turned many voters toward his rival, who was seen as a more independent politician unassociated with the negative legacy of Ardzinba's regime. As a result, during the October 3 elections, over 50 percent of voters, many of them ethnic Georgians from the Gali region, voted for Bagapsh.[110] Khadzhimba refused to accept the result, and a protracted period of instability followed, at points threatening to escalate to violence. With all major international organizations and foreign states denouncing the elections as illegitimate, Russia again stepped in as a mediator, but continued to pursue its own agenda by striving to delegitimize Bagapsh's victory and organize new elections from which Khadzhinba might yet emerge the winner. Russian senior officials called both candidates to Moscow and pressed for new elections. Bagapsh and his supporters refused to yield, claiming that they had won the election and that their victory had been recognized by the Abkhazian Parliament, Central Election Commission, and Supreme Court. Therefore, they intended to go ahead with the inauguration in early December. Moscow then sent Nodar Khazhba, an ethnic Abkhazian who worked with Sergei Shoigu at the Russian Ministry of Emergencies, to Sukhumi, while Ardzinba appointed Khazhba prime minister with the task of resolving the electoral deadlock. The appointment of Khazhba, who had long resided outside of the republic and had no popular following in Abkhazia, led to further anti-Russian protests among the Abkhazian elite.

At the same time, Russia continued to apply its economic leverage. First the governor of the Krasnodar region, Alexander Tkachev, issued a statement calling for the closing of the border between Abkhazia and

---

[109] "Samoprovozglashennyi Falstart."

[110] On October 11, the Abkhazian Central Election Commission announced that Bagapsh had won with 50.08 percent of votes. On October 28, the Abkhazian Supreme Court recognized the election results as valid, but was forced the following day to rescind its decision due to pressure from Khadzhimba's supporters. On November 12, Bagapsh supporters stormed government buildings and occupied them until November 15.

Russia "due to the direct threat to Russia's security and particularly its border regions," including his own.[111] Tkachev underscored that closing the border would have a direct economic impact on the Abkhazian economy "causing stagnation of the tourist industry and interrupting cross-border trade in agricultural products resulting in thousands of Abkhazian citizens losing income."[112] Tkachev's decision bewildered the Abkhazian opposition. When the border crossing was indeed restricted on November 19, consternation grew among the public. Rumors began to circulate that Russia was planning to send military forces into Abkhazia, although these appear not to have had any basis in fact.

Instead, President Putin dispatched two high-level representatives from the *siloviki*—Russia's deputy prosecutor general, Vladimir Kolesnikov (who had lived in Abkhazia and was well-known there), and the first deputy minister of the interior, Alexander Chekalin—to mediate between Bagapsh and Khadzhimba. After the first meeting between the two, no compromise was evident. Then came a second threat to close the border; this time from Gennady Bukaev, an adviser to the Russian prime minister.[113] It was Bukaev who threatened the Abkhazians that, "If Bagapsh continues his unconstitutional actions [i.e., goes ahead with the inauguration], the border between Russia and Abkhazia will be closed."[114] The Russian government also temporarily suspended train service between Abkhazia and Sochi. All of these measures were explained by the need "to protect Russian citizens" from the potential danger of instability.[115] It is interesting that no such concern was expressed for Russian citizens residing in Abkhazia, whose interests the Russian government had repeatedly pledged to protect.

---

[111] "Zaiavleniie gubernatora Krasnodarskogo kraia vyzvalo nedoumeniie mestnoy opozitsii," *Regnum.ru,* November 24, 2004.

[112] "Zaiavleniie gubernatora Krasnodarskogo kraia vyzvalo nedoumeniie mestnoy opozitsii."

[113] Anatoly Gordienko, "Abkhaziey zanialis' spetsialisty po nalogam," *Nezavisimaia Gazeta,* December 2, 2004.

[114] "Russia Blockades Abkhazia," *Alternatives,* December 1, 2004, http://www.alternatives.ca/article1568.html.

[115] Statement by Andrei Logunov, government representative in the State Duma. He further stated that "Russia does not want its citizens to travel to Abkhazia where [the] political crisis could escalate into bloodshed." See "Gruziia vystupaiet protiv vmeshatel'stva Rossii v dela Abkhazii," December 3, 2004, http://www.kavkaz.memo.ru/newstext/news/id/736646.html.

A final round of talks took place on December 4–5, just days before Bagapsh planned to carry out his inauguration.[116] An agreement was reached that stipulated that new elections would take place before January 13, and that in these elections Bagapsh would run for president and Khadzhimba for vice president. The compromise stunned Abkhazian society, which was bitterly divided between Bagapsh and Khadzhimba supporters. However, it helped to diffuse tensions and paved the way for trouble-free elections on January 12. Bagapsh won a decisive victory, taking over 90 percent of the vote.[117]

As a result, Bagapsh assumed real power, while Khadzhimba held a largely symbolic role. Contrary to initial expectations, Bagapsh denied reports that Khadzhimba would be put in charge of all security and foreign policy issues. All strategic decisions, he said, would be taken by the president, and the vice president would only oversee operational issues. Moreover, Bagapsh consolidated his power further by removing Nodar Khazhba and appointing Alexander Ankvab as prime minister, despite Moscow's opposition. The formal alliance between Bagapsh and Khadzhimba, who comes from the Ardzinba clan, could still become a source of trouble, because the two men represent different groups of interests and are unlikely to become true allies. Further tensions could lead to ongoing instability and prevent Abkhazia from carrying out internal reforms, nation-building, and a resolution of the conflict with Georgia.

Several conclusions can be drawn from Russia's actions during this period. Russia's active involvement in the election process, as explained by a variety of Russian politicians, stemmed from three factors: first, that instability or violence in Abkhazia could spill over into Russia's North Caucasus regions; second, that the majority of Abkhazian residents were now officially Russian citizens; and third, that Russian citizens and com-

---

[116] These talks were attended by Bagapsh, Khadzhimba, Khashba as well as Kolesnikov and a deputy speaker of the Russian State Duma, Sergei Baburin. The sides did reach an agreement on "Measures for Reaching National Unity in the Republic of Abkhazia." It was signed by Ardzinba as president.

[117] According to Central Electoral Commission Chairman Batal Tabagua, 129,298 people were put on the main and additional lists of voters, and 75,691 people, or 58.5 percent, took part in the voting. In the final count, 68,225 people, or 90.1 percent, voted for Sergei Bagapsh, and 3,467 people, or 4.5 percent, voted for alternative presidential candidate Yakub Lakoba.

panies had substantial economic interests in the area. These reasons may provide some justification for Russia's interest in the election, particularly among private individuals and businesses. The Russian government's active intervention in the electoral process, however, was not compatible with its role as one of the key facilitators of the Georgian–Abkhazian peace process under UN auspices. Events during this period graphically demonstrated the tension between the domestic impulses driving Russian policy and the international commitments that it has undertaken. Yet despite Russia's actions during the Abkhazian elections, its role as a mediator in the Georgia–Abkhazia peace process will likely still be accepted by the international community, if for no other reason than that Russia continues to hold the only real leverage over the Abkhazian side.

This leverage, however, has its limits, and this is the second obvious implication of the outcome of the Abkhazian elections. Indeed, Russia's involvement in the electoral process went beyond efforts to stabilize the situation and constituted a direct and sustained attempt to shape the outcome of the elections. But Moscow failed to bring Khadzhimba to power, despite the long-standing direct links between large segments of the Abkhazian population and Russia.

The limits to Russia's influence are not based on geopolitics. In contrast to the November–December 2004 elections in Ukraine, Russia was the only external power acting to influence the result of elections in Abkhazia. Nor do these limits stem from a lack of resources. Rather, they owe to the incompetence of those who conceived and implemented Russia's strategies. These individuals obviously lacked both an understanding of and a respect for the Abkhazian people and their aspirations. Although it is hard to pinpoint the architect of Russia's initial policy in Abkhazia, Russian newspapers claim that the strategy of supporting Khadzhimba was developed within the Foreign Policy Department of the Presidential Administration.[118] Later, the officials who were called in to implement "damage control" included the usual combination of nationalist politi-

---

[118] *Nezavisimaia Gazeta* reported that the Foreign Policy Department of the Presidental Administration was responsible for overseeing Russia's policy toward elections in Abkhazia. From this department, the head of section on relations with CIS states—Alexei Sitnin—spent a lot of time on the ground in Abkhazia. Reportedly, Russian *siloviki* also had an important influence over Russia's policy. Anatoly Gordienko and Natalya Melnikova, "Samoprovoz-glashennyi Falsstart," *Nezavisimaia Gazeta*, October 5, 2004.

cians and *siloviki*, the key domestic constituencies shaping Russia's relations with Abkhazia.

The actual mediation was carried out by Sergei Baburin, who is known for championing Abkhazian interests in the Duma, and former *siloviki*, Vladimir Kolesnikov and Alexander Chekalin. The outspoken governor of Krasnodar region, Alexander Tkachev, also played an important role by delivering threats of border closure. While Putin tried to distance the state from the actions of these mediators and originally claimed that they were acting in their own personal capacities, it was clear that they were seen as protecting Russian interests as the best means of projecting Russian influence.

In Moscow, the policymaking process was confused and badly coordinated. The Foreign Ministry issued contradictory statements, first indicating that Russia would defend its interests in Abkhazia, then later distancing the government from any threat of sanctions.[119]

The Foreign Ministry, which publicly supported Georgia's territorial integrity and took part in the Geneva meeting in the midst of the crisis in Sukhumi, was once again sidelined by the *siloviki*. The *siloviki* were the ones willing to play tough with the Abkhazians and to ignore Russia's international commitments within the UN-led peace process. Nonetheless, on the positive side, the election dispute did not result in major violence, nor did it spill over into Russia's own increasingly unstable North Caucasus region. Moreover, Russia's intervention was done without resorting to military pressure. And despite a short interlude when the border was closed, economic relations between Abkhazia and Russia remained unaffected.

Finally, Russia's heavy-handed interference during the elections produced widespread criticism among the Abkhazian population and political elite. Both now realized that any significant integration with Russia would mean less political freedom, including the right to elect the leaders they wanted and to develop civil society and a free press. While much of

---

[119] Ministry of Foreign Affairs Spokesman Alexander Yakovenko stated that Russia will protect its interests in Abkhazia (*Nezavisimaia Gazeta*, November 15, 2004). In December, Mikhail Troyansky, deputy head of the Information Department of the Foreign Ministry, confirmed that the issue of border closure with Abkhazia was not discussed with the Ministry of Foreign Affairs (*Nezavisimaia Gazeta*, December 2, 2004).

Abkhazian society does not embrace democratic values, Abkhazia's difficult existence as an "unrecognized" state has reinforced a strong sense of community. This distinguishes Abkhazia from many neighboring Russian regions that remain dependent on the federal center and that are ready to accept limits on their political autonomy in exchange for economic benefits. Bagapsh, who has declared a readiness to promote economic ties with Russia by harmonizing domestic legislation, is more reserved on the question of political ties.[120] At the same time, Abkhazia has reinforced the symbols of its political independence by issuing internal Abkhazian passports alongside Russian passports.[121]

Meanwhile, the growing authoritarian trends in Putin's domestic politics are increasingly at variance with developments inside Abkhazia. Elections showed that in Abkhazia civil society is ready to mobilize in protest against corrupt leaders no matter how much they wave the banner of patriotism. If these trends continue, closer association with Russia may come to seem a step back from realizing Abkhazia's national aspirations.

None of this, however, means that a major change is in store in Abkhazian–Russian relations. Given the absence of international recognition for Abkhazia or any near-term prospects for a significant improvement in Georgian–Abkhazian relations, Russia will remain Abkhazia's principal source of economic and political support.

Unlike the Orange Revolution in Ukraine, where the international community supported democratic forces protesting against a fraudulent election, the lack of international engagement in Abkhazia allowed external manipulation to go unchallenged. Moreover, the lack of a constructive strategy on the part of the new Georgian leadership coupled with Abkhazia's international isolation provided little room for maneuver for those parts of the Abkhazian elite who were dismayed by Russian interference.

---

[120] In his interview with *Nezavisimaia Gazeta*, Sergei Bagapsh stated that, "The people of Abkhazia decided to [build an] independent state and rapprochement with Russia will be pursued through economic cooperation," *Nezavisimaia Gazeta*, January 21, 2005, http://www.ng.ru/printed/courier/2005-01-24/9_georgia.html.

[121] According to Bagapsh, Abkhazia planned to start issuing new internal passports in March–April 2005. See "Vesnoy etogo goda v Abkhazii nachnetsia vvedeniie vnutrennih pasportov," http://www.kavkaz.memo.ru/newstext/news/id/760564.html.

Back in Russia, the Kremlin's actions provoked a vigorous debate among the Russian political elite. Regional experts (such as Sergei Arutiunov, Alexei Malashenko, and Alla Yazkova), prominent liberal politicians (such as Irina Khakamada and Valery Goreglyad), and even traditionally pro-Kremlin analysts (such as Sergei Markov and Stanislav Belkovsky), expressed strong criticism of Moscow's tactics.[122] Despite this criticism, Russia's leaders repeated many of the same mistakes during Ukraine's fall 2004 presidential elections.

Ultimately, detaching Abkhazia from Russia's political control can only happen if Georgia finds a way to demonstrate to Abkhazian society that it no longer represents a threat to Abkhazia's national survival. Saakashvili and his team have not yet managed to do this, although Moscow's missteps during the Abkhazian elections have been carefully noted in Tbilisi. Russia's control over Abkhazia, many Georgian commentators have noted, is more of a myth than many had thought. The problem is that Georgian leaders so far have failed to find a way of turning Russian weakness to Georgian advantage—that is, to open the path to a new constructive dialogue with Sukhumi.[123]

THE WAY AHEAD: BEYOND THE STATUS QUO?

For over a decade, Russia's strategy of "frozen uncertainty" helped to preserve the post–armed conflict status quo between Georgia and Abkhazia. This role not only allowed Russia to keep its presence and influence in the region, it also contributed to entrenching the de facto statehood of Abkhazia. While Russia's policy did little to advance a resolution of the conflict, it made ordinary Abkhazians feel more secure and allowed them to survive economically. It also prevented a further destabilization of Russia's North Caucasus.

At the same time, Russia's policy served as a major obstacle to the development of Georgian sovereignty. Georgia has had to endure years of interference in its internal affairs and carry the burden of supporting large

---

[122] Respectively, at http://grani.ru/Politics/World/Europe/Georgia/p.81031. html; http://www.ng.ru/printed/cis/2004-12-07/5_abkhazia.html; and http://www.ng.ru/politics/2004-10-18/2_abhazia.html.
[123] Paata Zakareishvili "Akhali Shvidi Dge," October 8–14, 2004.

numbers of IDPs. Despite the lack of progress in political negotiations, major changes have occurred within Georgia, Abkhazia, and Russia over the last decade. Georgia's President Saakashvili is determined to break the current impasse. Abkhazia is also developing a more sophisticated strategy, which is bound to reduce its dependency on Russia as it pursues its own national goals.

Russia's policy toward Georgia was already put through a severe test during the events in Ajara and South Ossetia in the spring and summer of 2004. More importantly, Russia's actions during the Abkhazian elections in fall 2004 exposed the limits of its power and its inability to conduct a well-coordinated policy. As a result, Russia lost the confidence of the Abkhazian elite, which is now more reluctant to pursue closer political relations with Moscow. Russia's influence in Abkhazia is and will remain economic, at least until Georgia and the international community decide to abandon efforts to isolate Abkhazia and to adopt a strategy promoting economic opportunities for the area in the hopes that this will provide a more solid foundation for a political dialogue leading to reconciliation. Perhaps the traces of such a shift can be seen in the EU's increased contribution to Abkhazia's economic rehabilitation and by voices within the Georgian NGO community calling for unilateral confidence-building measures on the part of the Georgian government. Russia, for its part, remains reactive in the peace process, largely due to the complex mix of actors and interests involved. Should that trend continue, Russia is likely to be further marginalized if and when the international community takes a second look at the Caucasus's legacy of "frozen conflicts."

CHAPTER 6

Georgian Security and the Role of the West

DAMIEN HELLY AND GIORGI GOGIA

W hen Mikheil Saakashvili was elected President in January 2004, Western governments celebrated him as a skillful and reform-oriented democrat. He would, in spite of all political challenges, lead his country toward stability, security, and development. A few months later, his violent intervention in South Ossetia demonstrated that the West may have nurtured exaggerated hopes. Saakashvili's success in leading a revolution did not necessarily mean that he would be equally successful in reforming the country's institutions. The new elites inherited a weak state, whose institutions were thoroughly permeated with corruption. The West failed to appreciate the depth of these problems. It had focused for too long on the narrowly defined interests it had in the region. This had led to a number of misunderstandings and misperceptions among external actors and Georgia's government.

A first misunderstanding concerns the depth of Western engagement. Despite frequent references to the geopolitical significance of Georgia and the South Caucasus, neither is an area of primary interest for the United States or the European Union.[1] Western policy in the region has sought to maintain the status quo and prevent new conflicts. But it has neither achieved peace nor built a comprehensive security framework for the South Caucasus region.[2]

---

[1] Fiona Hill, "A Not-So-Grand Strategy: United States Policy in the Caucasus and Central Asia since 1991," http://www.brook.edu/dybdocroot/views/ articles/fhill/2001politique.htm. This paper is the English version of a contribution to *Politique étrangère*, no. 1 (February 2001), pp. 95–108.

[2] There are also divergences between EU and U.S. policies in Georgia. In 1999, for instance, the EU strongly opposed U.S. and World Bank plans to privatize

Georgia's relations with both the United States and the European Union have furthermore been built upon other misperceptions. Since the collapse of the Soviet Union, the West and Georgians have labored to find a common language by which to convey each party's interests. In areas involving humanitarian aid or financial assistance, this effort has been partially successful. In other key areas, however, communication and common understanding have been in shorter supply. Several factors explain the distance between Westerners and their Georgian interlocutors.

First, Georgian elites have tended to pursue short-term gains, while the West, particularly the European Union (EU), has generally sought to implement long-term sustainable programs. Under Shevardnadze, political and governmental instability encouraged corrupt officials to make as much profit as possible in the shortest period of time. Security threats and violence, as well as Russian political pressure linked to the Chechen conflict, increased the feeling of political unpredictability and reinforced narrow, self-interested behavior. As a result, the West has found it difficult to promote mid-term solutions that do not afford Georgian officials short-term personal gains.

Second, neither the United States nor Western Europe can rely on a historical memory of close cooperation with Georgia. Some Western countries were only briefly interested in Georgia before the Soviet invasion in 1921.[3] This lack of common historical experience deprives the West and Georgia of common historical references for their present policies. In addition, there are difficulties introduced by the complexity of the decision-making process in Western countries and international organizations. This is particularly true in the case of the EU. Georgians, accustomed to the centralized politics of the Soviet system and unfamiliar with the long process of European integration, are baffled and frustrated by the way things get done (or do not get done) within the EU.

---

the strategic Georgian port of Poti. In general, however, the United States and Europe have sought to achieve coordination and burden sharing in the South Caucasus through a combination of bilateral and multilateral policies.

[3] S. Neil MacFarlane, "Caucasus and Central Asia: Towards a Non-Strategy," Geneva Center for Security Policy Occasional Paper Series no. 37 (Geneva: Geneva Center for Security Policy, 2002), http://www.gcsp.ch/e/publications/Occ-papers/2002/37-MacFarlane.pdf; Musa Gasimli, "The Role of the United States in the South Caucasus 1917–1918," *Caspian Crossroads Magazine*, vol. 6, no. 3 (2003), http://www.usazerbaijancouncil.org/caspiancrossroads/current.html#4.

Third, the rule of law is only weakly developed in Georgia. Traditions and informal practices are considered to be far more important than formal legal procedures. This has posed problems in the day-to-day implementation of foreign aid projects and other forms of cooperation with Western partners. The Saakashvili government is addressing this problem, but it will not be easily or quickly eliminated. Still, the arrival of a young generation of Georgian leaders educated abroad and more influenced by the Western commitment to rule of law may change methods of operation. However, differences remain between the discourses these new elites use for Western and for domestic consumption. Saakashvili himself, for instance, employs a far more nationalistic and populist language when speaking to audiences at home than when he speaks to international audiences.[4]

Fourth, misperceptions between Georgia and the West have been accentuated by both sides' exaggerated expectations. By telling Caucasian interlocutors that the South Caucasus was a key geopolitical area, the West supported unrealistic expectations in Georgia for Western political and military support. As a result of their military defeats in South Ossetia and Abkhazia, Georgians came to count on the Western powers to solve internal security problems that they were unable to solve on their own. It has been made very clear that with its internal conflicts and uncontrolled territories, Georgia is not ready for NATO membership. But NATO has been unwilling to clarify more concretely what Georgia's long-term prospects of being admitted to the organization are, in spite of Georgia's official application to NATO in 2002, although the Individual Partnership Action Plan (IPAP) approved by NATO in fall 2004 is meant to be a sign of encouragement.

The EU, for its part, has never offered membership to Georgia and was not even willing, until the regime change in November 2003, to consider Georgia as a part of its "new neighborhood" policies.[5] EU mem-

---

[4] On the question of Abkhazia for instance, President Saakashvili has repeatedly stated before international audiences in English that he would not use force to regain the breakaway region. In his statements in Georgian, however, he has been much more aggressive on this topic, raising concerns about his commitment to peaceful methods in Abkhazia.

[5] This EU policy framework was designed in 2003 to include all countries geographically bordering the enlarged European Union (with the exception of Turkey and those countries of the Balkans that are already candidates for European Union membership and therefore part of existing EU policy frameworks).

bership, however, is the main inducement Brussels has to stimulate institutional reforms in Georgia. The EU, in the framework of its neighborhood strategy, is offering prospects for closer cooperation with countries that implement policies in line with the union's objectives. However, it is questionable whether such general prospects are strong enough to convince Georgian elites to implement unpopular reforms.

The United States has raised immense hopes in Georgia by supporting energy projects, but there is no guarantee that the oil and gas projects will contribute significantly to Georgian growth. They will not draw other foreign investment as long as other conditions, such as legal and economic reforms or the resolution of Georgia's internal conflicts, are not met. Washington continually stresses Georgia's importance in the region and rallies to its side (at least rhetorically) when Russia becomes overbearing. At the same time, however, the United States regularly encourages Georgia to be more flexible in dealing with Russia. From the American perspective, Georgia will be permanently dependent on Russia in many areas and has no choice but to find a *modus vivendi* with its powerful neighbor. In short, Georgian leaders seem to believe that the West's chief concern is addressing Georgia's aspirations to be part of the Euro-Atlantic community, when in fact the West's main priority is for Georgia to put its own house in order and, in cooperation with Russia and its other neighbors, to find durable solutions to its domestic problems and those of its immediate region.

Over the course of the 1990s, Western security policies in Georgia have come to focus on three main objectives: securing energy supplies, achieving regional stability and integration through the resolution of local conflicts, and strengthening the Georgian state. These security objectives are tightly interconnected. They have all been addressed in multilateral and bilateral forums, leading to specific proposals for mitigating Georgia's security problems in the fields of energy independence, conflict resolution, regional integration, and state reform.[6] In this chapter, we will analyze the significance of each of these objectives for Western security policies in Georgia.

---

[6] Stephen J. Blank, *U.S. Military Engagement with Transcaucasia and Central Asia* (Carlisle, PA: Strategic Studies Institute, 2000), http://www.carlisle.army.mil/pdffiles/PubID=113/.

GEORGIA'S WESTERN PARTNERS

Georgia's main "Western partners" can be considered to be the EU and the United States. Neither of the two, however, has managed to develop a coherent, broad-based policy toward Georgia. Policy is the product of a range of actors, institutions, and states. This helps to explain why Georgia sees some of their decisions as confusing and uncoordinated.[7]

EU foreign policy depends on the interactions within the so-called institutional triangle of the Council, the Commission, and the Parliament. The Council's input is governed by the level of political cooperation among member states as they attempt to shape a common intergovernmental foreign policy. Some of the member states are particularly reluctant to get deeply involved in South Caucasus affairs.[8] The Commission, which is often more favorable to a genuinely common policy, cannot go beyond what the Council allows. This, however, has not prevented it from occasionally taking on ambitious external initiatives.[9] As far as the European Parliament is concerned, it may at times be influenced by lobbies, such as the Armenian lobby, but has generally supported stronger EU involvement in the South Caucasus and tried to push the Council forward, despite the lack of interest among the European

---

[7] Jan Zielonka, "Transatlantic Relations: Beyond the CFSP," in Hall Gardner and Radoslava Stefanova, eds., *Russia and China: The Risks of Uncoordinated Transatlantic Strategies* (Aldershot, UK: Ashgate, 2001), pp. 65–80. On Western policies in the South Caucasus region, see S. Neil MacFarlane, *Western Engagement in the Caucasus and Central Asia* (London: Royal Institute of International Affairs, 1999), and on Western policies regarding the conflict in Abkhazia, see Bruno Coppieters, "Western Security Policies and the Georgian–Abkhaz Conflict," in Bruno Coppieters, David Darchiashvili, Natella Akaba, eds., *Federal Practice: Exploring Alternatives for Georgia and Abkhazia* (Brussels: VUB Press, 2000), pp. 21–58.

[8] Europeans bring varied perspectives to the Caucasus. Some put more emphasis on the Russian and Soviet legacy, others on ethno-linguistic factors; some consider the Caucasus to be a part of Europe, others prefer to include it in the wider Caspian Basin region. For a more elaborate discussion of these approaches, see Damien Helly, "The Role of the EU in the Security of the South Caucasus: A Compromised Specificity?" *Connections,* vol. 1, no. 3 (July 2002), pp. 67–76, http://pfpconsortium.org/parser.cgi?file=/info-pages/pubs_en.htm.

[9] On the EU as an international actor and the Commission's external competencies, see (among others) Charlotte Bretherton and John Vogler, *The European Union as a Global Actor* (London: Routledge, 1999).

public for this part of the European periphery. In the minds of most Europeans, the South Caucasus is a remote area hidden beyond mountains and figuratively behind a mountain of problems.[10] Thus far, the EU has been a rather weak actor in the South Caucasus, leaving it to individual member states such as the United Kingdom, France, and Germany to take the lead.[11]

In the U.S. policymaking process, the Department of State and its many directorates, the White House and the National Security Council, and the Department of Defense each have distinctive perspectives on the South Caucasus, while Congress, influenced by oil and ethnic lobbies, often pushes in still other directions. Successive U.S. presidential administrations have elaborated their own priorities.[12] Until the late 1990s, U.S. policy was particularly unclear because of institutional confusion and a lack of coherence in the decision-making process. Only toward the end of Bill Clinton's second term did a "Caspian policy" emerge. In addition, the terrorist attacks of September 11, 2001, significantly modified important aspects of U.S. foreign policy. Georgia is now viewed as part of the "Greater Middle East," the primary area of potential terrorist threat. Georgia's role as a gateway to Central Asia was underscored by the wars in Afghanistan and Iraq. Outlaw regions within Georgia became a real concern, because Europeans and Americans alike saw them as refuges for terrorists. This terrorist threat had to be addressed as part of Georgia's overall state reform.

---

[10] As long as the question of Turkey's entry into the EU remains unresolved, the South Caucasus will not be a priority for the EU. But once Turkey becomes a member of the EU, the union will then border directly on the South Caucasus. See Christopher Hill, "The Geopolitical Implications of Enlargement," EUI Working Paper no. 30 (Florence: European University Institute, 2000).

[11] Dov Lynch, ed., *The South Caucasus: A Challenge for the EU*, Chaillot Papers no. 65 (Paris: Institute for Security Studies, European Union, December 2003), http://www.iss-eu.org/public/content/chaile.html. Germany and small EU states have been more in favor of a common EU policy than the United Kingdom and France (which is, together with Russia and the United States, a member of the so-called Minsk Group that mediates the conflict in Nagorno-Karabakh).

[12] Hill, "A Not-So-Grand Strategy." See also Simon Serfaty, "Les Etats-Unis, l'Europe et la France," *Revue française de géoéconomie*, no. 7 (1998), pp. 125–143; and Michael Brenner, "La diplomatie américaine et la sécurité en Europe," *Le Trimestre du Monde*, vol. 30 (1995), pp. 57–69.

ENERGY SECURITY

Beginning with the Clinton administration, Washington's approach to
the development and transport of Caspian Sea oil and gas has been driven
by more geopolitical than commercial calculations.[13] In the second half
of the 1990s, the United States, at the initiative of the National Security
Council, favored an Azerbaijan–Georgia–Turkey oil pipeline route over
other options for two reasons: first, the wish to bypass Russian territory
in order to reduce Moscow's influence over its southern neighbors, and
second, Washington's determination to prevent Iran from benefiting
from the transit of Caspian energy resources.[14] Beyond these two objectives, U.S. officials acted on the assumption that the Baku–Tbilisi–Ceyhan (BTC) Pipeline would help to stabilize the region by reducing rather
than stimulating conflict. This pipeline project was also supposed to be
a form of U.S. compensation to Turkey for its role in the 1991 Persian
Gulf war and the revenues it lost as a result of the war.[15] Additionally,
the Clinton administration justified the undertaking by citing the general
need to diversify U.S. energy supplies, even if Caspian oil reserves represent less than 5 percent of world reserves.

Moving the BTC Pipeline forward was never easy. Many of the major
oil companies originally opposed the Caucasian route, arguing that the
most viable economic pipeline option was through Iran or Russia.[16]
ExxonMobil, the lead U.S. company in Azerbaijan and Kazakhstan, never
joined the project. Even BP, eventually the decisive force behind the BTC

---

[13] Amy Jaffe noted that Clinton's Caspian policy had existed since 1994, but its
importance was emphasized by the nomination of a special envoy to the region
in 1998. See Amy Jaffe, "U.S. Policy towards the Caspian: Can the Wish-list
be Realized?" in Gennady Chufrin, ed., *The Security of the Caspian Sea Region*
(Oxford: Oxford University Press, 2001), pp. 136–150.

[14] Hill, "A Not-So-Grand Strategy." Hill explains, "By August 1996, with the
passage of the Iran Libya Sanctions Act (ILSA) imposing penalties on major
international investors in Iran's oil and gas industry, the U.S. had moved firmly
toward a policy of isolating Iran in the Persian Gulf and elsewhere—including
the Caspian. As a result, between 1995–1996, [National Security Council]
analysts were the architects of a U.S. policy to construct multiple pipelines for
the export of Caspian oil that would link the Caucasus and Central Asia to
global markets while minimizing links to Iran."

[15] Hill, "A Not-So-Grand Strategy."

[16] Jaffe, "U.S. Policy towards the Caspian."

Pipeline, had long resisted it, but finally yielded under considerable U.S. pressure. As late as 2000, BP still preferred to double the capacity of the Baku–Supsa Pipeline from its Chiraq field rather than to build BTC.[17]

Nor was this project the best solution for many EU countries. In the case of the EU's new members, it was more logical to import Caspian oil directly from the Black Sea through Romania, Bulgaria, or Greece in Southeastern Europe rather than through Turkey and the Mediterranean. But the absence of a common EU energy policy made it difficult for Brussels to affect the outcome. Because some EU countries (such as Great Britain, France, and Italy) stood to benefit along with their national oil companies (BP, TotalFinaElf, and ENI, respectively) from the BTC project and other investments in the Caspian, they had little reason to back a common approach to energy geopolitics.[18] Such a policy would have given opportunities in the region to their European competitors. Among European states, Great Britain was finally, despite BP's initial hesitations, the most supportive of the BTC route, notwithstanding a British nongovernmental organization (NGO) campaign against the project.

Leaders from Azerbaijan, Georgia, and Turkey gave strong support to the BTC Pipeline at a time when much of the international business community judged it to be commercially unviable. Azerbaijan's President Heydar Aliev and the oil consortium Azerbaijan International Operating Corporation (AIOC) lent assistance by involving prominent U.S. oil figures from the U.S.–Azerbaijan Chamber of Commerce in the project. Turkey's President Suleyman Demirel argued that BTC would help Turkey's environmental situation by bypassing the dangerously congested Bosporus Straits, and Georgia's President Eduard Shevardnadze insisted that the BTC project would help Georgia play the role of an energy bridge in the region.

In the South Caucasus, U.S. and European state interests are bound up with the commercial interests of major oil companies that form the principal Caspian energy consortia. To secure their investments in the Caspian Basin, these companies have found allies among U.S. geostrategists who support a strong U.S. presence among Russia's neighbors.[19]

---

[17] Jaffe, "U.S. Policy towards the Caspian."

[18] The agendas of other EU countries with diplomatic representation in Georgia and the South Caucasus but without major oil companies, such as Germany and Greece, were less influenced by oil interests.

[19] Jaffe, "U.S. Policy towards the Caspian."

High-level former officials such as Zbigniew Brzezinski, Brent Scowcroft, John Sununu, James Baker, and Richard Cheney (when he was head of Halliburton) have all visited Baku and the Caspian region and lobbied in favor of the oil companies.[20]

Because Russia (with reason) saw the BTC project as an attempt to circumvent its influence and to exclude it from the energy market in Azerbaijan and Georgia, it never warmed to the undertaking, even when the Russian oil company LukOil agreed in principle to take part in it. LukOil's participation, however, lasted only until 2002, when, for reasons that remain unclear, it withdrew.

The BTC Pipeline has also been strongly criticized by an array of Western and Georgian NGOs that are distressed by the project's likely environmental impact.[21] Project planners have had to deal with public protests within Georgia itself over the risk the pipeline as originally planned posed to the Borjomi natural reserve and its mineral water. The anti-BTC campaign continued into 2004, but with diminishing effect.

Without Washington's push, the BTC Pipeline would likely not have been built. Companies involved in the BTC needed U.S. intervention to secure support from the local governments and funding from international financial institutions. With U.S. encouragement, the International Finance Corporation (IFC)—the private sector arm of the World Bank—agreed to participate in the BTC project in November 2003.[22] Despite initial differences on pipeline issues between the United States on the one hand and European countries and oil companies on the other, these differences gradually diminished, and by 2004 the BTC project was largely a reality. The BTC Pipeline is now expected to be operational in 2005 and

---

[20] Svante E. Cornell, *Small Nations and Great Powers: A Study of Ethnopolitical Conflict in the Caucasus* (Richmond, UK: Curzon, 2001), p. 373.

[21] On NGOs' criticism of the Baku–Tbilisi–Ceyhan project, see the United Kingdom Parliament, House of Commons, Session 2002–03, *International Development Committee Publications, International Development—Written Evidence, Annex 1,* November 6, 2003, http://www.parliament.the-stationery-office.co.uk/pa/cm200203/cmselect/cmintdev/1266/1266we15.htm. On the Baku Ceyhan Campaign, see http://www.bakuceyhan.org.uk.

[22] "IFC's investment in the BTC pipeline consists of a loan up to $125 million for its own account and a loan of up to $125 million in commercial syndication. The total project cost of BTC is approximately $3.6 billion." See http://www.ifc.org/btc.

to reach its full capacity in 2010, when it is scheduled to transport a million barrels of oil a day.[23]

Despite its lack of a common energy security policy, the EU has always understood that Georgia would become a key transit country for bringing oil and gas to Europe and included the country in its 1997 Black Sea strategy, a part of which stressed the need to connect trans-European transportation networks with the Caucasian infrastructure. The Commission's 2001 Green Paper on the security of energy supplies, with its emphasis on the importance of finding alternative energy sources, reaffirmed this goal.[24] The EU also took a greater interest in projects to export Azerbaijani gas to Southeastern Europe via Georgia. Turkey was chosen as the destination of the Baku–Tbilisi–Erzerum Pipeline, which is intended to transport gas through Greece to EU countries and is scheduled for completion in 2006.[25]

The "nondecision" of the EU member states in the field of energy policy as well as foreign policy was further counterbalanced, at least until 1999, by the European Commission's attempt to fashion a collective effort in dealing with transportation and energy questions.[26] As export routes were being designed and pipelines planned in the South Caucasus,

---

[23] See http://www.caspiandevelopmentandexport.com/ASP/BTC.asp.

[24] European Commission's Communication, *Regional Cooperation in the Black Sea Area: State of Play, Perspectives for EU Action Encouraging Its Further Development*, November 14, 1997. On the Black Sea Petra project, see www.bs-petra.org. The main achievement of the European Commission's Black Sea policy, intended to help prepare for future EU expansion, has been the development of transportation networks around the Black Sea and the progressive economic integration of littoral states that are outside the framework of the EU. The Black Sea strategy, however, never became an EU priority. See also the European Commission Green Paper, *Towards a European Strategy for the Security of Energy Supply* (2001), http://europa.eu.int/comm/energy_transport/en/lpi_lv_en1.html. This document was adopted by the European Commission on November 29, 2000.

[25] Jean-Christophe Peuch, "Smell of Russian Gas Hangs over Georgian Election Campaign," *RFE/RL*, June 14, 2003, http://www.rferl.org/features/2003/06/13062003144514.asp.

[26] Peter Bachrach and Morton S. Baratz, "Decisions and Nondecisions: An Analytical Framework," *American Political Science Review*, vol. 57, no. 3 (1963), pp. 632–642. This concept was used in Damien Helly, "L'action extérieure de l'Union européenne dans le Caucase du Sud," Ph.D. diss., Institut d'Etudes Politiques de Paris, 2003.

the European Commission began its own initiative. It set in motion an alternative, temporary oil railway system between Azerbaijan and Georgia across the Transport Corridor Europe Caucasus Asia (TRACECA).[27] Through a multilateral technical agreement, this system is designed to link European transportation networks to Central Asia and the Caucasus and export extra Caspian oil that is not already carried by pipelines. Simultaneously, the EU has sought to provide the region with a collective legal framework for cooperation in oil and gas infrastructure sectors under the Interstate Oil and Gas Transport to Europe (INOGATE) program.

Western countries' interest in energy transportation links has forced them to look more energetically for ways of easing regional conflicts in the Caucasus. Border control, transport infrastructure, reliable revenue collection, and efficient law enforcement are crucial not only for Georgia, but for the entire region, because Georgia remains the key transit country. It is the hub through which Armenian and Azerbaijan trade reaches markets in Turkey, Russia, Iran, and the world beyond. Energy security, therefore, has become interdependent with Caucasian stability and the resolution of conflicts, difficult as these tasks are. It is not an accident that the linkage between oil and the Nagorno-Karabakh conflict moved to the head of the U.S. agenda in the second half of the 1990s, about the same time that the Clinton administration committed itself to the BTC Pipeline.

CONFLICT RESOLUTION

Georgia's record on conflict resolution is rather poor: Neither the Abkhazian nor the South Ossetian conflict has been overcome and the situation has even dramatically deteriorated on the ground with major crises in 1998 and 2004. The United States and Europe have been largely unable to prevent these resurgent crises. Their contributions to peace processes have been unsuccessful because of disagreements with other mediators, Russia in particular. Georgia has become a battleground for Russia and the United States where the cold war persists essentially as a "neither war nor peace" outcome and a frozen status quo. Non-recog-

---

[27] On TRACECA, see Damien Helly, "Un corridor de transport Asie-Europe: Traceca, l'Union européenne et sa Route de la Soie," *Courrier des Pays de l'Est*, no. 1019 (2001), pp. 52–64.

nized entities have played an obstructive role in attempts at mediation thanks to Moscow's direct support.

The South Caucasus has been consistently unstable since the collapse of the Soviet Union, threatening to spread trouble to Europe as well as to the Middle East.[28] To protect Europe's energy interests, the transport corridor through Azerbaijan and Georgia must be stabilized.[29] "Europe," as one observer has noted, "cannot be fully secure if the Caucasus remains outside [the framework of] European security."[30] Because security in the South Caucasus involves a ramified set of issues and many states, solutions are likely to be found only in multilateral frameworks, not least because only collective solutions are likely to work. Stability in the region requires the agreement of all concerned parties. Otherwise, those powers that are either marginalized or excluded are bound to become spoilers. Competition in mediation efforts can easily lead to deadlock. Russia has opposed a number of Western-led peace initiatives on Nagorno-Karabakh and Abkhazia, just as the West has opposed Russian attempts to be the sole mediator in Georgia's unresolved conflicts.

Caucasian regional stability and the internal stability of each of the South Caucasus states depend on how well local and external actors deal with a security complex in which every piece depends on every other piece.[31] Georgia's security thus depends very much on its relationship with its neighbors, especially with Russia. The West, therefore, has no choice but to take into account Russia's historical, geographical, military, and economic weight when dealing with Georgia. For the West, addressing the challenge in Georgia means not only mediating between belliger-

---

[28] On the geopolitical importance of the South Caucasus, see Ronald D. Asmus and Kenneth M. Pollack, "The New Transatlantic Project: A Response to Robert Kagan," *Policy Review*, no. 115 (2002), pp. 3–18, http://www.policyreview.org/OCT02/asmus.html; Bruno Coppieters, ed., *Contested Borders in the Caucasus* (Brussels: VUB Press, 1996); and Edmund Herzig, *The New Caucasus: Armenia, Azerbaijan, and Georgia* (London: Royal Institute of International Affairs, 1999).

[29] William E. Odom, "U.S. Policy toward Central Asia and the South Caucasus," *Caspian Crossroads Magazine*, vol. 3, no 1 (1997); and Graham Fuller, "Geopolitical Dynamics of the Caspian Region," *Caspian Crossroads Magazine*, vol. 3, no. 2 (1997), http://www.usazerbaijancouncil.org/caspiancrossroads/archive/archive.htm.

[30] Blank, *U.S. Military Engagement with Transcaucasia and Central Asia*, p. 8.

[31] Cornell, *Small Nations and Great Powers.*

ents, but also negotiating with Russia, Turkey, and Iran—each of which is directly affected by outcomes in conflict resolution efforts in Georgia. One also has to take the multinational security frameworks—the Organization for Security and Cooperation in Europe (OSCE), the Commonwealth of Independent States (CIS), and the North Atlantic Treaty Organization (NATO)—into account. Georgia is a neighbor of all the Black Sea littoral states, and all three Caucasian states are full members of the Black Sea Economic Cooperation (BSEC). [32]

But multilateralism is not the most prominent feature of security policies in the region, and external actors sometimes find themselves in conflict in the South Caucasus. For example, as NATO and the European Union expand, some Western analysts argue that the three South Caucasian counties should be treated as "the West's immediate neighborhood" instead of as Moscow's "near abroad."[33] Conservative Russian circles, meanwhile, are convinced that Moscow's position can only be salvaged through military power and the resurrection of Russia's previous imperial reach, including in the South Caucasus. Thus, Georgia has the dubious privilege of being one of the few countries in the world where the West and Russia are in direct competition.

Georgia's unresolved internal conflicts in Abkhazia and South Ossetia have seriously hampered the country's political and economic development and, in the process, its stability. Organized crime and the shadow economy have flourished in the breakaway territories, increased elsewhere in the country, and damaged national security both internally and externally. These conflicts have generated tension between Georgia and Russia, displaced hundreds of thousands of people, inflicted trauma on whole populations, and pitted community against community. It is impossible

---

[32] Armenia, despite its landlocked situation, is also a member of the eleven-member BSEC, whose membership is based on a regional approach rather than on a strictly geographical one. For more on this organization, see Thomas de Waal's chapter in this volume.

[33] This neo–cold war argument has been advanced by prominent American policymakers, such as Zbigniew Brzezinski and Bruce Jackson. See also Vladimir Socor, "Better For All than Alexander the Great," *The Wall Street Journal Europe*, January 10, 2003. Socor writes, "NATO has now secured the Black Sea's western rim in Romania and Bulgaria, and thus cemented the link with the southern, Turkish rim. From the east Balkan coast, the alliance is well positioned now to reach out directly to Georgia and the energy-rich Caspian basin, which have become the new neighborhood of the West."

to conceive of Georgian security without a settlement of these conflicts.

There have been many diplomatic initiatives to resolve the Abkhazian conflict, where the consequences of conflict have been most severe. In the process, all relevant foreign and domestic actors have come to understand that a solution, if it is to be found, requires a multilateral approach attuned to the interrelated nature of the problem. The UN is the framework organization where such a multilateral approach can take shape.

Concerning Abkhazia, UN involvement varied from "soft actions" (such as the first fact-finding mission in 1992) to the military observer role of the United Nations Observer Mission in Georgia (UNOMIG), which was originally established in August 1993 in order to monitor the July 1993 cease-fire agreement between Georgia and Abkhazia.[34] Until 1994, the West deferred to Russia in the region, seeking to avoid tensions over the intrusion of Western influence. For this reason, the UN only established an observer mission in Georgia (UNOMIG) rather than a full-fledged peacekeeping operation.[35]

UNOMIG deploys roughly 100 military observers in Abkhazia, whose main duty is to monitor and verify the implementation by the parties of the Agreement on Cease-fire and Separation of Forces signed in Moscow on May 14, 1994.[36] Its mandate includes: (1) overseeing a "security zone" (in which no military presence is permitted) and a "restricted zone" (where no heavy weapons may be deployed) on both

---

[34] On July 27, 1993, the government of Georgia and the Abkhazian authorities signed a cease-fire agreement in Gudauta. UN military observers started monitoring this agreement initially. The cease-fire broke down in September 1993, however, as Abkhazians launched an attack on Ochamchira and Sukhumi. A new cease-fire agreement was signed in 1994 in Moscow. The parties agreed on the deployment of CIS peacekeeping forces, with UNOMIG monitoring the implementation of the agreement and observing the operation of the CIS forces. For more, see Oliver Paye and Eric Remacle, "UN and CSCE Policies in Transcaucasia," in Coppieters, *Contested Borders in the Caucasus*, pp. 105–110. See also Rick Fawn and Sally N. Cummings, "Interests over Norms in Western Policy toward the Caucasus: How Abkhazia Is No One's Kosovo," *European Security*, vol. 10, no. 3 (autumn 2001), pp. 84–108.

[35] S. Neil MacFarlane, "The Role of the UN," *Accord*, issue 7 (September 1999), p. 36, http://www.c-r.org/accord/geor-ab/accord7/unrole.shtml; and Pierre Binette, "La crise en Abkhazie, acteurs et dynamique," *Revue Etudes Internationales*, vol. 29, no. 4 (1998), pp. 831–865.

[36] See the UNOMIG website, http://www.un.org/Depts/dpko/missions/unomig/.

sides of the cease-fire line along the Inguri River; (2) patrolling the
Kodori;[37] and (3) observing the operation of the Commonwealth of
Independent States (CIS) peacekeeping force within the framework of
the implementation of the Moscow Agreement.[38] UNOMIG is also
responsible for maintaining close contact with both parties to the conflict, cooperating with the CIS peacekeeping force, and, by its presence
in the area, contributing to conditions conducive to the safe and orderly
return of refugees and internally displaced persons (IDPs). UNOMIG
military officers, to a large extent coming from European countries, are
unarmed and their political and physical positions are tenuous.[39] For
example, UNOMIG had to suspend its monitoring operations in the
upper Kodori Valley after a hostage-taking incident in June 2003.

To achieve a comprehensive political settlement, UNOMIG developed a complex multifaceted mechanism for peace talks, often referred to
as the Geneva peace process.[40] The Geneva process is chaired by the UN.
Russia is expected to act as a facilitator—an ambiguous status, but evidently one implying the expectation that Russia will help to promote a
comprehensive settlement. The OSCE and the Group of Friends of the
Secretary-General—which includes the United States, Germany, the
United Kingdom, France, and Russia—have observer status in this
process. The agenda of the Geneva talks varies from political to humanitarian issues, including security and economic matters. In 1997, a more
complex mechanism consisting of a Coordinating Council and its three
issue-specific working groups devoted to the non-resumption of violence,
the return of refugees and IDPs, and economic issues was established
within the broader Geneva framework. At the same time, the UN has
developed a forum on confidence-building measures to enhance bilateral
contacts within an informal environment.[41] From 1993 to 1997, the UN
special envoy of the secretary-general visited Georgia and Abkhazia regu-

---

[37] The Kodori is a remote mountain area in Abkhazia. The upper part of Kodori
   is under Georgian control.
[38] See http://www.unomig.org.
[39] Fawn and Cummings, "Interests over Norms in Western Policy toward the
   Caucasus," pp. 84–108.
[40] The first round of talks between the parties was held in Geneva, November–
   December 1993.
[41] Three high-level meetings were organized within the context of the confidence-building measures: in Athens (October 1998), Istanbul (June 1999),
   and Yalta (March 2001).

larly, but did not have a permanent presence in the conflict zone. A special resident representative of the secretary-general of the UN (SRSG), appointed in July 1997, now chairs the Geneva process and heads UNOMIG.

The United States, Germany, Russia, Great Britain, and France have all taken part in the Group of Friends of the UN Secretary-General on Georgia, originally a French initiative designed to accelerate the languishing comprehensive settlement process and to counterbalance Russian predominance in the mediation between Georgia and Abkhazia. The Group of Friends is linked to the UN peacekeeping operation and the UN-led Geneva negotiation process. Abkhazians perceive it to be a biased actor pursuing the economic and geostrategic interests of Western powers, despite Russia's membership in this group.[42] This perception is not without merit. France, in particular, has never hidden its pro-Georgian position and on several occasions has conveyed this directly to the Abkhazians. The United Kingdom and Germany have played a more subtle game, actively participating in the Group of Friends on the one hand and funding NGO conflict resolution activities in Abkhazia on the other.[43]

The joint presence of UNOMIG and the Russian peacekeeping force in Abkhazia contributed to general stability and resulted in the spontaneous return of IDPs to the Georgian-populated district of Gali. In early 1998, the United Nations High Commissioner for Refugees (UNHCR) estimated that at least 50,000 people had returned to the Gali district. Confronted with this influx of IDPs, the international community increased humanitarian assistance to Abkhazia, especially for rebuilding schools and houses. In May 1998, however, fighting resumed when Abkhazian militias launched a large-scale sweep operation intending to drive out illegal Georgian armed groups, which ended in a new mass exodus of some 30,000 to 40,000 local residents. Over the course of five days, the results of several million dollars of foreign aid had been lost. Interna-

---

[42] Fawn and Cummings, "Interests over Norms in Western Policy toward the Caucasus," p. 94.

[43] Georgia has been a German priority since the collapse of the Soviet Union. The level of both German diplomatic activity and financial aid during the Shevardnadze era were exceptionally high, as compared to its involvement in other parts of the post-Soviet space. For more details, see Helly, "Un corridor de transport Asie-Europe."

tional donors grew reluctant to re-engage in Abkhazia because of this tragic and costly experience. These events dictated a clear need for regulating the return of refugees to Abkhazia. In fact, by the fall of 1998, the two sides had prepared a UN-brokered draft paper addressing the issue as well as steps to help with the Gali district's economic rehabilitation, but the Georgian and Abkhazian leaders, Eduard Shevardnadze and Vladislav Ardzinba, never met to sign it.[44]

Some Georgian politicians and officials continued to support guerrilla troops operating in Abkhazia, while Shevardnadze's government looked for Western support in order to implement a "Bosnian model," a term that referred to the forceful imposition of a constitutional arrangement by the international community in Bosnia in 1995. He also asked for the transformation of the peacekeeping operation in Abkhazia into a "peace-making operation," hoping to better guarantee a safe return of IDPs.[45] Some years later, in the wake of the 1999 NATO air campaign against Yugoslavia during the Kosovo crisis, officials in Tbilisi floated the idea of applying the "Kosovo model" to Georgia and evoked the "ethnic cleansing" committed against the Georgian population in Abkhazia with the aim of forcing a solution to the conflict. In response, the United States made it clear that there would be no replay of the "Kosovo scenario" in the South Caucasus.

The May 1998 crisis in Abkhazia demonstrated the inadequacy of the existing mechanisms for preventing violent eruptions. Rather than discuss a comprehensive solution to the conflict, the Coordinating Council and its substructures confined themselves to the narrower issues of non-resumption of hostilities, the exchange of hostages, and increased security measures for returnees.[46] In 1999, the UN's special representative, Liviu Bota, acted to revive the political negotiations on a new basis. After consultations with the Group of Friends in 2001, Bota's successor Dieter Boden, a German diplomat, elaborated "Basic Principles on the Distribution of Competences between Tbilisi and Sukhumi," a proposal

---

[44] MacFarlane, "The Role of the UN," p. 40.

[45] Liana Kvarchelia, "An Abkhaz Perspective," *Accord*, issue 7 (September 1999), p. 31, http://www.c-r.org/accord/geor-ab/accord7/unrole.shtml.

[46] Ketevan Tsikhelashvili, "The Case Studies of Abkhazia and South Ossetia," working paper prepared for the Carnegie Project on Complex Power-Sharing and Self-Determination, September 30, 2001, http://www.ecmi.de/cps/download/Abkhazia_SouthOssetia.pdf.

that has come to be known as the "Boden Document." It resulted from negotiations between Russia and the Western countries within the Group of Friends, rather than from a compromise between the parties to the conflict.[47] The Abkhazian side has refused to discuss the Boden Document, primarily because it proposes to keep Abkhazia as a part of Georgia, albeit as a sovereign entity based on the "rule of law." Western members of the Friends of the Secretary-General have failed to convince Russia to exert sufficient pressure on the Abkhazian authorities to start negotiations on this basis.

Despite the lack of progress in the negotiations, UNOMIG continued its work, but the situation in the security zone has not improved sufficiently to permit the safe return of IDPs to the Gali region.[48] In fact, the conflict has almost deteriorated into an open crisis on several occasions. Increased criminal activities on both sides of the Georgian–Abkhazian border have undermined the efficiency of the UNOMIG mission. There has been no agreement between Georgians and Abkhazians on the introduction of a UN civilian police group (CIVPOL) on both sides of the cease-fire line. In spring 2004, the CIVPOL was present only on the Zugdidi side of the security zone, which is controlled by Georgian authorities. Confidence-building measures between NGOs from Abkhazia and Georgia carried on, but with limited effect, largely because they reach only a small number of people on either side.

Although Russia is also a member of the Group of Friends of the Secretary-General, it has often assumed a reserved and sometimes obstructive approach in Abkhazia, urging the group not to interfere with its own separate negotiating efforts. Because of these differences within this organization, it is not surprising that it has made relatively little headway toward a sustainable solution. Alongside the UN framework, Russia has taken a number of independent initiatives. In March 2003, Russia's President Vladimir Putin met with Shevardnadze in the Black Sea resort of Sochi and signed an agreement addressed to improving the status quo. The

---

[47] Bruno Coppieters, "The Georgian–Abkhaz Conflict," in Bruno Coppieters, et al., *Europeanization and Conflict Resolution: Case Studies from the European Periphery* (Ghent: Academia Press, 2004), pp. 203–208, also published in the electronic *Journal on Ethnopolitics and Minority Issues in Europe*, issue 1 (2004), http://www.ecmi.de/jemie/.

[48] Domitilla Sagramoso, "The UN, the OSCE and NATO," in Lynch, *The South Caucasus*, pp. 63–89.

Sochi Agreement provided for the opening of the Gali district of Abkhazia to returning Georgian refugees, in parallel with the restoration of the railway link from Russia to Armenia through Abkhazia and the reconstruction of the Inguri electric power station.[49] To some, Shevardnadze's actions appeared to reflect a frustration over the slow pace of the UN-led mediation process and a readiness to transfer a greater mediating role to Russia without breaking, however, with the UN-led Geneva process.[50]

The OSCE is a player with a limited mandate in the Georgian–Abkhazian peace process. Its chief tasks are to maintain a liaison with UN operations in order to provide regular updates to OSCE headquarters and to observe and assist the UN-sponsored peace negotiations.[51] Through its human rights officer, the OSCE maintains a presence in Sukhumi where it concentrates on promoting confidence-building measures as part of an effort to strengthen civil society. The OSCE, however, suffers from a bad image among the Abkhazian authorities because the OSCE has accused Abkhazians of "ethnic cleansing" in several OSCE summit declarations.[52]

Organizations promoting initiatives aimed at developing confidence between Georgian and Abkhazian civil societies include International Alert, the London Information Network on Conflicts and State-building (LINKS), Conciliation Resources, as well as academics from the University of California–Irvine and the Vrije Universiteit Brussel (Free University of Brussels). They have sponsored meetings in neutral venues, providing opportunities for activists from the two sides to build relationships and foster dialogue.[53] While these programs have not achieved any significant breakthroughs, they have had a positive impact on the development of civil society on both sides of the dispute, by giving local leaders the

---

[49] The information on the Inguri power station comes from the authors' interviews in Abkhazia, spring 2004.

[50] Coppieters, "The Georgian–Abkhaz Conflict."

[51] In 1993, the UN and the CSCE (later OSCE) agreed that the UN should take the international lead on the conflict in Abkhazia, while the CSCE should take the lead in South Ossetia. See MacFarlane, "The Role of the UN," p. 36.

[52] See the OSCE declarations from the summits in Budapest (1993), Lisbon (1994), and Istanbul (1999).

[53] Susan Allen Nan, "Civic Initiatives," Accord, issue 7 (September 1999), p. 50. For information on International Alert, see http://www.international-alert. org/. For more on LINKS, see http://www.links-london.org/. For information on Conciliation Resources, see http://www.c-r.org/.

opportunity to travel, learn about the outside world, and dialogue with their counterparts.[54]

Still, mistrust and a deep disagreement over the future status of Abkhazia and the return of internally displaced persons persist. Beyond confidence-building measures, Western funding has also gone to humanitarian projects in Abkhazia, such as the work of the Halo Trust (mine clearance), Acción Contra el Hambre (rehabilitation of buildings), the International Red Cross (food to disabled persons), and Médecins Sans Frontières (medical aid).

Thus, it would appear that Western and UN peace efforts in Abkhazia have not brought nearer a political solution. Each of the Western initiatives—the progressive approach in 1997 with the creation of the Coordination Council, as well as the more comprehensive approach in 2000 broadened to address the political status of Abkhazia—have failed. Moreover, Russia, by multiplying negotiating channels, has simply confused the entire process.

As far as the unresolved conflict in South Ossetia is concerned, Western governments left the field at the outset of the conflict in 1992 to Russia (including North Ossetia) and the Conference on Security and Cooperation in Europe (CSCE, presently OSCE). As was the case in Abkhazia, the West supported the territorial integrity of Georgia from the beginning. The CSCE first established a mission in Georgia in 1992, in response to Georgia's request for assistance in the search for a settlement of the Georgian–Ossetian and Georgian–Abkhazian conflicts. At present, the OSCE, UNHCR, and EU work together with Russia, Georgia, and South Ossetia within a multilateral framework of peacekeeping and negotiation called the Joint Control Commission (JCC).

The OSCE's mandate in South Ossetia includes objectives such as the creation of a broad political framework within which a lasting political resolution can be achieved; the encouragement of an active dialogue between Georgia and South Ossetia through roundtable discussions; and an active role in the JCC's effort to craft proposals for resolving the conflict.[55] The OSCE also monitors the Joint Peacekeeping Forces by main-

---

[54] Abkhazian civil society was instrumental during the presidential elections in Abkhazia last fall, when a coalition of NGOs monitored the elections and rallied to defend the winner of the popular vote.

[55] See http://www.osce.org/georgia/mandate/.

taining contact with their Russian military command.[56] The peacekeeping forces (composed of Russian, Georgian, and Ossetian troops)
collaborate with the West inside multilateral mechanisms. The UN initially took the lead in reconstruction activities, but the European Commission has taken a prominent role since 2001 and was awarded a seat
on the JCC as the main funder of aid projects in the conflict area.[57]

Despite the OSCE's efforts to develop confidence-building measures
inside the JCC (such as the rehabilitation of infrastructure, the reduction
of small arms, and the fight against organized crime), it faced growing
criticism from all sides. For years, the Georgian side has argued that the
OSCE's presence, due to its failure to resolve the conflict, was adding
legitimacy to an independent South Ossetia. With the renewed flare-up
of violence in 2004, however, Georgian authorities altered their position.
They now favored the expansion of the OSCE mandate, urging the
organization to oversee the border between South Ossetia and Russia,
and, in particular, to monitor the road traffic through the Roki Tunnel.
Now it was Russia's turn to object.

The OSCE also until recently maintained border monitoring operations (BMOs) between Georgia and Russia (at the Chechen, Ingushetian,
and Dagestani sections of the Georgia–Russia territorial borders) to prevent a spillover from the Chechen conflict and to enhance contacts
between Russian and Georgian border guards. The BMO mandate
expired on December 31, 2004, and Russia vetoed its extension. Georgian authorities, however, continued lobbying for international monitors
on its border with Russia. On April 14, 2005, the OSCE Permanent
Council voted to allocate funds for an OSCE border guard training mission on the basis of a BMO. In addition, a three-person EU assessment
mission was deployed to Georgia in early April for a three-month period
to analyze threats on the border as well as Georgia's needs and capacities.[58]

---

[56] Under the Russia–Georgia Dagomis Accord and Sochi Cease-fire Agreement
of June/July 1992, a Joint Peacekeeping Force (JPKF) consisting of Russian,
Georgian, and Ossetian soldiers was deployed in the conflict zone.

[57] For more details on the European policies concerning South Ossetia, see
Damien Helly, "L'action extérieure de l'Union européenne dans le Caucase du
Sud," pp. 343–349. Officially, the peacekeeping operation in South Ossetia is
trilateral: Georgian, Russian, and Ossetian. However, the Ossetian contingent
over time came to be almost entirely staffed by South Ossetian soldiers, under
the command of a North Ossetian officer.

[58] "Three Experts from EU to Observe Russo-Georgian Border," *Civil Georgia*,

Although no comprehensive settlement of the South Ossetia conflict has been reached, the situation remained under control until recently, and a durable solution still seemed possible. In June–August 2004, however, the escalation of hostilities in this conflict zone, resulting in military and civilian casualties, revealed how fragile the status quo there was. Georgia's President Mikheil Saakashvili's successful reintegration of Ajara into the Georgian political fold led to attempts to bring about a similar outcome in South Ossetia. As with the case in Ajara, the Georgian government acted on the assumption that the South Ossetian authorities lacked popular legitimacy. In fact, however, Tbilisi failed to exploit the real discontent in the region, and the renewed hostilities had an opposite result from events in Ajara, leading to a consolidation of support around the South Ossetian de facto president, Eduard Kokoiti.[59] Facing the recrudescent threat of full-fledged war in the region, the West firmly warned Saakashvili that Georgia would be on its own if open hostilities erupted in South Ossetia.[60] An uneasy cease-fire was re-established on August 19, and Georgia withdrew its unsanctioned deployments from the conflict zone. Despite these setbacks in its attempt to reintegrate South Ossetia, Tbilisi had succeeded in unfreezing the Georgian–Ossetian conflict. In the process, the Georgian authorities openly pled for greater Western involvement and called for an international conference to address the question of a comprehensive settlement process.[61]

In 2003, the EU appointed Heike Talvitie, a Finnish diplomat, as its special envoy to the South Caucasus. His mandate, which included assisting in conflict resolution efforts, was criticized by some observers as too limited, because he was not allowed to be directly involved in mediation or conflict

---

April 8, 2005, http://www.civil.ge/eng/article.php?id=9557.

[59] International Crisis Group, "Georgia: Avoiding War in South Ossetia," Europe Report no.159, November 26, 2004.

[60] Authors' interviews with Western diplomats, Tbilisi, August–September 2004.

[61] At the Council of Europe's Parliamentary Assembly (PACE) session in January 2005, President Saakashvili announced the "Initiatives of the Georgian Government with Respect to the Peaceful Resolution of the Conflict in South Ossetia." The proposal primarily deals with the means to resolve South Ossetia's status within Georgia, but without prior confidence-building measures, it is not likely to produce results. See International Crisis Group Policy Briefing no. 38, "Georgia–South Ossetia: Refugee Return the Path to Peace," April 19, 2005, http://www.crisisgroup.org/home/index.cfm?id=3380&l=1.

resolution as such. Even with his limited mandate, however, Talvitie quickly managed to upgrade the EU's political profile in the region and did so without provoking the ire of big member states such as France or the United Kingdom. This reflected a more ambitious EU approach, despite disagreements over what the common policy in the region should be.

Georgia's preoccupation with the internal conflicts in Abkhazia and South Ossetia makes it hard for national leaders to respond to the West's other concerns. Both the United States and Europe have exhorted Georgia to seek greater regional cooperation with its immediate neighbors. Programs have been developed to increase customs, transportation, and environmental collaboration in the South Caucasus, but progress will be slow as long as Georgia is distracted by the fight to restore control over its breakaway territories (or, at least, to achieve some form of national reconciliation).

STATE REFORM

Internal security has been one of the West's main priorities in Georgia from the beginning, and foreign aid, both bilateral and multilateral, has been one of the primary tools for advancing this goal. It has evolved from purely humanitarian aid in the early 1990s to development aid focused on strengthening civil society and state structures.

Measured in per capita terms, Georgia ranks second among all U.S. aid recipients,[62] and much of this aid goes to address internal security, such as Georgia's border guards and customs controls.[63] Since 2001, the United States has put special stress on aiding in the struggle against organized crime.[64] In addition, U.S. concern over Georgia's internal security only increased following the Ministry of Interior's failed Gelayev operation in Kodori Gorge in summer 2001, when Chechen troops were

---

[62] Total U.S. aid to Georgia amounted to $778 million between 1992 and 2000, which is about five times the sum received by Azerbaijan. In addition, Georgia has received about $375 million in assistance from the U.S. Agency for International Development (USAID) since 1996. See "Country Report: Georgia," *The Economist Intelligence Unit*, November 2003.

[63] Office of the Secretary of State, *Congressional Budget Justification*, 2003. See also Ekaterine Metreveli and Ester Hakobyan, "The Political Underpinnings of U.S. Bilateral Aid to the Countries of Transcaucasus," *Demokratizatsia*, vol. 9, no. 3 (summer 2001), pp. 367–381.

[64] See Brenda Shaffer, "U.S. Policy," in Lynch, *The South Caucasus,* pp. 53–62.

supported by Georgian elements in an attempt to destabilize Abkhazia. This presence of Chechen warlords added intensity to U.S. preoccupations and shifted attention to Georgia's Pankisi Gorge, an area feared to be a safe heaven for global terrorists.[65] Both for this reason, and because Georgia was now seen as strategically relevant to the fight against terrorism, in April 2002, the United States launched the Georgia Train and Equip Program (GTEP) aimed at training special units of the Georgian army to deal with the terrorist threat and possibly to protect the BTC Pipeline.[66] Following Georgia's commitment to the anti-terrorist coalition and its decision to boost its presence in the coalition forces in Iraq, the United States announced a new military assistance program for Georgia to train its troops in peace support operations.[67] The Sustainment and Stability Operations Program (SSOP), as it is called, officially began in April 2005. It is designed to assist the Georgian armed forces to sustain their military participation in coalition efforts in Iraq by providing training and other support.[68]

NATO, through its Partnership for Peace Program, and its member countries (particularly the United States, Great Britain, Turkey, and Germany) have also been engaged in state reform, especially in army building and defense reform. NATO has organized peacekeeping training exercises in the Black Sea area in which Germany, Great Britain, and other European militaries (including Georgia's) have been active participants.[69]

---

[65] On the failed Gelayev operation in the Kodori Gorge, see the chapters in this volume by Oksana Antonenko and Jaba Devdariani. For more detail on the Pankisi Gorge question, see the chapter by Devdariani.

[66] See David Darchiashvili's chapter in this volume.

[67] "U.S. Announces New Military Assistance Program for Georgia," *Civil Georgia,* November 5, 2004, http://www.civil.ge/eng/article.php?id=8271. After completing the training provided under SSOP, the 558 soldiers are to deploy to Iraq in support of the global war on terrorism, replacing other Georgian units already serving as part of the coalition in support of Operation Iraqi Freedom. See "U.S. Announces New Military Assistance Program for Georgia."

[68] "Sustainment and Stability Operations Program (SSOP) Formally Begins," http://georgia.usembassy.gov/events/event20050423SSOPOpen.html.

[69] During his trip to Brussels on April 6, 2004, President Saakashvili stressed Georgia's aspiration to join NATO and announced that Georgia intended to finalize the individual partnership treaty with NATO at the alliance's Istanbul Summit in June 2004 (*RFE/RL Newsline,* April 7, 2004). In 2001 and 2002, Georgia joined in nine NATO Partnership for Peace (PfP) exercises, and eight exercises held in the spirit of the PfP. On Georgia's policies toward NATO, see

In addition, Georgia contributed to Turkish-led peacekeeping forces in Kosovo and hosted military exercises on its own territory. Defense reform in Georgia, however, has been slowed by severe economic constraints and rampant corruption. Tbilisi has made several requests for NATO to become more involved in Georgia's security affairs. Some of these requests were meant to counterbalance Russia's presence in the South Caucasus, whereas others were intended to create forms of cooperation with Russia. President Saakashvili has, for instance, officially proposed to set up a joint Russian–Georgian antiterrorism center in exchange for the withdrawal of Russian military bases from Georgia.[70] During its June 2004 summit in Istanbul, NATO decided to appoint a special representative for the Caucasus and Central Asia. On September 15, Robert Simmons, NATO's deputy assistant secretary-general, officially started fulfilling his duties as a special representative and appointed a permanent liaison officer in the Caucasus, based in Tbilisi.[71] In late October 2004 Georgia's Individual Partnership Action Plan (IPAP) was approved by NATO governments and a first evaluation of its implementation was carried out in spring 2005. The boost to Georgia-NATO relations is expected to accelerate state reforms in the country, thanks to the help of third countries, some of which have already gathered in a group of "New Friends of Georgia." Composed of Estonia, Latvia, Lithuania, Poland, Romania, and Bulgaria, this group reflects the growing interest of some of the EU's new members in the region. It is supposed to complement the older "Group of Friends" and focuses on Georgia's relations with NATO and the EU as well as on state reforms.[72]

Before the Rose Revolution of November 2003, the United States and Europe had been confronted with the Shevardnadze government's failure to build a state with credible authority, foster economic development, or

---

NATO's New Role in the NIS Area, Interim Project Report: NATO and its Partners in Eastern Europe and the Southern Caucasus (Warsaw: Osrodek Stuiow Wschodnich Centre for Eastern Studies, December 2003), at pp. 42–46, http://www.osw.waw.pl/en/epub/NATO/raport_en.pdf.

[70] "Georgia Proposes New 'Mechanics' for Relations with Russia," Civil Georgia, September 22, 2004, http://www.civil.ge/eng/article.php?id=7891.

[71] "NATO to Dispatch Liaison Officer to Georgia," Civil Georgia, September 9, 2004, http://www.civil.ge/eng/article.php?id=7846.

[72] Vladimir Socor, "New Group of Georgia's Friends Founded," Eurasia Daily Monitor, February 7, 2005.

achieve stability. The government's inability to implement any meaningful reform produced widespread donor fatigue.[73] In early 2003, the World Bank suspended energy and social programs in Georgia because of concerns over corruption, and in September 2003 the United States announced that it would begin to cut back its aid effort starting in 2004.[74] Increased Western criticism prompted Shevardnadze to seek a closer alliance with Russia, reflected principally in a series of strategic energy deals.[75] These deals stirred further U.S. wariness. Ambassador Steven Mann, the president's advisor for Caspian energy issues, publicly worried that such energy deals with Russia could undermine the South Caucasus Gas Pipeline Project, which is due to start in 2006 and is designed to transport gas from Azerbaijan's Shah Deniz gas field to Turkey via Georgia.[76]

The United States, or at least some American actors, also began investing more heavily in the Georgian political opposition, and these actors' role in the Rose Revolution was decisive. The U.S. government-funded National Democratic Institute (NDI) took part in the training, preparation, and unification of opposition leaders. Its sister institution, the International Republican Institute (IRI), and the International Foundation for Election Systems (IFES) also worked extensively to ensure free and fair elections. Organizations for Georgian election observers, particularly the International Society for Fair Elections and Democracy (ISFED), were set up and trained by American experts. This political expertise played a large role in politicizing the NGO sector and providing support to the democratic opposition.

---

[73] "Country Report: Georgia," *The Economist Intelligence Unit*, November 2003.

[74] Natalia Antelava, "United States Cuts Development Aid to Georgia," *Eurasia Insight*, September 29, 2003, http://www.eurasianet.org/departments/insight/articles/eav092903.shtml.

[75] In July 2003, Georgia signed a twenty-five-year cooperation agreement with Russia's gas giant Gazprom. The agreement envisaged supplying Georgia with gas and using Georgia's infrastructure for transit purposes. See *RFE/RL Newsline*, July 28, 2003, http://www.rferl.org/newsline/2003/07/2-TCA/tca-280703.asp.

[76] *RFE/RL Newsline*, July 28, 2003, http://www.rferl.org/newsline/2003/07/2-TCA/tca-280703.asp. The United States announced that it would cut aid to the Georgian energy sector from $30 million to $14 million. See "Country Report: Georgia," *The Economist Intelligence Unit*, November 2003. For more on this agreement with Gazprom, see Jaba Devdariani's chapter in this volume.

After his resignation, Shevardnadze went so far as to charge Washington with direct involvement in Georgia and accused American philanthropist George Soros of backing the opposition. Some Georgian journalists pointed to the fact that the U.S. ambassador to Georgia, Richard Miles, had been ambassador in Azerbaijan when President Abulfaz Elchibey was ousted and then in Serbia when President Slobodan Milošević was overthrown. It does appear that the American ambassador and other Western diplomats were in close contact with the Georgian opposition during key moments of the November 2003 upheaval. This does not mean, however, that they staged the ousting of Shevardnadze.

The United States gave its strong backing to the new regime. Secretary of State Colin Powell attended Saakashvili's presidential inauguration in January 2004 and brought word of a U.S. aid package of $166 million for 2004. In May 2004, Washington announced Georgia's inclusion in the Millennium Challenge Account (MCA).[77] Under this plan, Tbilisi is to receive $500 million over three years. MCA grants are awarded to governments, nongovernmental organizations, and private organizations to promote good governance, economic reform, anticorruption efforts, enterprise and private sector development, increased capacity for trade and investment, enhanced agricultural productivity, and improved health care and education.[78] Finally, President Bush traveled to Georgia as part of his trip to commemorate the sixtieth anniversary of the end of World War II. He came to Georgia from Russia on May 10, 2005, to "underscore his support for democracy, historic reform, and peaceful conflict resolution."[79]

As far as the EU is concerned, it has continuously provided Georgia with substantial aid, despite its failures in implementing programs and the lack of development prospects when Shevardnadze's corrupt team was in command. The European Commission has programs in the fields of humanitarian and food aid, rule of law, economic and judicial reform, and energy policy. To a lesser extent than the United States, European states—particularly the United Kingdom, Germany, Greece, and France—have

---

[77] Millennium Challenge Corporation, Press Release, http://www.mca.gov/public_affairs/press_releases/PR_Eligible.pdf.

[78] "U.S. to Grant Georgia $500 ml in Frames of MCA," *Civil Georgia*, May 28, 2004, http://www.civil.ge/eng/article.php?id=7021.

[79] "President Bush to Travel to Georgia," http://georgia.usembassy.gov/events/event20050325BushVisit.html.

also developed bilateral cooperation with Georgian authorities, especially with the military, customs officials, and the police. Since November 2003, the EU has developed a keener interest in Georgia and appears to have considerable expectations for the new leadership, despite misgivings over Saakashvili's commitment to the rule of law. At a donors conference in Brussels in June 2004, the European Commission and the World Bank— together with thirty-one countries and twelve international organizations—pledged nearly $1 billion in assistance to the new regime.[80] This aid is directed toward reforms in energy, governance, poverty reduction, child welfare, infrastructure, and agriculture for the years 2004–2006.

In December 2003, the European Parliament recommended the inclusion of the South Caucasus countries—Armenia, Azerbaijan and Georgia—in the European Neighborhood Policy (ENP), and the European Commission (EC) endorsed it in May 2004. Analysts argue that this somewhat delayed decision to include the South Caucasus into ENP was largely the result of the political changes in Georgia.[81] In March 2005, the EC recommended significantly intensifying relations with Georgia by developing an Action Plan under the ENP. The recommendation was based on the Commission's Country Report, which provided a comprehensive overview of the political and economic situation in Georgia and the state of its bilateral relations with the EU.[82]

---

[80] Joint Press Release by the European Commission and the World Bank, June 16, 2004, http://www.seerecon.org/Georgia/press_release.pdf.

[81] Jaba Devdariani, "Europe Remains Ambiguous in its South Caucasus Neighborhood," *Central Asia–Caucasus Analyst,* July 14, 2004.

[82] The European Commission's Delegation to Georgia and Armenia, http://www.delgeo.cec.eu.int/en/press/5_mart_ge_2005.htm. The key objectives of the Action Plan are to include: respect for the rule of law, strengthening democratic structures and pluralism, improvements in the business climate, reform of tax and customs administration, poverty reduction, conflict resolution, and enhanced regional cooperation. After the Rose Revolution the EU has paid particular attention to strengthening the institutions that protect the rule of law in the country. In summer 2004 the EU launched in Georgia its first ever Rule of Law mission, called EUJUST THEMIS, to help the country in reforming its criminal justice system. The mission is to assist the Georgian government in coordinating its overall approach to the reform process by placing eight civilian experts from the EU member states in relevant ministries. See "EU Launches 'Rule of Law' Mission, Amid Human Rights Concerns, *Civil Georgia,* July 17, 2004, http://www.civil.ge/eng/article. php?id=7439.

WHAT SHOULD THE WEST DO?

Western governments should place development challenges and state reforms at the head of the security agenda in Georgia. Thus, it is good that the "donor fatigue" of Shevardnadze's last years has given way to a new readiness to help, once the new Georgian leadership began invigorating the fight against corruption and moving forward with state reforms. In these circumstances, the West should continue to push for a comprehensive strategy of state reform achievable within Saakashvili's first term. The main guidelines must come from Georgia itself, but be consistent with EU standards and Euro-Atlantic practices. The basic principles are already in documents signed by previous Georgian governments or are about to be approved, such as the EU–Georgian Partnership and Cooperation Agreements, the New Neighborhood Policy (EU–Georgia Action Plan), and NATO's Individual Partnership Action Plan (IPAP).

The West must have a balanced strategy, however, attacking fundamental problems (including corruption) in a fashion that is mindful of the need for political stability during this period of reform. For example, broad social discontent might follow massive dismissals from state institutions. In addition, such a step is likely to expose the lack of qualified personnel for government positions in Georgia, particularly in the absence of an adequate human resources policy. These challenges will almost certainly be felt early on in the process, but they will linger much longer if the West does nothing to help. In March 2004, the Georgian government promised to provide dismissed civil servants with adequate compensation and new employment opportunities.[83] It has also elaborated an extremely ambitious plan of reform in all sectors of society for the 2004–2009 period. This plan includes enhancing democratic governance, refurbishing state institutions, upgrading education and public services, developing cultural institutions, restoring the nation's territorial integrity, safeguarding national security, and generating economic prosperity. The new leadership obviously needs to set priorities among these reforms, otherwise little is likely to be accomplished.

Urgent needs are nonetheless already apparent. Recruitment programs should be launched in Western countries to attract and recruit

---

[83] Georgian Ministry of Finance, "Strengthening and Uniting Georgia through Economic Growth, European Integration, and Long-Term Stability: Reform and Development Programme for the Government of Georgia 2004–2009."

young Georgians abroad who have trained in European or American universities or companies. These programs should help to create an administrative government staff based on competence, experience, and honesty. As part of the same effort, the government needs to establish and then follow a code of conduct for civil servants. In addition, the government needs to be careful in its decisions to fire civil servants. Even if corruption was widespread in the Shevardnadze era, some people managed not to be involved in it. These officials and their families would be victims of indiscriminate administrative purges. To be effective, state reforms and the recruitment of new staff must be matched by the payment of adequate salaries in a timely fashion. If this does not happen, corruption will soon reappear. A special fund for civil servants' salaries has been set up to receive grants from various donors. Soros and other U.S. foundations, as well as the United Nations Development Project, have begun contributing to this special fund.[84]

In addition, customs regulations and management need to be reformed if the revenue necessary for the state budget is to be secured, and existing Western programs in this field should be continued. Tax collection will depend on increased control of strategic border crossing points, such as South Ossetia and Megrelia. In order for this to happen, central authorities' political control will have to be strengthened. Customs reform is intricately entwined with state unity and territorial integrity. The government's crackdown on the Ergneti Market near the South Ossetia conflict zone in June 2004 was essential as a means of disrupting the activity of several criminal groups. This type of market, how-

---

[84] In 2004, the president, prime minister, parliamentary speaker, and head of the Supreme Court each received $1,500 from this fund, in addition to their official Georgian salaries. Fifteen ministers and four state ministers, as well as the National Security Council secretary and the head of presidential administration each received $1,200. The head of the Economic Council, the head of interior troops, the head of the army's General Staff, the head of the traffic police, the head of the State Protection Guard, the head of the Tax Department, and the head of the financial police each received $1,000. Sixty deputy ministers each received $700. National Security Council deputies each received $500. Traffic police staff members each received $150. It is planned that these salaries will be paid by the state budget. Other supplements will be given to the presidential administration, the Economic Council, and ministers. Approximately 5,000 civil servants are expected to receive additional salaries. See *Rezonansi*, March 25, 2004, p. 2.

ever, also provides jobs for the local population. Therefore, such a policy should be combined with economic development opportunities for the area.

Police reform in Georgia has to restore trust between citizens and the state. Training programs supported by outside donors are essential to improving police performance, as is advice on how Soviet-style police structures might be recast. Georgia has started police reform by firing thousands of traffic police staff. While the traffic police were widely corrupt and public sympathy toward them is minimal, the act of firing thousands of these people and leaving them without prospects for a new job or social benefits is not likely to improve the larger picture of crime in the country. Reform of the police's investigative structures in Georgia should also be a priority, because human rights concerns have not decreased since the change of leadership. Complaints about arbitrary arrests, the planting of drugs and weapons on suspects, and torture in the investigative and penitentiary system are frequent.

A productive dialogue between Tbilisi and the breakaway regions will only be possible if the West helps Abkhazia and South Ossetia to develop and to open up their own local political systems. Moreover, Western assistance to local civil society organizations and vulnerable populations should improve confidence between both sides. If trust is increased and populations in Abkhazia and South Ossetia believe that the West (and consequently Georgia too) is concerned about their future and their legitimate desire not to be assimilated into a hegemonic Georgian culture, a window of opportunity could reopen, allowing political dialogue to make headway. As long as the Western powers deny Abkhazian and Ossetian concerns, however, they will be seen in these areas as part of the threat, simply inclining the breakaway entities to lean ever more heavily on Russian support.

The international community must act collectively if it wants to stabilize Georgia. As a first step, the mandates of the CIS (Russian) peacekeeping force and UNOMIG in Abkhazia should be reconsidered. Russian troops need to be more involved in ensuring personal security of those individuals in the conflict zone. If Russian peacekeeping forces cannot provide a secure environment, the UN should seriously consider the possibility of sending an international peacekeeping force. As far as UNOMIG is concerned, it might serve as an umbrella for extended UN involvement in humanitarian and development projects aimed at diminishing tension between Georgians and Abkhazians. The UN-sponsored civil police project intended for the Georgian-populated Gali district in Abkhazia could provide such an opportunity.

In South Ossetia, efforts should be increased to encourage economic cooperation in the region, in particular, by supporting a local trade and banking system. EU proposals for joint customs or joint freight-monitoring mechanisms that have been turned down previously should again be brought forward. They could serve as a key confidence-building measure. The international community should also pressure Georgia into adopting a legal framework for refugee return and property restitution for about 60,000 Ossetian refugees who have fled Georgia during the conflict. Donors should also provide financial assistance to cover part of the operating costs, but most importantly to assist the Georgian government in meeting its compensation liability.

Attempts to develop regional cooperation in the South Caucasus have failed in part because of the Azerbaijani–Armenian conflict over Nagorno-Karabakh. In this case, rather than continue to labor fruitlessly for trilateral collaboration among Georgia, Armenia, and Azerbaijan, the West would be wise to push for workable forms of bilateral cooperation between Georgia and the other two South Caucasus countries. Useful projects could be organized in many areas: transportation, intelligence, customs, border security, and the campaign against organized crime.

To boost economic development and attract Western investors who are not likely to commit themselves without official institutional support (as well as to facilitate contacts among European and non-European economic actors), the EU should consider establishing a Caucasian bank and an EU-funded regional chamber of commerce. It need not (and, indeed, should not) be confined to Georgia, but could also be extended to Russia, Iran, and Turkey.

U.S. involvement in Georgia has significantly increased during the last few years. For instance, Georgia became a transit point for U.S. military flights supporting operations in Afghanistan. Georgia has looked for close military cooperation with the United States, including outside the NATO framework. In August 2003, Georgia sent a Special Forces platoon of 70 troops to Iraq and then the next April raised the figure of peacekeeping troops to 155.[85] Georgia's participation in the anti-terrorism coalition,

---

[85] "Georgian Peacekeeping Troops to Deploy in Iraq," *RFE/RL Newsline*.

therefore, enlarged the U.S. military presence in an area that Russia considered part of its sphere of influence, introducing another factor capable of heightening U.S.–Russian tensions.

Such an acceleration of U.S. involvement has inevitably led to Russian fears that Washington is trying to displace it in the South Caucasus. This feeling grows when the United States puts pressure on Moscow to fulfill the commitments it made in Istanbul in 1999 to withdraw its troops from Georgian bases. Tensions over the issue were particularly evident at the December 2003 OSCE summit in Maastricht, when Secretary of State Colin Powell criticized Russia for failing to respect the Istanbul agreement and warned Moscow against supporting separatist leaders of breakaway regions in the South Caucasus. The United States has indicated a willingness to provide financial aid to Russia to help facilitate Russia's withdrawal from its two remaining bases in Georgia at Akhalkalaki and Batumi. No matter how the United States tries to soften the impact of its increased role in Georgia and the region, however, it is too bitter of a pill for Russian nationalists and conservatives to swallow, and an emotional response is unavoidable. Beyond the psychological challenge of adjusting to a loss of influence, a broad spectrum of Russians worry that U.S. or NATO troops will replace Russian troops in Georgia when they are withdrawn from the remaining bases.

To minimize the risk of misleading Russia or Georgia, the United States must clarify the place of Georgia on its security agenda. If Washington hopes to enhance Georgia's role as a staging country in its military efforts elsewhere, it should say so unambiguously to both the Georgians and the Russians. NATO, for its part, should clearly set out the conditions and deadlines by which Georgia can strengthen its relationship with the alliance. A comprehensive framework comparable to the action plans established for NATO member-candidates should be officially proposed. NATO's intentions in Georgia should be made plain to Russia, and steps should be taken to reduce the risk that these intentions will be misread. Oksana Antonenko's proposal to transform the Russian base at Batumi into a NATO–Russia training center for the Caucasus or the Black Sea region would be one such step.[86] After all, a stable Georgia should be very much in Russia's long-term interest. A more secure Geor-

---

[86] Oksana Antonenko, senior fellow at the International Institute for Strategic Studies (IISS), interview with the author, March 27, 2004.

gia will present increased opportunities for Russian business interests. A Georgia free of domestic crises will be another element encouraging Russia to rely on its financial and economic rather than military power—and another reason to abandon its earlier inclination to exploit trouble as a means of building influence. Time will tell if the new Georgian leadership has the ability to nudge Russia in this direction, while also persuading the West that it is a fit partner.

CONCLUSION

The U.S. and European contributions to Georgia's security have long been diminished by a lack of understanding and common language, whether concerning Georgia's responsibility for its own stability or the West's readiness to confront Russia on sensitive issues such as the unresolved territorial conflicts. Tensions between Russia and the West over Georgian security are not likely to dissipate soon.

For economic as well as geopolitical reasons, the West is interested in stability on the periphery of Europe and in the Middle East, and Georgia is an essential factor in the stability of the Caucasus. But for Georgia to be a stabilizing influence in the Caucasus, its own security challenges must be met.

The United States has actively mixed energy-related and geopolitically grounded policies to achieve comprehensive regional stability in the South Caucasus. The EU has been much less proactive in the field of oil and gas projects, letting private actors take the lead, and has given priority to regional cooperation programs instead. In the field of conflict resolution, Europeans and Americans have failed to achieve tangible and sustainable results despite long-standing multilateral efforts within the framework of the OSCE and the United Nations.

Western-sponsored state reforms, especially under President Shevardnadze, achieved little success. The main Western success story is probably the 2003 Rose Revolution itself, which demonstrated that consistent efforts to support civil society, defend human rights, and the presence of a democratic opposition do pay off. The new Georgian leadership probably has too much to do to succeed in all instances, but it must at least strive to prevent the country's security situation from deteriorating further.

In the near term, Georgia's new leaders need to prove that they are capable of launching the kind of reform that will restore the state and

provide a basis for domestic stability. This means a significant modernization of state structures, including the implementation of the rule of law,
controlling and then rationalizing the military, and seriously reducing
corruption and organized crime. To accomplish these goals, customs officials, the police, and military forces must be trained and reshaped according to Western standards, a theme Saakashvili has often sounded when
expressing Georgia's desire to become a part of the Euro-Atlantic family.

The West can help Georgia by stressing the importance of shedding
non-democratic habits; softening the linguistic, ethnic, and religious
dimensions of Georgian nationalism; treating national minorities in an
enlightened fashion; and looking for ways to ease the mistrust between
the center and the breakaway regions. If progress is achieved on these
fronts, Georgian security, as well as security in the wider Caucasian
region, will be enhanced.

CHAPTER 7

Georgia and its Distant Neighbors

THOMAS DE WAAL

A t the end of 1919, a newly independent Georgia was struggling with a terrifying range of challenges on all fronts. A border dispute with Armenia remained unsolved; there was a small but troublesome list of bilateral problems with Azerbaijan; and the government in Tbilisi was asserting a contested claim to the region of Batumi, which the British were on the point of abandoning. Amid this chaos, Georgia's sophisticated foreign minister, Yevgeny Gegechkori, was still trying to keep the idea of a broad-based Transcaucasian confederation between Georgia, Armenia, and Azerbaijan alive. Gegechkori was the prime mover behind a series of conferences designed to re-establish ties between the three republics, which had been severed the year before. But British journalist C.E. Bechhofer, who met with Gegechkori in 1919, was struck both by how unready the Georgians were to compromise with their neighbors and by the inauspicious regional climate overall. He wrote:

> What he [Gegechkori] did not tell me, but what was evident enough to any one who knew a little of the inside of the Transcaucasian situation, was that Georgia could not count upon Azerbaijan['s] support in the event of a Turkish or pro-Turkish invasion of the Caucasus. Nor as time was to show was the Tartar–Armenian [Azerbaijani–Armenian] Treaty worth the paper it was written on.[1]

Bechhofer comments further that what he calls the "the recent Georgian–Armenian squabble" of December 1918 might have ended in Armenian occupation of the city of Tiflis (Tbilisi) if the British had not

---

[1] C. E. Bechhofer, *In Denikin's Russia and the Caucasus, 1919–1920* (London: Collins, 1921), p. 54.

intervened in defense of the Georgians.[2] Georgian historians have a different account of the same episode, asserting that British troops prevented Georgia's army from going on the offensive. In any event, it was an outside power that played the critical role in bringing the intra-Caucasian fighting of 1918 to a close.

Four external powers—Russia, Turkey, Germany, and Great Britain—were the big players in the South Caucasus in this period, and each of them at various times was seen as the protector of the three Caucasian states—Russia protected Armenia, Turkey protected Azerbaijan, and Great Britain and Germany protected Georgia, respectively. The continued quarrels between the states of the Caucasus make it clear that the promise of protection from a big military power superseded any feelings of regional solidarity or loyalty. Indeed, in a region of contested borders, the support of the most dominant power (in 1919, this was briefly Britain) could be exploited effectively to get the upper hand in disputes, such as the one over Batumi. In the case of Armenia, picking your allies carefully could make the difference between survival and annihilation.

In 2005, the three small recently independent post-Soviet states of the Caucasus are driven by similar calculations in their foreign and security policies, as they try to buy into security arrangements that strengthen their independence and borders. Armenia still relies on Russia as its main strategic ally, Georgia looks to the United States, while Azerbaijan's closest ally is Turkey. These protection agreements tend to work against cross-Caucasian cooperation. The need of the states of the Caucasus to obtain security from big external powers means that once again these outside powers, as well as other players such as international oil companies and the Islamic Republic of Iran, fracture the security picture of the region.

Pulled apart by conflicting interests, the South Caucasus and its immediate neighborhood has never formed an easily recognizable "region" in the way that, for example, the Baltic states or the Benelux countries have. The metaphor of a crossroads or meeting place of different cultures, rather than a region, is much more commonly applied to the South Caucasus. From 1918 to 1920, Gegechkori was one of the few people trying to facilitate some kind of regional cooperation in the South Caucasus. More recently, Georgia has displayed little interest in close cooperation with its neighbors. Modern Georgia's first president, Zviad

---

[2] Bechhofer, *In Denikin's Russia and the Caucasus*, p. 54.

Gamsakhurdia, promoted an image of Georgia as a special European country that should immediately sever all links with Russia and its Soviet past, and that would turn into a country like Austria or Switzerland within a matter of years. His eccentric ideas about the common ethnic and cultural basis of the Caucasian peoples and that the Georgian ethnos was part of an Ibero–Caucasian ethnocultural civilization distracted from regional integration. He ended by isolating his country from Russia, the West, and his South Caucasian neighbors. Gamsakhurdia's successor, Eduard Shevardnadze, intently focused his foreign policy on moving Georgia away from Russia and toward winning the protection of the United States, to the exclusion of both the European Union and Georgia's immediate neighbors. He showed almost no interest in enhancing political or economic integration with Georgia's neighbors and even his good relationship with Azerbaijan was based on high-level strategic and energy calculations rather than commercial links. Georgian political leaders have shown rhetorical support for their fellow leaders in Armenia or Azerbaijan or signed their name to initiatives, but these paper-thin commitments have been no substitute for the hard work of building a region.

My argument in this chapter is that Georgia's environment, both in the South Caucasus and in the wider region beyond, is not one of security, but of insecurity and that the failure of the three South Caucasian countries to imagine themselves as a region has deleterious effects on their long-term prospects. This is partly the fault of the Georgian government and the ambitions of the country's elites, and partly stems from deeper historical and geographical factors (such as the diverse and divisive history of the region and the role of Moscow) that have shaped political choices in the South Caucasus. The net result is that Georgia remains very much alone in its security arrangements. Even the much-vaunted energy pipelines being built across Georgia have negative aspects and do not necessarily contribute to a broader regional security architecture.

The regime change in Georgia in November 2003 that brought to power a new president, Mikheil Saakashvili, has changed many things, but the deep-rooted structure of regional insecurity is not one of them, at least not in the short term. Saakashvili's fight against black markets and corruption promises—if it works—to make cross-border trade more transparent. His vision of a more balanced foreign policy holds out the hope of a Georgia that is less of a hostage to Washington and Moscow. But with Saakashvili strongly concentrated on Georgia's internal prob-

lems and with the intractable security problems of the wider region unresolved, the road forward in the South Caucasus is going to be a long one.

SECURITY IN THE SOUTH CAUCASUS

The geographical definition of the "South Caucasus" has only enjoyed
wide currency since the mid 1990s. Bounded to the north by the defining landmark of the vast Caucasus Mountain range, the territories of
Georgia, Armenia, and Azerbaijan were formerly collectively called by the
Russocentric term "Transcaucasus" (or "*Zakavkaz'e*") before independence allowed the three countries to employ the more neutral term of
"South Caucasus." But while the mountains form a conclusive barrier to
the north (albeit one whose exact boundaries might be disputed by
groups such as the Abkhazians, Ossetians, or Lezgins), the southern limits of the region are more arbitrary. Broadly speaking, the southern frontier of the region was drawn by Russian imperial rulers, first in tsarist
times and then by the Soviet Union. Its exact borders have been defined
more by history than geography. The fact that the South Caucasus
includes Batumi but not Kars is a matter of historical contingency (stemming from the events of 1915–1921) that leaves Batumi far closer politically to Moscow than to the nearby Turkish port of Trabzon. Thus, the
Soviet legacy still defines the modern identity of this region as a region in
innumerable ways.[3]

From the security perspective, a brief glance at the history of the
region gives the impression that the phrase "Caucasian security" is actually an oxymoron. The South Caucasus has been a battlefield of empires
for centuries, with local peoples used as willing or unwilling combatants
in a seemingly endless series of wars. This imperial legacy of enforced
cohabitation and great power war by proxy has never provided the region
with a stable security framework, except for one imposed from above.

Georgia, with Tiflis/Tbilisi as its capital, has frequently been acknowledged as the center of the region. Tiflis was the administrative capital of
the region when it was part of the Russian Empire and again during the
short-lived Transcaucasian Federation of 1918. With the border between

---

[3] For a detailed discussion about geographical terminology for the region, see
Tamaz V. Gamkrelidze, "'Transcaucasia' or 'South Caucasus'? Towards a More
Exact Geopolitical Nomenclature," *Marco Polo Magazine*, vol. 4–5 (1999),
http://www.traceca.org/marcopolo/mp40.pdf.

Armenia and Azerbaijan, the longest in the South Caucasus, closed by
the Nagorno-Karabakh dispute, Georgia is again (by default) the regional
center for any international organizations, businesses, and nongovernmental organizations (NGOs) that want to deal in all three countries.

It is worth stressing that the Georgians themselves have generally not
laid claim to a leading role in the South Caucasus, and Georgia as such
has no tradition of dominance in the region. The status of Tiflis/Tbilisi
as a capital city was conferred by Russia in tsarist times, but neither
Armenians nor Azerbaijanis regard the city as the capital of the Caucasus.
Over the last century, Georgia's nation-building has consistently clashed
with the ambitions of its ethnic minorities, who have looked for protection not to Tbilisi but to Moscow (the Abkhazians and the Ossetians), to
Baku (the Azerbaijanis), or to Yerevan (the Armenians). At the same
time, there is no comparable Georgian diaspora scattered across the rest
of the South Caucasus that might have given Tbilisi the status of a protector for citizens outside the borders of Georgia. In the Caucasus family,
you could say, Georgia has been one of the competing children, not a
parent. Indeed, the problem might be defined as a family that *has* no par-
ents, only intervening uncles and stepmothers.

The Caucasus's traditional stepmother has been Moscow. In Soviet
times, 50 percent of the region's trade was with Russia (the Russian
Soviet Federal Socialist Republic), and economic relations among the
three Caucasian republics were poorly developed. Political negotiations
for resources and favors were generally conducted in Moscow rather than
in collaboration with comrades from Baku or Yerevan.

The role (or lack thereof) of Georgia in the Nagorno-Karabakh dispute illustrates this dysfunctional regional dynamic. When the Nagorno-
Karabakh conflict first erupted in 1988, Georgia was a Soviet republic
and in no position to mediate. At the first signs of trouble in Nagorno-
Karabakh in February 1988, the Politburo dispatched a motorized battalion of 160 Soviet Interior Ministry troops from Georgia to Nagorno-
Karabakh to keep order. Even at this early stage, it was already deemed
too risky to send a battalion from Armenia or Azerbaijan to the region.
However, even if many of the personnel of that first battalion sent to
Nagorno-Karabakh were Georgian, it is safe to assume that its commander was a Slav.

Politburo transcripts (released in 1992) show that the only Georgian
in the Politburo, Eduard Shevardnadze, was the first to offer a proposal

for resolving the conflict. Shevardnadze's proposal was to upgrade the status of Nagorno-Karabakh to that of autonomous republic. But his advice was not heeded and his involvement seems to have ended there. Shevardnadze's proposal was taken up again later in 1988, but by then it was already too late.

With the disintegration of the Soviet Union, a dispassionate observer might have expected a newly independent Georgia to be a useful intermediary between the Armenians and Azerbaijanis when the Karabakh dispute escalated once again into a full-fledged interstate war in 1991. Instead it was Russia's President Boris Yeltsin and his Kazakhstani counterpart, Nursultan Nazarbaev, who launched the most high-profile peace initiative of that year, as both of them visited Stepanakert, the regional capital of Nagorno-Karabakh.

Georgia's failure to mediate between its warring neighbors was probably due in part to the fact that it was too immersed in its own troubles from 1991 to 1994 to have the political will to resolve anyone else's problems. Of greater importance was the fact that Georgia, which was confronting the attempted secessions of the regions of South Ossetia and Abkhazia, supported Azerbaijan's fundamental position in the Karabakh dispute—that the territorial integrity of the new post-Soviet states must be upheld and separatism must be curtailed. Forging a close strategic relationship with Heydar Aliev of Azerbaijan, Shevardnadze therefore essentially supported Azerbaijan on the Karabakh issue.

A look at the tangled web of relations between the South Caucasian countries and their immediate neighbors suggests that hard realist calculations are much more important than culturally or historically determined factors in defining priorities. For example, despite all their rich cultural and historical interconnections over two centuries, Georgia's relations with Russia are currently very poor. In addition, Georgia's often troubled history with predominantly Muslim Azerbaijan has not prevented these two countries from developing a good relationship over the last ten years; and although Russia and Armenia both talk up the age-old affinities that supposedly underlie their alliance, those same types of considerations do not explain why Armenia (which has a population that is approximately 98 percent Christian) has a good strategic partnership with the Islamic Republic of Iran. The same types of pragmatic considerations inform Georgia's relations with Armenia—two nations with an ancient Christian heritage whose foreign policies are not, however, governed by this common historical experience. Landlocked Armenia relies on the Georgian Black Sea ports of Poti and Batumi for most of its foreign imports.[4] Georgia is also the conduit for Russian gas and oil exports to Armenia. But this link is not backed up by broader political or economic cooperation between Georgia and Armenia. The main road on the Georgian side of the border with Armenia in the Javakheti region is one of the worst in the Caucasus and there are currently no commercial flights at all between Yerevan and Tbilisi.

The Georgian–Armenian conflict of December 1918, over the Lori and Akhalkalaki regions, lasted only two weeks. But tension remains around the Georgian region of Javakheti in general and around the town of Akhalkalaki in particular. Approximately 5 to 6 percent of the population of Georgia is Armenian, and in Javakheti the figure is more than 90 percent. Javakheti Armenians' discontent with Tbilisi is a simmering problem that, while it does not conspicuously hurt top-level relations between Armenia and Georgia, creates suspicions lower down in Georgian society.

Strategically, Armenia and Georgia look in opposite directions— toward Moscow and Washington, respectively. In 1995, Armenia signed an agreement allowing the Russian military to remain at the base in Gyumri for twenty-five more years. Two years later, this agreement was supplemented by a comprehensive "Treaty on Friendship, Cooperation, and Mutual Assistance." The Armenian and Russian armies train together and cooperate closely. On an economic level, Russia is affecting a gradual takeover of many of Armenia's most important assets, including Armenia's nuclear power station and many of its industrial plants. In sharp contrast, Georgian leaders consistently say they want to join the North Atlantic Treaty Organization (NATO) and have made it a priority for Russia to close its two remaining military bases in the country. It is in Armenia's strategic interest for the bases at Batumi and Akhalkalaki in Georgia to remain open, as these bases help allow the Russian military to supply the Russian base in Gyumri, Armenia. There has also been plenty of both human and technical Russian military traffic across the Georgian-

---

[4] Evgeny Polyakov, *Changing Trade Patterns after Conflict Resolution in the South Caucasus* (Washington, DC: World Bank Poverty Reduction and Economic Management Sector Unit, Europe and Central Asia Region, 2000), p. 33, http://lnweb18.worldbank.org/eca/eca.nsf/0/23ac8865ee0dc 520852568fc005ba956/$FILE/ATT00ZE9/Trade+flows3.pdf.

Armenian border (although this has decreased since Russia and Georgia set up their mutual visa regime in 2000). In addition, the Akhalkalaki base is virtually the only employer for the local Armenian population in the district, and its closure may have a catastrophic effect on the local economy.

Georgia's relations with Azerbaijan appear to be much better than its relations with Armenia. Although the two countries have had border disputes over the Zakatala region in the past, they have not flared up in recent memory. Both countries now have a declared strategic orientation toward the West, embodied in their commitment to the highly politicized Baku–Tbilisi–Ceyhan (BTC) oil pipeline project (which is discussed in more detail later in this chapter). In addition, the countries' two previous long serving presidents, Shevardnadze and Aliev, also forged a very public alliance during the 1990s—even though they had been ideological opponents when they were members of Mikhail Gorbachev's Politburo in the 1980s. Aliev even "donated" Azerbaijan's transit fees for the BTC Pipeline to Georgia at a time when the project appeared to be in trouble.

Yet the Georgian–Azerbaijani partnership is not as close as it seems. Cooperation on the huge infrastructure project of the BTC Pipeline has not translated into substantial lower-level economic collaboration. In line with the particular traditions of the South Caucasus, Azerbaijan's strategic priorities are proving to be different from Georgia's. Azerbaijani-Russian relations have thawed since President Vladimir Putin came to power in Russia. As two former KGB officers, Putin and Heydar Aliev were able to strike up a good relationship, which was in strong contrast to the strained relations between Putin and Shevardnadze. In 2000, Russia conspicuously imposed visa requirements on Georgia while continuing to waive them for Azerbaijan. And Moscow's prompt and warm congratulations to Ilham Aliev in October 2003, following his victory in Azerbaijan's disputed presidential election, were in strong contrast to Russia's ten-day silence following Mikheil Saakashvili's overwhelming—and entirely undisputed— victory in the presidential elections in Georgia in January 2004. Azerbaijan and Georgia's different relationships with Russia suggest that Baku and Tbilisi do not see eye to eye on all strategic issues.

The experience of postwar Europe demonstrates that a close trading relationship and open borders between countries are prerequisites for closer strategic alignment. Measured against this yardstick, the three Caucasian countries are painfully estranged from one another. Indeed, the semi-isolation of Georgia from its two South Caucasian neighbors is most obvious at the borders. Passing from one former Soviet republic to another in this region can take many hours: commercial traffic is subject to heavy tariff fees plus substantial bribes; drivers with cars bearing the license plate of one country are reluctant to cross into another, for fear of being harassed for bribes by the traffic police across the border.

As a result, legitimate trade between Georgia and its neighbors is mainly restricted to timber, wheat, and energy products. The disincentives to any kind of joint ventures, let alone to any broader Caucasian common market, are huge. What is more, this does not appear to be a case of corrupt local officials sabotaging the grand plans of their leaders. This isolation seems to be *intrinsic* to the political and economic structure of the South Caucasus. These problems are not merely unfortunate bureaucratic obstacles which, when removed, will release pent-up entrepreneurial energy, but are products of a deep-rooted political economy where short-term political interests oppose longer-term economic progress.

The economy of the South Caucasus is divided up among a number of powerful players who seek stable monopolies to keep their political power well-funded and secure. In Georgia, a situation has developed whereby widespread poverty, an informally privatized economy, and weak and corrupt law enforcement agencies have made the black economy all-pervasive, endangering any attempts to build up a properly funded and functioning state. Zurab Zhvania, Georgia's late prime minister, said that because of smuggling and non-payment of taxes, the Georgian government had lost 60 million lari ($29 million) from uncollected tobacco revenue alone in 2003 and almost $200 million from non-declared oil products.[5] An American specialist puts the issue even more starkly, saying that, "The [Georgian] government could eliminate its fiscal deficit if it would just fully collect the taxes on two products, imported gasoline and cigarettes."[6] A Georgian expert on organized crime, Giorgi Glonti, estimates that the Georgian economy "is 60 to 70 percent dependent on the black

---

[5] Shorena Ratiani, "Georgia: Corruption Crackdown Makes Waves," *IWPR Caucasus Reporting Service* no. 231, March 4, 2004, http://www.iwpr.net/index.pl?archive/cau/cau_200403_221_1_eng.txt.

[6] Craig MacPhee, "Expert on Georgia Explores 'Can Saakashvili Outdo Shevardnadze?'" *Newswise*, January 5, 2004.

market, which sells mostly smuggled goods such as food, alcohol, cigarettes, and other manufactured goods."[7]

Often the distinction between legal and illegal is less clear-cut. Tony
Vaux has argued, "Despite the appearance of being a crumbling post-
Soviet state, Georgia is really a thriving free-market economy. The problem is that regulation of that economy depends on the influence of clan
and criminal networks rather than on the rational actions of the state."[8]
Perhaps it would be better to say that the market is not "free" at all, but
regulated by the narrow political considerations of a few individuals
(some of them state actors) who are not interested in the long-term economic development of the state as a whole.

In regions where the rule of law is weak, the question of the legality
of some economic activity is hard to define. But the people who control
timber in northern Armenia or western Georgia, hazelnuts or cigarettes
in Ajara, petroleum products of all kinds in Azerbaijan, or scrap metal all
over Georgia have good reasons to fear free trade. As a result, Georgia's
ambitions to be a transportation corridor have so far made it into an
attractive route for criminals. For example, the country has become a
transit zone for the international drug trade. Louise Shelley of the
Transnational Crime and Corruption Center (TRACC) writes that,
"According to analysts at Interpol, in the 1990s the southern route
[across the South Caucasus] for the drug trade now carries 10 percent of
the drugs trafficked from Afghanistan to European markets, a non-exis-
tent share before the end of the USSR."[9] Some of the illicit drugs—
heroin and raw opium from Afghanistan—appear to be crossing from
Iran into the South Caucasus before passing onward to the Balkans.
Other drugs almost certainly make their way through Turkmenistan and
across the Caspian Sea, although obtaining data from the highly secretive
state of Turkmenistan makes this hard to verify. Svante Cornell makes the
point that Georgia is particularly hard hit by the use of this narcotics
route, not least because the "Georgian security services are ill-equipped

---

[7] Giorgi Glonti, "Problems Associated with Organized Crime in Georgia,"
http://www.traccc.cdn.ge/publications/publication2.html.

[8] Tony Vaux, *Strategic Conflict Assessment, Georgia* (Timbertop, UK: Humanitarian Initiatives, 2003), p. 6.

[9] Louise Shelley, "Organized Crime in the Former Soviet Union: The Distinctiveness of Georgia," http://www.traccc.cdn.ge/publications/
publication1.html.

to deal with the problem, and have apparently been infiltrated by trafficking networks to a greater extent than in Azerbaijan."[10]

With Georgia's borders all too often closed to the poor but honest businessman, but disturbingly open to organized crime, state authority is constantly vulnerable. The presence of several dozen "professional *mujahedeen*" (some with ties to al-Qaeda) in the Pankisi Gorge from 2001 to 2002 can probably be attributed to Georgia's weak and corrupt security forces and borders officials. Georgia thus became for a while a haven for international terrorists, and the Pankisi region also became the launching pad for the disastrous expedition led by Chechen commander Ruslan Gelayev to the Kodori Gorge in Abkhazia in October 2001 that severely undermined the Georgian–Abkhazian peace process.[11] This was a blatant case of the country's endemic corruption undermining its own statehood.

Corruption and border issues are perhaps the biggest challenges that Saakashvili has pledged to tackle. The arrest of powerful figures associated with the Shevardnadze regime on corruption charges, a drive to clean up the customs services, operations against smuggling on the Georgian–Azerbaijani border and in Ajara—all these actions suggest that he understands the scale of the problem, if not necessarily which methods need to be used to combat it. The case of South Ossetia highlights the dilemma facing Saakashvili: nothing can be treated in isolation, yet the Georgian government lacks the resources to fight all of its problems simultaneously. Georgia's "anti-smuggling operation" against South Ossetia in June 2004 quickly escalated into the worst political standoff between Tbilisi and Tskhinvali in more than a decade.

As well as providing Tbilisi with its biggest security headache, the inability to resolve the conflicts of the 1990s also, needless to say, continues to undermine the formation of a healthier economic environment in the South Caucasus. A negotiated end to the Nagorno-Karabakh, Abkhazia, and South Ossetia conflicts would weaken a number of powerful cartels in the region. To name three examples: (1) the Armenian military, which has control over much of the Armenian economy and the

---

10 Svante Cornell, "The Growing Threat of Transnational Crime," in Dov Lynch, ed., *The South Caucasus: A Challenge for the EU*, Chaillot Papers no. 65 (December 2003), p. 33, http://www.iss-eu.org/public/content/chaile.html.

11 For more detail on the Gelayev expedition in the Kodori Gorge, see the chapter in this volume by Oksana Antonenko. For more detail on the Pankisi Gorge question, see the chapter by Jaba Devdariani.

traffic that travels on the single road between Armenia and Armenian-controlled Nagorno-Karabakh, would lose out if the border with Azerbaijan, closed since 1990, were to reopen; (2) the authorities and security structures in Samegrelo district complicit in smuggling gasoline, cigarettes, and hazelnuts across the border between western Georgia and Abkhazia would lose a great deal were that border to be fully open to road and rail traffic; and (3) if the main north-south rail route from Russia to Georgia and Armenia across Abkhazia were to reopen as a result of progress over the Georgian–Abkhazian dispute, that would also hurt those who are making millions of dollars a year in profit from the semi-legal road trade across South Ossetia.

In other words, strong vested criminal interests oppose the development of a Caucasian common market. The only big cross-Caucasian projects currently underway are two energy pipelines being built across Georgia and Azerbaijan, which are funded by Western oil companies and thus mainly immune to parochial economic interests. However—and I turn to a more detailed discussion of the strategic impact of the pipelines later in this chapter—their potential for boosting regional trade is mixed at best. Once construction of the two pipelines is finished and the final compensation payments to landowners in Azerbaijan and Georgia are handed out, no one along the route stands to derive further special economic benefits. The profits will go to oil companies and governments in Baku, Tbilisi, Ankara, and the West.

At the same time, there is a real risk that the pipeline projects will skew the cross-Caucasian economy. This is because of the "Dutch Disease" syndrome. Three experts writing about the potential risks to Azerbaijan define this syndrome as follows:

> Dutch Disease occurs when large amounts of foreign exchange earned from the sale of a commodity such as oil are converted into local currency. The effect is to raise the demand for local currency, leading to appreciation of the exchange rate. As a result, imports become cheaper and exports more expensive. This decline in price competitiveness weakens the labor-intensive manufacturing sector.[12]

---

[12] Sabit Bagirov, Ingilab Akhmedov, and Svetlana Tsalik, "State Oil Fund of the Azerbaijan Republic," in Svetlana Tsalik, ed., *Caspian Oil Windfalls: Who Will Benefit?* (New York: Caspian Revenue Watch, Open Society Institute, 2003), p. 94.

In 2001, Azerbaijan's oil sector accounted for 67.5 percent of the country's industrial production. Output in the non-oil sector has declined sharply, and exports of goods to Russia, the country's largest trading partner, more than halved between 1997 and 2001. This trend is only likely to intensify as a large tide of foreign currency revenues begins to enter Azerbaijan in the next few years. Azerbaijan's non-oil economy could simply collapse. The implications for Georgia of such a scenario are not clear: it could lead to an increase in Georgian exports to Azerbaijan, although Georgian production is still so low that this seems unlikely. The important point is a more general one: a sharp boost in the energy sector is likely to have a dramatic (and not necessarily positive) effect on the economies of the South Caucasus. The environment in which these big energy profits will be made, one of cartel-dominated economies and obstructive borders, is not one where free trade will develop any time soon.

PIPELINES, OPPORTUNITIES, AND THREATS

In 2005 and 2006, two new energy pipelines will comprehensively change the energy profile and strategic shape of the South Caucasus. The Baku–Tbilisi–Ceyhan (BTC) oil pipeline is due to be completed in early 2005 and is scheduled to be followed a year later by the Baku–Tbilisi–Erzerum (or South Caucasus) gas pipeline, which will run parallel to BTC through Azerbaijan and Georgia before diverging from it in Turkey. Each of these pipelines is by itself larger than any infrastructure project ever to be built in the region. These projects will transform Georgia's place in the world in a strategic if not an economic sense, binding the country closely to Turkey and the West and giving Western countries an added interest in the stability of a country through which oil and gas must be safely delivered to their markets. Yet such a high-profile project also inevitably carries security risks, and Georgia has probably underestimated the long-term security challenge that the pipelines will present.

In purely economic terms, the BTC Pipeline will not make a big impact on Georgia. This is in contrast to Azerbaijan, where the rewards will be huge. It has been estimated that at an oil price of only $25 a barrel, Azerbaijan already could earn total revenues of more than $17 billion from oil production and shipment by the year 2010. If the current, much higher price of oil is maintained, the revenues will be even greater. Georgia stands to earn far less—it will only receive approximately $50 million dollars a year from tariff fees along its comparatively small section of the route. This has led to accusations against Shevardnadze from people such as his successor Mikheil Saakashvili that he "oversold" BTC to the Georgian population.

The Baku–Erzerum gas pipeline will certainly bring greater immediate benefits to Georgia by providing a reliable supply of Caspian Sea gas to whole areas of the country that were previously dependent on irregular Russian gas supplies or entirely without gas. The fate of the Baku–Erzerum Pipeline still depends on whether an energy deal signed by the Shevardnadze government and the Russian gas giant Gazprom in 2003—the full implications of which are not yet clear—undermines the new pipeline. In addition, as Armenia continues to rely on Russian gas shipped via Georgia and was negotiating with Iran for the construction of an Iran–Armenia gas pipeline, Georgia found itself at the center of two gas routes planned by politically opposed blocs: Azerbaijan–Georgia–Turkey versus Russia–Georgia–Armenia–Iran.

BTC has had two incarnations. The first project was initiated by Turkey, which stood to gain by it because the ultimate destination point at the Turkish port of Ceyhan on the Mediterranean Sea would reduce the constant environmental threat posed by oil tankers from the Black Sea ports of Novorossiisk and Poti passing through the narrow channel of the Bosporus next to Istanbul. The idea really took flight, however, when it won strong support from the Clinton administration in Washington in 1997 and 1998. In Congressional testimonies during those years, top U.S. officials such as Steve Sestanovich, Richard Morningstar, Federico Pena, and Bill Richardson promoted BTC as a project that would improve U.S. energy security while buttressing Azerbaijan and Georgia.

From the beginning, many were worried that the initial plans for BTC were too driven by political interests and were an example of the "flag leading trade." Wayne Merry, a former Pentagon and State Department official who was present at some of the initial discussions about the pipeline, said that thinking about the project was extremely muddled. According to Merry, the initial motivation was to compensate Turkey for the revenues it was losing as a result of sanctions against Iraq after the 1991 Persian Gulf war:

> Only [later] did other issues—and other personal and institutional prejudices—come into play. The oil companies always wanted a southern route through Iran to make use of their

existing local and global distribution infrastructure. This con-
flicted with powerful interests in Washington—the anti-Iran
faction (who remain capable of blocking initiatives).   Then
came interest in a [northwestern] route to Novorossiisk,
which ran into the anti-Russian faction who feared "neo-
imperialism" (although there were significant voices favoring
Russian involvement). Then came interest in doing something
to help "Shevy" [Shevardnadze] for his often-compensated
actions as Soviet foreign minister and to bolster Aliev—in
both cases without considering that neither would live long
enough to see such a project come on line.[13]

Where the BTC Pipeline did not go was as important as where it did,
and it could perhaps have been described as the "not-Russia, not-Iran
pipeline." In Congressional testimony in March 1998, the top U.S.
strategist for the former Soviet Union, Strobe Talbott, gave an overt
warning to Iran, which he termed a "state sponsor of terrorism," and a
veiled one to Russia about their perceived interests in the Caucasus. He
said, "We continue to caution nations throughout the region about the
development of close relations with Iran…Moreover, we are against any
state in the region being allowed to dominate the region politically or
economically. We will continue to work with all the states of the Caucasus
to thwart the growth of Iran's influence in the region."[14]

The oil industry was not fully convinced by all these arguments. Terry
Adams, who headed the first multinational oil consortium in Baku, the
Azerbaijan International Operating Company (AIOC), said that the
scheme was too politicized and had not demonstrated its economic via-
bility. Writing in 2000, Adams said:

> [T]he support of any national independence, by definition,
> engages the external player in the broader geopolitical arena.
> For the U.S. this meant constraining Russian and Iranian
> influence in the region, whilst simultaneously requiring an
> increased presence in the region by the U.S. itself. This
> inevitably led to regional diplomatic and commercial conflicts,

---

[13] Wayne Merry, letter to the author, November 4, 2003.
[14] Strobe Talbott, U.S. Congress, Senate, Testimony before the Subcommittee
on Foreign Operations, Appropriations Committee, 105th Congress, 2nd Session, March 31, 1998.

which almost by default became focused on the pipeline issue. All was based on an untested perception that enforced selection of pipeline routes for petroleum export from the Caspian would determine the long-term geopolitical outcomes.[15]

Around the year 2000, however, as circumstances changed in and around the region, oil companies (particularly BP Amoco) began to believe in the commercial possibilities of BTC. Construction finally began in 2003. The combination of promised oil reserves from the Caspian, a continuing high oil price, and increased uncertainty about the Middle East were the decisive factors. As "energy security" became a bigger priority for Western companies and governments, the attractions of a source of energy that was outside OPEC and controlled almost directly by international companies boosted the rating of the Caspian once again. As John Roberts has written, "The Caspian is important not because it is one of the world's major producing areas, but because it is likely to become one of the biggest producing areas in the world in which actual oil production remains essentially in the hands of market-oriented international energy companies."[16] In this sense, BTC has transformed from the "not-Iran, not-Russia pipeline" into the "not-Iraq, not-Saudi Arabia pipeline"—an attractive alternative source of energy security that is under the full control of Western companies.

For Azerbaijan and Georgia, the three-country route of BTC had evident political benefits. For Azerbaijan, to have its politically weak neighbor Georgia as a transit country was attractive, as long as the jealousy of Iran and Russia could be handled. For Georgians, the pipeline has an overwhelmingly political character and has come to symbolize their independence as a state. Georgia's former President Eduard Shevardnadze made it clear that he saw the building of BTC as perhaps the most important achievement of his presidency. "Everyone recognizes that Georgia is a key link in this project," Shevardnadze said in August 2003. "The functioning of the pipeline will largely depend on our country. Georgia has

---

[15] Terry Adams, "Caspian Hydrocarbons, The Politicisation of Regional Pipelines and the Economic Destabilisation of the Caucasus," *Caucasian Regional Studies,* vol. 5, issue 1 & 2 (2000), http://poli.vub.ac.be./publi/crs/eng/0501-00.htm.

[16] John Roberts, "Energy Reserves, Pipeline Politics and Security Implications," in Lynch, *The South Caucasus,* p. 91.

become part of a sphere of global interests, which is a serious factor in strengthening our state independence." [17]

According to Gela Charkviani, one of Shevardnadze's closest aides and his chief adviser on foreign policy, both Georgians and Russians recognized the important symbolism of a major pipeline that avoided Russia. Charkviani regarded it as a bulwark of Georgian sovereignty:

> The Soviet Union was the most centralized country in the world and all movement in the Soviet Union was from the periphery to the center, not the other way round. There was never any connection from the periphery outside, from Tbilisi to Turkey. Turkey is much nearer than Moscow, but everything had to go via Moscow. Nothing had the right to cross the border until it got the blessing of the center. That mentality is still there.[18]

Despite its confused origins and delays, BTC now has near-universal backing in Azerbaijan and Georgia. No significant political voices have been raised against it in either country and opposition parties support it. Even concerned NGOs in Georgia such as Green Alternative have reservations not so much about the project itself as about what they maintain is its flawed or hasty implementation.

The notion that the two pipelines will help Georgia become an east-west transit corridor and win more independence from Russia is almost universally accepted. However, BTC is having other strategic repercussions for Georgia that are more uncomfortable and have not yet been widely appreciated. This is because the very political nature of the pipelines divides the region into "winners" and "losers" and is likely to exacerbate some existing arguments and tensions.

From the beginning, it was clear that the BTC Pipeline was unlikely to go through Armenia. The quickest and cheapest way of running a pipeline from Baku to Ceyhan would have been to build it along the Araxes River valley beside the Azerbaijani–Iranian border, through the Azerbaijani exclave of Nakhichevan and across into eastern Turkey. How-

---

[17] Quoted in Leila Amirova, Nurlana Gulieva, Gennady Abramovich, and Giorgy Kupatadze, "Special Report: Trans-Caucasus Pipeline Underway at Last," *IWPR Caucasus Reporting Service* no. 211, December 23, 2003, http://www.iwpr.net/index.pl?archive/cau/cau_200312_211_2_eng.txt.

[18] Gela Charkviani, interview with the author, October 24, 2003.

ever, that would have meant sending it through a thirty-kilometer stretch of territory either in Iran—unacceptable to the United States—or across a similar distance in Armenia. The Armenia option enjoyed popularity among some in the West who saw it as a potential "peace pipeline." John Maresca, formerly U.S. co-chairman in the Organization for Security and Cooperation in Europe (OSCE)'s Minsk Group responsible for the Nagorno-Karabakh peace process, argued for this idea in 1995, saying that it would have the positive benefit of involving Armenia in a shared cross-regional economic project. Maresca wrote that, "The possibility that a pipeline could be built across Armenia could encourage rational Armenians to join in an honest effort to find a solution to the Karabakh conflict, in order to capitalize on this unique opportunity. It will be a foolish mistake if the pipeline is not used with this possibility in mind."[19]

This did not happen, because the dynamics of the Nagorno-Karabakh peace process were deemed far too uncertain to drive a fundamentally commercial project, and oil companies were understandably reluctant to allow the fate of Nagorno-Karabakh to determine the fate of their pipeline. As energy specialist Robert Ebel memorably put it, "Peace can bring a pipeline but a pipeline can't bring peace."[20] Even more importantly, without a solution to the Karabakh dispute, the notion of building a pipeline across a hostile state was *a priori* unacceptable in Azerbaijan. Domestic political opinion would simply not countenance a route that was perceived as rewarding the enemy or, practically speaking, inviting sabotage.

Thus, BTC excludes Armenia—but in a way that has been evident for several years. Its impact on the Karabakh dispute is likely to be mixed. To take the more positive side first, the construction of a $3 billion project gives BP Amoco and other foreign investors a stake in a peaceful resolution of the conflict. At its nearest point, BTC will run just twelve kilometers north of the Karabakh cease-fire line. Azerbaijani officials have made fairly implausible claims about the threat "Armenian terrorism" poses to the pipeline. Azerbaijan's Defense Minister Safar Abiev said, "Armenia is building up its arms stocks and poses a real security threat to the pipeline,"

---

[19] John Maresca, "A 'Peace Pipeline' to End the Nagorno-Karabakh Conflict," *Caspian Crossroads,* vol. 1 (winter 1995).
[20] Quoted, among other places, in Inga Saffron, "Black Gold, Once Red, Fuels an Oil Rush," *Knight-Ridder Newspapers,* July 20, 1997.

while Deputy National Security Minister Fuad Iskenderov said that his organization had information about "Armenian terrorist organizations" that represented a threat.[21] These comments both overestimate Armenian destructive capacity and intent, and underestimate the vast and complex security features that the investors are installing to protect the pipeline. Most importantly, the Armenians have been made aware that any sabotage of the pipeline by anyone associated with Armenia would be an international diplomatic disaster for them—and are no doubt acting accordingly.

Energy expert John Roberts has written:

> Both the BTC and SCGP [South Caucasus Gas Pipeline] will be buried at least one meter underground for their entire length, so this should shield them against casual attacks. But there will be two pumping stations above ground in Azerbaijan, another two in Georgia, and various pumping stations and pressure reduction facilities in Turkey. Although these could constitute targets for guerrillas or terrorists, attacks on such installations are far more likely to occur as elements in a much more wide-ranging conflict than as part of a direct campaign against the pipelines themselves. So the underlying issue is the stability of the countries through which they pass.[22]

To take the terrorist threat first, two hypothetical dangers can be identified (although over the projected forty-year lifespan of BTC, many others can be expected to emerge). One is that the pipelines, Western-led projects in a pro-American country, could be targets for al-Qaeda or its allies. Militant Islamists have come and gone freely across Georgian borders over the last few years and a few dozen are still believed to be in and around the Pankisi Gorge area. This perceived danger has led to discussion as to whether Georgian Special Forces trained under the U.S. Georgia Train and Equip Program might be deployed to protect the pipeline.

The other hypothesis is that if Russia becomes a more authoritarian state and more hostile toward Georgia, then rogue Russian security elements or their allies—if not, it should be emphasized, official Russian forces themselves—could try to disrupt the pipelines. Many Georgians believe that some elements of the Russian security forces were complicit

21 Amirova et al., "Special Report: Trans-Caucasus Pipeline Underway at Last."
22 Roberts, "Energy Reserves," p. 99.

in the two assassination attempts against Shevardnadze in 1995 and 1999—and that Russia's refusal to extradite Georgia's former security chief Igor Giorgadze is a partial admission of guilt in this. Moscow appears to have moved away from the kind of covert action it used in the Caucasus in the early and mid-1990s, but it could still return to it in the future. In both of these scenarios, the pipelines would become a security liability for Georgia, turning its territory into a battleground in which the Georgian government itself would be one of the weakest players—as happened in the row over the Pankisi Gorge in 2002, when both the United States and Russia argued out their security concerns in front of a confused Georgian government.

If we consider Roberts's warning of a "wide-ranging conflict" in the Caucasus, the most serious danger is that of an overall resumption of hostilities in the Nagorno-Karabakh conflict. Before his arrest in March 2000, the former Karabakh Armenian military commander, Samvel Babayan, talked of the need for a "fourth round" of the conflict in which the Azerbaijanis would be made to acknowledge their defeat. Shortly before his arrest, Babayan said, "If there is this fourth round, it will be decisive and then we won't have to stop the war and sit down at the negotiating table. In the course of the war, both sides will have to make concessions and come up with a solution. If we stop again as we did in 1994, then we will forget again what this problem was."[23]

Although the line of the more moderate Karabakh Armenian government prevails, the views of Babayan, now released from prison, continue to enjoy popularity among many military men in the breakaway Armenian-ruled statelet. The danger is that if hostilities were to start again, these Armenian officers, unrestrained by the cease-fire, would identify the BTC Pipeline as a target.

This leads to another possible negative scenario that could result from BTC. Paradoxically, as has happened to several states in Africa and Latin America, energy wealth could do Azerbaijan more harm than good, by allowing the government to spend heavily on weapons and the country's own security apparatus. If that were to happen and Azerbaijan were to buy itself an expensively re-equipped army, its bellicose rhetoric might become a self-fulfilling prophecy and lead to a new military offensive against Karabakh. Almost all outside observers agree that if two well-

---

[23] Samvel Babayan, interview with the author, February 26, 2000.

armed belligerents renewed the destructive conflict in Nagorno-Karabakh, it would be a disaster for all sides. One likely outcome is that the Armenians would respond to an Azerbaijani offensive—some of them enthusiastically seeing this as Babayan's "fourth round" of the conflict—and the South Caucasus would then be plunged into another regional war, with the Russian military drawn in on the Armenian side. The most immediate devastating consequences would be felt in Armenia and Azerbaijan, but Georgia and the pipelines would also suffer.

The prospect of another Karabakh war is fortunately remote—at least for the next few years. A more immediate problem that could develop into something more serious lies in Georgia's southern Armenian-majority province of Javakheti. This is a problem that BTC may exacerbate. The Javakheti Armenians have long felt alienated from Tbilisi. Few of them speak Georgian, their transportation links to the rest of Georgia are poor, and the currency of choice tends to be the Armenian dram or the Russian ruble rather than the Georgian lari. Two Armenian nationalist parties campaign for official autonomy—but not yet (as some Armenian nationalists outside the region want) for outright secession from Georgia. Following the election of Mikheil Saakashvili in January 2004, some Javakheti Armenians again raised the issue of being granted a politically autonomous structure within Georgia.

Initially, when the Georgian section of the route for BTC was under discussion, there was widespread support for a route via Javakheti following the quickest path to the Turkish border. However, when the decision was finally taken, it was for a longer route through more difficult terrain to the north. The new route passed close to Borjomi, home to Georgia's famous mineral water springs and to a national park that is trying to attract tourists. This has become the most controversial aspect of the whole BTC project so far, with the main mineral water producer in Borjomi, Georgian Glass and Mineral Water, and a group of Georgian environmental NGOs (supported by the World Wildlife Fund) opposing the Borjomi route.

The decision-making process behind the choice of the pipeline's route was opaque. The project's institutional investors maintain that the Borjomi route makes good sense. The then-head of the Georgian state oil company GIOC, Giorgi Chanturia, and the then-head of the Georgian Security Council, Tedo Japaridze, said in 2002 that it was unacceptable to build the pipeline close to the Russian base at Akhalkalaki—even though the base is due to close within the next few years, while BTC is intended to last for forty years. Many Georgians are still equivocal about the choice of the Borjomi route. For example, Ramaz Jabauri, Georgia's deputy intelligence chief, said the decision to place the pipeline around Akhalkalaki "was made when the nation was facing a different set of threats." He added that, "At this point, it might stand to reason to run the pipeline through Akhalkalaki to boost local employment opportunities there."[24]

Given the division of opinion in Georgia, it is highly likely—although still unproven—that Azerbaijan's view of a Javakheti route was critical and that the government in Baku vetoed the idea of its pipeline going through an Armenian-populated area for political reasons. Azerbaijani officials have not commented directly on the issue, but given Azerbaijan's extreme sensitivity to any project that is seen to have any benefit to Armenia or Armenians, support for a Javakheti route would have made the government politically vulnerable. For example, opposition leader Ali Kerimli, head of the reformist wing of the Popular Front Party, said that, "It was impossible to lay [the pipeline] through Javakheti. This region is populated by Armenians and so it represents a threat to the project. Running the pipeline through Borjomi is more secure."[25]

An immediate consequence of the choice of the Borjomi route has been an increase in feelings of alienation among the Javakheti Armenians. The mayor of Akhalkalaki, Nairi Iritsian, said in an interview that he was disappointed that his region had been ignored. He said that around 2,000 of the town's residents go to Russia every year to look for work and the only jobs to be had in his city are at the Russian military base. BTC would have provided construction jobs and compensation payments to the region.[26] Given that the short-term benefits of the pipeline to the local economy would be limited, perceptions may be more important than reality. A local NGO leader, Ararat Esoyan, put the political context of the decision to bypass Javakheti more starkly: "In Javakheti, people say that by choosing this route they have drawn the future border of Georgia."[27]

Taken overall, the two pipelines present Georgia, a country with only weak sovereignty, with both enormous opportunities and daunting responsibilities. The long-term security challenge will come when the two

---

[24] Amirova et al., "Special Report: Trans-Caucasus Pipeline Underway at Last."
[25] Amirova et al., "Special Report: Trans-Caucasus Pipeline Underway at Last."
[26] Amirova et al., "Special Report: Trans-Caucasus Pipeline Underway at Last."
[27] Ararat Esoyan, interview with the author, October 24, 2003.

pipelines are built and begin operating for up to forty years and the Georgian state will have prime responsibility for protecting them on its territory. The wider sociopolitical context is just as important, however. If Georgian society as a whole (and not just certain sections of it) is seen to be benefiting from the pipelines, the projects will receive the public support that guarantees their political durability.

FINDING A PLACE IN THE GREATER MIDDLE EAST

Under the Soviet Union, Georgia was relegated from being a sovereign state to being one region in a highly centralized state. During Soviet times, most contacts between union republics went through Moscow, and the non-Russian republics had very limited bilateral relations. It was unthinkable for Georgia to have anything approaching "bilateral relations" with Turkey, and traffic across the Georgian–Turkish border was very restricted. In the Gorbachev era of the late 1980s, locked doors suddenly began to open. But since then, Georgia has (to change metaphors) spent the last fifteen years like a dancer in a bewilderingly choreographed performance, in which its partners keep changing quickly.

The whirlwind of events has not allowed stable relationships to form. From 1989 to 1991, the Soviet republics most hostile toward the center formed an informal alliance against Gorbachev and Moscow. Georgia joined five other republics—Armenia, Moldova, and the three Baltic republics—in boycotting the March 1991 referendum on the preservation of the Soviet Union. That list, however, gave no clue to how relations would develop, as the alignment of the former Soviet republics has frequently changed. Although they formed a common front against Moscow in 1991, the Baltic and Caucasian republics have little direct contact now—and also have very contrasting fortunes. As noted, Armenia now has a very different strategic orientation from Georgia. Only Moldova, hardly a major ally of Georgia's, shares something of the same orientation.

This is a useful lens through which to view the GUUAM alliance. Formed in 1996–1997 as GUAM by Georgia, Ukraine, Azerbaijan, and Moldova, it was, broadly speaking, an attempt to form an informal alliance of Commonwealth of Independent States (CIS) countries who wanted to resist Russian influence collectively. In April 1999, GUAM became GUUAM with the accession of Uzbekistan. At the same time, three of its members—Georgia, Azerbaijan, and Uzbekistan—quit the CIS Collective Security Treaty. The venue for this (re-)formation of GUUAM was significant—it was done at NATO's Fiftieth Anniversary Summit in Washington.

At this Washington meeting, the GUUAM leaders set out an agenda that declared a shared commitment to four main ideas. The first two were a commitment to uphold the territorial integrity of states and to reject "aggressive separatism"—a reference to Georgia, Azerbaijan, and Moldova's claim to recover their lost secessionist territories, Abkhazia, South Ossetia, Nagorno-Karabakh, and Transnistria. The third was a common will to fight "religious extremism"—a reference to the Uzbek government's campaign against its Islamist opposition. The final point was a common commitment to prevent an arms buildup in conflict areas, a reference (although not by name) to Russian bases in Georgia, Armenia, and Moldova.

The location of this meeting of GUUAM was intended to be symbolic, and it paralleled the agenda of a Russosceptic strand of opinion then very much in the ascendant in Washington. The conservative *Jamestown Foundation Prism* commented approvingly that, "The venue and setting were doubly significant: first, for dramatizing Moscow's failure to persuade the CIS countries to fall into line with Russian policy toward NATO; and second—just as important—for symbolizing the five governments' strategic orientation toward the West."[28]

GUUAM, however, has proved to be a mirage. It was never institutionalized, and no treaty was ever signed by the member states. There is no evidence that trade between them increased substantially as a result of the alliance. As noted earlier in this chapter, even relations between Georgia and Azerbaijan are not as deep as an initial glance would suggest. GUUAM suffered heavily from the events of September 11, 2001, when strategic priorities in the United States changed with regard to the former Soviet Union. Suddenly, containment of Russia's perceived neo-imperial ambitions was no longer such a popular policy in Washington. In combating the new threat of Islamic terrorism, U.S. relations with Vladimir Putin's Russia improved and Moscow's relations with Azerbaijan and Uzbekistan took a turn for the better. Most of the GUUAM countries now saw no contradiction in cultivating good relations with Russia as well

---

[28] "From GUAM to GUUAM: A Growing Centrifugal Force in the CIS," *The Jamestown Foundation Prism*, May 7, 1999.

as the United States—although Georgia, for very understandable reasons, proved to be an exception. Symptomatic of the constantly shifting political terrain, in May 2005 GUUAM again became GUAM, when Uzbekistan, alarmed over the Rose and Orange revolutions, pulled out.

GUUAM has, if nothing else, underlined the redundancy of another international grouping, the Moscow-led Commonwealth of Independent States (CIS). The CIS turned out to be less of a "commonwealth" and more of an instrument for Russia to continue to exert control over its former Soviet neighbors—an institutionalization of the phrase, "Russia's near abroad." When the CIS has been called upon to play an active security role, as with manning the 1,600-strong peacekeeping mission for postwar Abkhazia, its real status has been revealed: no other CIS country except Russia has supplied troops to the peacekeeping force in Abkhazia.

Thus, the hard reality is that even Georgia's relations with its former Soviet neighbors are largely dependent on the variations of U.S.–Russian relations, with Washington and Moscow representing the two security poles between which the former Soviet republics fluctuate. This provides the context in which Georgia's membership in a whole series of ambitious but poorly funded regional organizations has to be seen. What is the worth of the modest budget and grand declarations of a GUUAM when a real crisis confronts a government in Tbilisi, Gali, or the Pankisi Gorge?

Outside the borders of the former Soviet Union and to the south and west, Georgia is part of a region that has been variously classified, perhaps most usefully as "the Greater Middle East." Tbilisi is closer geographically to Baghdad and Damascus than to Moscow. Its best transportation links with any of its neighbors—by road, rail, sea, and air—are with Turkey. Over the last thousand years, the Persian and Ottoman empires have frequently controlled the South Caucasus and determined its history, and it is reasonable to expect their successors, Iran and Turkey, to have interests in doing the same.

Since formally regaining independence in 1992, however, Georgia's place in this wider non-Soviet region must count as "unused potential." The primary reason for this is obviously the fact that Georgia needs time to cultivate relations with neighbors with whom all direct relations were severed during seventy years of Soviet rule when the Soviet Union's southern borders were virtually closed. Moreover, the experience of Soviet rule made Georgians more educated, secular, and Europeanized than their southern neighbors. Syria, Turkey, or Iran hardly offers a state model that Georgian elites would want to copy, and almost no young Georgians take an interest in studying in these countries that are far from the Christian European civilization to which Georgia aspires.

Politics between these countries lag behind in the same way. Georgia's relationships with its neighbors to the south, superficially at least, embed Georgia within a complex network of alliances that defines this larger area. Turkey is, after all, a member of NATO and has a strong relationship with Israel. Iran and Armenia have sought to build a trilateral relationship with Greece. The further reaches of these arrangements, however, appear to have little impact on Georgia. Israel and its problems barely cause a flicker of interest in Georgia, while President Shevardnadze's offer of Georgian air bases in 2003 to the United States for the Iraq war was politely declined. As for Greece, the primary bilateral issue between Tbilisi and Athens is the large number of migrants and guest workers (most but not all of them ethnic Greeks) traveling between the two countries. Neither "Christian solidarity" nor historical suspicions of Turkey are enough to stop Greece from having an active embassy in Azerbaijan and displaying a strong interest in consuming Azerbaijani gas.

Iran, despite its relative geographical proximity, is remote from Georgia and its strategic concerns. Iran's strategic interest in the South Caucasus is concentrated mainly on Armenia and Azerbaijan. Tehran worries about the influence of Azerbaijan on its own Azerbaijani population in northern Iran and cultivates a good relationship with Armenia, a relationship which may be cemented by a new gas pipeline. Even Armenia and Azerbaijan, however, keep Iranian diplomacy at a distance: Iran made one effort to negotiate the Armenian–Azerbaijani conflict in May 1992, which was cut short by the Armenian capture of Shusha and was never resumed.

Georgia's relationship with Iran is even more remote. The Islamic Republic's semi-authoritarian political system is not a model that any Georgians want to follow, and its status as part of President Bush's "axis of evil" puts it in a camp opposite to the one with which Georgia sympathizes over the big world issues of the day. Moreover, Iran is not a member of any of the pan-European institutions that Georgia is either part of or wants to be part of: the European Union, the Council of Europe, the OSCE, and NATO.

Another instance of undeveloped potential is Georgia's muted relations with its neighbors across the Black Sea, as symbolized in the relative failure of the eleven-member Black Sea Economic Cooperation (BSEC) organization. Article 8 of BSEC's founding Summit Declaration signed in Istanbul on June 25, 1992, asserts that the organization's aim is to "ensure that the Black Sea becomes a sea of peace, stability, and prosperity, striving to promote friendly and good-neighborly relations." The organization was conceived by Turkey's President Turgut Ozal as an institution that could mobilize 330 million people in a group of contiguous countries with a joint trade balance of more than $300 billion into a new free-trade area. While it has formed a bureaucracy capable of holding meetings and passing declarations, it is not an organization that is capable of more substantial cooperation. In an embittered June 1999 interview, BSEC's International Permanent Secretary Nurver Nures lamented that since the death of Ozal, even Turkish politicians had failed to support his organization. He said two of BSEC's offices—supposedly those of an international organization—were commandeered by Prime Minister Tansu Ciller for the Turkish government's use. Nures also said:

> If Ozal had lived, perhaps we would have overcome the obstacles and reached more advanced levels, because Ozal could argue the attractiveness of this idea very well. If we weren't able to open the doors to these purposes sufficiently enough, the mistake was not in his thinking but lay rather with the people. The idea is marvelous. Turkey has had to play the role of the locomotive within this organization.[29]

BSEC is making efforts to acquire new teeth with the appointment of a second Georgian secretary-general in succession, former foreign minister Tedo Japaridze, but it has only a tiny budget, and it is a fair assumption that few Georgians could say what the organization does. This is not to say that a Black Sea regional association is not a good idea. The Black Sea has recently become a route for aid to be shipped to Afghanistan, with the first cargo leaving Bulgaria for Georgia and then Afghanistan in September 2003. In April 2001, the six littoral states of the Black Sea formed BLACKSEAFOR, an organization to coordinate search-and-rescue and humanitarian operations on the sea. The point is that without a serious agenda of economic cooperation and a well-funded organizational structure, BSEC, like GUUAM and the CIS, is doomed to be no

---

[29] Nurver Nures, "Lack of Interest, Not Lack of Success vis-à-vis Black Sea Economic Cooperation," *Turkish Daily News,* June 22, 1999.

more than a talking shop.

Georgia does not need BSEC in order to develop its relationship with Turkey, a country of growing importance for the South Caucasus. Like Russia, Turkey is a country of a different order to its neighbors. Its population of 68 million inhabitants contrasts with a combined total of around 15 million people for all three South Caucasus countries, and its enormous land area and much greater GDP dwarf those of Georgia, Armenia, and Azerbaijan combined.

Turkey and Georgia have strong shared interests that are being strengthened by the BTC and Baku–Erzerum pipelines. Both Turkey and Georgia aspire to European Union membership (with Turkey's ambition much more plausible than Georgia's), and Georgia wants to follow Turkey into NATO. In contrast to Turkey's other eastern neighbors— Iran, Iraq, Syria, and Armenia—Georgia promises to be a trouble-free political and commercial partner, and Turkey is already Georgia's second biggest trading partner. A military partnership is developing between the two countries, with Turkish military trainers moving into barracks recently vacated by the Russians in the Vaziani airbase outside Tbilisi. In April 2003, a large Turkish military delegation, led by military Chief of Staff Hilmi Ozkok, flew to Tbilisi and discussed, among other things, the training of Georgian military personnel by Turkish military experts, increased Turkish funding for the Georgian army, the renovation of a Georgian military air facility, and Turkish assistance in training a marine anti-terrorism unit for Georgia's Black Sea flotilla.[30]

Even so, Turkey still lags far behind Russia in its economic importance for Georgia. Historical and linguistic factors appear to outweigh contemporary political ones in that at least half a million Georgians are living as guest workers in Russia, a country where Georgians now need to apply for a visa well in advance to visit, while the numbers for Turkey— where visas are obtainable within minutes—are much smaller.

In part, of course, Turkey is simply poorer than Russia, but that does not appear to be the whole story. A comparison of the responses of Ankara and Moscow to Georgia's Rose Revolution of November 2003 points up how Georgia is far more enmeshed in Russia and its concerns than in those of Turkey, whether it likes it or not. As soon as the Shevard-

---

[30] Igor Torbakov, "Expanding Turkish–Georgian Strategic Ties Rankle Russia," *Eurasia Insight*, April 25, 2003.

nadze regime was tottering, it was Russia's (Georgian-born) Foreign Minister Igor Ivanov who flew to Tbilisi to mediate between the president and the opposition. Ivanov had crisis talks with both sides and even talked to a rally of demonstrators on Rustaveli Avenue. The same scenario was repeated in May 2004, this time right on Turkey's doorstep in Ajara, when Ivanov, now the secretary of the Russian National Security Council, again flew in to negotiate the peaceful surrender of veteran Ajaran leader Aslan Abashidze.

It would be hard to imagine Turkey playing such a significant role in a crisis in Georgia. In fact, the Rose Revolution seems to have caught the Turkish government by surprise, with its prime minister and foreign minister both away and unwilling to comment. Newspaper columnist Tuncay Ozkan noted that Turkey and Georgia had maintained strong and friendly ties ever since Georgia's independence and their two militaries were cooperating closely. But, wrote Ozkan in the center-right daily *Aksam*, "Turkey is now unable to even understand the developments [in the Caucasus], let alone to manipulate them."[31] It seems that Turkey simply lacks the language and framework to move its relationship with Georgia into an everyday political conversation—something that cannot be said of either Russia or the United States.

Recent history and the powerful institutional frameworks offered by Russia and the West thus still outweigh all the claims of geography and older history in Georgia. Paradoxically, an indicator of the strategic disengagement of both Turkey and Iran from the South Caucasus is the interest of both in the now-moribund concept of a "Security Pact for the Caucasus." President Suleyman Demirel backed the idea at the OSCE summit in 1999, and Iran's Foreign Minister Kamal Kharrazi tried to revive the plan in a tour of the South Caucasus in April 2003. For both countries, a "security pact" would have given them a role in the region that they currently do not have.

CONCLUSION

More than ten years after it gained full independence, Georgia finds itself in the curious situation of still looking to two distant capitals, Washing-

---

31 Mevlut Katik, "Will Turkey Meet The Strategic Challenge In Georgia?" *Eurasia Insight*, December 12, 2003.

ton and Moscow, to define its foreign policy choices and has done surprisingly little to further cooperation with its more immediate neighbors. The European flag flying over government buildings in Tbilisi under Saakashvili proclaims a new declaration of intent, which may eventually provide Georgia with a more stable security environment but so far has resulted only in increased economic aid: the EU, after all, has no history of extended involvement in the security of far-flung regions. Georgia's immediate neighborhood remains troubled. For various reasons, Georgia has failed to win any strategic advantage from its central position in the South Caucasus and proximity to Turkey and Iran. Detached from the Nagorno-Karabakh dispute, it has open borders with Armenia, Azerbaijan, and Turkey, as well as its fourth neighbor, Russia—but does not have long-term security arrangements with any of these countries. In some respects, Georgia's central geographical position can be uncomfortable. Georgia finds itself caught between two competing alliances, Turkey–Azerbaijan and Russia–Armenia–Iran, both of which are promoting energy corridors. Although Georgia's preference is clearly for the former alliance, it cannot ignore the latter and will have to reckon with Russia's continuing desire for access to Armenia.[32]

Georgia's lack of interest in regional cooperation is a major factor in its own strategic vulnerability. The theme of "unused potential" recurs throughout this chapter. While the ebbs and flows of the U.S.–Russian relationship have dominated Georgian foreign policy for the last thirteen years, Georgia's relations with its neighbors have not advanced significantly. Great-power rivalry has contributed to this trend, and it may be unreasonable to expect a "regional identity" to form and drive forward economic integration in an area of such great diversity and historical suspicions. But the Georgian elite must also share responsibility for the choices it has and has not made. Legitimate trade, the prerequisite to a closer relationship, is still depressingly limited among South Caucasus countries. In 2003, Georgia's two biggest exports were scrap metal and

---

[32] An Iran–Armenian pipeline would cut against Gazprom's interests, but *Interfax* reported on February 2, 2004, that Russia's Deputy Prime Minister Boris Alyoshin had told a press conference in Yerevan that an Iranian–Armenian gas pipeline was in Russia's interests because of increased Russian ownership of energy-generating facilities in Armenia. He said Gazprom might become operator of part of the pipeline through Armenia and that the line might be extended to the Georgian border.

timber, marking it as a largely non-industrial country without a strong economic profile or strong sovereignty. Border restrictions, smuggling, and crime undermine any tenuous hopes for free trade and open markets. These problems have deprived Georgia of the economic power or stability to exploit its regional potential, while corrupt local and national leaders have taken more interest in their own economic well-being than in the long-term interest of the state.

The most hopeful development for Georgia is the two new energy pipelines under construction. Although they will help free Georgia from energy dependence on Russia and build a link to Europe, these pipelines also entail new risks and responsibilities for the Georgian state. Providing protection for a Western-backed pipeline draws Georgia into wider security issues it has not had to deal with hitherto.

In short, the lack of ground-level regional cooperation in the wider region in general and between Georgia and its South Caucasus neighbors in particular serves to magnify the influence of both the United States and Russia and their own disputes. It makes Georgia unhappily vulnerable to shifts in relations between Moscow and Washington. Georgia alone is not responsible for the fractured condition of its neighborhood and its uncertain future, but it has done little to mend the cracks and break down the barriers.

CONCLUSION

Locating Georgian Security

BRUNO COPPIETERS

G eorgia is a weak state in a fragmented region. Since its secession from the Soviet Union in April 1991, observers have repeatedly questioned the ability of this newly independent state to overcome the threat of anarchy and to establish sovereign statehood. In security terms, Georgia and its South Caucasus neighbors, Armenia and Azerbaijan, are part of a region—the wider Caucasus region—where these three weak South Caucasus states have a difficult time coexisting with three stronger neighbors—Russia, Iran, and Turkey. Three "de facto"

* I would like to thank Viacheslav Chirikba, George Hewitt, Magaly Rodriguez, Xiaokun Song, Dmitri Trenin, and the contributors to this volume for their comments to a first draft of this paper. The idea of applying a center–periphery model to Georgia's domestic and international security environment was presented at the conferences, "Armenia: The South Caucasus and Foreign Policy Challenges," Ann Arbor, Michigan, October 21–24, 2004; and "Sortir de l'Empire: le cas des Etats sud-caucasiens," Paris, November 25–26 2004. On the distinction between the various meanings of a periphery, as applied to relations between the EU and Georgia in the early years after Georgian independence in 1991, see also Bruno Coppieters, "Georgia in Europe: The Idea of a Periphery in International Relations," in Bruno Coppieters, Alexei Zverev, and Dmitri Trenin, eds., *Commonwealth and Independence in Post-Soviet Eurasia* (London: Frank Cass, 1998), pp. 44–68. This approach has been updated in Bruno Coppieters, "An EU Special Representative to a New Periphery," in Dov Lynch, ed., *The South Caucasus: A Challenge for the EU,* Chaillot Papers no. 65 (December 2003), pp. 161–170, http://www.iss-eu.org/chaillot/chai65e.pdf; and in Michael Emerson, Marius Vahl, Bruno Coppieters, Michel Huysseune, Tamara Kovziridze, Gergana Noutcheva and Nathalie Tocci, "Elements of Comparison and Synthesis," in Bruno Coppieters et al., "Europeanization and Conflict Resolution: Case Studies from the European Periphery," *Journal on Ethnopolitics and Minority Issues in Europe,* issue 1 (2004), http://www.ecmi. de/jemie/.

states—Nagorno-Karabakh, Abkhazia, and South Ossetia[1]—survive in this unstable region, which is largely due to external support from neighboring countries. This situation is indicative of the extent to which the political relations between all these nations are fractured.

The introduction to this volume described "the security of statehood" within a deeply "insecure neighborhood" as the twin security challenge Georgia has to address. Its state leadership still has to prove that it is able to deliver basic public goods to its citizens. Such a performance is inextricably bound up with the creation of a secure regional environment.

Some chapters in this volume primarily addressed the "domestic" security concerns in Georgia, such as the consequences of the 1991–1992 civil war, the emergence of secessionist movements in the autonomous entities South Ossetia and Abkhazia, or civilian control over the military. Other chapters focused on international relations in the South Caucasus. They dealt with the involvement of neighboring countries, external powers, and international organizations, or explored the question of whether the South Caucasus can be called a region in its own right or if it should be conceived of as part of a larger regional entity. Domestic and international perspectives presented in this volume converge in the thesis that the divisive history of the region finds an expression in the fault lines and conflicts within Georgia itself and that any progress in regional integration is undoubtedly connected to the domestic process of state- and nation-building in the South Caucasus.

Security studies on Georgia are generally based on a broad definition of security. They assess the vast range of threats to state institutions and regional stability, ranging from the breakdown of cease-fire agreements in secessionist conflicts to the proliferation of small arms and the penetration of organized crime into state structures. The last years of the Shevardnadze regime were dominated by public discussions about how corruption and the failure to reform posed a threat to the development of the economy and to the survival of the Georgian state.

One of the most worrisome aspects of the late Shevardnadze years was the abandoning of all serious attempts at improving state efficacy. External pressures from "friendly" forces, particularly the U.S. govern-

---

[1] Chechnya has been destroyed as a de facto state as a consequence of the Russian military intervention of 1999. This does not mean that this war has erased the Chechen independence movement or the conflict over sovereignty.

ment, on the Georgian government to restructure its armed forces or its financial policies did not have any significant results. Georgia ceased to be perceived as merely temporarily weak because of particular circumstances, such as the transition from a planned to a market economy, tensions with Russia, or the failure to reach a peace settlement concerning the political status of the breakaway entities. Its failure to perform was increasingly perceived as having an enduring character for structural reasons. There were increasing fears that the transition to the post-Shevardnadze era would not be peaceful and that it might reproduce many of the features Georgia had exhibited earlier in its independence.

In the first half of the 1990s, Georgia had not only been a "weak state" with respect to the various performance criteria of statehood— such as the capacity to extract the necessary resources for performing core state functions, to regulate social relations, to use public resources in purposeful ways, and to establish legitimate rule[2]—but had at certain moments moved into the subcategory of weakness known as "failing states." This happened when it confronted breakaway movements in South Ossetia and Abkhazia and when civil unrest erupted at the time of Zviad Gamsakhurdia's ouster, its first democratically elected president.

The concept of a "failing state" indicates an institutional profile where the political institutions are threatening to collapse entirely. Such a total collapse, turning Georgia into a "failed state," could have been the consequence of a struggle for succession to Shevardnadze's presidency. It could also have been the result of a spillover of the Russian–Chechen war into Georgia or of a breakdown of the fragile cease-fires in Abkhazia or South Ossetia. Furthermore, protest movements against poverty and corruption could have led to popular uprisings, fueling public disorder and mass violence. But these worst-case scenarios did not happen. The dramatic events of November 2003 following rigged parliamentary elections resulted in another type of regime change. Georgia's incapacity to reform

---

[2] Ghia Nodia's definition of "weak state" in this volume draws on Joel S. Migdal, *Strong Societies and Weak States: State–Society Relations and State Capabilities in the Third World* (Princeton, NJ: Princeton University Press, 1988), p. 4. For my analysis, I am also including some of the criteria of the efficiency of state performance presented by Byungki Kim at the conference "Comparative Regionalism: Cases in Europe and East Asia" organized by the Renmin University of China, Beijing, April 8–9, 2005. See also Robert I. Rotberg, ed., *When States Fail. Causes and Consequences* (Princeton, NJ: Princeton University Press, 2004).

did not generate anarchy and state failure. To the contrary, it produced a well-organized democratic revolt against the government and the replacement of a large part of the political elite.

In this chapter, I will draw some conclusions from the contributions to this volume concerning the interplay of factors that have been shaping Georgia's national and regional security relations, particularly in the multi-faceted transition from Eduard Shevardnadze to Mikheil Saakashvili. As stated by Robert Legvold in the introduction to this volume, the many dimensions that bear on national and regional security policy come together in Georgia in a highly complex fashion. This concluding chapter makes a systematic attempt to unravel the most salient elements of analysis presented in this book, particularly concerning the relationship between Georgia's security policies in the domestic and international fields.

For this purpose, I will make use of the concepts of "center" and "periphery," and consider Georgia from the perspective of both a center and a periphery. As a sovereign state, Georgia is expected to exercise its authority over its whole territory. From this perspective, the Georgian state may be seen as a center in relation to particular peripheries. However, Georgia is also a small state confronting stronger states active in the region as it strives to be recognized on the international legal level as an equal among others. From this perspective of international relations, Georgia may be seen as in the position of a periphery. The concept of sovereignty—both as the control of a state over a particular territory and its population and the right to claim equal legal status with other states in the international arena—is crucial to both types of relationships.

THE CENTER–PERIPHERY MODEL

The center–periphery model can be helpful for analyzing the domestic and international conflicts over sovereignty and hegemony in which Georgia is involved. This model is traditionally used to analyze various types of processes resulting from spatial partitioning by borders.[3] It has its origins

---

[3] See Jean Gottmann, ed., *Center and Periphery: Spatial Variations in Politics* (London: Sage, 1980); Georges Prevelakis, "Jean Gottmann's Relevance in Today's World," paper presented at The Earhart Foundation Conference on the State of the Social Sciences, Boston University, December 6–7, 2002, http://www.bu.edu/uni/iass/conf/George%20Prevelakis.pdf; Claude Grasland, "Center/Periphery," http://hypergeo.free.fr/article.php3?id_article=186.

in geometry, but has been applied metaphorically in many other disciplines, including political geography,[4] archeology,[5] political economy,[6] and comparative federalism.[7] In political geography, the opposition between a center and a periphery is closely related to other dichotomies such as "heartland" and "rimland." The concept of a center is also connected to terms such as "core," "nucleus," "pivot area," and the concept of a periphery is linked to "frontiers," "boundaries," and "borders." All these words evoke similar ideas and have heuristic potential.[8]

The center–periphery scheme will first be applied to Georgia's domestic order and then to Georgia's place in the international order. But center–periphery relations have a very different meaning in the literature on domestic relations—for instance, in the literature on comparative federalism—and in the literature on international relations—for instance, in the literature on international political economy. For our comparative purposes, it makes sense to standardize these meanings. I therefore make a general distinction between various types of center–periphery relations in the domestic and international fields. This distinction then is used as the

---

[4] Jean Gottmann, "Confronting Center and Periphery," in Gottmann, ed., pp. 11–25; Paul Claval, "Center/Periphery and Space: Models of Political Geography," in Gottmann, ed., pp. 63–71; George W. Hoffman, "Variations in Center–Periphery Relations in Southeast Europe," in Gottmann, ed., pp. 111–133.

[5] Tim C. Champion, ed., *Center and Periphery: Comparative Studies in Archaeology* (London: Routledge, 1995).

[6] See, among many others, Raimondo Strassoldo, "Center–Periphery and System–Boundary: Culturological Perspectives," in Gottmann, ed., pp. 42–44 and Immanuel Wallerstein, *The Modern World System: Capitalist Agriculture and the Origins of the European World Economy in the Sixteenth Century* (New York: Academic Press, 1974).

[7] The use of the concepts of center and periphery is traditional in the analysis of domestic politics, especially in the analysis of federal relations. This formulation is found, for instance, in the analysis of the relationship between national governments and lower levels of governments with smaller geographic jurisdictions in Russia. See among others, Daniel R. Kempton and Terry D. Clark, eds., *Unity or Separation: Center–Periphery Relations in the Former Soviet Union* (London: Praeger, 2002). For an application in the history of sciences, see "Center and Periphery Revisited: The Structures of European Science, 1750–1914," *Revue de la Maison Française d'Oxford*, vol. I, no 2 (2003), http://www.mfo.ac.uk/Publications/Revue%20Fox/introduction.htm. For an application on the general theory of systems, see Strassoldo, p. 50.

[8] Claval, p. 64.

main conceptual instrument to describe the profound changes in domestic relations between Tbilisi and various autonomous entities in Georgia, and between Tbilisi and the main external powers active in the region under Georgia's three successive presidential regimes (Gamsakhurdia 1991–1992, Shevardnadze, 1992–2003 and Saakashvili 2004–).

It is possible to distinguish four different types of center–periphery relations. All four types can be situated either on the internal or external level and have in common a clear spatial dimension. Furthermore, they all express, on the domestic and international level, a basic asymmetry in material and normative resources leading to dependency and hierarchical relations between the center and the periphery. Concepts such as sovereignty and hegemony illustrate the point because in both cases the center exercises dominance over a periphery.

First, the term "periphery" in center–periphery relations refers to particular lines of *confrontation*—to boundaries where the center has to defend itself or to fault lines where the center has to confront external threats. Second, the terms "center" and "periphery" may be used to express processes of *integration* or even the progressive assimilation of the periphery by the center. In this case, the model reflects a constant flux in the spatial interaction between the two poles and particularly a movement toward the center.[9] Third, "periphery" may refer to something of marginal importance to the center. The center would then maintain an attitude of *indifference* toward the periphery. And in a fourth type of center–periphery relationship, a periphery is a *bridgehead*, linking one micro-region (on the domestic level) or one macro-region (on the international level) to another micro- or macro-region.

A basic inequality in material and normative resources between center and periphery is common to all four types of center–periphery relations. The meaning of the term periphery when referring to boundaries, particularly lines of conflict or fault lines along which the center confronts external threats, entails an asymmetrical and hierarchical relationship between center and periphery. This is likewise the case for the use of these two terms to express processes of integration or assimilation, or the function of the periphery as a bridgehead for the center. Indifference is another expression of an asymmetrical relationship between center and

---

[9] On the dynamic character of the center–periphery relations, see Hoffman, pp. 111–133.

periphery. It may be that the periphery has a marginal importance to the center, but the reverse rarely holds true.

The asymmetrical and hierarchical relationship between both poles may reflect more than a situation of inequality. The concept of the center is often associated—both in Western civilization and in archaic cultures—with eternity, the sacred, and the transcendent, while periphery is associated with temporality, the profane, and material reality. In the modern conceptions of the state, sovereignty is at the center. The authority of the state is imposed on the whole territory under its jurisdiction. The boundaries indicate the limits of the power of the center, but also of external actors by preventing them from unauthorized forms of interference in domestic affairs. This gives a "sacred" significance to the principle of territorial integrity.

As is the case with any ideal type distinction, these different types of center–periphery relations do not reflect empirical realities, but accentuate, exaggerate, or idealize particular empirical traits with the aim of developing a better understanding of social reality. These various types of relationships do not exclude each other. Relationships of domination characterized by conflict, by integration, or by indifference may very well intermingle in domestic or international relations. If the center, as the seat of authority and power, generates values and norms that are assimilated by the periphery, the center–periphery relationship is defined by integration. As an alternative to the assimilation of a powerless periphery, the periphery may formulate grievances and mobilize protest actions, entering into a relationship of confrontation with the center.

As all types of center–periphery relations are asymmetrical and hierarchical, it may be assumed that the transformation in the relationship between both poles is affected by changes in each of the poles, but more fundamentally by changes at the center than at the periphery. The use of a center–periphery model further assumes that the transformation of the relationship between both poles will more substantially affect the periphery than the center.

The identity of the center is largely defined at the periphery and the identity of the periphery by its relationship to the center. The center is the nucleus that creates itself through the reproduction of one or more types of the relationships mentioned above, such as the assimilation of its periphery, the maintenance of its borders, or the use of its peripheries as a bridgehead to other areas.[10] But peripheries are also active creators of their own identities, either through the reproduction of their dependency relations with a center, through integration, or by resisting integration through confrontation.

The reproduction of center-periphery relations should not be understood as static. Polarity reversals cannot be excluded. A periphery may, under particular circumstances, start to take an innovative role and acquire more crucial roles in the whole system, modifying its structure, and even come to acquire centrality. Such a reversal in polarity may come about as a consequence of a radical transformation in the relationship between center and periphery that strengthens the latter to the point that it becomes the dominant center. The emergence of the former periphery as a new center may also result if the imperial center disappears. A more gradual transformation from dependency to interdependency is also conceivable, if both poles acquire relatively equal functions in the political system. Examples of shifts of dominance from center to periphery are numerous in history, ranging from the ascendancy of former peripheries over the Chinese, Macedonian, and Roman empires up to the emergence of the former British colonies in North America as the dominant pole in the modern world system.[11] Examples of polarity reversals are likewise numerous in economic history, both between regions within one state and between macro-regions in the world system.

Individuals within a political elite too play a key role in spatial relationships. Peripheries may serve as bridgeheads between different centers, and political leaders from these peripheries may, under circumstances favoring regional cooperation, play an integrative role. Raimondo Strassoldo points out that "marginal" individuals such as Jean Monnet or Konrad Adenauer, coming from peripheral regions such as Alsace-Lorraine or the Rheingebiet, were crucial in integrating France and Germany into a European framework. But political leaders from the periphery may also stress their unconditional loyalty to the center, as was the case with Napoleon (from Corsica) or Stalin (from Georgia).[12]

---

[10] Strassoldo, pp. 27–61.

[11] See Owen Lattimore, "The Periphery as Locus of Innovation," in Gottmann, ed., pp. 205–215; and Jean Gottmann, "Organizing and Reorganizing Space," in Gottmann, ed., pp. 217–224.

[12] Strassoldo, p. 50.

The center–periphery model is a spatial model and spatial relations are crucial when national movements are attempting to remove specific territories and their populations from the authority of a government. They in effect are protests by peripheries against their subordinated status. But the separation they are striving for is not necessarily absolute. Partial forms of withdrawal also exist. Peripheries may thus strive to diminish their dependency on a center by seeking self-government through various forms of autonomy or federal relations. Means to diminish dependency relations range from incorporation into the center by obtaining a share in the central functions of decision-making (through the creation of a federation) up to the creation of an internationally recognized sovereign state on a par with the center (through, for instance, the creation of a confederation).

The creation of de facto states—whose definition includes the control over a defined territory[13]—and the redrawing of international boundaries—when a secessionist movement is successful in achieving recogni-

---

[13] Control over a territory is crucial to the definitions of a state—including definitions of de facto states in juridical and political science literature. According to Article 1 of the Montevideo Convention from 1933, "The state as a person of international law should possess the following qualifications: (a) a permanent population; (b) a defined territory; (c) government; and (d) capacity to enter into relations with the other states." See The Avalon Project at Yale Law School, Documents in Law, History and Diplomacy, 20th Century Documents, Convention on Rights and Duties of States (inter-American), December 26, 1933, http://www.yale.edu/lawweb/avalon/intdip/interam/intam03. htm#art1. Scott Pegg gives a more encompassing definition of the de facto state: "In essence, a de facto state exists where there is an organized political leadership which has risen to power through some degree of indigenous capability; receives popular support; and has achieved sufficient capacity to provide governmental services to a given population in a defined territorial area, over which effective control is maintained for an extended period of time. The de facto state views itself as capable of entering into relations with other states and it seeks full constitutional independence and widespread international recognition as a sovereign state. It is, however, unable to achieve any degree of substantive recognition and therefore remains illegitimate in the eyes of international society." See Scott Pegg, *De Facto States in the International System*, Working Paper no. 21, (Vancouver: Institute of International Relations, The University of British Columbia, February 1998), p. 1, http://www.iir.ubc.ca/pdffiles/webwp21.pdf. See also Scott Pegg, *International Society and the De Facto State* (Aldershot, UK: Ashgate, 1998) and Dov Lynch, *Engaging Eurasia's Separatist States: Unresolved Conflicts and De Facto States* (Washington, DC: United States Institute of Peace Press, 2004).

tion—can both have consequences for domestic relations between majorities and minorities within a state, and for the external regional balance of power.[14] Secessionist conflicts may lead to a re-centering of the international order, when dependency relations move from one center to another, or to a realignment of dependency relations by creating a multiplicity of centers within a more pluralistic network.

THE APPLICATION OF THE MODEL

Various types of relations between state institutions characterize Georgia's domestic center–periphery order. For each of these types, political authority operates within spatial limits. First are state-to-state relations, where the Georgian government represents an internationally recognized state and where the authorities from South Ossetia and Abkhazia constitute de facto states. Second, the current Georgian Constitution provides for federal relations between Tbilisi and the Autonomous Republic of Ajara.[15] Third, the process of regionalization in Georgia has to be taken into account. The "regions," which were created under the Shevardnadze regime and where so-called governors represent presidential authority on the local level, never received a proper constitutional status. The question of self-government on the regional level remained therefore

---

[14] See Prevelakis.

[15] An amendment to Article 3.3 of the Georgian Constitution provided that, "The status of the Autonomous Republic of Ajara shall be determined by the Constitutional Law of Georgia." Until May 2004, when Ajaran leader Aslan Abashidze was forced into exile, no such law was approved by the Georgian Parliament. A law on the status of Ajara was passed on July 7, 2004, granting the region only nominal autonomy, but formally confirming its statehood as an autonomous republic. On Georgia's policies in Ajara, see the International Crisis Group, "Saakashvili's Ajara Success: Repeatable Elsewhere in Georgia?" *Europe Briefing*, August 18, 2004, http://www.crisisgroup.org/home/index. cfm?id=2907&l=1. On Ajara's constitutional status, see *The Report of the Committee on the Honouring of Obligations and Commitments by Member States of the Council of Europe (Monitoring Committee)*, Parliamentary Assembly, Council of Europe, Honouring of Obligations and Commitments by Georgia, Doc. 10383, December 21, 2004, particularly pp. 3, 10–11, http://assembly.coe. int/Documents/WorkingDocs/doc04/EDOC10383.htm. In 2002, according to official statistics, Ajara had a population of 376,016.

on the political agenda after the Rose Revolution.[16] Fourth, there are some regions with a high proportion of national minorities, such as the Azerbaijanis in Georgia's southern Kvemo Kartli region bordering Azerbaijan; the Armenians in the Samtskhe–Javakheti region, particularly in and around the town of Akhalkalaki; and the Kists, who are related to the Chechens, in the Pankisi Gorge. The political and economic integration of these minority populations within Georgian state structures remains weak. Claims for political autonomy among some of these territorially concentrated minorities could lead to a further fragmentation of Georgian statehood. In all of these cases, there is a clear spatial dimension to the security problematic: the territories of Abkhazia and South Ossetia constitute nearly 15 percent of Georgia's territory. In the rest of Georgia's territory, minorities represent 16.3 percent of the population.[17]

The same conceptual center–periphery scheme can be applied to the international order in the Caucasus, and more particularly to the "peripheral" security policies that Georgia, under successive presidents, developed toward Moscow, Washington, and Brussels.[18] Here too a spatial dimension applies. Georgia is conceived of as a single center in relation to various domestic peripheries and as a single periphery in relation to various international centers. This twofold application of the center–periphery model provides insights into the mutual linkages between domestic and international security threats under each of the three Georgian presidential regimes.[19]

---

[16] On the problematic of Georgia's regionalization, see Bruno Coppieters, Tamara Kovziridze, and Uwe Leonardy, "Federalization of Foreign Relations: Discussing Alternatives for the Georgian–Abkhaz Conflict," Caspian Studies Program Working Paper no. 2, (Cambridge, MA: Caspian Studies Program, Harvard University, October 2003), p. 16, http://bcsia.ksg.harvard.edu/publication.cfm?program=CSP&ctype=paper&item_id=405.

[17] See Ghia Nodia's contribution to this volume.

[18] For an analysis of the role of culture in Georgian foreign policy orientations, see Stephen Jones, "The Role of Cultural Paradigms in Georgian Foreign Policy," in Rick Fawn, ed., *Ideology and National Identity in Post-Communist Foreign Policies* (London: Frank Cass, 2004), pp. 83–110.

[19] Here the center–periphery model is used for spatially located security threats. This does not exclude its application to security threats created by widespread corruption, the criminalization of state structures and poverty, or civil–military relations when these have a spatial dimension. All such threats, indeed, have had an impact on the relations between Tbilisi and the breakaway states.

The analysis in preceding chapters provides a basis for testing assumptions implied by the center–periphery model. Thus, in terms of Georgia's domestic security policies, have changes between the center and the peripheries been induced by transformations at the center rather than at the periphery? With respect to Georgia's international security policies, do profound policy changes in Moscow, Washington, and Brussels have a stronger impact on their relationships with Tbilisi than events in Georgia have on these relationships?

These assumptions have direct consequences for an assessment of Georgia's future policy options—for example, concerning its chances of reintegrating the breakaway entities or coming closer to the European Union (EU). The chance of successfully negotiating the political status of South Ossetia or Abkhazia will depend, of course, in part, on political dynamics in Sukhum(i) or Tskhinval(i)[20] but more crucially on those in Tbilisi. The chance of Georgia being drawn into Western organizations, particularly NATO and the EU, will likewise largely depend on its capacity to reform its state structures, but even more fundamentally on the capacity of these organizations to address the problems of Georgia as a peripheral state.

The assumptions involved in the use of a center–periphery model to locate Georgian security does not mean that the outcome of its secessionist conflicts has to be exclusively conceived of as the result of shifts in the balance of power between the main external actors in the South Caucasus. On the contrary, the use of the center–periphery model to analyze secessionist conflicts within Georgia focuses on both the role of centers in international relations—referring to those actors which have the greatest impact on Georgia's foreign policy choices—and of the center at the domestic level—referring to the policies of the Georgian state. But the main key to a resolution of domestic conflicts between center and periphery remains the transformation of the Georgian center.

In addition, the synergy between insecurity within Georgia and instability within the wider Caucasus has resulted in two movements of the periphery away from the center. First, the Georgian center is being challenged by the periphery—by the claims of the former Soviet

---

[20] Abkhazians write "Sukhum" and Georgians write "Sokhumi" or "Sukhumi" in English-language publications. Ossetians use "Tskhinval," whereas Georgians refer to the city as "Tskhinvali."

autonomous entities on the one hand and by its national minorities on the other. These challenges could be resolved by integrating these peripheries into the center—through political representation, minority rights, or federal arrangements. They may also be addressed through a policy of confrontation. This, however, could lead to a weakening of the center and, if secessionist entities are able to take full advantage of this weakening, to the emergence of new sovereign centers. So far, the center in Tbilisi has failed to integrate the breakaway states at its periphery or to subdue them through a policy of confrontation. But the breakaway states in the periphery have likewise failed to free themselves from the Georgian center by securing international recognition of their sovereignty.

Second, a conflictual process that can be described as a movement from the periphery away from the center exists on the international level: Georgia resists its peripheral status vis-à-vis Moscow by claiming membership in Western organizations. It strives for a change of status from dependency on a single center toward interdependency with a multi-tiered network of centers within a larger Euro-Atlantic environment. Georgia's aspiration for membership in NATO and the European Union symbolizes this longing. Moscow has responded to this challenge by mixing policies of integration and confrontation. In this case, the center failed to stop the growing dissociation of the periphery. But the periphery has also failed to complete its emancipation by severing its dependency on the center and by achieving inclusion into new centers, such as NATO and the EU. Georgia remains peripheral to the Western security system. Its profound instability can thus be understood as the result of two failed attempts by peripheries to change their relationship to a center—in one case, national, in the other, international.

Integration and confrontation are two possible conditions of center–periphery relationships. The other types of center–periphery relations also provide useful analytical tools for understanding Georgian security policies. For instance, in comparing the state- and nation-building strategies that Georgia has employed toward its autonomous entities since its independence, it is interesting to see not only the extent to which these strategies have been based on confrontational policies, but also in what measure they have taken other options into account. In this regard, several questions can be raised. To what extent did nationalist elements under Gamsakhurdia, Shevardnadze, or Saakashvili treat the autonomous entities as fault lines where a severe confrontation with minority nations or external powers was taking place? Did they ever conceive these autonomous entities—even after a settlement of the present conflicts—as potential bridgeheads to other regions in the wider Caucasus—favoring, for instance, cooperation with Turkey, Russia, or particular regions in the North Caucasus? On the other hand, did these autonomous entities—for instance, Ajara or Abkhazia—strive for such a role? Similar questions can be raised on the level of international relations when Georgia is defined as a periphery and the center is located in Washington, Brussels, or Moscow. Thus, for instance, which policies have Brussels and Washington followed to support Georgia's role as a bridgehead between Asia and Europe?

The national and international levels are linked by the extent to which various "national projects" in this multinational country, to use Nodia's concept, have been framed by a confrontation between the Georgian nation and the nations on the periphery, as well as between the Georgian periphery and the Russian center. What are the domestic consequences for Georgia of having Washington treat Georgia as a country located on a fault line near "rogue" states such as Iran or as a country whose failure to establish full control over its territory opens the door to international terrorist elements? Finally, it may be asked to what extent the nature of Georgian policies toward its domestic periphery is affected by the evolution of Russian, U.S., or EU policy and actions.

While the contributors to this volume do not frame their analyses in terms of center–periphery relations, they supply the evidence for such an analysis. The book has thus been conceived of as "layered." The inner layers deal with the internal and historical sources of the national security challenge facing Georgia. The outer layers deal with the external sources of the challenge, including Russia, the West, and the complex configuration of other players and problems that make the environment so intricate. Nodia includes both layers in his analysis of the Georgian national project, which includes the unification of the nation and the center's control over its periphery on the one hand and full integration into the Western world on the other. Both layers are also more or less explicitly included in all other contributions to be found in this book, even if their main focus is on either the internal or the external sources of insecurity.

CENTER–PERIPHERY RELATIONS IN THE DOMESTIC REALM

Center–periphery relations on the domestic level in Georgia encompass the various dependencies between Tbilisi and different territorial autonomies as well as territorially concentrated minorities. Several types of interaction are relevant in this context. First there are the confrontations between national communities that have taken place on the South Ossetian and Abkhazian peripheries, leading in both cases to full-scale war with the center. Until May 2004, confrontation also characterized the relationship between Tbilisi and Ajara. Confrontation has been avoided but remains a risk with territorially concentrated minorities. Second is the failure to integrate the Georgian periphery into the state- and nation-building efforts of the center. The authorities at the center generally lacked the political will to engage in radical compromises for resolving outstanding conflicts with the periphery, because such compromises risk a loss of domestic legitimacy or could stir up other sources of state instability. Third, despite the recurrent eruption of crises due to the lack of resolution of the Georgian national question, the interaction between center and periphery remains largely characterized by indifference. This results from the failures of both the policies of confrontation and accommodation. Fourth, there is the untapped potential of the periphery to serve as a bridgehead toward other regions and states. All four patterns of interaction are elements in the creation and transformation of national identities.

The center–periphery model assumes that changes in the interaction between poles will be more heavily shaped by changes at the center than at the periphery. This means, for example, that the accession to power of Gamsakhurdia, Shevardnadze, and Saakashvili had a greater impact on the relationship between Tbilisi and its peripheries than any political change within the periphery could have had. The asymmetrical and hierarchical relationship between the poles also implies that each transformation of the relationship between the poles will have a more profound effect on the periphery than on the center. Dramatic changes in the center–periphery relationship in Georgia include the failed restructuring of the Georgian state at the time of independence and its consequences for Tbilisi's control over South Ossetia and Abkhazia. They also include the 2003 Rose Revolution and the consequences for Ajara and South Ossetia.

The Soviet Period

Integration was the declared aim, domination the main characteristic, and confrontation the final result of ethno-federalism in the Soviet Union. It had been conceived of as a form of integration of the various nations previously held together by tsarist imperial rule. A complex federal structure including a supranational level of governance and various types of federated entities (union republics, autonomous republics, and autonomous regions) was meant to solve the problem of national self-determination. Relations between Moscow and the union republics constituted a first tier of center–periphery relations within a multilevel structure, whereas relations between union and autonomous republics constituted a second tier, and between union republics and autonomous regions a third tier. The Soviet center remained the arbiter of all center–periphery disputes on the second and third tier.

The Soviet ethno-federal institutions failed, however, to integrate the national communities, due in part to the lack of equality among nations in this multi-tiered framework. Shared sovereignty, one of the specific characteristics of federations, was also missing. Nodia describes this structure as quasi-federal, where the exercise of sovereignty in fact occurred in a highly centralized form through the Communist Party. Confrontation between national communities on the second and third tiers resulted largely from a breakdown at the Soviet center. Moreover, when confrontation erupted, Soviet ethno-federal traditions that had strengthened separate identities and provided state resources to nationalist elites added to its intensity.[21]

Abkhazians and South Ossetians defined their identity largely in opposition to the Georgian authorities, but they were also involved in a confrontation with the local Georgian population in their area. After the collapse of the Soviet Union, the Georgian government could not stay indifferent toward these conflicts at its periphery. In the face of this challenge, it sought to re-establish Georgian cultural and political hegemony

---

[21] On the discussion regarding the unifying aims and divisive effects of ethno-federalism, see Henry E. Hale, "Divided We Stand. Institutional Sources of Ethnofederal State Survival and Collapse," *World Politics*, vol. 56 (January 2004), pp. 165–193 and Nancy Bermeo, "Position Paper for the Working Group on Federalism, Conflict Prevention, and Settlement," presented at the Third International Conference on Federalism, Brussels, March 3–5, 2005.

over the whole of its territory, a hegemony that it claimed to have lost during the Soviet period.

The justification for Georgian territorial claims on Abkhazia and South Ossetia has a temporal dimension. According to a popular Georgian historical narrative, these territories were first settled by proto-Georgian tribes, and over time they have been developed by an indigenous Georgian population.[22] The Georgians, it is asserted, are the only population "native" to the South Ossetian region, whereas the Ossetians were "latecomers" to Georgian territory, since they migrated from North Ossetia "only a few centuries ago." This difference in origins would give the Georgians a greater historical claim to the region than the Ossetians, despite local demographics that leave Georgians in the minority. Concerning Abkhazia, a different argument is used to justify Georgian hegemony. While Abkhazians are, in the eyes of many Georgians, correct to claim an autochthonous status, they are a minority in Abkhazia (18 percent of the population in 1989), and their numbers do not, in Georgian eyes, warrant the overrepresentation they enjoy in the institutions of the republic nor special political privileges as a titular nation.

Moreover, not all Georgian nationalists accepted the view of Abkhazians as an autochthonous nation. As early as 1954, the literary historian, Pavle Ingoroqva, maintained that the Abkhazians were not indigenous to Abkhazia, but had migrated from the Northern Caucasus. His thesis has a large following in Georgia. Basically it denies the right of the Abkhazians to be considered as a titular nation, and, therefore, delegitimizes their political overrepresentation.

Abkhazian discourses on the ethnogenesis of the Abkhazian nation, in turn, also invoke the issue of sovereignty. Their historians deny an indigenous status to the Georgian population in Abkhazia, characterizing them as settlers and migrants. They refer to migration policies implemented by the tsarist and Soviet regimes that turned the local Abkhazian population into a minority.[23] Abkhazians rely on this historical interpretation to jus-

---

[22] Bruno Coppieters, "In Defence of the Homeland: Intellectuals and the Georgian–Abkhazian Conflict," in Bruno Coppieters and Michel Huysseune, eds., *Secession, History, and the Social Sciences* (Brussels: VUB University Press, 2002), p. 105, http://poli.vub.ac.be/.

[23] See the various contributions to George Hewitt, ed., *The Abkhazians* (Richmond, UK: Curzon, 1999).

tify an exclusive status for the Abkhazian nation and its claim to international sovereignty. They also use it to delegitimize Georgian claims for proportional representation.

Gamsakhurdia

With the weakening of Soviet institutions, both Georgians and Abkhazians attempted to reshape center–periphery relations according to their respective national projects. These colliding projects rested on opposite discourses concerning historical injustices, national identity, and state sovereignty. From the Georgian perspective, the primary aim of the Soviet approach to federalism and of the creation of federal entities within Georgia was to divide their country and to restrain their sovereignty. The Abkhazians and the Ossetians, the titular nations of federal entities that were subordinated to the Union Republic of Georgia, resisted what they perceived as forms of oppression and discrimination. They feared that Georgian independence would put an end to the constraints previously imposed by the Soviet center on Georgian nationalism. As demonstrated by Nodia, it was far easier for these two minority nations than for the other minority groups without autonomous state institutions to articulate their grievances, formulate a national project, mobilize state resources, and receive external support to confront the center.

Nationalist mobilization took place both at the center and at the periphery among Georgians, Ossetians, and Abkhazians. It took the form of a series of unilateral moves corresponding to comparable moves at the other pole, such as unilateral declarations of sovereignty or independence, the organization of elections in which one side refused to participate, constitutional changes that were considered illegitimate by the other side, the introduction of new language policies enhancing the status of one language and culture while degrading the status of the other, and eventually the use of military force.

The eruption of violence in this confrontation between center and periphery in Georgia was part of a series of unilateral actions and may thus be understood as the result of a multitude of factors. David Darchiashvili points out that the weakening and then final breakdown of the Soviet center permitted the creation of paramilitary units, which emerged to deal with the internal ethnic conflicts underway by the end of 1980s. The Georgian authorities, however, failed to turn the professed loyalty of these paramilitary groups to the nation into a loyalty to the state's institutions. For Christoph Zürcher, this situation provided a favorable environment for "entrepreneurs of violence" to exploit violence in advancing their own profit seeking. Gamsakhurdia used these forces to consolidate his political power and to wage war in South Ossetia. But the weakness of the Georgian state left him unable to control their actions or even to prevent them from eventually turning against him.

The Georgian national project and nationalist mobilization at the time of independence did not favor policies allowing the peripheries to act as bridgeheads with other centers. As noted by Thomas de Waal, Gamsakhurdia defended eccentric ideas about the common ethnic and cultural basis of the Caucasian peoples, but failed to take practical initiatives toward regional integration. Such initiatives would have had to include Georgia's peripheries in cooperative frameworks. The confrontation with South Ossetia prevented the strengthening of cooperative links with North Ossetia. In the case of Abkhazia, Gamsakhurdia helped to popularize the notion that the Abkhazian population was not indigenous to the territory, but had migrated from the Northern Caucasus, beyond the borders of Georgia.[24] Cross-border cooperation only happened on the military level. During the wars in South Ossetia and Abkhazia, armed support was given to the Ossetians and the Abkhazians by ethnic kin and political allies from beyond the Georgian borders.

Shevardnadze

Gamsakhurdia's ouster in January 1992 and the return of Eduard Shevardnadze to Georgia a few months later had dramatic consequences for Tbilisi's relationship with the periphery. Shevardnadze's accession to power permitted, with Russia's support, the implementation of a ceasefire in South Ossetia. Still, one of the main reasons that Shevardnadze supported the August 1992 military intervention in Abkhazia was to demonstrate his nationalistic credentials in the face of the continuing threat from Gamsakhurdia, who had mobilized armed groups in western Georgia. Zürcher notes that there had been cases of intercommunal violence in Abkhazia before August 1992, but these had not escalated into a full-scale civil war. Such a war only became possible through the center's outside intervention.

---

[24] See Coppieters, in Coppieters and Huysseune, eds., pp. 91–94.

The armed groups loyal to Gamsakhurdia were only defeated at the end of the Abkhazian war in October 1993, and then only with Russian support. Despite the loss of large parts of territory, the Shevardnadze government managed to restore some of the elements of statehood. The end of the "Times of Troubles," as Zürcher phrases it, was symbolized by the introduction of a new constitution in 1995 and the reinforcement of the government's monopoly of power. Paramilitary organizations were marginalized or reintegrated into the new armed forces.

Reunifying the Georgian multinational state became the Shevardnadze regime's main challenge. The military defeat in Abkhazia, the weakness of the Georgian Army, and the Russian refusal to help solve the issue by force left diplomacy as the only option for resolving the political status of Abkhazia and South Ossetia. Negotiations, however, were quickly deadlocked and remain so today.

The Georgian approach to reunification entails an asymmetrical federal model, in which Abkhazia and South Ossetia, together with Ajara and the Georgian regions, would receive differing degrees of autonomy. This is unacceptable to the secessionist leaderships. Such federal ties would in their view perpetuate a relationship of dependency and confrontation between center and periphery. The Abkhazian authorities, for their part, initially preferred a confederation or the status of a "free associated state" with Georgia. Either option would permit the recognition of Abkhazia as a subject of international law with a full international legal personality, sovereignty, and a unilateral right to secession. It would also radically change the nature of the center–periphery relationship with Georgia. Tbilisi has refused, considering this position to be incompatible with preserving the country's territorial integrity.

With Abkhazia, confrontation between center and periphery remained predominant throughout the Shevardnadze era. In 1999, the Abkhazian leadership radicalized its position, insisting that independence or a free association with the Russian Federation were the only acceptable options. The Georgian authorities, in turn, repeatedly threatened to use military force if negotiations remained stalled, and provided undercover support to Georgian guerilla forces operating in Abkhazia. Georgian and Abkhazian authorities have talked of economic cooperation since 1997, on the assumption that, if progress could be achieved in areas of common economic interest, confrontation could be avoided. [25] But the deadlock

---

[25] On the following, see Coppieters, Kovziridze, and Leonardy.

over Abkhazia's political status stood in the way of economic or any other form of cooperation.

The prospect of developing a policy of economic integration with South Ossetia appeared better than with Abkhazia. In this case too, however, the question of political status overshadowed all efforts at economic integration. In the political negotiations between the South Ossetian authorities and the Shevardnadze government, the issue of passports and travel documents constituted a key point of contention. For the South Ossetian authorities, the issue was crucial to communication and trade with the Russian Federation. South Ossetian leaders asked to be allowed to issue their own identity cards and legal documents, but the Georgian government refused.

From the Abkhazian and South Ossetian perspectives, cross-border trade with Russia must be facilitated before a final political settlement can be reached. Increased contact with Russian regions, particularly in the North Caucasus, in their view, will not only be beneficial for their economic development, but will also enhance their leverage in future negotiations with the Georgian authorities. During the Shevardnadze era, the absence of a legal regime, however, did not halt the trade of large quantities of goods through South Ossetia, much of it smuggled. The Shevardnadze government preferred to tolerate rather than suppress such activities, and sometimes even treated them as hopeful forms of an emerging cooperation between Georgians and Ossetians as well as proof that ethnic hostility between the populations did not exist.

As explained by Nodia, the tensions between Tbilisi and the former Autonomous Republic of Ajara did not result from secessionist claims or from conflicts over national identity. There is a sharp contrast, in this respect, between the case of Ajara and the two previous cases. Center–periphery conflicts in this case resulted mainly from the refusal of Ajaran Supreme Council Head Aslan Abashidze to accept the formal authority of Tbilisi. On fiscal matters, Ajara prevented Tbilisi from controlling customs points at the Turkish border and refused to transfer tax revenues. In the security field, Abashidze developed close cooperation with the Russians stationed at the military base in Ajara and set about creating an independent local army. According to Darchiashvili, in 2003, Ajara had twenty tanks and armored vehicles at its disposal, as well as helicopters, coastal cutters, and special armed units.

Leaders coming from the periphery may portray themselves as patriots and demonstrate unconditional loyalty to the national cause. Such was the case with Abashidze. As noted by Nodia, he never defended an Ajaran national project, but "loved to portray himself as a champion of Georgian unity." He also managed to become a powerful figure on the national level through elections, largely by distorting the number of eligible voters and voter turnout in Ajara. This electoral manipulation gave a significant number of seats to his political party (the Revival Party) in the Georgian Parliament.

Ajara had extensive trade relations with neighboring Turkey, signed several bilateral agreements with regions in the Russian Federation, and developed, as a member of the Assembly of European Regions (AER), bilateral ties with a number of other European regions.[26] Ajara was the first region in the Caucasus to make a serious attempt to be integrated into the pan-European network of interregional cooperation. But Ajara failed to play the role of a bridgehead to other countries or regions, because Batumi and Tbilisi could never formalize their federal relationship, and, therefore, resolve the matter of custom duties or that of Ajara's international legal status. Moreover, domestic conflicts between Tbilisi and Ajara were reproduced on the international level. Ajara's membership in the AER, for example, was swiftly followed by the membership of the Georgian region of Imereti, whose governor was an appointee of the Georgian president, to the same organization. Tbilisi made this move in order to counterbalance Batumi's activity on the interregional level. The representatives of these two Georgian regions were soon in conflict with each other, openly airing their domestic divergences. This hindered their cooperation with other AER members.

There were thus sufficient grounds for a severe confrontation between the center and the Ajaran periphery, but Shevardnadze and Abashidze also shared common interests that at times allowed political agreement. The Ajaran leader, for example, traded his personal support for Shevardnadze in the April 2000 presidential elections for the introduction of the name "Ajaran Autonomous Republic" into the Georgian Constitution. Shevardnadze's views on the future federalization of the

---

[26] Created in 1985, the Assembly of European Regions (AER) is a forum that facilitates cooperation among 250 regions of thirty different European countries. In November 2004, Ajara and two Georgian regions (Imereti and Shida Kartli) were members of the AER and two regions (Guria and Kakheti) had the status of observers. See http://www.are-regions-europe.org/.

state were another factor impeding the normalization of Tbilisi's relations with Batumi. From Shevardnadze's perspective, the formalization of federal ties with Batumi should follow, rather then precede, the reintegration of Abkhazia and South Ossetia. Shevardnadze's unwillingness to try to solve this question implied a policy of powerlessness in the face of Ajara's de facto withdrawal from central authority. His relative indifference constituted one of the main points of contention for the Georgian parliamentary opposition in the last years of his regime.

Regionalization was much debated under Shevardnadze, but actual reform remained tentative and inconclusive. Without taking Ajara and Abkhazia into account, Georgia consists of ten regions, each of which includes a number of rayons.[27] The *presidentis rtsmunebuli* (representatives of the president of Georgia) or so-called governors wield great executive power over the lower entities on the rayon and municipal level. The process of democratization and state consolidation in the second half of the 1990s failed to establish a proper constitutional status for the regions or the principle of self-government. The unresolved secessionist conflicts constituted one of the regime's main arguments against a clear and democratic division of powers between the central government and the regional authorities. Tbilisi insisted that such a reform had to be postponed until Georgia's territorial integrity had been restored. Shevardnadze also feared losing control over the lower levels of government, particularly over the electoral process, a process with which his governors regularly interfered.

In the debate on the future of the administrative–territorial arrangement of Georgia, the "rayonists" were opposed to the "regionalists." For the rayonists, control was said to be central to preserving the stability of the state and even the survival of the existing political regime. They believed that Abkhazian and South Ossetian secessionism and the threat to stability they represented made radical reforms impossible. According to the regionalists, undemocratic electoral practices at the regional level

---

[27] These ten regions (excluding Ajara and Abkhazia) are: (1) Imereti (with 669,666 inhabitants), (2) Kvemo Kartli (497,530), (3) Samegrelo and Zemo Svaneti (466,100), (4) Kakheti (407,182), (5) Shida Kartli (without South Ossetia, 314,039), (6) Samtskhe-Javakheti (207,598), (7) Guria (143,357), (8) Mckheta-Mtianeti (125,443), and (9) Racha-Lechkhumi and Kvemo Svaneti (50,969) (10) Tbilisi (1,081,679). I am thankful to Ghia Nodia for these data, which he received from the State Department for Statistics of Georgia.

would be more difficult to maintain once regional decentralization had taken place and local self-government was established. Both currents were represented in the Georgian government and parliament. Until the end of the Shevardnadze regime, the far-reaching reform urged by the regionalists seemed impossible.

Under Shevardnadze, unlike in the Gamsakhurdia period, ethnic minorities were no longer assigned the threatening status of "guests." The Shevardnadze regime failed, however, to develop an inclusive civic concept of Georgian citizenship and the Georgian nation. Minority elites were simply co-opted into patronage networks. This perpetuated the Soviet practice of tolerating elite corruption in exchange for political loyalty.

Saakashvili

The political leadership that came to power in Georgia following the Rose Revolution put the struggle against corruption, Georgia's integration into the Euro-Atlantic community, the normalization of relations with Russia, and the reunification of the country at the top of its political agenda. In the new leaders' view, the previous leadership under Shevardnadze had only paid lip service to these objectives. The new leadership sought radical changes. It seemed at first that the most spectacular results could be achieved on the question of national reunification. Once again, as had been the case with Saakashvili's two predecessors, progress was to come through a policy of confrontation. Saakashvili was convinced that the new regime could make a clear break with the previous regime by pursuing a different policy toward Ajara, whose leader had strongly opposed the Rose Revolution. Saakashvili succeeded and Abashidze was forced from power in May 2004.[28]

---

[28] To understand the lack of Russian full support to Abashidze in his confrontation with Saakashvili in May 2004, one has to make a distinction between Russia's attitude toward conflicts between national communities in Georgia on the one hand and toward intra-Georgian disputes on the other. As compared to its involvement in the ethnic conflicts in South Ossetia and Abkhazia, where Russia has taken the side of the national minorities, Moscow has been far more careful as far as intra-Georgian disputes—including violent ones—were concerned. It did not attempt to destabilize the domestic situation in Georgia during the *coup d'état* against Gamsakhurdia at the end of 1991 by giving substantial support to the forces loyal to the ousted president. It further supported Shevardnadze at the end of 1993 against the pro-Gamsakhurdia forces at a

In Shevardnadze's order of priorities, the Abkhazian question had ranked first, followed by the questions of South Ossetia and Ajara. Saakashvili reversed this order. After its success in Ajara, the new regime confronted the authorities of South Ossetia, combining a policy of force with an extended hand toward the population of the South Ossetia. As the International Crisis Group Report on South Ossetia described, the Georgian government combined a policy of "attacking greed" on the elite level with one of "addressing grievance" at the level of the population at large.[29]

Anti-smuggling operations were mounted in and around South Ossetia in December 2003 and reinforced in May 2004. The most spectacular were attempts at military intimidation by moving in troops and cracking down on the Ergneti Market, which functioned as a trading post between Russia and Georgia. This trade, which involved both Ossetians and Georgians, had been considered by the previous regime as a way to facilitate contacts between the communities. Accordingly, it was thought to have long-term positive effects on Tbilisi's conflict resolution efforts. From the perspective of the Saakashvili government, however, the primary effect of this market was to criminalize the economy and to prevent a settlement of the conflict. Moreover, it destabilized the Georgian budget and impeded necessary customs and tax reforms. Shevardnadze's indifference, the new people believed, stemmed from the degree to which parts of the Georgian establishment had materially profited from this trade.

At the same time that the new Georgian government increased the physical pressure on the South Ossetian authorities, it also sought to appeal to the South Ossetian population by paying retirement pensions and launching television and radio broadcasts in the Ossetian language.

---

moment when Georgia was not strong, but rather, as Shevardnadze's suggested, "on its knees." In November 2003, Russia abstained from direct involvement against the revolutionary mobilization against Shevardnadze, and in May 2004 it also refused military support to Aslan Abashidze's regime in Ajara, mediating his departure from the country. This distinction between the two types of conflicts may be explained by a fear of a total destabilization of Georgia, which would be a far greater risk if Russia intervened in intra-Georgian disputes than in secessionist conflicts.

[29] International Crisis Group, "Georgia: Avoiding War in South Ossetia," *Europe Report,* no. 159, November 26, 2004, pp. 11–12, http://www.icg.org/home/index.cfm?l=1.

Saakashvili and his people were acting on the conviction that the Georgian–Ossetian conflict was primarily driven by greed rather than by genuine grievances, and, therefore, that the South Ossetian authorities lacked popular legitimacy. Seen from this perspective, they assumed that a few well-chosen concessions to the population would remove the issue of grievances.

These initiatives, however, failed. On the military level, the confrontation led in August 2004 to a series of armed clashes with casualties, particularly on the Georgian side. As a result, Saakashvili decided to end the military confrontation and to withdraw Georgian troops from the conflict area.[30] On the economic level, as Damien Helly and Giorgi Gogia note, the closure of the Ergneti Market disrupted the activities of several criminal groups, but failed to address the problem of the local population's economic survival. Thus, both the policy of military confrontation with the South Ossetian authorities and the attempt to integrate the local population backfired. According to the International Crisis Group, the remilitarization of the conflict reversed a decade of relative progress.

The situation in South Ossetia has been radically affected by the deterioration in relations with Tbilisi, which underscores South Ossetia's status as a periphery more than ever. Because of the breach in trade relations with Georgia, it has become entirely dependent on another center, Russia. At the moment, Moscow sustains the South Ossetian budget, infrastructure, and even its pension system.[31]

Darchiashvili shows how the absence of central authority over breakaway states has led to the loss of authority over adjacent territories. This has surely been the case for territories along the Georgian–Abkhazian cease-fire line. The new government has sought to control the Georgian partisan groups operating in Abkhazia and pursued them for their alleged involvement in criminal activities. According to Oksana Antonenko, police operations against such groups in February 2004 have helped to improve the security situation in both Georgia and Abkhazia.

---

[30] See Ghia Nodia, "Europeanisation and (Not) Resolving Secessionist Conflicts," *Journal on Ethnopolitics and Minority Studies in Europe,* issue 1 (2004), http://www.ecmi.de/jemie.

[31] Interviews with South Ossetian participants in the first expert meeting of the "Georgian–Ossetian Dialogue," which took place on March 15–18, 2005, in Brdo, Slovenia. The meeting was organized by Oksana Antonenko from the International Institute for Strategic Studies.

Despite the eagerness of the Saakashvili regime to solve the problem of national reunification, it realized that unilateral measures would not work in the Abkhazian case. On the military level, operations such as the one in South Ossetia would have been obstructed by Russian peacekeeping forces. Offering the Abkhazians economic concessions or opportunities would require a mutually agreed-to framework, which at that time seemed impossible. For more than a decade, Abkhazia had been separated from Georgia, and all meaningful trade links between Georgia and Abkhazia had been severed.

The low level of social, cultural, and economic interaction between Abkhazia and Georgia had a direct impact on the process of state- and nation-building in Abkhazia. It explains why the negotiations with Georgia played no role in the first round of the presidential elections in Abkhazia in October 3, 2004, and in the crisis that emerged afterward. The two main candidates in this election expressed no disagreement on the question of Abkhazian sovereignty or the position to be adopted toward Georgia. Here, it was the periphery that expressed an attitude of indifference toward the center, reflecting the basic change in the nature of this relationship and the shift of Abkhazian dependency to the Russian center. Georgia could only pretend to be the center with authority over the Abkhazian periphery by blocking Abkhazia's international recognition and by creating severe security threats. Antonenko notes that Russia, having brokered an agreement between the two main candidates in the 2004 Abkhazian presidential election, remained the only external force with direct influence on Abkhazian affairs. The fact that Russia's preferred candidate did not become president of the republic, however, highlights the limits of its power. The relationship between Abkhazia and Russia, therefore, is asymmetrical and hierarchical, but not a full dependency.

Concerning the possibility of integrating the peripheries, the new Georgian regime promotes ideas of national identity, nation-building, and citizenship that differ from the nationalist ideology of its predecessors, who had been socialized under the Soviet regime. A distinction thus has to be made in this particular respect between the policies of Saakashvili on the one hand and those of his predecessors. During the Soviet period, Shevardnadze, as a Georgian Communist Party leader, had defended "orthodox" nationalist positions. On the preservation of the Georgian language, for example, his position was in a Soviet context the orthodox view. Gamsakhurdia, a major dissident during Soviet times, represented an "unorthodox" nationalism. That is, he criticized the many concessions made by the

Soviet—including Georgian—authorities to national minorities. Both camps, however, agreed that the Georgian titular nation should preserve its cultural hegemony over other nationalities in the Georgian Republic.

As president, Gamsakhurdia did make concessions to the Abkhazian titular nation, but these attempts at integration were in the Soviet political tradition of power-sharing, which ignored the question of a separation of powers as well as the political differentiation within national communities. In 1991, he proposed that the Abkhazian leadership implement an electoral law based on ethnic quotas that would guarantee them a similar degree of overrepresentation to that enjoyed under the Soviet regime. This proposal was accepted by the Abkhazian side and implemented in the ensuing local elections, but failed to lead to a pacification of the conflict between the two major national communities in Abkhazia. Shevardnadze, after his defeat in Abkhazia, likewise searched for a compromise formula with breakaway states and national minorities that remained in the Soviet tradition. Beginning in 1995, Shevardnadze made several proposals to the Abkhazian and South Ossetian leaderships for the creation of an asymmetrical federal state. His proposals in fact basically reframed the Soviet practice of granting autonomous rights to territorially concentrated minorities while co-opting their elites. He had no idea of how federal mechanisms could be designed that went beyond this Soviet tradition and no notion of the role a multiparty system would have to play in upholding the unity of the state. Leaders in the breakaway states described his offers as a "return to the past."

The new leadership under Saakashvili and a predominantly Western-educated elite has discussed more pluralistic and civic strategies for integrating the periphery and building the nation. But Darchiashvili and Nodia stress the contradiction between the liberal and democratic inclinations of the new elite and the widely popular traditional nationalist sentiments and practices with which they must contend. One may also add that the fears of the new elite do not radically differ from their predecessors. The new leadership still faces the old dilemma: how to transcend the legacy of Soviet ethno-federalist practices with democratic forms when a new democratically based federalism risks a further disintegration of the country.

As a result, when drawing a blueprint of a future federal system uniting Georgia, South Ossetia, and Abkhazia, the new leadership prefers to stress the cooperative features of a federal arrangement and is reluctant to depict the constitutional mechanisms that would guarantee a separation of powers. The necessary involvement of foreign powers, particularly the Russian Federation, in providing security guarantees for Abkhazia and South Ossetia creates another delicate problem that the Georgian authorities prefer not to address.[32] Furthermore, the unwillingness of the Abkhazian and South Ossetian leaderships to discuss how federal arrangements could attenuate or even abolish hierarchical relations between national communities and provide for international security guarantees for federated states does not favor a political settlement.

More interesting is Saakashvili's proposal in January 2005 to link the question of the political status of South Ossetia to the prospect of cross-border cooperation with the Russian Federation.[33] In Saakashvili's view, the constitutional autonomy of South Ossetia should be broader than in the Soviet era and, indeed, broader than the autonomy enjoyed at present by the Republic of North Ossetia in the Russian Federation. The competencies granted to South Ossetia would include control of the local economy. Saakashvili further stated that a peace agreement would lead to the easing of border crossings between North and South Ossetia and to the creation of a free economic zone. But these views on the federal status of South Ossetia, as presented before the Council of Europe, remained very vague.

In July 2004, the Georgian Parliament adopted a constitutional Law on the Status of the Autonomous Republic of Ajara.[34] It confirmed the

---

[32] In his speech before the Council of Europe on a peace plan on South Ossetia, Saakashvili described the OSCE as a "peace monitor," the EU as a "peace guarantor," the United States as a "peace supporter," and Russia as "a welcomed and constructive peace partner." This formula may be rhetorically well-formulated, but fails entirely to address the question how the various international actors could be involved in future mechanisms for security guarantees in politically realistic terms. See Mikheil Saakashvili, "Address by the President of Georgia on the Occasion of the First Part of the 2005 Ordinary Session of the Council of Europe Parliamentary Assembly," Strasbourg, January 24–28, 2005, http://www.coe.int/T/E/Com/Files/PA-Sessions/janv-2005/Saakashvili.pdf.

[33] See Liz Fuller, "South Ossetia Rejects Georgian President's Offer of Autonomy," *RFE/RL Caucasus Report*, vol. 8, no. 4, January 28, 2005, http://www.rferl.org/reports/caucasus-report/2005/01/4-280105.asp; and Saakashvili, "Address by the President of Georgia."

[34] See The International Crisis Group, "Saakashvili's Ajara Success: Repeatable Elsewhere in Georgia?"

principle of Ajara's federal autonomy, but at the same time reflected the new leadership's fear of delegating governmental responsibility to regional bodies. The Council of Europe, basing its assessment on a critical report of the Venice Commission,[35] expressed severe concerns over the "excessively limited autonomy" granted to Ajara, and more specifically over the fact "that the President of Georgia may dissolve the Ajaran Supreme Council if the latter repeatedly refuses to accept his candidate for the region's Prime Minister and that members of his or her executive are literally appointed by the Ministers in Tbilisi. These restrictions reduce the status of Ajara to a nominal autonomy with little if any practical consequence."[36]

The Rose Revolution, therefore, has not led to radical reforms in regionalism or local self-government. This is partly due to the unresolved problem of restoring the country's territorial integrity. The Georgian Parliament ratified the European Charter of Local Self-Government in October 2004, but significantly refrained from accepting a paragraph that envisages the cooperation of local authorities with their counterparts in other countries.[37] The future potential of regions to serve as bridgeheads to other regions and countries does not seem to be very appealing to the Georgian political elites.

Saakashvili has created a commission on territorial-administrative reform intended to rationalize the complex system of territorial organization. The government stated that in the future, all leading positions in local government would be elective.[38] But the question of integration of national minorities remains a difficult one, particularly in those regions

---

[35] See the European Commission for Democracy through Law (Venice Commission), *Opinion on the Draft Constitutional Law of Georgia on the Status of the Autonomous Republic of Ajara,* Adopted by the Venice Commission at its 59th Plenary Session (Venice, June 18-19, 2004), CDL-AD(2004)018, Strasbourg, June 21, 2004, http://66.102.9.104/search?q=cache:j1bAtuP3w4IJ:www. venice.coe.int/docs/2004/CDL-AD(2004)018-e.asp+Opinion+on+the+ draft+constitutional+law+of+Georgia+&hl=nl.

[36] *Report of the Committee on the Honouring of Obligations and Commitments by Member States of the Council of Europe.*

[37] *Civil Georgia,* October 26, 2004, http://www.civil.ge/eng/article.php?id =8174.

[38] *Report of the Committee on the Honouring of Obligations and Commitments by Member States of the Council of Europe,* p. 11.

where they are geographically concentrated. According to Nodia, the presence of national minorities in the 2004 Georgian Parliament remained purely ceremonial.

Still, the transformation of the center through the Rose Revolution has had a profound impact on Georgia's periphery, even if confrontation and lack of integration continue. The new leadership is using a more civic and inclusive nationalist rhetoric and has changed the order of priorities in its strategy of national reunification. In the case of Ajara, a democratic process of change has taken place, but Ajara's reintegration has been made according to a strict hierarchical pattern, leaving only nominal autonomy to the Ajaran Republic. The failed attempt to force reunification with South Ossetia has seriously retarded efforts at confidence-building and cooperation. Confrontation is still the main characteristic of Tbilisi's relations with both Abkhazia and South Ossetia. The questions of territorial integrity, regionalization, and the integration of national minorities remain unresolved, but the impatience with which the present leadership addresses these questions—leading, as in the case of South Ossetia, to hasty or even foolhardy actions—contrasts with the relative indifference with which the late Shevardnadze regime addressed these problems.[39]

---

[39] The Parliamentary Assembly of the Council of Europe adopted in January 2005 a resolution on Georgia, which includes an excellent synthesis of the challenge Georgia confronts in its attempt at national integration and state-building: "The Rose Revolution and the two subsequent elections resulted in a very strong government, which may be an asset in dealing with the country's political, economic, and security problems, provided that a strong government is accompanied by a strong and functioning system of checks and balances. This is not yet the case. Today, Georgia has a semi-presidential system with very strong powers of the President, basically no parliamentary opposition, a weaker civil society, a judicial system which is not yet sufficiently independent and functioning, underdeveloped or non-existing local democracy, a self-censored media and an inadequate model of autonomy in Ajara." Parliamentary Assembly, Resolution 1415 (2005), "Honouring of Obligations and Commitments by Georgia," http://assembly.coe.int/Main.asp?link=http://assembly.coe.int/Documents/AdoptedText/ta05/ERES1415.htm. This resolution is based on the report of the Committee on the Honouring of Obligations and Commitments by Member States of the Council of Europe mentioned above (Doc. 10383).

CENTER–PERIPHERY RELATIONS IN THE INTERNATIONAL ORDER

The assumption that Georgia's relations toward Moscow, Washington, and Brussels can be described as dependency relations according to a center–periphery pattern presumes first that changes at the center will have a more profound impact than changes at the periphery on the interaction between both poles, and second that changes in the interaction pattern will have a greater impact on the periphery than on the center. Five developments, in particular, put these assumptions to a test: the breakdown of the Soviet multinational framework; the progressive emergence of a Caspian energy security policy in the United States in the second half of the 1990s; the transformation of Russia's security environment at its southern borders at the start of the second Chechen war in 1999 and Vladimir Putin's accession to the Russian presidency; the turn taken by American global security policies after September 11, 2001; and the consequences of EU enlargement for the EU's South Caucasus policies.

All five cases demonstrate that Georgia's security environment has been more deeply affected by a reorientation of the policies of each of these three centers than by any of Georgia's domestic changes. In each of these five cases, policymakers in Tbilisi had, as a consequence, to change the parameters of the national security agenda. This confirms Georgia's position as a peripheral country in international relations.

The Dissolution of the Soviet Union

The contributions to this book describe how the relations between Moscow and Tbilisi were primarily determined by the transformation and the eventual dissolution of the Soviet Union, which opened a window of opportunity for national liberation movements in Georgia both at the center (in Tbilisi) and at its periphery (in South Ossetia and Abkhazia). The Georgian independence movement conceived of the re-establishment of political and cultural hegemony over Georgia as indivisible from its attempt to emancipate itself from Soviet and later from Russian rule. Internal sovereignty was not to be dissociated from external sovereignty. But the loosening of links with Moscow did not lead to greater control over the autonomous entities within Georgia. The mobilization of the Georgian national movement at the end of the 1980s subsequently led to Tbilisi's confrontation with the domestic periphery. But as long as Georgia was a part of the Soviet Union, Tbilisi could not create genuine

armed forces to intervene in domestic conflicts. According to Darchiashvili, the gendarmerie-like National Guard, which was created for such
a purpose, circumvented the risk of confronting the Soviet center.

A confrontation with Moscow was not avoided, however, due to unilateral steps taken on both sides. The Soviet center started to revise its
previous position concerning the status of the Georgian autonomous
entities. The Soviet Communist Party had previously always refused to
accept the repeated demands of the Abkhazians to secede from Georgia
and to be directly subordinated to the Soviet Union. As described by
Zürcher, Mikhail Gorbachev's attempt to reform the Soviet federal system needed the support of national movements in autonomous entities
within union republics, including Georgia. One of the aims of the 1990
Soviet Law on Secession was to forge such an alliance. It gave minorities
within union republics that were opting for independence the right to
remain in the Soviet Union. Such a move hardened Tbilisi's view that its
territorial integrity was not only threatened from within but also from
without, that the interests of Russia and Georgia were incompatible, and
that the Soviet Union had to be conceived of as Georgia's "oppressive
other" (Devdariani). As a consequence, it took further unilateral steps,
culminating in a declaration of independence in April 1991.

The loosening of Soviet control and the eventual demise of centralized Communist Party rule thus led to the breakdown of the federal institutions on all levels of the Soviet framework where center–periphery
negotiations and regulation could have taken place.[40] This also had particular consequences for the relations between the newly independent
republics that emerged from the Soviet Union. At the end of 1991, there
was no foreign policy apparatus in Georgia or the Russian Federation that
could have regulated any confrontation or avoided unilateral steps
through diplomatic means.

Gamsakhurdia's short exercise of power after his victory in the Georgian parliamentary elections in October 1990 until the civil war in the
winter of 1991–1992 was a period of confrontation with Russia, particularly through Moscow's direct and indirect intervention in the armed
conflict in South Ossetia, which started in January 1991 and lasted dur-

---

[40] Nancy Bermeo, "Position Paper for the Working Group on Federalism, Conflict Prevention, and Settlement," presented at the Third International Conference on Federalism, Brussels, March 3–5, 2005.

ing the whole period Gamsakhurdia was in power.[41] What is more, Gamsakhurdia refused to join the Commonwealth of Independent States (CIS). Devdariani writes that Gamsakhurdia was challenging Moscow's security interests in the whole of the Caucasus.

Georgia has been building what Devdariani calls a "resistance identity" against external domination. But the rising confrontation between Georgia and Russia cannot be explained solely by the Georgian national project and search for identity. Devdariani points out how the collapse of the Soviet Union went together with a severe identity crisis within Russia itself. Russia's leadership conceived of the dissolution of the Soviet Union as a form of self-liberation, but its elites felt a deep ambivalence about the past. Some still thought in terms of the country's great-power status or *derzhavnost* and deeply regretted the lost grandeur of the Soviet Union, a goal that could only be pursued in Russia's relations with the weaker states at its periphery. As Robert Legvold notes in the introduction, Russia was weak compared to its former Soviet self, but retained the capacity to dominate its neighbors.

During the same period, Western governments were indifferent toward the internal conflicts in Georgia and the confrontation between the new leaderships in Tbilisi and Moscow. They disliked Gamsakhurdia's nationalism, which resembled the new radical discourses emerging in the Balkans, but they did not perceive these conflicts as touching core Western security interests. They refused to establish diplomatic relations with Gamsakhurdia's government or accept the country's membership in international security organizations. This led to Georgia's international isolation, which lasted until Shevardnadze's return to Tbilisi in March 1992. In explaining Georgia's situation, Devdariani writes that the country had inherited the aspiration to share European political practice but no experience with it.[42] This lack of common history with Europe means

---

[41] A cease-fire agreement in South Ossetia was signed in June 1992, after Gamsakhurdia's removal from power.

[42] The only exceptions in this regard were the brief years of Georgian independence in 1918–1921 and the aftermath of the Bolshevik occupation of Georgia in 1921, when European social democracy developed an active campaign of cooperation and solidarity with the Georgian Mensheviks. But this brief experience did not create any positive legacy: there was not any sympathy in the Georgian independence movement in the 1980s and 1990s for the Menshevik ideological tradition.

that it is not possible—as it is in the Baltic states, for instance—to speak about Georgia's independence as a return to Europe or to the Western community.

At the time of the Abkhazian war, Georgia's troubles did not rank high on the security agenda of Moscow, Washington, or Brussels. None of these capitals had a clear view of how to intervene in this troubled neighborhood, and this was no less true for Russia. Antonenko describes the confusion and compartmentalization of decision-making characteristic of Russia's policies toward Georgia, particularly in its intervention in the Abkhazian war. Some parts of the Russian leadership wanted to uphold the principle of territorial integrity, particularly on Russia's fragile southern border. But Russian military commanders in Abkhazia supported the local resistance against the Georgian military intervention, and this support progressively became the main feature of the Russian role in the course of the 1992–1993 war. The incapacity of the Russian leadership to have more of a constraining effect on the local Russian military can partly be explained by the political crisis in Moscow over the standoff between the executive and the parliament. This conflict between President Yeltsin and the Russian Supreme Soviet, which came to a climax in October 1993 and had the potential to turn into a genuine civil war, overshadowed all possibilities for a more balanced Russian role in mediating the conflict in Abkhazia.

After the defeat of the Georgian troops in Abkhazia in September 1993, Russian military support for the Abkhazian side did not lead to a confrontation with the Georgian authorities. Georgia was brought to its knees, as Shevardnadze said at the time. He agreed to join the CIS and to accept the further stationing of Russian troops on Georgian territory. These concessions gave him the necessary Russian support to disband the forces loyal to Gamsakhurdia. Further concessions to Russia were to follow. Vardiko Nadibaidze, an active-duty Russian officer, was appointed as Georgia's minister of defense in April 1994. In addition, Shevardnadze gave unconditional support to the Russian military intervention in Chechnya at the end of the same year.

Western governments remained indifferent toward the fate of Abkhazia.[43] As noted by Helly and Gogia, these governments primarily

---

[43] Antonenko makes the observation that Boris Yeltsin does not speak in his memoirs about the Georgian–Abkhazian conflict, which contrasts with the

sought to avoid tensions in the region and deferred the main responsibility for peacekeeping operations to Russia. The West only supported the establishment of a UN observer mission in Abkhazia, which included military from several Western countries, and expressed concern about the impact of the Russian military presence in the South Caucasus on the Conventional Forces in Europe (CFE) Treaty.[44] Regional stability was thus from the start a Western security interest, even if this was not then seen as necessitating direct Western involvement. There were, however, also Western energy security interests encouraging a greater Western presence in the South Caucasus. A third area of concern that required greater Western involvement was the fear of failing states in the South Caucasus. As noted by Helly and Gogia, Western humanitarian aid in the beginning of the 1990s was progressively replaced for these various reasons by broader development aid, support for democratization, and other state reform policies.

Western Energy Security Policies

According to Darchiashvili, Western interest in a more direct involvement in Georgian affairs started in 1995 after the consolidation of the Shevardnadze regime. The Georgian government tried to overcome the Western attitude of indifference by playing on Georgia's geographical location and potential role as a bridgehead for communication and transport between Europe and Asia. Georgian leaders also hoped that a confrontational policy with Russia could lead to greater Western attention. But neither the United States nor EU member states wanted to engage in such a policy vis-à-vis Russia. When Georgia put forward the idea of future membership in NATO, the North Atlantic Alliance did not explicitly reject it, despite the poor state of the Georgian armed forces and the lack

---

importance he attaches to the CIS. This demonstrates an attitude of relative indifference. A similar observation could be made concerning Germany's former Minister of Foreign Affairs Hans-Dieter Genscher. Despite his reputation as a "friend of Georgia" and the fact that Germany has given substantial aid to Georgia since the return of Shevardnadze to Georgia in 1992, Georgia is barely mentioned in Genscher's memoirs. This seems to reflect a marginal interest in Georgia and its problems, much as in Yeltsin's case. See Hans-Dieter Genscher, *Erinnerungen* (Berlin: Siedler, 1995).

[44] See Alexei Zverev and Bruno Coppieters, "Verloren evenwicht. Georgië tussen Rusland en het Westen," in *Oost-Europa Verkenningen*, no 134 (August 1994), pp. 38–47.

of democratic standards in its defense policies. As noted by Legvold, Georgia's membership aspirations gave NATO leverage to promote domestic reforms in line with Western interests.

The increasing Western involvement in Georgian affairs in the second half of the 1990s—particularly through American energy politics as symbolized by the Baku–Tbilisi–Ceyhan (BTC) project—had a decisive impact on Georgia's security strategy. Darchiashvili situates Tbilisi's unambiguous choice for alignment with the West in 1998. During that year, Georgia intensified its cooperation with NATO. A year later, it withdrew from the CIS Collective Treaty and became a member of the Council of Europe. This membership was conditional upon the realization of democratic state reforms and respect for minority rights. Western governments asserted leverage in various policy domains. In the military field, U.S. and other Western experts pushed for radical reform of the Georgian armed forces. This included a reduction in military personnel, the elimination of corruption, civilian control over the military, and the development of a national security concept. These attempts at reform failed.

A Western orientation should not be equated with a choice for radical democratic reforms, at least not during Shevardnadze's tenure. According to Darchiashvili, transparent defense policies would have endangered a corrupt system of patronage. A similar conclusion can be drawn in other policy fields, such as regional cooperation in the South Caucasus, which was an EU priority. Georgia remained deaf to all calls for exploiting this "unused potential"(de Waal) for its development policies.

Consequently, Western efforts to promote regional integration had little success in Georgia. Only the BTC Pipeline project could be implemented as planned by its American backers. But even this project cannot be considered a success from the point-of-view of regional integration, although it did create long-term material incentives for Western support to regional stability. As de Waal points out, this pipeline can best be described as a non-Russia, non-Iran pipeline.

Shevardnadze's hope that Georgia would get external support for resolving the question of Abkhazia and South Ossetia went unrealized. In the first Chechen war he fully supported the Russian government's attempt to reintegrate Chechnya by force, hoping that Russia would help Georgia to enforce a similar policy toward Abkhazia. This support contrasted with the West's severe criticism of the Russian military's disregard for international humanitarian law during this war, particularly for the

indiscriminate bombing of Chechnya's capital Grozny. But Shevardnadze's support was of no avail.

A few years later, in 1999, Shevardnadze would give full support to
NATO's war in Kosovo, despite the fact that the Yugoslavian authorities
were engaged in a war against secession and that the UN Security Council
had not endorsed NATO's intervention. He was hoping that the United
States might also endorse a unilateral military action in Abkhazia. As noted
by Helly and Gogia, the U.S. government made clear, however, that it
would not accept a replay of the Kosovo scenario in Abkhazia. Washington's refusal was not a matter of principle or a reflection of indifference. It
was simply impossible for the United States or European governments to
engage unilaterally in a military resolution of the secessionist conflicts in
Georgia without risking a direct military confrontation with Russia.

Georgian diplomatic efforts in the UN framework to enforce a military solution to the Abkhazian problem did not have any reasonable
chance of success either. Proposals to have a Security Council resolution
supporting the use of force in restoring the principle of Georgian territorial integrity never got the support of the Western permanent council
members.

The Second Chechen War and Putin's Presidency

Confrontation remained the main characteristic of Georgian–Russian
relations in the second half of the 1990s. From the Georgian perspective,
any Russian attempt at integration with its southern neighbor was perceived as threatening domination, nourishing Georgia's "resistance identity" and providing a new motive for confrontational policies toward
Russia. An increased Western presence in the South Caucasus also led to
a more assertive Russian role in the region, particularly during Yevgeny
Primakov's tenure as minister of foreign affairs (1996–1998). This
assertiveness had consequences for the competition between the UN and
Russia for a leading role in the mediation between Georgia and Abkhazia.
Primakov actively tried to mediate between the presidents of Georgia and
Abkhazia, organizing meetings such as the one he arranged between
Vladislav Ardzinba and Eduard Shevardnadze in Tbilisi in 1997. As
described by Antonenko, Russia's involvement in the Georgian–Abkhazian conflict was facilitated by its federal framework. Russian regional elites
were highly active in cooperating with Abkhazia. This eroded the sanctions regime implemented by the CIS.

The start of the second Chechen war in 1999 and the succession of Boris Yeltsin by Vladimir Putin in the Russian presidency led, according to the research results presented in this volume, to a shift of policies toward Georgia and to a reordering of priorities on Georgia's security agenda. First, as far as Russia's perception of threats was concerned, Islamic fundamentalism ranked first. The second Chechen war was not legitimized as a conflict over sovereignty, contrary to the previous war, but as a military operation against Islamic terrorism. This necessitated a new relationship with Washington, which in turn affected Georgia's relationship with the United States. In order to understand this triangular relationship in the framework of center–periphery relations, one has to be careful not to assume that all centers have an equal capacity to determine Georgia's security agenda. Asymmetry and hierarchy are not only characteristic of the relations between center and periphery, but also—albeit to a lesser degree—of the relations among centers.[45] The dramatic impact of the shift in American security strategy after September 11 has not only created a very different international environment for Georgia's security policies, including at home, but also for Russia's security policies toward Georgia. Devdariani shows how Putin started to use principles and terminology drawn from U.S. anti-terrorist discourse, particularly regarding a right of preemptive strikes across Georgian borders and Russia's right to self-defense against terrorist threats under the UN Charter. Furthermore, Putin did not radically oppose enhanced U.S. military involvement in the post-Soviet space, such as the GTEP in Georgia, and interpreted it as a kind of burden-sharing.

Second, Putin's accession to power radically changed the forms of Russian decision-making on Georgia and toward the Georgian–Abkhazian conflict. Antonenko writes that Russia's Minister of Defense Sergei Ivanov, who was appointed in 2001, became the most frequent spokesman on Moscow's policies toward Georgia. But the military apparatus did not have the same degree of autonomy under Putin as it did

---

[45] Some of the literature on center–periphery relations has made an attempt to differentiate among semi-peripheries, central peripheries, and peripheral centers. Such a differentiation, however, is not helpful in situating Georgia and identifying the security challenge that it faces. It does not make sense to characterize Russia or the European Union as semi-peripheries or as peripheral centers with respect to the United States and Georgia, despite the asymmetries and hierarchy among these various poles.

during the Yeltsin era. A parallel centralization took place with respect to the foreign policy of the regions. Governors lost much of their autonomy in establishing links with Abkhazia. This did not lead, however, to a cessation of their activities. On the contrary, Russian authorities continued to use these para-diplomatic activities as a way of avoiding international criticism for the support they provided the breakaway states.

Third, Putin made an attempt to expand Russia's influence in the South Caucasus region by intensifying relations with the de facto states. Devdariani describes these new policies as the creation of a specific normative regime only partially compatible with international law; one that aims at exploiting the existence of these unrecognized states to the maximum extent possible. According to Antonenko, this can be seen as one of the results of the destruction of Chechnya as a de facto state. Because of this perceived success, Russia was no longer as concerned with the consequences of its support for breakaway states despite the threat they posed to the principle of territorial integrity. This shift of policies led to the reopening of the Russian border with Abkhazia (although Russia's earlier blocade had long been eroded by cross-border trade and cooperation with Russian regions). New visa requirements for Georgian citizens were waved for the residents of Abkhazia and South Ossetia, from whom Moscow also accepted Russian citizenship requests on a very large scale. These citizenship policies gave Russia the opportunity to legitimize a durable presence in the breakaway states and leverage in pursuing its own security concerns in these conflicts.

Georgia had to change security priorities as a consequence of this shift in Russian policies. The risk of Russian preemptive strikes on Georgian territory became a main security concern. But Western governments—as observed by Devdariani—drew a redline against direct Russian interference in Georgia and opposed all attempts at implementing preemptive anti-terrorist operations on Georgian territory. Diplomatic efforts were initiated in the multilateral framework of the Organization for Security and Cooperation in Europe (OSCE), which in December 1999 began to monitor an eighty-one kilometer stretch of border between Georgia and the Chechen Republic of the Russian Federation.[46]

---

[46] OSCE Press Release, "OSCE Georgia Mission Expands Border Monitoring Operation," January 2, 2002, http://www.osce.org/item/6491.html. In December 2001, this mission was expanded to include the border between Georgia and the Ingush Republic in the Russian Federation to the west of Chechnya.

September 11

The reorientation of U.S. security policies as a result of the events of September 11 had a direct impact on U.S. relations with Georgia. According to Helly and Gogia, it led to the inclusion of the South Caucasus into the "Greater Middle East," defined as an area of potential threat. It also prompted a rearrangement of U.S. security policies with the Russian Federation, leading, as mentioned by de Waal, to a devaluing of the GUUAM alliance. The most significant step by Washington was its support for the development of modern armed forces and stabilization of the Russian–Georgian border through the Georgia Train and Equip Program (GTEP). Georgia thus received increased attention in the West, particularly in the United States. Helly and Gogia note that Georgia turned into a transit point for U.S. aircraft supporting military operations in Afghanistan.

Despite increased U.S. attention toward Georgia and its new geopolitical significance as a transit country, confrontation became increasingly frequent in Western, particularly American, relations with Georgia. There was, as analyzed by Antonenko as well as Helly and Gogia, strong Western criticism of Georgia's support for guerilla activities in Abkhazia, such as the failed Gelayev operation in the Kodori Gorge in summer 2001. Aborted attempts to go against corruption and the failure of institutional reforms in Georgia weakened the overall capacity of the state, threatening to turn the country into a failing or even failed state. According to Devdariani, the incapacity of the Georgian armed forces to control the Pankisi Gorge came close to a sign of state failure. In October 2001, Georgia had to acknowledge the presence of foreign guerillas in Pankisi after Washington insisted that it apply a "zero tolerance policy" toward such security threats.

But Shevardnadze found it increasingly difficult to accept Western recommendations and criticism. Devdariani and Darchiashvili both note that this led to a softening of Shevardnadze's opposition to Moscow, including on the question of Russian bases in Georgia. Shevardnadze even stated that future NATO membership could be combined with membership in the CIS. This went together with the lack of a security strategy that clearly defined values and threats, and with the strengthening of nationalist movements challenging Georgia's Western orientation.[47]

---

[47] Such movements, which criticized the implementation of Western democratic standards and called for a unique Georgian way to development, remained, as noted by Nodia, in the minority and could not challenge Western cultural hegemony.

The impact of September 11 and of the reorientation of U.S. security policies on Georgia should not be underestimated. The prospect of Georgia becoming a failed state, a state that would breed terrorism at the border with Chechnya and otherwise destabilize U.S. relations with Russia, explains not only the increased U.S. insistence that the Shevardnadze government implement reform policies, but also the lack of strong Western support for Shevardnadze when he was confronted with domestic opposition in November 2003, which ultimately resulted in his downfall.

As far as the question of Abkhazia is concerned, Helly, Gogia, and Antonenko describe how Russia's greater assertiveness in this breakaway republic combined with Georgia's growing frustration over the lack of progress in the UN's mediation efforts led Shevardnadze to accept of a more prominent mediating role for Russia. The result was the so-called Sochi process, bringing together Russia and Georgia, albeit without abandoning the UN-led Geneva negotiations.

The Rose Revolution of November 2003 brought a new leadership to power in Tbilisi. Regime change in this case not only demonstrates that the transformation at the Georgian center had a profound impact on the relationship with Georgia's peripheries—particularly Ajara and South Ossetia. It also shows that a transformation even as great as the Rose Revolution has a limited capacity to fundamentally alter the pattern of relations with a key external center like Moscow. Contrary to the expectations of the new Georgian leaders, they were unable to integrate more deeply with Western structures while normalizing relations with the Russian Federation. Their hopes were reflected in the simultaneous appointment of Salome Zourabichvili, a French diplomat of Georgian origin, as minister of foreign affairs and Kakha Bendukidze, a Georgian entrepreneur who had been highly successful as an industrialist in Russia, as minister of economics. These expectations were also shared by Western observers, but, significantly, not by Russian observers and journalists, who generally pointed out that Saakashvili's radicalism and nationalism could become a new source of conflict with the breakaway states, with Georgia's national minorities, and with Russia itself.

The Enlargement of the European Union

The most significant progress toward integration with the West was probably Georgia's inclusion in the European Neighborhood Policy (ENP) of the European Union. This progress was, however, not primarily due to

Georgia's change of regime, but to the new geopolitical situation in which the European Union found itself after its May 2004 enlargement. Its expansion to the east and the inclusion of new member states that had either been part of the Soviet Union or of the Warsaw Pact increased European interest in the South Caucasus, also in the process confirming my thesis that changes in the relationship between the European Union and Georgia are induced by a transformation at the center rather than at the periphery. It may be added, however, that the Rose Revolution has enhanced European interest in the South Caucasus region, which has thus helped to overcome the marginal importance previously attached by EU policymakers to Georgia and facilitated its rapid inclusion in the ENP.[48]

As Helly and Gogia report, a further sign of a significant improvement in Georgia's cooperation with Western governments and organizations was the announcement by the United States in May 2004 of $500 million in grants, largely in the field of state reform. In June 2004, the European Union and the World Bank pledged nearly $1 billion to Georgia. The same year, NATO endorsed Georgia's Individual Partnership Action Plan (IPAP) and appointed a special representative for the Caucasus and Central Asia, who was to be stationed in Tbilisi. In May 2005, U.S. President George W. Bush visited the Georgian capital.

The contributors to this volume—particularly the Georgian contributors Nodia, Darchiashvili, and Devdariani—point to the various obstacles to Georgia's full integration into the West. The new leadership largely consists of Western-educated elites with no or few ties to former Soviet networks. In their public discourse, they favor international integration, and have proclaimed a crusade against corruption. But they also respond to Georgian public opinion, particularly with respect to a quick resolution of the Abkhazian and South Ossetian question. Saakashvili's uncompromising attitude in addressing the conflict with South Ossetia in the summer of 2004 was not appreciated by Western governments. According to Helly and Gogia, Saakashvili was warned that he would not receive any Western support and would be isolated if he used military force in this crisis.

---

[48] The European Commission had initially proposed in 2003 that the countries of the South Caucasus could only be integrated at a later stage in this new EU strategy toward its periphery.

Georgian authorities are reluctant to implement reforms granting self-government to regional and local authorities consistent with existing formal European standards, as already noted with respect to the Council of Europe recommendations. A profound contradiction between aspirations and existing practice can also be observed in the reform of the defense and security sectors. Thus, while Georgia has been pursuing its policies of Western integration, severe tensions remain between aspiration and practice.

Relations between Russia and Georgia have not been normalized as a result of the West's increased effort to promote Georgian reform. The OSCE monitoring mission at the Georgian border with Russia was halted. Russia's overall criticism of this organization, which it had once favored but later saw as an instrument of Western expansion in the post-Soviet space, has made it more difficult for Western governments to ameliorate Russia's relations with Georgia within a multilateral framework.

Legvold argues that Russia is out to preserve its influence in Georgia both over the center and the periphery. Moscow respects the principles of territorial integrity and non-intervention in internal affairs, but not at the cost of lessening its influence. It could be added that Russia would not want to support a peace settlement in Abkhazia or South Ossetia that was unlikely to succeed thereby failing to guarantee stability on its borders.

Devdariani has stressed the importance of Russia's economic penetration in Georgia, particularly in the energy sphere. Georgian economic cooperation with Russia would, if Moscow does not ask for preferential treatment but accepts the principles of free trade, give better prospects for a normalization of their relations. But economic cooperation efforts that involve Abkhazia may be very difficult to realize. For instance, Russian economic projects linking southern Russia with Armenia through the reconstruction of existing railway networks would require the agreement of the Georgian government on terms that are also acceptable to the Abkhazian authorities. Attempts to come to such an agreement have not been successful in the past.

SUMMARY AND OUTLOOK

Georgia's relations with Russia, the United States and the European Union—and toward its various domestic peripheries—are both asymmetrical and hierarchical. Transformations in the relationship between the poles are more influenced by changes at the center than at the periphery.

In the case of relations with Moscow, Washington, or Brussels, the remaking of Georgia's international security environment as a result of major shifts in the security policies of these states—from the dissolution of the Soviet Union in 1991 to the enlargement of the European Union in 2004—had a greater impact on Georgia's foreign relations than either of the two regime changes within Georgia had.

This does not mean, of course, that the *coup d'état* against Gamsakhurdia in 1991 and the Rose Revolution in 2003 had no effect on the country's international position. Shevardnadze's arrival in power in 1992 facilitated the development of diplomatic relations with the outside world and admission to the UN and other international organizations. Similarly, the Rose Revolution sped the inclusion of the South Caucasus in the ENP.

The Georgian government, however, has not always used well these major shifts in the international environment to strengthen its position and to achieve a safer and more productive relationship with the Russian Federation by energetically fostering ties with the Western world. After the Soviet Union collapsed, Zviad Gamsakhurdia failed to secure broad international support for Georgia, and in fact deepened his regime's isolation until it was violently overthrown. Shevardnadze more skillfully exploited the emergence of a Western energy policy in the South Caucasus in the second half of the 1990s, a second major shift in Georgia's international security environment, but chose not to use Russia's plight during the second Chechen war to establish better diplomatic relations with the new Moscow leadership. Instead, he preferred to mobilize his domestic constituency on the basis of anti-Russian rhetoric and policies. The question of Pankisi and the irresponsibility of the Georgian authorities in the Gelayev operation did much to increase anti-Georgian sentiment in Moscow. True, the Russian government also ignored legitimate Georgian security interests, choosing instead to rely on threats. If diplomacy can be said to be the art of dealing with difficult neighbors in difficult situations, diplomacy was largely missing on both sides.

At the point in Russian–Georgian relations when Georgia came close to state failure, the events of September 11 forced Tbilisi to reorient its security policies. It re-established state control over the Pankisi Gorge, went after guerilla forces operating in Abkhazia, and initiated a program of institutional reforms. But the Shevardnadze regime was incapable of seeing democratic reforms through. The result was the Rose Revolution and at last the chance to make good use of the changing security policies of an enlarged European Union and of renewed U.S. support for democratic progress in the post-Soviet world.

As for Georgia's domestic relations, the advent of independence, the *coup d'état* against Gamsakhurdia, and the Rose revolution also had a more profound impact on the relationship with the peripheries than any internal change taking place within these territories. This is most clearly illustrated by the recent history of South Ossetia, where violent clashes took place as a result of the mobilization organized by Gamsakhurdia and other nationalist leaders in 1989. Shevardnadze's return to Tbilisi in 1992 permitted the establishment of a cease-fire, which held for more than a decade, but the Rose Revolution resulted in new violent confrontations.

In 1991, the Abkhazian national movement, determined to achieve equal status with Georgia, profited from the Gamsakhurdia government's entanglement in South Ossetia and strengthened its position within Abkhazia by accepting a new electoral law, guaranteeing overrepresentation to its parliamentary representatives. The 1992–1993 military intervention in Abkhazia was initiated by the Georgian government a few months after Shevardnadze's return to Tbilisi, and led to an Abkhazian military victory and the creation of one more de facto state on Georgia's periphery.

A center–periphery model further assumes that changes in the relationship between both poles will affect more substantially the periphery than the center. The conspicuous exception is the dissolution of the Soviet Union, where the center was destroyed and the various peripheries emerged as independent states. This book shows the deep impact on Georgia of shifts in the international setting, including obviously the end of the Cold War and the breakup of the Soviet Union. But less obviously so is it affected by a changing relationship with the West as a result of increased U.S. and European interest in their own energy security. In this case, not only has Georgia's foreign and security policy been deeply influenced, but its entire development strategy. Georgia's shifting relations with Moscow, Washington, and Brussels— produced by the dramatic developments in Russia in 1999, in the United States in 2001, and within the European Union in 2004—had similar far-reaching consequences for Georgia. For these countries, however, the place of relations with Georgia and the other Caucasian states was far less significant.

When it comes to Georgia's domestic conflicts, the point that changes in the relationship between the poles have a greater impact at the periphery than at the center is reflected in the emergence of South Ossetia and

Abkhazia into de facto states as the result of their military victory over the center. Other examples include the reintegration of Ajara into the Georgian fold and the increased dependency of South Ossetia on the Russian Federation, both of which resulted from confrontations with Tbilisi after the Rose Revolution.

The contributions to this volume also demonstrate that peripheries on both the domestic and international levels may try to transform themselves into centers. This has happened in two separate, but parallel cases. On the international level, Tbilisi has striven to move away from Moscow, while on the domestic level Sukhum(i) and Tskhinval(i) have struggled to free themselves from Tbilisi. Other center–periphery relations on both international and domestic levels are far less conflictual, even when neither pole supports a high level of integration.

The conflicts between the poles are also marked by the failure of the peripheries to emancipate themselves entirely from a center perceived as oppressive by establishing themselves as an alternative center or by connecting themselves with another center seen as more protective. As the separation of Abkhazia and South Ossetia from Georgia has deepened, each breakaway state has been more thoroughly integrated into the Russian fold, yet without formally or legally emancipating itself from Georgia. For this to happen, they need international recognition of their sovereignty, which they have not yet achieved.

A similar problem arises in Georgia's international relations. For more than a decade, Tbilisi seemed to assume that further integration into Western institutions would be sufficient to change the balance of power with Moscow, and thus permit a normalization of their mutual relationship, including the resolution of outstanding conflicts. The contributions to this book only partially confirm this assumption. Georgia's alliance with Western governments, its progressive integration into Western institutions, and its parallel policy of confrontation with Russia have led to a lessening of dependency on Moscow. However, these developments have not ameliorated crucial issues for Georgia, such as Russian visa requirements or key questions regarding Abkhazia and South Ossetia.

On the international level, a transformation of Georgian–Russian relations may, if one thinks in terms of a center–periphery model, be expected to follow more from profound changes in Moscow's security environment than in Tbilisi's. If Russia were to reorient its policies towards the EU or the United States, this could have a profound influence on its relations with Georgia. Or if the situation in the Northern Caucasus were to deteriorate seriously or if massive terrorist attacks occurred on Russian territory, the effects would also likely be significant.

A transformation of Georgian–Russian relations might also come from a radical change in Georgian–Western relations, for instance through Georgia's inclusion in NATO or the EU. A comparison with the Baltics is relevant in this respect. Russia is the single most powerful external influence on all the post-Soviet states, except the Baltic states. The three Baltic states are also the only post-Soviet states for which security "does not start at home," to repeat Legvold's formulation in the introduction, and, which, despite difficult relations with Moscow, "enjoy anything approaching a secure existence." This is largely due, of course, to their membership in NATO and the EU, and, therefore, they represent a role model for the kind of security Georgia wishes to achieve.

The timeframe for these prospects, however, is not only difficult to pin down, but in the case of the EU, hard to conceive of, not only because of the state of Georgia's economy and the incapacity of its state institutions but also because of the difficulties the EU is facing in the negotiations with prospective new members. Georgia's membership seems easier to imagine in the case of NATO, but Georgia's incorporation would require that both NATO's policy objectives and its membership criteria be modified. In either instance, however, change would again mean that a transformation at the center was largely responsible for a new relationship with the periphery.

If the attempts by Georgia, Abkhazia, and South Ossetia to emancipate themselves from a perceived exploitative center seem to be only partially successful, a normalization of their relationship with this center by compromise does not then easily follow. On the Georgian domestic level, any federal arrangement based on the principle of Georgia's territorial integrity will have to include some element of hierarchy among state institutions, and this will have direct consequences for relations with Georgia's national communities. From the perspective of the Abkhazian and Ossetian national projects, even if their inclusion in an ethno-federal framework permits them to realize to a large extent their right to national self-determination, the principle of hierarchy would be difficult to accept. The principle of shared sovereignty would include some severe constraints on the exercise of power by the Georgian majority, which would be similarly difficult to accept from the perspective of the Georgian national project.

An even more difficult task in the transformation of the conflictual center–periphery relations within Georgia into a stable federation is overcoming the profound instability of the center. None of the presidential successions in Georgia has followed constitutional procedures, and it remains unclear to what extent the new elite will be able to build a core statehood based on the rule of law. Weak statehood and chronic instability reflected in *coups d'état* and popular revolts[49] inevitably have a profound effect on the relationship with peripheries. Still more importantly, any change in center–periphery relations as a result of instability at the center affects the peripheries more profoundly than it affects the center itself. In Georgia, successful democratic reforms and institutional stability, of course, cannot be ruled out, but one must be realistic when contemplating a federal solution, and with Abkhazia and South Ossetia, avoiding the worst-case scenario becomes key. Any federal arrangement in Georgia must provide for security mechanisms that are able to resist spillover effects. A high degree of separation between the competences of the domestic center and those of the periphery, as well as strong international security guarantees, will be necessary to achieve a stable federal outcome. Russian involvement in guaranteeing security for Abkhazia and South Ossetia will be crucial, but so will Russian restraint, if international guarantees are not to become unilateral guarantees.

The fact that the future relationship between Georgia and Russia depends more on transformations at the center than at the periphery and that Abkhazia and South Ossetia have turned themselves into peripheries of the Russian Federation does not mean that a resolution of Georgia's conflicts is only to be found in Moscow. Tbilisi's claim to sovereignty over Abkhazia and South Ossetia means that it too must assume an active role in the search for a settlement. This in turn requires a normalization of its relations with the Russian Federation. There must also be confidence-building steps between the center and Abkhazia and South Ossetia. The Georgian authorities need to convince people in both territories of the center's capacity to reform and readiness to resolve national conflicts through peaceful means. Much of this will undoubtedly be difficult, but if Georgian leaders can persuade themselves to move in this direction, they have a chance of persuading the Abkhazians and Ossetians as well.

---

[49] The Rose Revolution has generally been analyzed in the framework of post-communist transitions. But a comparison between Georgia and some countries of Latin America, such as Ecuador, may also reveal crucial parallels.

Contributors

OKSANA ANTONENKO is a senior fellow and the program director for Russia and Eurasia at the International Institute for Strategic Studies (IISS). She joined the IISS in 1996 and frequently contributes to IISS publications (*Survival*, *Strategic Survey*, and *The Military Balance*), provides briefings for IISS members worldwide, presents papers and reports at international conferences, and comments on developments in Eurasia for the international media. Her recent publications include *Russia and the European Union: Prospects for a New Relationship* (2004); "Russia's Southern Border: Western Siberia–Central Asia" (IISS, 2003); and "North-West Russia in the Baltic Sea Region" (IISS, 2003).

BRUNO COPPIETERS is associate professor at the Vrije Universiteit Brussel. His research focuses on normative theories on war and secession. He has largely been publishing on the conflicts in the Caucasus, and particularly on the case of Georgia and Abkhazia. His recent publications include *Federalism and Conflict in the Caucasus* (2001); co-editor, *Secession, History, and the Social Sciences* (2002), also published electronically at http://poli.vub.ac.be/; *Moral Constraints on War: Principles and Cases* (2002); *Contextualizing Secession: Normative Studies in Comparative Perspective* (2003); and co-author, *Europeanization and Conflict Resolution: Case Studies from the European Periphery* (2004), published as a special issue of the electronic *Journal on Ethnopolitics and Minority Issues in Europe* on http://www.ecmi.de/jemie/.

DAVID DARCHIASHVILI is an executive director of the Open Society Georgia Foundation, a part of the Soros Foundations Network, and a teacher at Ilia Chavchavadze University of Language and Culture. Until recently, he worked for the Caucasus Institute for Peace, Democracy, and Development. His research focuses on ethnic conflicts and regional relations in the South Caucasus and the national security problems of Georgia. His publications include "Georgian Security Problems and Policies," in *The South Caucasus: A Challenge for the EU* (2003); and "Trends of Strategic Thinking in Georgia: Achievements, Problems, and Prospects," in *Crossroads and Conflict: Security and Foreign Policy in the Caucasus and Central Asia* (2000).

THOMAS DE WAAL is Caucasus editor at the Institute for War and Peace Reporting in London. As a writer and journalist, he has specialized in Russia and the Caucasus for the past fourteen years. He studied Russian and Modern Greek at Oxford University and has worked for the BBC World Service, *The Moscow Times*, and *The Times of London*, and has been a frequent contributor to *The Economist*. He is co-author with Carlotta Gall of *Chechnya: Calamity in the Caucasus* (1998) and author of *Black Garden: Armenia and Azerbaijan through Peace and War* (2003), an in-depth study of the Nagorno-Karabakh conflict.

JABA DEVDARIANI is a founding director of the United Nations Association of Georgia. He co-founded the Internet magazine *Civil Georgia* and served as its editor-in-chief. His research includes democratization and development issues in the Caucasus and the Balkans, as well as security issues in the South Caucasus. Currently, he serves as head of field office and human rights officer at the Organization for Security and Cooperation in Europe (OSCE) Mission to Bosnia and Herzegovina. His latest publication, "Georgia: Rise and Fall of the Façade Democracy" (*Demokratizatsiya*, winter 2004), discussed political party development in Georgia since its independence.

GIORGI GOGIA is a Caucasus analyst for the International Crisis Group. His research examines the causes of conflict, and international and domestic responses to conflict, in the three countries of the South Caucasus: Armenia, Azerbaijan and Georgia. His focus is on three "frozen conflicts" of the region— South Ossetia, Abkhazia, and Nagorno-Karabakh—and he prepares reports with policy and program recommendations for governments, multi-lateral organizations, and international groups. He holds an M.A. in political science from Central European University, Budapest.

DAMIEN HELLY has a Ph.D. in political science from Sciences Po, Paris and worked as Caucasus Project Director for the International Crisis Group. His main areas of research are European foreign policy, conflict prevention and management, as well as foreign aid. His recent publications include: *L'Union européenne, acteur international* (2005); and, for the International Crisis Group, *Georgia: What Now?* (2003), *Azerbaijan: Turning over a New Leaf?* (2004), and *Moldova and Transdniestria: Democracy at Stake* (forthcoming 2005).

ROBERT LEGVOLD is professor of political science at Columbia University where he specializes in the foreign policies of Russia and the other new states of the former Soviet Union, U.S. relations with the post-Soviet states, and the impact of the post-Soviet region on the international politics of Asia and Europe. He is a member of the Committee on International Security Studies of the American Academy of Arts and Sciences and director of its project on International Security in the Post-Soviet Space. From 1986 to 1992, he was director of Columbia University's Harriman Institute. His recent publications include: *Swords and Sustenance: The Economics of National Security in Belarus and Ukraine* (2004), *Thinking Strategically: The Major Powers, Kazakhstan, and the Central Asian Nexus* (2003), and *Belarus at the Crossroads* (1999).

GHIA NODIA is the chairman of the Caucasus Institute for Peace, Democracy, and Development, an independent think tank in Tbilisi, Georgia, and a professor of political science at Ilia Chavchavadze University of Culture and Language. His international fellowships include: the Woodrow Wilson Center, Washington, D.C.; the University of California–Berkeley; Wissenschaftskolleg zu Berlin; and the Emile Franqui Chair in Belgium. He writes primarily on regional security, state building and democratization in the Caucasus, and theories of nationalism and democratic transition in the post–Cold War context. He is co-author of *Georgia Lurching to Democracy. From Agnostic Tolerance to Pious Jacobinism: Societal Change and People's Reactions* (2000) and has written several contributions to the *Journal of Democracy.*

CHRISTOPH ZÜRCHER is lecturer and senior researcher at the Otto-Suhr Institute for Political Science of Free University Berlin. He holds the chair for Peace and Conflict Research at the Institute of East European Studies at Free University Berlin. His research focuses on peace and conflict research. He was educated in Bern, Switzerland, and studied in Moscow, Vilnius, Khabarowsk, and Lviv. He is the co-editor of *Potentials of Disorder: Explaining Violence in the Caucasus and in the Former Yugoslavia* (2003).

Index

THE AMERICAN ACADEMY OF ARTS & SCIENCES

Founded in 1780, the American Academy of Arts and Sciences is an international learned society composed of the world's leading scientists, scholars, artists, business people, and public leaders. With a current membership of 4,000 American Fellows and 600 Foreign Honorary Members, the Academy has four major goals:

- Promoting service and study through analysis of critical social and intellectual issues and the development of practical policy alternatives;

- Fostering public engagement and the exchange of ideas with meetings, conferences, and symposia bringing diverse perspectives to the examination of issues of common concern;

- Mentoring a new generation of scholars and thinkers through the newly established Visiting Scholars Program;

- Honoring excellence by electing to membership men and women in a broad range of disciplines and professions.

The Academy's main headquarters are in Cambridge, Massachusetts. With its geographically diverse membership, it has also established regional centers at the University of Chicago and the University of California, Irvine, and conducts activities in the United States and abroad.

THE COMMITTEE ON INTERNATIONAL SECURITY STUDIES

The Academy's Committee on International Security Studies (CISS), founded in 1982, plans and sponsors multi-disciplinary studies of current and emerging challenges to global peace and security. Recent and ongoing CISS projects examine: the governance of outer space, international security relationships in the region of the former Soviet Union, the costs and consequences of the war in Iraq, the global security implications of joint missile surveillance, and the implications of the International Criminal Court for U.S. national security. For more information on CISS, visit our website: http://www.amacad.org/projects/ciss.aspx.

Recent CISS publications include:

United States Space Policy: Challenges and Opportunities, by George Abbey and Neal Lane (2005).

The Physics of Space Security: A Reference Manual, by David Wright, Laura Grego, and Lisbeth Gronlund (2005).

War with Iraq: Costs, Consequences, and Alternatives, by Carl Kaysen, Steven E. Miller, Martin B. Malin, William D. Nordhaus, and John D. Steinbruner (2002).

The Significance of Joint Missile Surveillance, by John D. Steinbruner (2001).

The United States and the International Criminal Court, edited by Sarah Sewall and Carl Kaysen, eds. (2000).

To order publications or for more information, please contact CISS at the American Academy of Arts & Sciences, 136 Irving Street, Cambridge, MA 02138.

Phone: 617-576-5024; email: ciss@amacad.org; Website: www.amacad.org.